Genealogy Online For Dummies, 3rd Edition

P9-CEE-912

How to Use Helm's Genealogy Toolbox

You can use Helm's Genealogy Toolbox to identify genealogical resources on the Internet in two different ways: using the Global Search engine or browsing through categories. To do either, go to Helm's Genealogy Toolbox at www.genealogytoolbox.com.

Using the Global Search engine

1. **In the left column, you find a blue box with a Global Search graphic.**
2. **Type the keyword that you're looking for in the box, or type the first and/or last names that you're looking for, and click the Search button.**

   The Search Results page contains several areas. The top section lists the Helm's Genealogy Toolbox categories that match your search terms. The second section lists the links on the Toolbox that contain your search terms. The third section shows the results of a full-text search using the Toolbox with your terms.

3. **Choose a link that appears to have information on your topic.**

Browsing by category in the directory

On the home page for Helm's Genealogy Toolbox is a gray box labeled Site Categories. Each category has a small description to help you figure out which category contains the information that you're looking for. These categories include:

- Computers
- How-To and Help
- Media
- People
- Places
- Supplies and Services

1. **Click the category that interests you.**
2. **If a listing of subcategories appears, browse through it and click the subcategory that interests you.**

   On subcategory pages, you find lists of hand-picked links relating to that topic, a list of URLs generated from the Toolbox's full-text search, queries, and software related to the topic (if appropriate). For each link to another site, you're provided with the name and a brief abstract of the link's content.

Here are a couple of hints to remember when you browse through categories:

- **Looking for information about a surname?** Click the People category in the main directory.
- **Looking for information about a geographic location?** Click the Places category in the main directory.

For Dummies: Bestselling Book Series for Beginners

Genealogy Online
For Dummies, 3rd Edition

Some Genealogical Web Sites to Remember

For news and information about developments in genealogy

Eastman's Online Genealogy Newsletter	`www.ancestry.com/library/view/columns/eastman/d_p_1_archive.asp`
Journal of Online Genealogy	`www.onlinegenealogy.com`

For links to lots of other genealogical sites

Genealogy Home Page	`www.genhomepage.com`
Helm's Genealogy Toolbox	`www.genealogytoolbox.com`

For surname resources

Genealogy Resources on Internet Mailing Lists	`www.rootsweb.com/~jfuller/gen_mail.html`
Roots Surname List search page	`rsl.rootsweb.com/cgi-bin/rslsql.cgi`

To post queries and share genealogical research success

Genealogy's Most Wanted	`www.citynet.net/mostwanted/`
Genealogy Toolbox: Query Central	`query.genealogytoolbox.com`
FamilyHistory.com	`www.familyhistory.com`
FamilySearch.org	`www.familysearch.org`
GenForum	`www.genforum.com`

For United States government resources

Immigration and Naturalization Service	`www.ins.gov`
Library of Congress	`www.loc.gov`
National Archives and Records Administration	`www.nara.gov`

For Dummies: Bestselling Book Series for Beginners

Genealogy Online

FOR

DUMMIES®

3RD EDITION

Genealogy Online

FOR DUMMIES®

3RD EDITION

by Matthew L. Helm and April Leigh Helm

Wiley Publishing, Inc.

Genealogy Online For Dummies,® 3rd Edition

Published by
Wiley Publishing, Inc.
909 Third Avenue
New York, NY 10022
www.wiley.com

Copyright © 2001 Wiley Publishing, Inc., Indianapolis, Indiana

Published simultaneously in Canada

For general information on our other products and services or to obtain technical support, please contact our Customer Care Department within the U.S. at 800-762-2974, outside the U.S. at 317-572-3993, or fax 317-572-4002.

Wiley also publishes its books in a variety of electronic formats. Some content that appears in print may not be available in electronic books.

Library of Congress Cataloging-in-Publication Data:

Library of Congress Control Number: 00-109247

ISBN: 0-7645-0807-5

Manufactured in the United States of America

10 9 8 7 6 5 4 3

About the Authors

Matthew L. Helm is the Executive Vice President and Chief Technology Officer for FamilyToolbox.net, Inc. Also, he is the publisher of the *Journal of Online Genealogy*. He's the creator and maintainer of the award-winning Helm's Genealogy Toolbox, Helm/Helms Family Research Page, and a variety of other Web sites. Matthew has spoken at several national genealogical conventions, and has lectured to various genealogical and historical societies. Matthew holds an A.B. in History and an M.S. in Library and Information Science from the University of Illinois at Urbana-Champaign.

April Leigh Helm is the President of FamilyToolbox.net, Inc. She's also the editor and maintainer of the *Journal of Online Genealogy*. April has lectured on genealogy and other topics for various conventions, conferences, and groups. She holds a B.S. in Journalism and an Ed.M. in Higher Education Administration from the University of Illinois at Urbana-Champaign.

Together, the Helms have coauthored several books in addition to the three editions of *Genealogy Online For Dummies*. They include *Family Tree Maker For Dummies*, *CliffsNotes Tracing Your Family Roots Online*, *Your Official America Online Guide to Genealogy Online*, and *Get Your Degree Online*.

Although they collected notes on family members and old photographs for many years, it wasn't until 1990, while living and working in the Washington, D.C. area, that the Helms began seriously researching their family lines. Upon returning to central Illinois in 1994, the Helms found themselves with limited historical and genealogical resources to continue their research. It was then that they jumped into online genealogy.

Here's a little more information about a few of the genealogical Web sites maintained by the Helms:

Helm's Genealogy Toolbox (www.genealogytoolbox.com): An online clearinghouse of genealogical tools and links.

Genealogy Toolbox DigiSources (digisources.genealogytoolbox.com): An online archive of digitized records and documents that enable genealogists to conduct primary research on the Internet.

GenealogyPortal.com (www.genealogyportal.com): A site containing eight separate search engines that index sites of interest to genealogists. It was created as a joint project between Matthew and Stephen Wood, the creator and maintainer of the Genealogy Home Page.

Dedication

For Brynn Kyleakin

Authors' Acknowledgments

We wish to acknowledge the following people, without whom this book wouldn't exist:

Lisa Swayne, who sought us out to write our very first book and has been beside us ever since.

John Scroggins, a good friend, advisor, and fellow genealogist.

Carol, Sheri, Rebekah, Bill, Carmen, Megan, and Marisa, who logged a lot of hours pulling together this book and its CD.

Our respective parents and ancestors, without whom our own genealogies wouldn't be possible.

Publisher's Acknowledgments

We're proud of this book; please send us your comments through our online registration form located at www.dummies.com/register/.

Some of the people who helped bring this book to market include the following:

Acquisitions, Editorial, and Media Development

Project Editor: Sheri Replin

(Previous Edition: Wendy Hatch)

Acquisitions Editor: Carol Sheehan

Copy Editor: Rebekah Mancilla

Proof Editor: Mary SeRine

Technical Editor: John Scroggins

Senior Permissions Editor: Carmen Krikorian

Media Development Specialist: Angie Denny

Associate Media Development Specialist: Megan Decraene

Media Development Coordinator: Marisa E. Pearman

Editorial Manager: Jeanne S. Criswell

Media Development Manager: Laura Carpenter

Media Development Supervisor: Richard Graves

Editorial Assistant: Candace Nicholson

Production

Project Coordinator: Maridee Ennis

Layout and Graphics: John Greenough, Gabriele McCann, Kristin Pickett, Heather Pope, Jacque Schneider, Kendra Span, Brian Torwelle, Julie Trippetti, Jeremey Unger, Erin Zeltner

Proofreaders: Laura Albert, Vickie Broyles, Susan Moritz, Dwight Ramsey, York Production Services, Inc.

Indexer: York Production Services, Inc.

General and Administrative

Wiley Technology Publishing Group: Richard Swadley, Vice President and Executive Group Publisher; Bob Ipsen, Vice President and Group Publisher; Joseph Wikert, Vice President and Publisher; Barry Pruett, Vice President and Publisher; Mary Bednarek, Editorial Director; Mary C. Corder, Editorial Director; Andy Cummings, Editorial Director

Wiley Manufacturing: Carol Tobin, Director of Manufacturing

Wiley Marketing: John Helmus, Assistant Vice President, Director of Marketing

Wiley Composition Services: Gerry Fahey, Executive Director of Production Services; Debbie Stailey, Director of Composition Services

Contents at a Glance

Cartoons at a Glance

By Rich Tennant

The 5th Wave — By Rich Tennant

"Well, shoot! This eggplant chart is just as confusing as the butternut squash chart and the gourd chart. Can't you make a family chart like everyone else?"

page 201

The 5th Wave — By Rich Tennant

"I'm not sure I want to be claimed by a family whose home page has a link to the Zang Zone."

page 101

The 5th Wave — By Rich Tennant

"Well, she now claims she's a descendant of the royal Egyptian line of cats, but I'm not buying that just yet."

page 165

The 5th Wave — By Rich Tennant

"Hold your horses. It takes time to locate the ancestors for someone of your background."

page D-1

The 5th Wave — By Rich Tennant

"It's really quite an interesting site. There's roller coaster action, suspense, and drama where skill and strategy are matched against winning and losing. And I thought researching geneology online would be dull."

page 7

The 5th Wave — By Rich Tennant

"THAT'S A LOVELY SCANNED IMAGE OF YOUR SISTER'S PORTRAIT. NOW TAKE IT OFF THE BODY OF THAT PIT VIPER BEFORE SHE COMES IN THE ROOM."

page 243

Cartoon Information:
Fax: 978-546-7747
E-Mail: richtennant@the5thwave.com
World Wide Web: www.the5thwave.com

Table of Contents

Introduction

● ●

The world of online genealogy has undergone a tremendous amount of changes since *Genealogy Online For Dummies*, 2nd Edition, was published. The quantity and quality of research material and the number of people conducting research online have grown drastically. Also, some of the fundamental ways that online family history research is conducted have changed. To keep up with these changes, we wrote this new edition.

Over the last three years, interest in genealogical research has continued to boom. Everywhere you turn, magazines and newspapers run stories and columns about family history. Computer use and the rise of the Internet have helped to encourage this growing interest and have changed the nature of genealogy. To be a genealogist these days doesn't necessarily mean that you have to pack the kids in the car and travel a thousand miles to find details on that elusive ancestor. In fact, sometimes you don't even have to leave the comfort of your home in order to discover valuable information.

If you have an interest in genealogy, a wealth of information is at your fingertips. You can correspond with family members who live in far-off lands. You can research the history of a particular area and find images of historical documents without setting foot outside your home. You can discover resources that you never suspected to be helpful in your pursuit of your family history. And you can do all of it using your computer and a hookup to the Internet.

About This Book

Having so many resources available on the Internet is great, but you have to be careful not to overload yourself with information and get so frustrated that your interest in genealogy becomes a burden. The number of genealogy-related sites on the Internet is growing so rapidly that becoming overwhelmed is easy to do. This is where we come in to help you.

Of course, you're probably asking yourself how this book differs from the many other genealogy books on the shelf. Some books tell you only the traditional methods of genealogical research — which have you traveling hundreds of miles to visit courthouses and using the good old typewriter to summarize your results. Unfortunately, these books neglect the many opportunities that online research provides. Other books that do cover online genealogy tend to group resources by how users access them (all FTP sites are listed together, all World Wide Web sites are listed together, and so on), rather than telling you how you can integrate the many Internet resources to achieve your genealogical goal. As genealogists, we understand that researchers don't conduct searches by trying, for example, all the FTP sites and then all the World Wide Web sites. We search by looking for surnames or places anywhere we can find them — through FTP sites, World Wide Web sites, e-mail, newsgroups, or whatever.

Also, some books become too computer heavy — giving you lots of overkill about the ins and outs of each kind of Internet resource — and neglecting to help you with basic research techniques online and offline that you need to successfully meet your goal. We don't want you to have a bad experience online. So rather than focus on just one thing — genealogy or online resources — we try to balance the act. In this book, we show you how to integrate genealogical research with the use of online resources so that you can learn to effectively and efficiently use your computer and the Internet in your family research.

What are the requirements for becoming an official genealogist? Well, do you have a mirror nearby? If so, go to the mirror and look at yourself. Now say out loud, "I declare myself an official genealogist." There you go. It's official — you're a genealogist, and it's time to start pulling together the puzzle pieces of your family history.

Seriously, being a genealogist has no formal requirements. You simply need an interest in your ancestry and a willingness to devote the rest of your life to pursuing information and documents.

Foolish Assumptions

In writing and revising this book, we made a couple of assumptions. If you fit one of these assumptions, this book is for you:

- ✔ You've done at least a little genealogy groundwork, and now you're ready to use the Internet to pursue (and better prepare yourself for) your genealogy research both online and offline.

- ✔ You have at least a little computer experience, are now interested in pursuing your family tree, and want to know where and how to start.

- ✔ You have a little experience in genealogy and some experience with computers, but you want to learn how to put them together.

Of course, you can have a lot of computer experience and be a novice to genealogy or to online genealogy and still benefit from this book. In this case, you may still want to skim some of the basic sections on computers and the Internet in case you can find something else to use.

How to Use This Book

We know that you may not read this book from cover to cover, in order. (No, you're not hurting our feelings by skipping through the sections looking only for the information that you're interested in at that particular moment!) In fact, we've tried to write this book to accommodate you. Each section within each chapter can stand alone as a separate entity, so you can pick up the book and flip directly to a section that deals with what you want to know. If we think something relevant in another section can supplement your knowledge on the particular topic, we provide a note or reference telling you the other place(s) we think you should look. However, we've tried very hard to do this referencing in a manner that isn't obnoxious to those of you who choose to read the book from cover to cover. We hope we've succeeded in addressing both types of readers!

We use a couple of conventions in this book to make it easier for you to follow a set of specific instructions. Commands for menus appear with arrows between each selection. (For example, the command Format⇨ Tree Format tells you to choose Tree Format from the Format menu.)

If you need to type something, the explanation uses **bold type** to indicate what you need to type.

How This Book Is Organized

To help you get a better picture of what this book has to offer, we explain a little about how we organized it and what you can expect to find in each part.

Part 1: Getting Your Act Together

You need to have a good foundation before starting your online genealogical research. This part explores the fundamental family information that you need to collect first, how to form an online research plan, and how to start searching the Internet for information about ancestors and geographic locations.

Part II: Finding the Elusive Records

Searching online for information about members of a particular ethnic or religious group can pose a great deal of difficulty even for the most skilled genealogist. Likewise, looking for a specialized type of record can do the same. For this reason, Part II examines resources that are available online to help you find those elusive ancestors.

Part III: Keeping Your Ancestors in Line: Organizing and Presenting Your Findings

What you do with the information that you find is just as important as finding it in the first place. So, in this part, we look at how to store and organize your documents and photographs, as well as how to store research results in a genealogical database. We also give you methods of retrieving that information through reports that can help you with your future research.

Part IV: Share and Share Alike

One of the most important aspects of genealogical research is using a coordinated effort to achieve success. This part takes a look at what goes into this effort, including using all available online resources, cooperating with other researchers, coordinating with groups and societies, and sharing the fruits of your research with the online community.

Part V: The Part of Tens

Ah, the infamous Part of Tens (infamous because every ...*For Dummies* book has one of these sections with profound advice or lists of things to do). Here you find a series of quick-reference chapters that give you useful genealogical hints and reminders. We include a list of online database sites we think you should know about, some tips for creating a genealogical Web page, hints to keep your online research sailing smoothly, and a list of sites we think every beginner to genealogy should visit.

Appendixes

As you read this book (or skip from chapter to chapter, section to section, looking over only those parts that interest you), you may have additional questions in some areas. That's why we include the appendixes. One appendix helps you get some clarification or further information about going online. Another appendix provides definitions of many terms that you're likely to encounter in your genealogical research. And the last appendix gives you an overview of the software that we include on the CD-ROM that accompanies this book, as well as basic instructions for installing and using it.

The Genealogy Online For Dummies Internet Directory

This directory (on the yellow paper) lists selected Internet sites that are of use and interest to genealogists. You can find sites for everything — from surnames to government to geographic-specific to comprehensive genealogical indexes to big search engines to commercial endeavors. For each site that we identify, we provide the name, URL (Uniform Resource Locator), and a brief overview of what the site has to offer.

We want you to be able to see immediately whether a site in the directory has a particular type of information or service of interest to you. For this reason, we created some mini-icons — or, if you prefer, *micons* (see The *Genealogy Online For Dummies* Internet Directory for details).

Icons Used in This Book

To help you get the most out of this book, we created some icons that tell you at a glance if a section or paragraph has important information of a particular kind.

Here, we refer you to other books or materials if you'd like additional information.

This icon signals a Web site that has a search engine you can use to look for content within the site.

Here you can find concepts or terms that are unique to genealogy.

When you see this icon, you know we're offering advice or shortcuts to make your researching easier.

This icon points out software that's included on the CD-ROM.

We walk readers step by step through an example of something.

Look out! This is something tricky or unusual to watch for.

This icon marks important genealogical stuff, so don't forget it.

Where to Go from Here

Depending on where you're reading this introduction, your next step is one of two possibilities:

- ✔ You need to go to the front of the bookstore and pay for this book so that you can take it home and use it. (Many bookstores are pretty understanding about your sitting and reading through parts of books — that's why they provide the comfortable chairs, right? But we're not sure they would look highly upon you whipping out your laptop computer, asking to borrow an Internet connection from them, and proceeding to go through this entire book right there in the store. Then again, we could be mistaken — so use your best judgment based on your knowledge of the bookstore in which you're standing.)

- ✔ If you already bought the book and you're at home (or wherever), you can go ahead and start reading, following the steps for the online activities in the book as they come along.

Part I
Getting Your Act Together

The 5th Wave   By Rich Tennant

"It's really quite an interesting site. There's roller coaster action, suspense, and drama where skill and strategy are matched against winning and losing. And I thought researching geneology online would be dull."

In this part . . .

So you wanna be an online genealogist? Well, you need to prepare yourself for that first online research trip by finding out about the basics of genealogy and how to form a research plan. When you're ready to take the online plunge, we help you find worthwhile surname and geographic-specific resources on the Internet.

Chapter 1

You Gotta Have Groundwork

Wouldn't you know it — one of the most successful keys to researching your family history online doesn't even include turning on the computer. That's right, we said, "doesn't include the computer!" You may ask yourself, "How can people writing a book about online genealogy say that?" Well, our experience is that you need to know a few details about your family before you try to find all those great nuggets of information online. However, the good thing about the Internet is that it not only contains information on the family history of individuals, but it also has details on how to get started on your family history.

Before we begin, we need to give you the following disclaimer (so that we don't get scolded by other genealogists who know what it takes to produce a solid genealogical work): As you venture into online genealogy, keep in mind that you can't complete your entire genealogy by using only online resources. Many crucial records simply haven't been converted into electronic format. In fact, you should think of online research methods as only one of many tools that you can use to gather the information for a complete picture of your ancestors.

In this chapter, we give an overview of several resources that you can rely on for information before you begin your online genealogical research. We also provide some Web sites that can assist you in accessing these resources.

Starting Your Research with What You Already Know

Sometimes, beginning genealogists start their search by trying to discover the identities of their great-great-grandfathers or their families' first immigrants. Such a strategy often becomes frustrating because they either can't find any information or they find something that they assume is true, only to find out later that the information doesn't apply to their family branch. To avoid this mess, we recommend that you conduct your genealogical research one step at a time — and that you begin your genealogical research with yourself.

Making a few notes about yourself — the biographical sketch

You already know a great deal about yourself — probably more than anyone else knows about you. (Unless you're married. Then your spouse knows more about you, right?) You probably know your birth date, place of birth, parents' names, and where you've lived. (We recognize that not everyone knows all this information; adoptions or other extenuating circumstances may require you to do the best that you can with what you know until you can discover additional information about yourself.) So, sit down at that computer, open your word processor, and create an autobiographical sketch. (Of course, if you prefer, you can take out a piece of paper and write down all those details instead.)

You can approach the sketch in several ways. Sometimes, the easiest method is to begin with current events and work back through your life. For instance, first note the basics: your current occupation, residence, and activities. Then move back to your last residence, occupation, and so on until you arrive at your birth date. Make sure that you include milestones like children's birth dates, marriage dates, military service dates, and other significant events in your life. If you prefer, you can cover your life by beginning with your birth and working forward to the present. Either way is fine, as long as all the important events are listed in the sketch.

Another method is to use 3-x-5-inch cards or a word processor to make notes on things that you recall over a certain period of time. Then you can arrange the cards or the paragraphs in the word-processing file to create a biographical sketch.

Finding primary sources

Although you may know a lot about yourself, someone else may have difficulty discovering these facts about you (if they were to research you at some point in the future). This is where primary sources come in handy.

Primary sources are documents, oral accounts (if the account is made soon after the actual event and witnessed by the person who created the account), photographs, or any other items created at the time of a certain event's occurrence.

For example, a primary source for your birth date is your birth certificate. Typically, a birth certificate is prepared within a few days of the actual event and is signed by an actual witness to the birth. Because of this, the information (like the time, date, and parents' names) is a reliable firsthand account of the event — unless, of course, someone lied about the parents' names. Even if a record was prepared near the time of an event, this doesn't mean that every fact provided on the record is correct. Cases arise where typographical errors occurred or incorrect information was provided to the creator of the record. So it's always a good idea to try to find other primary records that can corroborate the information found in any record.

Secondary sources are documents, oral accounts, and so on that are created some length of time after the event or for which information is supplied by someone who wasn't an eyewitness to the event. (A secondary source can be a person who was an eyewitness to the event but recalls it after a significant period of time passes.)

Some records may be considered both primary and secondary sources. For example, a death certificate contains both primary and secondary source information. The primary source information is the death date and cause of death. These facts are primary because the certificate was prepared around the time of death and the information is usually provided by a medical professional who pronounced the death. The secondary source information on the death certificate includes the birth date and place of birth of the deceased individual. These details are secondary because the certificate was issued at a time significantly later than the birth (assuming that the birth and death dates are at least a few years apart). Secondary sources don't have the degree of reliability or surety of primary sources. Often secondary source information, such as that found on death certificates, is provided by an individual's children or descendants who may or may not know the exact date or place of birth. So, backing up your secondary sources with reliable primary sources is always a good idea.

You can familiarize yourself with primary sources by collecting some information for your own biographical profile. Try to match up primary sources for each event in the sketch — for example, birth and marriage certificates, deeds, leases, military records, and tax records. For more information on finding these types of documents, see the appropriate sections later in this chapter. If you can't locate primary source documents for each event in your life, don't fret! Your biographical sketch can serve as a primary source document because you write it about yourself.

For additional information on primary sources, see The Historian's Sources page at the Library of Congress Web site (`lcweb2.loc.gov/ammem/ndlpedu/ lessons/psources/pshome.html`).

Chatting with Papa and Aunt Lola: Interviewing Your Family Members

After you complete your autobiographical sketch, you may want to take the next step and begin interviewing your family members to collect information about them and other relatives. You want to collect the same type of information about their lives that you provided about your own. Your parents, brothers, sisters, grandparents, aunts, uncles, and cousins are all good candidates for information about your family's most recent generations. Talking to relatives provides you with leads that you can use later to find primary sources. For more information on primary sources, see "Finding primary sources" in the preceding section. You can complete family interviews in person or through a questionnaire — although we strongly recommend that you conduct them in person. For an example of a cover letter to send your family, go to this Web site: `www.familytreemaker.com/00000059.html`.

There's no easy way to say this, so please excuse us for being blunt — you may want to begin interviewing some of your older relatives as soon as possible, depending on their ages and health. If a family member passes on before you arrange to interview him or her, you may miss the opportunity of a lifetime to learn more about his or her personal experiences and knowledge of previous generations.

Here are a few tips to remember as you plan a family interview:

- ✔ **Prepare a list of questions that you want to ask:** Knowing what you want to achieve during the discussion helps you get started and keeps your interview focused. (See the sidebar "Good interviewing questions" for some ideas.)

- ✔ **Bring a tape recorder to the interview:** Make sure that you get permission from each participant before you start recording.

- ✔ **Use photographs and documents to help your family members recall events.**

- ✔ **Try to limit your interviews to two hours or less:** You don't want to be overwhelmed with information, and you don't want the interviewee to get worn out by your visit. Within two hours, you can collect a lot of information to guide your research. And remember, you can always do another interview if you want more information from the family member. (Actually, we strongly encourage you to do subsequent interviews — often the first interview stimulates memories for the individual that you can cover during a later interview.)

TIP

Good interviewing questions

Before you conduct a family interview, pull together a set of questions to guide the discussion. Your planning makes the difference between an interview in which the family member stays focused, or a question-and-answer session that invites bouncing from one unrelated topic to another. Here are examples of some questions that you may want to ask:

- ✔ What is your full name and do you know why you were named that?

- ✔ Where were you born and when? Do you remember any stories that your parents told you about the event?

- ✔ What do you remember about your childhood?

- ✔ Where did you go to school? Did you finish school? If not, why? (Remember to ask about all levels of schooling through college.)

- ✔ What were your brothers and sisters like?

- ✔ Where and when were your parents born? What did they look like? What were their occupations?

- ✔ Did your parents tell you how they met?

- ✔ Do you remember your grandparents? Do you recall any stories about them? What did they look like?

- ✔ Did you hear any stories about your great-grandparents? Did you ever meet your great-grandparents?

- ✔ When you were a child, who was the oldest person in your family?

- ✔ Did any relatives (other than your immediate family) live with you?

- ✔ Do you remember who your neighbors were when you were a child?

- ✔ Did your family have any traditions or celebrate any special holidays?

- ✔ Have any items (stories, traditions, or physical items) been handed down through several generations of the family?

- ✔ When did you leave home? Where did you live?

- ✔ Did you join the military? If so, what branch of service were you in? What units were you a part of? Did you serve overseas?

- ✔ What occupations have you had? Did you have any special training?

- ✔ How did you meet your spouse?

- ✔ When and where did you get married? Did you go on a honeymoon? Where?

(continued)

(continued)

✔ When were your children born? Do you have any stories about their births?

✔ Do you know who in the family originally immigrated to this country? Where did they come from? Why did they leave their native land?

You can probably think of more questions that are likely to draw responses from your family.

During the interview, stay flexible. Explore specific family events, share family legends, or ask for photographs that picture the events that you discuss. If you want to see additional hints for conducting interviews, see Recording Oral Histories: Tips and Topics (`www.familytreemaker.com/00000028.html`).

Looking for Love Letters, Laundry Receipts, and Other Important Documents

Are you, or have you ever been, accused of being a pack rat? You know what we mean — someone who keeps every little scrap of paper that they touch. Ah, you know who you are. (And we know how to recognize you because — and here's a deep, dark confession — we're both pack rats of the serious variety!) If you are, then you're well suited for genealogy. In fact, if you're lucky, you descended from a whole family of pack rats who saved all those scraps from the past in their attics or basements. You can dig through their treasures to find things that can further your genealogy research. For example, pay a visit to grandma's attic and you may discover an old suitcase or cigar box full of documents like driver's licenses, war ration cards, and letters. These items may contain original signatures and other information that you can use to construct your ancestor's past.

When you go through old family files, look for things that can serve as primary sources for facts that you want to verify. For more info on primary sources, see "Finding primary sources," earlier in this chapter. Look for documents to verify addresses, occupations, church membership, and military service. Here's a list of some specific things to look for:

✔ Family Bibles

✔ Legal documents (such as mortgages, titles, and deeds)

✔ Insurance policies

✔ Wills

✔ Family letters

✔ Obituaries and newspaper articles

- Diaries

- Naturalization records

- Baptismal certificates and other church records

- Copies of vital records (such as birth, marriage, and death certificates, and divorce decrees)

- Occupational or personnel records

- Membership cards

For a list of other items to look for around the home, see Treasures in the Attic (www.ancestry.com/library/view/ancmag/673.asp), Finding Information at Home (www.familytreemaker.com/00000027.html), and Family and Home Information Sources Checklist (www.kbyu.org/ancestors/charts/oldpdf/checklist1.pdf) [requires Adobe Acrobat].

Dusting Off the Old Photo Albums

A picture is worth a thousand words — so the saying goes. That's certainly true in genealogy. Photographs are among the most treasured documents for genealogists. Pictures show how your ancestors looked and what conditions they lived in. Sometimes, the flip side of the photo is more important than the picture itself. On the back, you may find crucial information, like names, dates, and descriptions of places.

Photographs are also useful as memory-joggers for your family members. Pictures can help others recollect the past and bring up long-forgotten memories. Just be forewarned — sometimes the memories are good, and sometimes they're not so good! Although you may stimulate thoughts of some great moments long ago, you may also open a can of worms when you ask grandma about a particular person in a picture. On the plus side, in the end she may give you the lowdown on not only that person but every single individual in the family who has ever made her angry — this can provide lots of genealogical leads.

You may run into several different types of photographs in your research. Knowing when certain kinds of photographs were produced can help you associate a time frame with a picture. Here are some examples:

- **Daguerreotypes:** Daguerreotype photos were taken from 1839 to 1860. They required a long exposure time and were taken on silver-plated copper. The photographic image appears to change from a positive to a negative when tilted.

- **Ambrotypes:** Ambrotypes used a much shorter exposure time and were produced from 1858 to 1866. The image was made on thin glass and usually had a black backing.

- **Tintypes:** Tintypes were produced from 1858 to 1910. They were made on a metal sheet and the image was often coated with a varnish. You can usually find them in a paper cover.

- **Cartes-de-visite:** Cartes-de-visite were small paper prints mounted on a card. They were often bound together into a photo album. They were produced between 1858 and 1891.

- **Cabinet cards:** Cabinet cards were larger versions of cartes-de-visite. They sometimes included dates on the borders of the cards. The pictures themselves were usually mounted on cardboard. They were manufactured primarily between 1865 and 1906.

- **Albumen prints:** These were produced on a thin piece of paper that was coated with albumen and silver nitrate. They were usually mounted on cardboard. These prints were used between 1858 and 1910 and were the types of photographs found in cartes-de-visite and cabinet cards.

- **Stereographic cards:** Stereographic cards were curved photographs that rendered a three-dimensional effect when used with a stereographic viewer. They were prevalent from 1850 to 1925.

- **Platinum prints:** Platinum prints have a matte surface that appears embedded in the paper. The images were often highlighted with artistic chalk. They were produced mainly between 1880 and 1930.

- **Glass-plate negatives:** Glass-plate negatives were used between 1848 and 1930. They were made from light-sensitive silver bromide immersed in gelatin.

When you deal with photographs, keep in mind that too much light or humidity can easily destroy them. For more information on preserving photographs, see Chapter 8. Also, some online resources can help you identify types of pictures. See the City Gallery Web site (`www.city-gallery.com/`) for 19th-century photography information, and visit Photography as a Tool in Genealogy (`freepages.genealogy.rootsweb.com/~fgriffin/photos.txt`) for descriptions of several types of photographs.

Sifting through Birth, Death, Marriage, and Divorce Records

Vital records are among the first sets of primary sources typically used by genealogists (for more on primary sources, see "Finding primary sources," earlier in this chapter). Vital records include birth, marriage, divorce, and death records, and, for the most part, local governments keep the originals (although some governments have microfilmed them and stored them centrally). These records contain key and usually reliable information because they were produced near the time that the event occurred and a witness to the actual event provided the information. (Outside the United States, vital records are often called *civil registrations.*)

Vital records are usually maintained in the county where the event occurred. Normally, you must contact the county clerk to receive a copy of a record. Some states centrally collect or microfilm their vital records, and they're available for public use at the state archives or library. You can find an online list of centralized vital record repositories in each of the United States at the Vital Records Information site (vitalrec.com). For information on where to find vital record (and civil registration) information online, see Chapter 6.

Each state has different laws regarding the release of vital records. It's a good idea to check the policy of the governing agency before making the trip or ordering a vital record. In some cases, the agency may only release a record for a good cause or to a close relative.

Birth records

Birth records are good primary sources for verifying — at a minimum — the date of birth, birthplace, and names of an individual's parents. Depending on the information requirements for a particular birth certificate, you may also learn the birthplace of the parents, their ages, occupations, addresses at the time of birth, whether the mother had given birth previously, date of marriage of the parents, and the names and ages of any previous children. Sometimes, instead of a birth certificate, you may find another record in the family's possession that verifies the existence of the birth record. For example, instead of having a certified copy of a birth certificate, Matthew's grandmother had a Certificate of Record of Birth. This certificate attests to the fact that the county has a certificate of birth and notes its location. These certificates were used primarily before photocopiers became commonplace and it became easier to get a certified copy of the original record.

Birth records are less formal in older sources. Before modern record-keeping, a simple handwritten entry in a book sufficed as an official record of an individual's birth. So be very specific when citing a birth record in your genealogical notes. Include any numbers that you find on the record and where the record is located (including not only the physical location of the building, but also the book number and page number).

Marriage records

Marriage records come in several forms. Early marriage records may include the following:

- **Marriage bonds:** Financial guarantees that a marriage was going to take place
- **Marriage banns:** Proclamations of the intent to marry someone in front of a church congregation
- **Marriage licenses:** Documents granting permission to marry
- **Marriage records or certificates:** Documents certifying the union of two people

These records contain — at a minimum — the groom's name, the bride's name, and the location of the ceremony. They may also contain occupation information, birthplaces of the bride and groom, parents' names and birthplaces, names of witnesses, and information on previous marriages.

Here's one thing to be careful about when using marriage records: Don't confuse the date of the marriage with the date of the marriage bond, bann, or license — it's easy to do. The latter records were often filed anywhere from a couple of days to several weeks before the actual marriage date. Also, do not assume that because you found a bond, bann, or license that a marriage actually took place. Some people got *cold feet* then (as they do today) and backed out of the marriage at the last minute.

Divorce records

Genealogists often overlook divorce records. Later generations may not be aware that an early ancestor was divorced, and the records recounting the event can be difficult to find. However, divorce records can be quite valuable. They contain many important facts, including the age of the petitioners, birthplace, address, occupations, names and ages of children, property, and the grounds for the divorce.

Death records

Death records are excellent resources for verifying the date of death, but are less reliable for other data elements like birth date and birthplace, because people who were not witnesses to the birth often supply the information. However, information on the death record can point you in the right direction for records that can verify other events. More recent death records include the name of the individual, place of death, residence, parents' names, name of spouse, occupation, and cause of death. Early death records may only contain the date of death, cause, and residence.

Was Your Ancestor a Criminal? Using Civil and Court Records

There's good news — your ancestor may not have been a criminal for civil and court records to be useful in your genealogical research. Civil and court records may also contain information about your model-citizen ancestors — those fine, upstanding citizens who made good witnesses.

Civil records

Generally, civil records include information on your ancestors' civic duties, and family members' interaction with local government. For example, several members of Matthew's branch of the Abell family held local posts in St. Mary's County, Maryland, including sheriff, inspector of tobacco, justice of the peace, and member of the legislature. Several civil records show when these Abells were sworn into office and some of the actions that they took within the community. Civil records are often found in local and state archives or libraries.

Court records

Court cases and trials aren't just a phenomenon of today's world. Your ancestor may have participated in the judicial system as a plaintiff, defendant, or witness. Some court records can provide a glimpse into the character of your ancestors — whether they were frequently on trial for misbehavior or called as character witnesses. You can also find a lot of information on your ancestors if they were involved in land disputes — a common problem in some areas where land transferred hands often. Again, your ancestor may not have been directly involved in a dispute but may have been called as a witness. Another type of court record that may involve your ancestor is a probate case. Often, members of families contested wills or were called upon as executors or witnesses, and the resulting file of testimonies and rulings can be found in a probate record.

Marching to a Different Drummer: Searching for Military Records

Although your ancestors may not have marched to a different drummer, at least one of them probably kept pace with a military beat at some point in life. Military records contain a variety of information; the two major types of records that you're likely to find are service and pension records. Draft or conscription records may also surface in your exploration.

Service records

Service records chronicle the military career of an individual. They often contain details about where your ancestors lived, when they enlisted or were *drafted* (conscripted), their ages, their discharge dates, and, in some instances, their birthplaces and occupations. You may also find pay records (including muster records that state when your ancestors had to report to military units) and notes on any injuries that they sustained while serving in the military. Although most of the information contained in service records seems to be of little genealogical value, you can use these records to determine the unit in which your ancestor served. This information can lead you to pension records that do have genealogical importance. Also, service records can give you an appreciation of your ancestor's place within history — especially the dates and places where your ancestor fought or served as a member of the armed forces.

Pension records

Pensions were often granted to veterans who were disabled or who demonstrated financial need after service in a particular war or campaign; widows or orphans of veterans also may have received benefits. These records are valuable because, in order to receive pensions, your ancestors had to prove that they served in the military. Proof entailed a discharge certificate or the sworn testimony of the veteran and witnesses. Pieces of information that you can find in pension records include your ancestor's rank, period of service, unit, residence at the time of the pension application, age, marriage date, spouse's name, names of children, and the nature of the veteran's financial need or disability. If a widow submitted a pension application, you may also find records verifying her marriage to the veteran and death records (depending on when the veteran ancestor died).

Locating military records

Some military records (such as a discharge certificate or copy of orders) may turn up in your own home or in the home of a relative. For other military records, you may need to visit a national archive or contact the appropriate military department. These Web sites contain general information on military records:

- ✔ **Australia:** If you're interested in researching Australian military records, see Australian Genealogy — Researching Armed Services Personnel (`www.pcug.org.au/~mjsparke/mj_page1.html`). Also, for unit histories, see Australian Army Regiments — Index of Web Sites (`regiments.org/milhist/anzpac/aargxref.htm`).

- ✔ **Austria:** You can find a list of the collections maintained in the Austrian State Archives War Archive (`www2.genealogy.net/gene/reg/AUT/krainf-e.htm`).

- ✔ **Bangladesh:** For unit histories, see India, Pakistan, and Bangladesh Army Regiments — Index of Web Sites (`regiments.org/milhist/asia/iargxref.htm`).

- ✔ **Canada:** For a description of the military records that you can find in the Archives of Canada, see `www.archives.ca/exec/naweb.dll?fs&02020203&e&top&0`. To see regimental histories, see Canadian Army Regiments — Index of Web Sites (`regiments.org/milhist/america/cargxref.htm`).

- ✔ **Germany:** A few addresses for military archives in Germany are available at `w3g.med.uni-giessen.de/gene/reg/SUD/sudet_miarch.html` and `my.bawue.de/~hanacek/info/earchive.htm`.

- ✔ **India:** For unit histories, see India, Pakistan, and Bangladesh Army Regiments — Index of Web Sites (`regiments.org/milhist/asia/iargxref.htm`).

- ✔ **Malawi:** For unit histories, see British Central Africa Army Regiments — Index of Web Sites (`regiments.org/milhist/africa/cafrgxref.htm`).

- ✔ **New Zealand:** For unit histories, see New Zealand Army Regiments — Index of Web Sites (`regiments.org/milhist/anzpac/nzrgxref.htm`).

- ✔ **Pakistan:** For unit histories, see India, Pakistan, and Bangladesh Army Regiments — Index of Web Sites (`regiments.org/milhist/asia/iargxref.htm`).

- ✔ **South Africa:** For unit histories, see South African Army Regiments — Index of Web Sites (`regiments.org/milhist/africa/sargxref.htm`).

- ✔ **United Kingdom:** In general, you can find military records at the Public Record Office that has a series of Family Fact Sheets on British military records (`www.pro.gov.uk/readers/genealogists/familyfacts.htm`). You can also view a brief introduction to military records at `midas.ac.uk/genuki/big/BritMilRecs.html`. For regimental histories, see British Army Regiments — Index of Web Sites (`regiments.org/milhist/uk/bargxref.htm`).

- ✔ **United States:** The National Archives and Records Administration (`www.nara.gov`) houses several types of military records including service and pension records. For guides on the types of military records kept by the National Archives, see `www.nara.gov/genealogy/genindex.html#guides`. You can also request information from the National Personnel Records Center (`www.nara.gov/regional/stlouis.html`) for more recent military records.

- ✔ **Zambia:** For unit histories, see British Central Africa Army Regiments — Index of Web Sites (`regiments.org/milhist/africa/cafrgxref.htm`).

- ✔ **Zimbabwe:** For unit histories, see British Central Africa Army Regiments — Index of Web Sites (`regiments.org/milhist/africa/cafrgxref.htm`).

A useful guide to military records is "Military Service Records in the National Archives," General Information Leaflet 7, available from the National Archives and Records Administration, Room G-7, 700 Pennsylvania Avenue, NW, Washington, DC 20408.

Coming to Your Census

Finding genealogical records in your relatives' attics can take you only so far in the pursuit of your ancestors. Although vital records (see "Sifting through Birth, Death, Marriage, and Divorce Records," earlier in this chapter for more details) can fill in some of the gaps, eventually you need a set of records that provides information on your ancestors that was taken at regular intervals. This type of record is called a *census record*.

United States census schedules

Federal census records in the United States have been around since 1790. Censuses were conducted every ten years to count the population for a couple of reasons — to divide up the number of seats in the U.S. House of Representatives, and to assess federal taxes. Although census collections are still done to this day, privacy restrictions prevent the release of any detailed census information on individuals for 72 years. Currently, you can find federal census data only for the census years 1790 to 1920 (however, practically all the 1890 census was destroyed due to actions taken after a fire in the Commerce building in 1921 — for more on this, see "First in the Path of the Firemen," The Fate of the 1890 Population Census at `www.nara.gov/publications/prologue/1890cen1.html`). The 1930 census is scheduled to be released in April 2002.

Census records are valuable in that you can use them to take historical "snapshots" of your ancestors in ten-year increments. These snapshots enable you to track your ancestors as they moved from county to county or state to state, and to identify the names of parents and siblings of your ancestors that you may not have previously known. Each census year contains a different amount of information, with more modern census returns (also called *schedules*) containing the most information.

The people who collected details on individuals were called *enumerators*. Traveling door to door, these census-takers worked within an assigned district where they stopped at each residence to ask questions about the household. Being a census enumerator was not the most glamorous work. They were typically paid small amounts of money — usually barely enough to cover their expenses. Enumerators possessed differing levels of training and penmanship. These variations resulted in census returns that contained some readable information and some that had illegible entries and notes. Of course, on the plus side for genealogists, some enumerators went beyond the call of duty and made interesting notes on the families that they visited.

Using Soundex to search United States census records

For the censuses conducted from 1880 to 1920, you can use microfilmed indices organized under the Soundex system. The *Soundex* system is a method of indexing that takes names that are pronounced in a similar way but spelled differently and places them in groups. This indexing procedure allows you to find ancestors who may have changed the spelling of their names over the years. For example, you may find names like Helm, Helme, Holm, and Holme grouped together in the Soundex.

The Soundex code for a name consists of a letter and then three numbers. (Double letters count for only one number, and if your surname is short, you use zeros on the end to bring the total numbers to three.) To convert your surname to Soundex, use the first letter of your surname as the first letter of the Soundex code, and then substitute numbers for the next three consonants according to the following table. (For example, the Soundex code for the surname Helm is H450.)

1	B, P, F, V
2	C, S, K, G, J, Q, X, Z
3	D, T
4	L
5	M, N
6	R

We know that sounds confusing, so just follow these steps to convert your surname to a Soundex code:

1. **Write down your surname on a piece of paper.**

   As an example, we convert the surname *Abell*.

2. **Keep the first letter of the surname and then cross out any remaining vowels (A, E, I, O, U) and the letters *W, Y,* and *H*.**

   If your surname begins with a vowel, keep the first vowel. If your surname does not begin with a vowel, cross out all the vowels in the surname. So, in the surname *Abell,* we keep the letters *A, B, L,* and *L*.

3. **If the surname has double letters, cross out the second letter.**

   For example, the surname Abell has a double *L,* so we cross out the second *L,* which leaves us with the letters *A, B,* and *L*.

4. **Convert your letters to the Soundex code numbers according to the preceding chart.**

   We have the letters *A, B,* and *L* remaining. Because *A* is the first letter of the surname, it remains an *A*. The *B* converts to the number 1 and the *L* to the number 4. That leaves us with A14.

5. **Cross out any numbers that are the same side by side.**

   The remaining numbers of the Abell (A14) surname do not have the same numerical code next to each other. But it could happen with a name like Schaefer. Ordinarily, the name Schaefer would have the Soundex code of S216. However, because the *S* and the *C* both have the code of 2 and are side by side, you would eliminate the second 2 and come up with a Soundex code of S160.

6. **If you do not have three numbers remaining, fill in the rest with zeros.**

Only two numbers remain in the Abell surname after we cross out the vowels and double letters. Because the Soundex system requires a total of three numbers to complete the code, we must fill in the remaining numerical spot with a zero. Thus, our result for Abell is A140.

Even though converting names to Soundex is really easy to do on paper (as you've just seen), we would be remiss if we didn't tell you about some online sites that offer free programs to do the conversions for you! Here are a few you may want to check out:

- **National Archives and Records Administration's Soundex Machine:** www.nara.gov/genealogy/soundex/soundex.html

- **Surname to Soundex Code:** searches.rootsweb.com/cgi-bin/Genea/soundex.sh

- **Surname to Soundex Converter:** www.geocities.com/Heartland/Hills/3916/soundex.html

Soundex indexes are subject to human error and in some cases are incomplete — for example, the 1880 Federal Census Soundex primarily focuses on indexing those households with children age 10 years or younger. And those who carried out the actual indexing did not always handle Soundex codes correctly or consistently. So the indexer may have made a coding error or failed to include some information. Therefore, if you're relatively certain that an ancestor should show up in a particular county in a census that uses Soundex, but the Soundex microfilm doesn't reflect that person, you may want to go through the census microfilm for that county anyway and look line-by-line for your ancestor.

Other census records in the United States

You may also find census records at the state, territorial, and local level for certain areas of the United States. For example, the state of Illinois has Federal Census records for 1810 (one county), 1820, 1830, 1840, 1850, 1860, 1870, 1880, 1890 (small fragment), 1900, 1910, and 1920. In addition to these, Illinois has two territorial censuses taken in 1810 and 1818 and eight state censuses taken in 1820, 1825, 1830, 1835, 1840, 1845, 1855, and 1865. Some city census enumerations were taken in the 1930s, and a military census was taken in 1862.

These non-Federal census records can often help you piece together your ancestors' migration patterns or account for ancestors who may not have been enumerated in the Federal censuses. Sometimes, these censuses can also provide more detail on your ancestors than the Federal census schedules.

A good guide to census returns at the local and state level is *Red Book: American State, County & Town Sources,* edited by Alice Eicholz and published by Ancestry.

Searching census records from other countries

The United States isn't the only country that has collected information on its population. Census counts have taken place in several countries throughout history. Here are examples of a few countries with census records.

Australia

Australia has taken a census every ten years since 1901. However, every return has been destroyed in accordance with law. There are other records that you can substitute for census returns in the form of convict returns and musters and post office directories. These returns are available for some states for the years 1788, 1792, 1796, 1800, 1801, 1805, 1806, 1811, 1814, 1816, 1817, 1818, 1819, 1820, 1821, 1822, 1823, 1825, 1826, and 1837. Some of these records can be found in the Mitchell Library in Sydney (`www.slnsw.gov.au/ml/mitchell.htm`), Archives Office of Tasmania (`www.archives.tas.gov.au/`), Latrobe Library in Melbourne, Public Records Office of Victoria, Battye Library in Perth, and State Archives of Western Australia. For more information on locating census returns, see Censuses in Australian Colonies (`www.users.on.net/proformat/census.html`).

Austria

Austrian censuses were taken in the years 1857, 1869, 1880, 1890, 1900, and 1910. The first census that listed individuals by name was the 1869 Census. These returns include surname, sex, year of birth, place of birth, district, religion, marital status, language, occupation, literacy, mental and physical defects, residence, and whether the household had farm animals. For more information on Austrian censuses, see Austrian Census Returns 1869-1910 with Emphasis on Galicia (`www.feefhs.org/ah/gal/jshea-ac.html`) or Austrian Census for Galicia (`www.feefhs.org/ah/gal/1880-gal.html`).

Canada

Census returns are available for the years 1851, 1861, 1871, 1881, 1891, and 1901. The returns from 1851 to 1891 contain the individual's name, age, sex, province or country of birth, religion, race, occupation, marital status, and education. The returns for 1901 also include birth date, year of immigration, and address. For more information on data elements in the 1901 Census, see

Description of Columns on the 1901 Census Schedule (www.geocities.com/ Heartland/9332/census.htm). These returns are stored at the National Archives of Canada (www.archives.ca/). If you're looking for online information on specific census records, see the Bob's Your Uncle, Eh! genealogy search engine (indexes.tpl.toronto.on.ca/genealogy/index.asp). By selecting Census from the drop-down box marked *Topic,* you can see a variety of sites on census records including the 1753, 1921, 1935, and 1945 censuses of Newfoundland, French Canadian Heads of Households in the Province of Quebec in 1871, Index to the 1871 Census of Ontario, Index to the 1744 Quebec City Census, Nova Scotia Census Records, and the Toronto Census of 1837.

Denmark

The Danish Archives (www.sa.dk/ra/engelsk/default.htm) has census returns for the years 1787, 1801, 1834, and 1840 (as well as other years up to 1916). The returns contain name, age, occupation, and relationship for each individual in the household. After 1845, census returns include information on the individual's place of birth. Census returns are available when they're 80 years old.

Germany

The German central government held censuses in 1871, 1880, 1885, 1890, 1895, 1900, 1905, 1910, 1919, 1925, 1933, and 1939. Unfortunately, these census returns do not have much genealogical value because they were statistical in nature. For more information on the German census, see What About the German Census? (www.genealogy.net/gene/faqs/sgg. html#census).

Ireland

Country-wide censuses have been conducted every ten years since 1821. Unfortunately, the census returns from 1821 to 1851 were largely destroyed in a fire at the Public Record Office in 1922. Fragments of these census returns are available at the National Archives of Ireland (an online searchable index of the 1851 County Antrim return is available at www.genealogy.org/ ~liam/sea2.html). The government destroyed the returns from 1861 and 1871. Returns for 1901 and 1911 still survive and are available at the National Archives of Ireland (www.nationalarchives.ie/). Ireland suspended its law prohibiting the release of census returns for 100 years to make the 1901 and 1911 returns available to the public. For more information on censuses in Ireland, see Census Records (scripts.ireland.com/ancestor/browse/ records/census/index.htm). If you are interested in Northern Ireland, see the Public Record Office of Northern Ireland site (proni.nics.gov.uk/ research/family/family.htm).

Italy

The Italian State Archives (www.archivi.beniculturali.it/) contains national censuses for the years 1861, 1871, 1881, 1891, and 1901.

Norway

The first census in Norway was conducted in 1769. A census by name was conducted for the first time in 1801, but was not repeated again until 1865. Each census after 1865 contained information such as name, sex, age, relationship to head of household, civil status, occupation, religion, and place of birth. For more information on Norwegian censuses, see The Norwegian Census (www.rhd.uit.no/census.htm). An online searchable index of the 1801, 1865, and 1900 Censuses of Norway is available (digitalarkivet.uib.no/index-eng.htm). The 1900 Census of Norway (draug.rhd.isv.uit.no/rhd/engel1900.html) is also available from the Norwegian Historical Data Centre.

United Kingdom

Since 1801, censuses have been taken in the United Kingdom every ten years (except 1941). Most of the returns from 1801 to 1831 were statistical and did not contain names, making them useless for genealogists. Beginning in 1841, the administration of the census became the responsibility of the Registrar General and the Superintendent Registrars, who were responsible for recording civil registrations (vital records). This changed the focus of the census from the size of the population to details on individuals and families. The Public Records Office (www.pro.gov.uk) releases information in the census only after 100 years. You can find census returns for England and Wales at the Family Records Centre (www.pro.gov.uk/about/frc/default.htm) in London and for Scotland at the New Register House in Edinburgh. If you are not in either of those places, you can find copies of area returns at district libraries or Family History Centers. The 1891 Census for Scotland is available online for a fee in the Scots Origins database from the General Register Office for Scotland Web site (www.open.gov.uk/gros/groshome.htm).

Location, Location, Location: Researching Land Records

In the past, ownership of land measured the success of individuals. The more land that your ancestors possessed, the more powerful and wealthy they were. This concept often encouraged people to migrate to new countries in the search for land.

Land records may tell you where your ancestor lived prior to purchasing the land, spouse's name, and the names of children, grandchildren, parents, or siblings. However, to effectively use land records, you need to have a good idea of where your ancestors lived and possess a little background information on the history of the areas in which they lived. Land records are especially useful for tracking the migration of families in the United States before the 1790 Census.

Most land records are maintained at the local level — in the town or county where the property was located. These records can come in multiple forms based upon the type of land record and the location in which it exists.

Finding land records in the United States

Your ancestors may have received land in the early United States in several different ways. Your ancestor may have purchased land or received a grant of land in the public domain — often called *bounty lands* — in exchange for military service or some other service for the country. Either way, the process probably started when your ancestor petitioned (or submitted an application) for the land. Your ancestor may have also laid claim to the land, rather than petitioning for it.

If the application was approved, your ancestor was given a *warrant* — a certificate that allowed him or her to receive an amount of land. (Sometimes a warrant was called a *right.*) After your ancestor presented the warrant to a land office, an individual was appointed to make a *survey* — or detailed drawing and legal description of the boundaries — of the land. The land office then recorded your ancestor's name and information from the survey into a *tract book* (a book describing the lots within a township or other geographic area) and on a *plat map* (a map of lots within a tract).

After the land was recorded, your ancestors may have been required to meet certain conditions, such as living on the land for a certain period of time or making payments on the land. After they met the requirements, they were eligible for a *patent* — a document that conveyed title of the land to the new owner.

The Bureau of Land Management, Eastern States Land Office (www. glorecords.blm.gov), holds land records for public domain land east of the Mississippi River. The National Archives holds the land records for the western states (www.nara.gov). For secondary land transactions (those made after the original grant of land), you probably need to contact the recorder of deeds for the county in which the land was held.

Here are some Web sites with information on land records:

- **History and Use of Land Records:** main.nc.us/OBCGS/searchland-rec.htm

- **Legal Land Descriptions in the USA:** www.outfitters.com/genealogy/land/land.html

- **California:** Bureau of Land Management in California (www.ca.blm.gov/landpatents/)

- **Georgia:** Georgia Department of Archives and History Land Records (www.sos.state.ga.us/archives/rs/land.htm)

- **Illinois:** Illinois Public Domain Land Tract Sales (www.sos.state.il.us:80/depts/archives/data_lan.html)

- **Indiana:** Land Office Records at the Indiana State Archives (www.ai.org/icpr/webfile/land/land_off.html)

- **Oklahoma:** Federal Tract Books of Oklahoma Territory (www.sirinet.net/~lgarris/swogs/tract.html)

- **South Dakota:** Homesteading Records Information Page (members.aol.com/~gkrell/homestead/)

- **Tennessee:** An Introduction to the History of Tennessee's Confusing Land Laws (web.utk.edu/~kizzer/genehist/research/landlaws.htm)

- **Texas:** Texas General Land Office Archives (www.glo.state.tx.us/central/arc/index.html)

- **Virginia:** Introduction to Virginia Land History (www.ultranet.com/~deeds/virg.htm)

Because the topic of land records is so expansive, many books have been devoted to the subject. When you're ready to tackle land records in more depth, you may want to look at William Thorndale's "Land and Tax Records" in *The Source: A Guidebook of American Genealogy,* edited by Loretto Dennis Szucs and Sandra Hargreaves Luebking, and published by Ancestry.

Finding land records in other countries

Depending on the country that you research, you may find a number of ways that land transactions occurred. These links can assist you in figuring out how to research land records in a particular country:

- **Canada:** Land Records — Genealogical Sources in Canada (www.archives.ca/02/020202/LandRecords.html)

- **Ireland:** Land Records (scripts.ireland.com/ancestor/browse/records/land/index.htm)

Visiting Libraries, Archives, and Historical Societies

Collecting additional information on the area where your ancestor lived may inspire you to search for information in public (and some private) libraries. Although local history sections are not generally targeted toward genealogists, the information you can find there is quite valuable. For example, public libraries often have city directories and phone books, past issues of newspapers (good for obituary hunting), and old map collections. Libraries may also have extensive collections of local history books that can give you a flavor of what life was like for your ancestor in that area. For a list of libraries with online catalogs, see the webCATS site (www.lights.com/webcats/).

Archives are another place to find good information. They exist at several different levels (national, state, and local) and have different owners (public or private). Each archive varies — some may have a large collection of certain types of documents, while others may just contain documents from a certain geographical area. To find archives see Repositories of Primary Sources (www.uidaho.edu/special-collections/Other.Repositories.html).

A third place to find additional information is at a historical society. Generally, historical societies have nice collections of maps, documents, and local history books pertaining to the area in which the society is located. Also, they are repositories for collections of papers of significant people who lived in the community. Often, you can find references to your ancestors in these collections, especially if the person whose personal documents are in the collection wrote a letter or transacted some business with your ancestor. You can find links to historical societies on the Yahoo! site (www.yahoo.com/Arts/Humanities/History/Organizations/Historical_Societies/).

Discovering Family History Centers

You may be surprised to discover that your own hometown has a resource for local genealogical research! Sponsored by the Church of Jesus Christ of Latter-day Saints (LDS), over 2,500 Family History Centers worldwide provide support for genealogical research. The FamilySearch collection of CD-ROMs is among the important resources found in Family History Centers. They contain databases with the following information:

- ✔ **Ancestral File:** A database with over 29 million names available in family group sheets and pedigree charts.
- ✔ **International Genealogical Index:** A list of over 284 million individuals who are reflected in records collected by the LDS.

- ✔ **United States Social Security Death Index:** An index of those persons for whom Social Security death claims have been filed.

- ✔ **Military Index:** A list of United States soldiers killed in the Korean and Vietnam Wars.

- ✔ **Family History Library Catalog:** A catalog of over two million rolls of microfilm, one-half million pieces of microfiche, and 400,000 books and CD-ROMs available at the Family History Library in Salt Lake City.

Many other resources are available from Family History Centers, including their collection of microfilmed records and indices.

You don't need to be a member of the LDS church to use a Family History Center; the resources contained within them are available to everyone. Keep in mind that the workers at a Family History Center cannot research your genealogy for you, although they're willing to point you in the right direction. To find a Family History Center, use the FamilySearch search interface (`www.familysearch.org/Search/searchfhc2.asp`) or consult your local telephone directory.

Chapter 2

Planning for Genealogical Success

In This Chapter

▶ Using the Helm Family Tree Research Cycle

▶ Taking your time

*I*t wouldn't be a normal day in the Helm household If we didn't receive at least one e-mail message saying something like "Looking for information about the Smiths. My great-granny was Lucy Smith." Although we would love to have an all-encompassing library that contained everyone's genealogy, we regret to tell you that we don't. Unless the individual in question is an ancestor of ours, we can do little to assist you except to point you to resources that may help. And the sad fact (one we hate to admit) is that we receive so many of these messages each day that we can't reply to them all — so some of them never get answered. Our solution to this problem was to write this book!

If you're a novice genealogist, you may not know where and how to start your research because you're unsure of the standard process. This is where we come in to help. This chapter covers some of the basic things to keep in mind when you begin your research journey and offers some tips on what you can do when you hit *research bumps* along the way.

Introducing the Helm Online Family Tree Research Cycle

No book on research would be complete without some sort of model to follow, so we created one just for you. Of course, wanting to take credit for our fabulous model, we like to call it the *Helm Online Family Tree Research Cycle*. Sounds impressive, doesn't it? Figure 2-1 shows the five phases of the cycle: planning, collecting, researching, consolidating, and distilling.

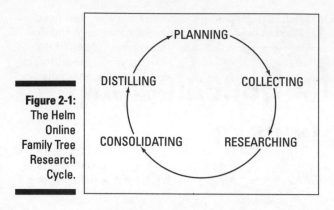

Figure 2-1:
The Helm
Online
Family Tree
Research
Cycle.

Sticking with the *family tree* motif here, we liken the cycle to the steps you take to plant and sustain a tree:

✔ **Planning:** The first step in planting a tree is figuring out what kind of tree you want and then finding a good place in your yard for the tree to grow. This step in the cycle is the *planning* phase. You want to select a family that you know enough about to begin a search and then think about the resources you want to use to find the information that you're looking for.

✔ **Collecting:** After you plan the location for the tree, you go to a nursery and pick out a suitable sapling and other necessary materials to ensure that the tree's roots take hold. The second phase of the cycle, *collecting,* is the same — you collect information on the family that you're researching by conducting interviews in person, on the phone, or through e-mail, and by finding documents in attics, basements, and other home-front repositories.

✔ **Researching:** The next step is to actually plant the tree. You dig a hole, place the tree in it, and then cover the roots. Similarly, you spend the *researching* phase of the cycle digging for clues, finding information that can support your family tree, and obtaining documentation. You can use traditional and technological tools to dig — tools like libraries, court-houses, your computer, and the World Wide Web.

✔ **Consolidating:** You planted the tree and covered its roots. However, to make sure that the tree grows, you mulch around it and provide the nour-ishment the tree needs to survive. The *consolidating* phase of the cycle is similar in that you take the information you find and place it into your computer-based genealogical database or your filing system. These sys-tems protect your findings by keeping them in a centralized location and provide an environment in which you can see the fruits of your labor.

> ✔ **Distilling:** After your tree has taken root and begins to grow, you need to prune the old growth, allowing new growth to appear. Similarly, the *distilling* phase is where you use your computer-based genealogical database to generate reports showing the current state of your research. You can use these reports to prune from your database those individuals you've proven don't fit into your family lines — and perhaps find room for new genealogical growth by finding clues to other lines you need to follow up.

We think that using this model makes researching a lot easier and more fulfilling. However, this model is merely a guide. Feel free to use whatever methods work best for you — as long as those methods make it possible for someone else to verify your research (through sources you cite and so on).

Planning your research

You may have heard that the Internet puts the world at your fingertips. Discovering all the wonderful online resources that exist makes you feel like a kid in a candy store. You click around from site to site with wide eyes, amazed by what you see, tempted to record everything for your genealogy — whether it relates to one of your family lines or not.

Because of the immense wealth of information available to you, putting together a research plan before going online is very important — it can save you a lot of time and frustration by keeping you focused. Tens of thousands of genealogical sites are on the Internet. If you don't have a good idea of what exactly you're looking for to fill in the blanks in your genealogy, you can get lost online. And getting lost is even easier when you see a name that looks familiar and start following its links, only to discover hours later (when you finally get around to pulling out the genealogical notes you already had) that you've been tracking the wrong person and family line.

Now that we've convinced you that you need a research plan, you're probably wondering what a research plan is. Basically, a *research plan* is a common-sense approach to looking for information about your ancestors online. A research plan entails knowing what you're looking for and what your priorities are for finding information.

If you're the kind of person who likes detailed organization (like lists and steps that you can follow to the tee), you can write your research plan on paper or keep it on your computer. If you're the kind of person who knows exactly what you want and need at all times, and you have an excellent memory of where you leave off when doing projects, your research plan can exist solely in your mind. In other words, your research plan can be as formal or informal as you like — as long as it helps you plot what you're looking for.

For example, say you're interested in finding some information on your great-grandmother. Here are some steps you can take to form a research plan:

1. **Write down what you already know about the person you want to research — in this case, your great-grandmother.**

   Include details like the dates and places of birth, marriage, and death; spouse's name; children's names; and any other details you think may help you distinguish your ancestor from other individuals. Of course, it's possible that all you know at this time is great-grandma's name.

2. **Conduct a search using a genealogically focused search engine to get an overview of what's available.**

   Visit sites like the GenealogyPortal.com (www.genealogyportal.com) to search for information by name and location. Using great-grandma's name and the names of some of the locations where she lived provides you with search results that give you an idea of what kind of resources are available. (Chapters 3 and 4 go into more detail about online trips and searching for this type of information.) You may want to make a list of the sites that you find on a sheet of paper or in your word processor.

3. **Prioritize the resources that you want to use.**

   Your search on a genealogically focused search engine may turn up several different types of resources, such as newsgroups, mailing lists, and Web sites. We recommend that you prioritize which resources you plan to use first. You may want to visit a Web site that specifically names great-grandma prior to signing up for a mailing list for all researchers interested in great-grandma's surname. (For more on using these resources, take a look at Appendix A.)

4. **Schedule time to use the various resources that you identify.**

   Genealogy is truly a life-long pursuit and, as such, you can't download every bit of information and documentation that you need all at once. Because researching your genealogy requires time and effort on your part, we recommend that you schedule time to work on specific parts of your research. (Scheduling time is especially useful if you're paying by the hour for an Internet connection.)

Collecting useful information

After you generate a research plan (see the preceding section, "Planning your research," for more information), you may need to fill in a few details like dates and locations of births, marriages, and deaths. You can collect this information by interviewing family members and by looking through family documents and photographs (see Chapter 1 for tips on interviewing and using family documents and photographs). You may also need to look up a few things in an atlas or *gazetteer* (a geographical dictionary) if you aren't sure where certain locations are. (Chapter 4 provides more information on online gazetteers.)

For a list of things that may be useful to collect, see Chapter 1. In the meantime, here are a few online resources that identify items to collect for your genealogy:

- **Ancestry.com: Getting Started — The First Steps:**
  www.ancestry.com/learn/start/memories.htm

- **Family Tree Maker's Genealogy Site: A Trip Down Memory Lane:**
  www.familytreemaker.com/00000025.html

- **Step-by-Step Guide to Finding Family Information:**
  www.familytreemaker.com/00000394.html

Researching: Through the brick wall and beyond

Of course, researching your family history online is the topic of this entire book, so you can find the necessary resources to do a great deal of your online research in these pages.

A time will undoubtedly come when you run into what genealogists affectionately call the brick wall syndrome. The *brick wall syndrome* is when you think you have exhausted every possible way of finding an ancestor. The most important thing you can do is to keep the faith — don't give up! Web sites are known to change frequently (especially as more people come online and begin sharing their information), so although you may not find exactly what you need today, you may find it next week at a site you've visited several times before or at a new site altogether. And fortunately, a few people post some suggestions on how to get through a brick wall when you run into it. Check out these sites:

- **How to Get Past Genealogy Road Blocks:**
  www.firstct.com/fv/stone.html

- **When Your Family History Research Hits the Wall:**
  www.parkbooks.com/Html/res_guid.html

Using a database to consolidate your information

After you get rolling on your research, you often find so much information that it feels like you don't have enough time to put it all into your computer-based genealogical database.

A *genealogical database* is a software program that allows you to enter, organize, store, and use all sorts of genealogical information on your computer.

When possible, try to set aside some time to update your database with the information that you recently gathered. This process of putting your information together in one central place, which we call *consolidating*, helps you gain a perspective on the work that you've completed and provides a place for you to store all those nuggets you'll need when you begin researching again. By storing your information in a database, you can always refer to it for a quick answer the next time you try to remember where you found a reference to a marriage certificate for your great-great-grandparents.

Distilling the information that you gather

The final step in the cycle is distilling the information that you gather into a report, chart, organized database, or detailed research log that you can use to find additional genealogical leads. Frequently, you can complete the distillation process by producing a report from your computer-based genealogical database. Most genealogical software programs allow you to generate reports in a variety of formats. For example, you can pull up a pedigree chart or an outline of descendants from information that you entered in the database about each ancestor. You can use these reports to see what holes still exist in your research, and you can add these missing pieces to the planning phase for your next research effort (starting the whole cycle over again).

Another advantage to genealogical reports is having the information readily available so that you can *toggle* back to look at the report while researching online, which can help you stay focused. (*Toggling* is flipping back and forth between open programs on your computer. For example, in Windows you press Alt+Tab to toggle, or you can click the appropriate task-bar item on the toolbar at the bottom of the screen. On a Macintosh, you can use the Application Switcher in the upper-right corner of the screen.) Of course, if you prefer, printing copies of the reports and keeping them next to the computer while you're researching on the Internet serves the same purpose.

Too Many Ancestor Irons in the Research Fire

One last piece of advice: When you begin your research, take your time and don't get in a big hurry. Keep things simple and look for one piece of information at a time. If you try to do too much too fast, you risk getting confused, having no online success, and getting frustrated with the Internet. This result isn't very encouraging and certainly doesn't make you feel like jumping back into your research, which would be a shame because you can find a lot of valuable research help online.

Chapter 3

What's in a Name?

....

....

As a genealogist, you may experience sleepless nights trying to figure out all the important things in life — the maiden name of your great-great-grandmother, whether great-grandpa was run out of town, and just how you're related to Daniel Boone (well, isn't everyone?). Okay, so you may not have sleepless nights, but you undoubtedly spend a significant amount of time thinking about and trying to find resources that can give you the answers to these crucial questions.

In the past, finding information on individual ancestors online was compared with finding a needle in a haystack. You browsed through long lists of links in the hopes of finding a site that contained a nugget of information to aid your search. Well, looking for your ancestors online has become easier than ever. Instead of merely browsing links, you can now use search engines and online databases to pinpoint information on your ancestors.

This chapter helps you with your first online search by covering the basics of a search for an ancestor by name, presenting some good surname resource sites and showing you how to combine several different Internet resources to successfully find information on your family. If you need a refresher on how to use a Web browser, take a look at Appendix A before you read this chapter.

Selecting a Person to Begin Your Search

Selecting a person sounds easy, doesn't it? Just select your great-great-great-grandfather's name and you're off to the races. But what if your great-great-great-grandfather's name was John Smith? You may encounter thousands of sites with information on John Smith — unless you know some facts about the John Smith you're looking for, you may have a frustrating time online.

Trying a unique name

The first time you research online, try to start with a person whose name is, for lack of a better term, semi-unique. By this, we mean a person with a name that doesn't take up ten pages in your local phone book, but is common enough that you can find some information on it the first time you conduct a search. If you're really brave, you can begin with someone with a very common surname, such as Smith or Jones, but you have to do a lot more groundwork up-front so that you can easily determine whether any of the multiple findings relate to your ancestor. (For more on groundwork, see Chapter 1.)

Also, consider any variations in spelling that your ancestor's name may have. Often, you can find more information on the mainstream spelling of their surname than on one of its rarer variants. For example, if you research someone with the surname Helme, you may have better luck finding information under the spellings *Helm* or *Helms.* If your family members immigrated to the United States in the last two centuries, they may have *Americanized* their surname. Americanizing a name was often done so that the name could be easily pronounced in English, or sometimes the surname was simply misspelled and adopted by the family.

To find various spellings of the surname, you may need to dig through some family records or look at a site like Table of Common Surname Variations & Surname Misspellings (www.ingeneas.com/alternate.html).

Narrowing your starting point

If you aren't sure how popular a name is, try visiting a site like Hamrick Software's surname distribution site (www.hamrick.com/names). At Hamrick's site, you can find the distribution of surnames in the United States based on the 1850 Census, 1880 Census, 1920 Census, and phone books from 1990 to the present. Here's what you do:

1. **Open your World Wide Web browser and go to Hamrick Software's surname distribution site** (www.hamrick.com/names).

   The Hamrick site appears with instructions and a form to use for searching.

Note: Need information on how to use a browser? Go to Appendix A.

2. **Type the surname you're researching into the Surname field in the search form.**

   For help choosing a surname, see the preceding section.

3. **Use the drop-down menu to select the year(s) for which you want to see the surname distribution.**

   You can choose 1850, 1880, 1920, 1990, or all these years.

4. **Click the Display button.**

   A color map displaying the distribution of your surname appears.

Figure 3-1 shows a distribution map for the surname Abell in 1990. According to the map, only one out of every 1,000 individuals uses this surname in two states. In the remaining states, the name is even rarer. This gives you a good indication that the surname Abell is semi-unique. In contrast, during the same year, the surname Smith was held by at least one out of every 300 individuals in each state.

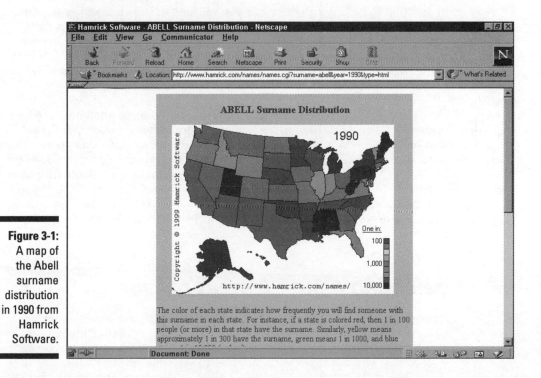

Figure 3-1: A map of the Abell surname distribution in 1990 from Hamrick Software.

Note: Looking at Figure 3-1, you may find it difficult to determine which two states have one out of 1,000 individuals using the surname Abell because of the way the colors show up as black, white, or shades of gray. If you visit Hamrick's site, the maps come up in color and are easier to read. (And just in case you're curious, the two states were Maryland and Kentucky.)

A good reason to check out the distribution maps is that you can use them to identify potential geographic areas where you can look for your family later in your research. This is especially true for maps generated from 1850 and 1880 Census data. For example, we generated another map on the Abell surname for the 1880 Census. We discovered that the name appeared more frequently in six states than in the rest of the country. If we hit a wall and can't find additional information online about a particular individual or the surname, we know that we can start looking at records in these states to find more clues about our particular branch of the family.

Using a person that you know about

In addition to picking a person that you're likely to have success researching, you want to use a person that you know something about. If you have a family line for which you know some basic information on your great-great-grandparents, use one of their names rather than a name for which you only know a few scattered details. The more details that you know about a person, the more successful your initial search is likely to be.

For example, Matthew used his great-grandfather William Abell because he knew more about that side of his family. His grandmother once mentioned that her father was born in Larue County, Kentucky, in 1876. This gives him a point of reference for judging whether a site has any relevant information on his family. A site is relevant if it contains any information on Abells who were located in Larue County, Kentucky, prior to or around the year 1876. Try to use the same technique with your ancestor. For more information on how to extract genealogical information from your family to use in your research, see Chapter 1.

Selecting a grandparent's name

Having trouble selecting a name? Why not try one of your grandparent's names? Using a grandparent's name can have several benefits. If you find some information on an individual but you aren't sure whether it's relevant to your family, you can check with relatives to see whether they know any additional information that can help you. This may also spur interest in genealogy in other family members who can then assist you with some of your research burden or produce some family documents that you never knew existed.

With a name in hand, you're ready to see how much information is currently available on the Internet about that individual. Because this is just one step in a long journey to discover your family history, you should keep in mind that you want to begin slowly. *Don't try to examine every resource right from the start.* You're more likely to become overloaded with information if you try to find too many resources too quickly. Your best approach is to begin searching a few sites until you get the hang of how to find information about your ancestors online. And keep in mind that you can always bookmark sites so that you can easily return to them later when you're ready for more in-depth researching. (A little rusty on how to set bookmarks on your Web browser? See Appendix A for a refresher.)

Finding the Site That's Best for You

Your dream as an online genealogist is to find a site that contains all the information that you ever wanted to know about your family. Unfortunately, these sites are few and far between (if they exist at all). Before you find a *golden site,* you may discover a variety of other sites that vary greatly in the amount and quality of genealogical information. Knowing ahead of time what kinds of sites are available and what common types of information you may encounter is useful.

Personal genealogical sites

The vast majority of sites that you encounter on the Internet are personal genealogical sites. Individuals and families who have specific research interests establish these pages. You're likely to find information on the site maintainer's immediate family or on particular branches of several different families, rather than on a surname as a whole. That doesn't mean that valuable information isn't present on these sites — just that they have a more personal focus.

You can find a wide variety of information on personal genealogical sites. Some pages list only a few surnames that the maintainer is researching; others contain extensive online genealogical databases and narratives. A site's content depends on the amount of research, time, and computer skills the maintainer possesses. Some common items that you see on most sites include a list of surnames, an online genealogical database, Pedigree and Descendant charts (for information on these charts, see Chapter 8), family photographs, and the obligatory list of the maintainer's favorite genealogical Internet links.

Personal genealogical sites vary not only in content, but also in presentation. Some sites are neatly constructed and use soft backgrounds and aesthetically pleasing colors. Others sites, however, require you to bring out your sunglasses to tone down the fluorescent colors, or they use link colors that blend in with the background, making it very difficult to navigate through the site. You should also be aware that many personal sites use JavaScript, music players, and animated icons that can significantly increase your download times.

An example of a personal genealogical site is the Mastin Family Genealogy Site (`members.nbci.com/mdm812/`). The site includes transcribed family obituaries, American Civil War diaries, a description of the migration of the Mastin family from Pennsylvania to Iowa and Missouri, family photographs, cemetery records, family documents, and a descendant chart (see Figure 3-2).

After you find a site that contains useful information, write down the maintainer's name and e-mail address and contact him or her as soon as possible if you have any questions or want to exchange information. Personal genealogical sites have a way of disappearing without a trace as individuals frequently switch Internet service providers or stop maintaining sites.

Figure 3-2:
A typical
personal
site: the
Mastin
Family
Genealogy
Site.

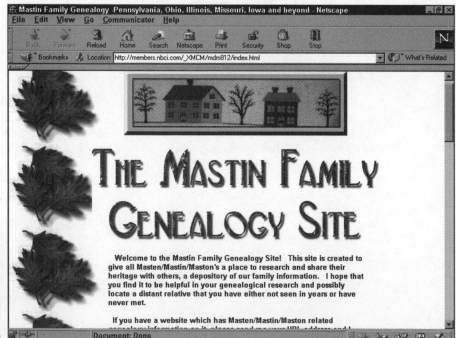

One-name study sites

If you're looking for a wide range of information on one particular surname, a one-name study site may be the place to look. These sites usually focus on one surname regardless of the geographic location where the surname appears. In other words, they welcome information about people with the surname worldwide. These sites are quite helpful because they contain all sorts of information about the surname, even if they don't have specific information about your branch of a family with that surname. Frequently, they have information on the variations in spelling, origins, history, and heraldry of the surname. One-name studies have some of the same resources you find in personal genealogical sites, including online genealogy databases and narratives.

Although one-name study sites welcome all surname information regardless of geographic location, the information presented at one-name study sites is often organized around geographic lines. For example, a one-name study site may categorize all the information about people with the surname by continent or country — such as Helms in the United States, England, Canada, Europe, and Africa. Or the site may be even more specific and categorize information by state, province, county, or parish. So, you're better off if you have a general idea of where your family originated or migrated. But if you don't know, browsing through the site may lead to some useful information.

The Iseli Family World Wide Web site (www.iseli.org/) is a one-name study site with an international focus. From the home page (see Figure 3-3), you can choose to view the site in German, English, French or Afrikaans. The site's divided into several categories, including variations in surname spelling, family branches, notable Iselis, family heraldry, and links to Iseli researchers' Web sites.

A notable portion of the Iseli site is the Iseli Millennium Project. This project seeks to produce a worldwide family genealogy to the year 2001 using the combined knowledge and research abilities of the users of the site.

The maintainers of one-name study sites welcome any information you have on the surname. These sites are often a good place to join research groups that can be instrumental in assisting your personal genealogical effort.

The *Genealogy Online For Dummies* Internet Directory in this book identifies some one-name study sites you may want to visit. It gives you just a sampling, though. To find one-name study sites pertaining to the surnames you're researching, you have to go elsewhere. Where, you say? Two sites that can help you determine whether any one-name study sites are devoted to surnames you're researching are SurnameWeb (www.surnameweb.org) and The Guild of One-Name Studies (www.one-name.org/top.htm).

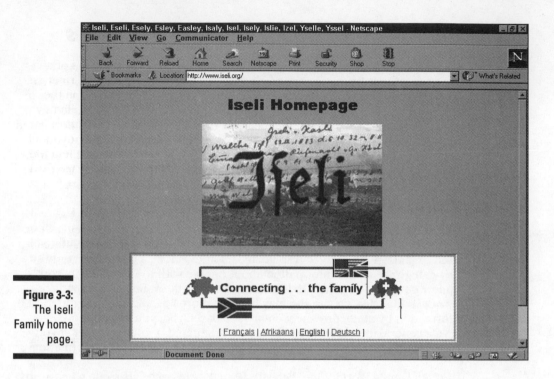

Figure 3-3:
The Iseli
Family home
page.

The Guild of One-Name Studies

Gee, we bet you can't figure out what the Guild of One-Name Studies is! It's exactly as it sounds — an online organization of registered sites, each of which focuses on one particular surname. The Guild has information about more than 7,000 surnames. Follow these steps to find out whether any of the Guild's members focus on the surname of the person you're researching:

1. **Open your Web browser and go to** www.one-name.org.

2. **Scroll to <u>The On-Line Searchable Register of One-Name Studies</u> link.**

   You're taken to a page called Register of One-Name Studies. Near the bottom of the page is a field where you can type in the surname you're researching or you can select a link of the letter of the alphabet corresponding to your search interest.

3. **Type a surname into the field and click Search.**

   The Results page contains entries from the database that match your search.

Family associations and organizations

Family association sites are similar to one-name study sites in terms of content, but they usually have an organizational structure (such as a formal association, society, or club) backing them. The association may focus on the surname as a whole or just one branch of a family. The goals for the family association site may differ from those for a one-name study. The maintainers may be creating a family history in book form or a database of all individuals descended from a particular person. Some sites may require you to join the association before you can fully participate in their activities, but this is usually at a minimal cost or free.

The Wingfield Family Society site (`www.wingfield.org`), shown in Figure 3-4, has several items that are common to family association sites. The site's contents include a family history, newsletter subscription details, a membership form, reunion news, queries, mailing list information, and a directory of the society's members who are online. Some of the resources at the Wingfield Family Society site require you to be a member of the society in order to access them.

Figure 3-4:
The home page of the Wingfield Family Society.

To find a family association Web site, your best bet is to use a search engine or a comprehensive genealogical index. For more on search engines see the sections "Focusing on Genealogically Focused Search Engines" and "Browsing Comprehensive Genealogical Indexes" later in this chapter.

Surnames connected to events or places

Another place where you may discover surnames is a site that has a collection of names connected with a particular event or geographic location. The level of information available on these sites varies greatly among sites and among surnames on the same site. Often, the maintainers of such sites include more information on their personal research interests than other surnames, simply because they have more information on their own lines.

Typically, you need to know events that your ancestors were involved in or geographic areas where they lived to use these sites effectively. This way, you have an interest in the particular event or location even if the Web site contains squat on your surname. Finding Web sites about events is easiest if you use a search engine or go to a comprehensive Web site. Because we devote an entire chapter to researching geographic locations (Chapter 4), we won't delve into that here.

Letting Your Computer Do the Walking: Using Search Engines

Imagine spending several hours clicking from link to link and not finding anything that related to your research. Wouldn't it be nice to be able to just type in your ancestor's name and see if there are any sites that contain that name? Well, that's exactly what search engines allow you to do.

Search engines are programs that search huge indexes of information generated by robots. *Robots* are programs that travel throughout the Internet and collect information on the sites and resources that they run across. You can access the information contained in search engines through an interface, usually through a form on a Web page.

The real strength of search engines is that they allow you to search the full text of Web pages instead of just the title or a brief abstract of the site. For example, say that we're looking for information on Jacob Helm who lived around the turn of the nineteenth century in Frederick County, Virginia. We could consult a comprehensive genealogical index site (for more on comprehensive genealogical indexes, see "Browsing comprehensive genealogical indexes" later in this chapter) and look for a Web site with Jacob Helm in the title or abstract of the site. Even if the comprehensive index contains tens of thousands of links, the chances of a Web site having Jacob Helm in its title or abstract is relatively small. But, by conducting a search through a search engine that indexes the full text of Web sites, we can find Jacob Helm listed in a tax list from Grayson County, Virginia in 1800 (along with 611 other individuals at `www.ls.net/~newriver/gray1800.htm`). Not only do we find information on Jacob Helm on a Web site — we find him in an unexpected county.

A few different kinds of search engines are available to aid your search. These include genealogically focused search engines, genealogy meta-search engines, general Internet search engines, and general Internet meta-search engines.

Focusing on genealogically focused search engines

Your first stop on a search for a particular ancestor should be a genealogically focused search engine. Genealogically focused search engines are sites that send out robots that index the full text of only sites that contain information of interest to genealogists. By indexing just such sites, you receive fewer extraneous results when you type in your ancestor's name as a search term. Currently, three principal genealogically focused search engines exist: GenealogyPortal.com, Internet FamilyFinder, and GenPageFinder.

GenealogyPortal.com

Technically, GenealogyPortal.com (`www.genealogyportal.com`) contains eight separate genealogically focused search engines. It includes search engines for archives and libraries, guides to research, historical sites, location-specific sites, names and personal sites, primary records, research supplies, and software and utilities. The GenealogyPortal.com search interface allows free-form text (your entry doesn't have to be a name) and Boolean searching. (*Boolean* searches involve using the terms *and*, *or*, or *not* to narrow your results.) You may have to use more than one of the GenealogyPortal.com's search engines to get complete coverage. For example, if you're searching for an individual, it's best to search the names and personal sites, location-specific sites, and primary records engines.

1. **Using your browser, go to** `www.genealogyportal.com`.

   The home page for GenealogyPortal.com contains a Search for Names and Personal Sites search box. If you want to switch to one of the other seven search engines, click one of the links located at the bottom of the search box.

2. **Type your search term in the field located in the gray box and click the Search button.**

   For example, we typed **George Helm** and clicked Search. The Results page appeared with 500 results — with 10 results on each page (see Figure 3-5).

3. **Click a link that interests you.**

   The Results page shows the title of the page and an abstract of the site. Within the abstract are bolded words that show you where your search terms appear on the page. Also, on the left side of the page title are green trees that show you the relevancy of the site to your search (the more trees, the more relevant the site is to your search).

Internet FamilyFinder

The Internet FamilyFinder (`www.genealogy.com/ifftop.html`) by Genealogy.com has a number of resources that can be searched at the same time. For example, at the time we visited the Internet FamilyFinder, you could search sites on the Internet, user home pages on Genealogy.com's site, message boards, classified advertisements, and some of Genealogy.com's CD-ROMs. Each of these types of sites are individually selectable — you can turn them off or on as you like.

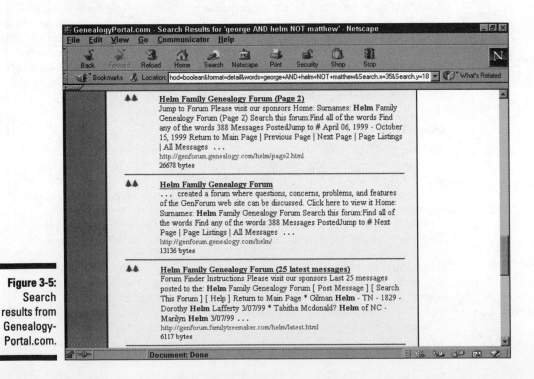

Figure 3-5:
Search
results from
Genealogy-
Portal.com.

To find information through the Internet FamilyFinder, follow these steps:

1. **Using your Web browser, go to** `www.genealogy.com/ifftop.html`.

   Note: See Appendix A for details on using a Web browser.

2. **Type the name of the individual you're researching into the First Name, Middle, and Last Name text boxes.**

   If you're looking for only general resources on a surname, just type the surname in the Last Name text box.

   Because we're interested in finding information on Joseph McSwain, we type **joseph** in the First Name and **mcswain** in the Last Name text box.

3. **Click the Search button.**

   The search form processes your request and shows you a page titled List of Matching Pages, which includes a table with five columns: Name, Date, Location, Found On, and Link. (Figure 3-6 shows an example of a list.)

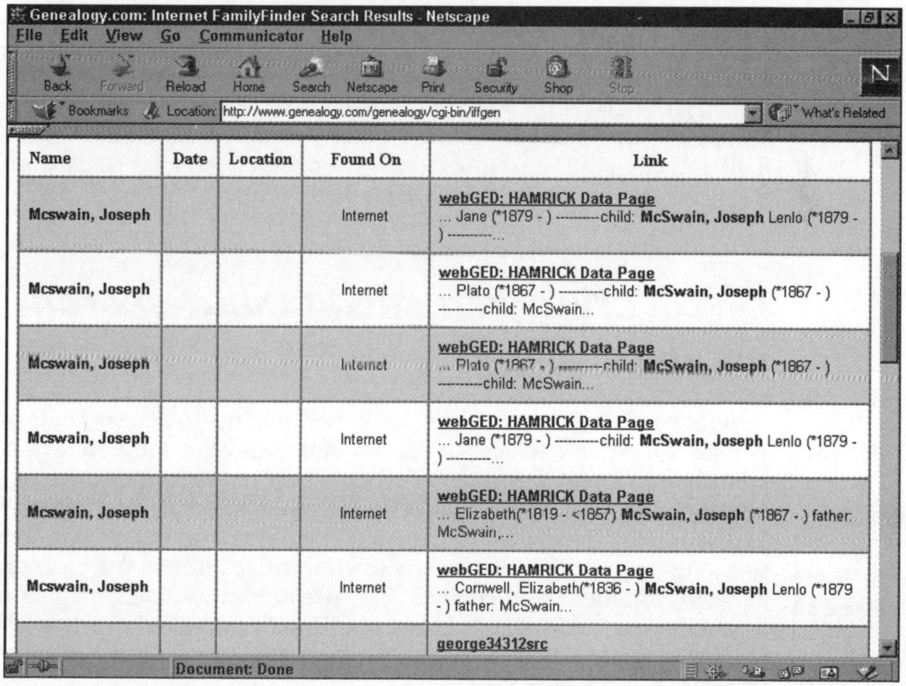

Genealogy.com: Internet FamilyFinder Search Results - Netscape

File Edit View Go Communicator Help

Back Forward Reload Home Search Netscape Print Security Shop Stop   N

Bookmarks Location: http://www.genealogy.com/genealogy/cgi-bin/ifgen   What's Related

Name	Date	Location	Found On	Link
Mcswain, Joseph			Internet	**webGED: HAMRICK Data Page** ... Jane (*1879 -) ----------child: **McSwain, Joseph** Lenlo (*1879 -) ----------...
Mcswain, Joseph			Internet	**webGED: HAMRICK Data Page** ... Plato (*1867 -) --------child: **McSwain, Joseph** (*1867 -) ----------child: McSwain...
Mcswain, Joseph			Internet	**webGED: HAMRICK Data Page** ... Plato (*1867 -) --------child: **McSwain, Joseph** (*1867 -) ----------child: McSwain...
Mcswain, Joseph			Internet	**webGED: HAMRICK Data Page** ... Jane (*1879 -) ----------child: **McSwain, Joseph** Lenlo (*1879 -) ----------...
Mcswain, Joseph			Internet	**webGED: HAMRICK Data Page** ... Elizabeth(*1819 - <1857) **McSwain, Joseph** (*1867 -) father: McSwain,...
Mcswain, Joseph			Internet	**webGED: HAMRICK Data Page** ... Cornwell, Elizabeth(*1836 -) **McSwain, Joseph** Lenlo (*1879 -) father: McSwain...
				george34312src

Document: Done

Figure 3-6: A table of results from Genealogy. com's Internet FamilyFinder.

The Name column is the full name of a person that the robot finds on the site. This can sometimes be misleading; the robot doesn't always understand the structure of the Web page. For example, if you were to do a search on the surname Helm, you'd find some interesting results. Several sites have links to other Web sites — in particular, Helm's Genealogy Toolbox. Another quirk of the program is that the robot sometimes combines the last word of the previous line in the list with the name Helm to form a name. On several sites, the last word of the previous line was the name of a state. So, the Internet FamilyFinder has an entry in the name field for Alabama Helm, Alaska Helm, and so on, for every state.

The other important column is the Link column, which displays a link to the site where the name was found and provides a few lines for the site that puts the name in perspective. This helps you avoid going to sites that result from the robot not understanding how the Web page was constructed. If the robot finds more results than can be displayed on one screen, you can click Next Page of Hits to see more results.

 4. **Click a link in the Link column to go to a site.**

You can return to the Internet FamilyFinder index by clicking your Web browser's Back button.

GenPageFinder

GenPageFinder (`www.ancestry.com/search/rectype/directories/ gpf/main.htm`) is the newest of the genealogically focused search engines. To use the search engine, simply enter your ancestor's name in the keyword field and click the Search button. If your search isn't successful, you should try to adjust the drop-down box marked Proximity.

Discovering genealogy meta-search engines

Several genealogy sites have search mechanisms to access their data. Wouldn't it be nice to search several of these at the same time? That's where meta-search engines come in. Technically, meta-search engines use a single interface (or form) to execute searches using several different search engines. They then return the results of all the individual search engines back to a single page that you can use to view the results. In the case of the two genealogy meta-search engines, they use not only some genealogically focused search engines, but they use the regular search mechanisms found on genealogical database sites. Two genealogy meta-search engines include Intelliseek and MetaIQ.

Intelliseek

Intelliseek Genealogy (`www.intelliseek.com/adv_genealogy.htm`) is a meta-search engine that searches twelve online genealogical resources including Family Tree Maker, Social Security Death Index, Connect with Surnames, GENDEX, RootsWeb Surname Helper, Genealogy Resources on the Internet Surnames, GenGateway, FamilySearch, Ancestry.com, Family History Library, I Found It!, and Cemetery Records Online.

To use the meta-search engine, type the name of your ancestor into the fields marked First Name, Middle Name, and Last Name. Under Search Sources, select the number of results that you want, whether you want links to be verified, and choose the resources to be search by checking the appropriate checkbox(es). After you have the desired search configuration, click the Just Find It button. After the search is executed, the Results page is returned (see Figure 3-7). Click the yellow box containing the site URL to go to a Web site that interests you.

MetalQ

MetalQ's (`www.metaiq.com/gen1/gen.html`) genealogy meta-search engine searches fewer sites but with a simpler interface. It searches Common Threads, FamilySearch, GenForum, Ancestry.com, SurnameWeb, RootsWeb, and GENDEX.

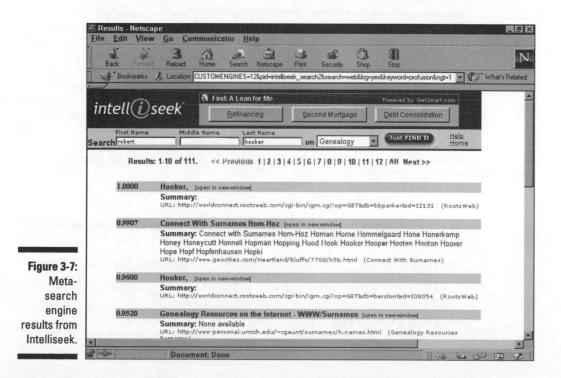

Figure 3-7: Meta-search engine results from Intelliseek.

Using the MetaIQ search form is easy: Just enter your ancestor's name into the field marked Enter First Name (Optional) or/and Surname (Required) Below and click the Seek button. After the Results page appears, click the link to a site that looks promising.

Meta-search engines do have some drawbacks. First of all, depending on how many search engines you decide to search at the same time, the processing of the results can be slow. So, you may have to exercise some patience. One way to speed things up is to select only a few search engines to be used during any given search. Second, meta-search engines don't always present the most relevant results first. This means that you may need to view several pages of results to find something that relates directly to your ancestor.

Using general Internet search engines

General search engines send out robots to catalog the Internet as a whole regardless of the content of the site. Therefore, on any given search you're likely to receive a lot of hits, perhaps only a few of which hold any genealogical value — that is, unless you refine your search terms to give you a better chance at receiving relevant results.

You can conduct several different types of searches with most search engines. Looking at the Help link for any search engine to see the most effective way to search is always a good idea. Also, search engines often have two search interfaces — a simple search and an advanced search. With the simple search, you normally just type your query and click the Submit button. With advanced searches, you can usually use a variety of options to refine your search. The best way to become familiar with using a search engine is to experiment on a couple of searches and see what kinds of results you get.

One search engine that has proven successful for us when we search for genealogical data is Google (`www.google.com`). To conduct a search on Google, do the following:

1. **Point your Web browser to** `www.google.com`.

   The Google home page is simple. It consists of a field to enter search terms and two buttons marked Google Search and I'm Feeling Lucky.

2. **Type your ancestor's name into the search field and click Google Search.**

   The Results page appears with a list of URLs and an abstract of the site with the search term bolded (see Figure 3-8).

3. **Click a search result that relates to your ancestor.**

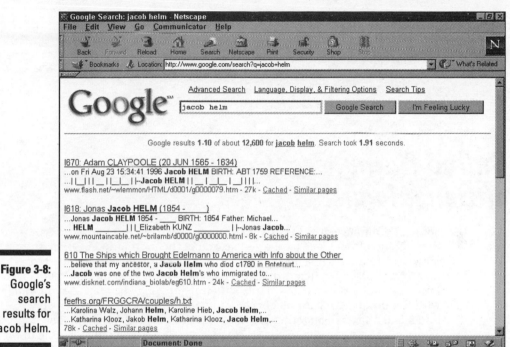

Figure 3-8:
Google's
search
results for
Jacob Helm.

If you're looking for additional leads, Google allows you to view other pages that are similar to results that you receive from your original search. You can also refine your search by using quotation marks in order to search for a phrase. For more search hints, you can click the <u>Search Tips</u> link available at the top of the Results page.

Looking at general Internet meta-search engines

Just like the genealogy meta-search engines, there are also meta-search engines that search the Internet as a whole. The number of results from meta-search engines can be overwhelming, so it's important for you to have a good search term and to know something substantial about the person you're researching. That way, you can quickly determine whether a result is relevant to your search. You also need to have patience because you may have to trudge through several sets of results before you find something useful. Some general Internet meta-search engines include the following:

✔ **C4:** `home.sprintmail.com/~debflanagan/cyber.html`

✔ **Debriefing:** `www.debriefing.com`

✔ **Dogpile:** `www.dogpile.com`

✔ **MetaCrawler:** `www.metacrawler.com`

✔ **Search.com:** `www.search.com`

Online Databases: Gold Mines of Genealogy?

Some of your ancestors may have been prospectors. You know the type — they roamed from place to place in search of the mother lode. Often, they may have found a small nugget here or there, but they never seemed to locate that one mine that provided a lifetime supply of gold. Searching on the Internet can be very similar to this situation. You may be able to sympathize with the prospectors as you check out results from search engines only to find small nuggets of information here and there. However, don't lose hope. There may be some goldmines waiting for you if you can only stumble upon the right site — and the right site may just be in the form of an online database.

Online databases are repositories of information that you can retrieve to assist you in compiling your family history. Most online databases are searchable and allow you to type in your ancestor's name and execute a search to determine whether any information stored in the database relates to that particular name. Databases can be large or small, they can focus on a small geographic area or have a broad scope that encompasses many different areas, and they can be fee-based or free. Each database may also have its own unique search method and present its information in its own format.

You can find online databases in many ways. You can find references to them through search engines (see the section "Letting Your Computer Do the Walking: Using Search Engines" earlier in this chapter), comprehensive genealogical indexes (see "Browsing Comprehensive Genealogical Indexes" later in this chapter), and links that appear on personal and geographic-specific Web sites. To give you a flavor of the type of goldmines that are available, we take a look at some of the larger online databases and some unique ones.

Social Security Death Index

If you're just beginning your genealogical journey, you may want to start with a search of the *Social Security Death Index (SSDI)*. The SSDI (as of the writing of this book) contains over 64 million records of deaths of individuals having a Social Security number beginning in 1962 (although a few scattered records pre-date 1962). Each entry includes the following:

- Name of deceased
- Birth date
- Death date
- Last residence
- Last benefit received
- Social Security Number
- State of issue

Several places exist online where the SSDI can be searched. Probably the most up-to-date version is found at ssdi.genealogy.rootsweb.com/cgi-bin/ssdi.cgi.

GENDEX

Many genealogists have posted their personal genealogical databases on the Web. However, locating all these independent databases can be challenging. Fortunately, some databases index all these individual efforts. One of the oldest is the GENDEX World Wide Web Genealogical Index (www.gendex.com/gendex/). This index was created to search the many online genealogical databases created through the GED2HTML program. (For more on posting genealogical databases to the Web and GED2HTML, see Chapter 12. And for even more about the GED2HTML program, see the section on genealogical software utilities in The *Genealogy Online For Dummies* Internet Directory in this book.) At press time, the database contained an index of over 16 million individuals in 4,226 databases.

1. **Type the address** www.gendex.com/gendex/ **into your Web browser.**

   The GENDEX — WWW Genealogical Index page appears.

2. **On the GENDEX — WWW Genealogical Index page, click Access the Index.**

   Another page appears, with links to Surname Index, Site Index, and Site Information.

3. **Click the <u>Surname Index</u> link.**

    The GENDEX — Index of Surnames page appears. This page includes text boxes labeled Enter A Prefix Of A Surname You Wish To Search For and Or, Enter A Surname And Search For Soundex-Equivalents.

4. **Enter the surname you're searching for in the Enter A Surname And Search For Soundex-Equivalents text box. Click the Submit button.**

    The Soundex page appears, showing a detailed breakdown of the surnames that meet your request. (For more information on Soundex, see Chapter 1.)

    We choose April's maiden name, Sanders. The Soundex page shows us the Soundex number for the name and a list of links to surnames with the number of instances of the surname in brackets following the link. For the surname Sanders, 6,128 entries are in the index. The results are listed in order of numbers of entries, rather than by the surname you entered. (For instance, if Sanders hadn't been the most frequently occurring surname for that Soundex code, it wouldn't have appeared as the first link on the results page. Therefore, you may have to look through the entire Results page to see whether your surname has an entry.)

5. **Click the appropriate link for your surname.**

    In our case, Sanders appears exactly as we want it on the page, so we click the <u>Sanders</u> link. The Surname page appears, with alphabetical ranges of given names for you to choose from. In our case, the page is called GENDEX — Surname: SANDERS.

6. **Click the given name range for the individual you're looking for.**

    Clicking Sanders brings us to an index with a range of names. Each link is arranged alphabetically by the first name of the individual possessing the last name Sanders. We were looking for April's great-grandfather, John Sanders, so we selected the link John /SANDERS/ - to - Lois /SANDERS/.

    Clicking the range of names takes you to another page that breaks down all the names within the first range into more ranges. For our example, the new index range offers two links to pages with information on people with the name John Sanders.

7. **Click the appropriate link for the range of names in which the name you're looking for would fit.**

    This takes you to a Web page that lists all the individuals in the database with names that fit in the range you've selected. In our case, we click the <u>John A. /SANDERS/ - to - John F. /SANDERS/</u> link because we believe April's great-grandfather's middle name was Duff. This takes us to a page that has links for 50 people with the name John Sanders and various middle names or initials beginning with letters between A and L.

8. On the Individuals page, click the name of the individual you're searching for.

Figure 3-9 shows a list of individuals in the range from John A. Sanders to John F. Sanders. Each surname is a link that takes you to the original database where the name appears. Also on the Individuals page, to help you decide whether the person is who you're looking for, you can see the dates and places of that person's birth and death if those dates were included in the original database. After you're taken to the original database, you can return to the GENDEX page by clicking the Back button on your Web browser.

GENDEX only indexes a small portion of the online databases available on the Internet. It's a good idea to check other sources such as search engines to find the locations of other online databases.

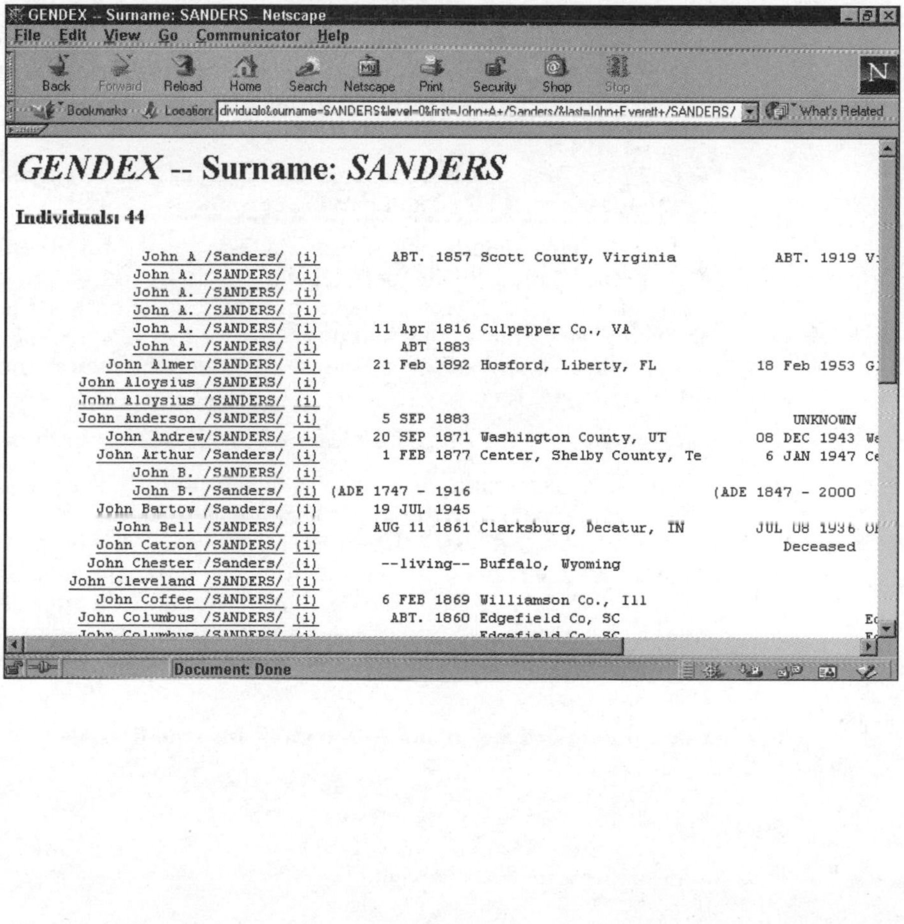

Figure 3-9:
A listing of individuals from the GENDEX site.

GENDEX -- Surname: *SANDERS*

Individuals: 44

John A /Sanders/ (i)	ABT. 1857 Scott County, Virginia	ABT. 1919 V:
John A. /SANDERS/ (i)		
John A. /SANDERS/ (i)		
John A. /SANDERS/ (i)		
John A. /SANDERS/ (i)	11 Apr 1816 Culpepper Co., VA	
John A. /SANDERS/ (i)	ABT 1883	
John Almer /SANDERS/ (i)	21 Feb 1892 Hosford, Liberty, FL	18 Feb 1953 G:
John Aloysius /SANDERS/ (i)		
John Aloysius /SANDERS/ (i)		
John Anderson /SANDERS/ (i)	5 SEP 1883	UNKNOWN
John Andrew/SANDERS/ (i)	20 SEP 1871 Washington County, UT	08 DEC 1943 We
John Arthur /Sanders/ (i)	1 FEB 1877 Center, Shelby County, Te	6 JAN 1947 Ce
John B. /SANDERS/ (i)		
John B. /Sanders/ (i)	(ADE 1747 - 1916	(ADE 1847 - 2000
John Bartow /Sanders/ (i)	19 JUL 1945	
John Bell /SANDERS/ (i)	AUG 11 1861 Clarksburg, Decatur, IN	JUL 08 1936 Of
John Catron /SANDERS/ (i)		Deceased
John Chester /Sanders/ (i)	--living-- Buffalo, Wyoming	
John Cleveland /SANDERS/ (i)		
John Coffee /SANDERS/ (i)	6 FEB 1869 Williamson Co., Ill	
John Columbus /SANDERS/ (i)	ABT. 1860 Edgefield Co, SC	Ed
John Columbus /SANDERS/ (i)	Edgefield Co, SC	Fo

FamilySearch

The FamilySearch Internet Genealogy Service (`www.familysearch.org`) is the official research site for the Church of Jesus Christ of Latter-day Saints (LDS). This free Web site allows you to search several of the LDS databases including the Ancestral File, International Genealogical Index, Family History Catalog, SourceGuide, and a collection of abstracted Web sites, all of which are currently free. To search the FamilySearch site do the following:

1. **Open your Web browser and go to** `www.familysearch.org`.

   The home page for FamilySearch contains three columns under the Features label: Search for Ancestors, Share Information, and Family History Library System.

2. **Click the Search for Ancestors column.**

   You can click anywhere in the column — the graphic or any part of the text description. This takes you to a page showing several fields that you can fill in to conduct a search on the site (the fields form a small pedigree chart).

3. **Type in the first and last name of the ancestor you're researching in the fields marked First Name and Last Name.**

   If you decide to include information on the spouse or mother or father and you don't receive adequate results, try doing the search just on the name of the ancestor. You can also fill in any of the optional fields such as Event, Year, Year Range, Country, State, or Use Exact Spelling. (Keep in mind filling in any of these fields may reduce the overall number of results that you receive.)

4. **After you select the search options, click the Search button.**

   The Results page contains links with descriptions to the resources that met your search criteria. For example, we search for information on Jacob Helm and check the option for Use Exact Spelling. We receive 74 matches from such resources as the International Genealogical Index, Ancestral File, Pedigree Resource File, and Web Sites. The far-right column entitled Sources Searched provides a breakdown of the number of results that you received from each FamilySearch resource (see Figure 3-10).

5. **Click the link of any result to see more information.**

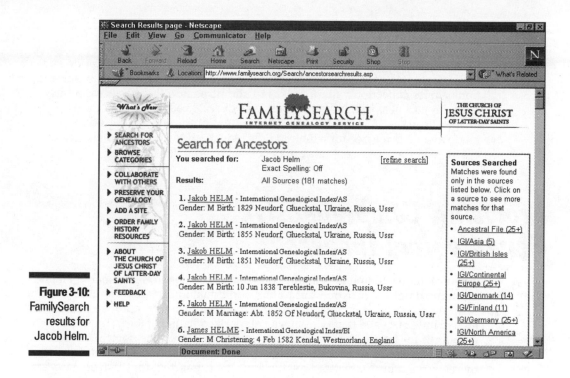

Figure 3-10: FamilySearch results for Jacob Helm.

Although the LDS is well known for its large genealogical collection, don't expect to find the complete collection online. Also, you need to verify (through original records) any information that you do find online. Much of the information currently on the site was contributed by other family history researchers, who may or may not have been careful in researching and documenting their family history.

Ancestry.com

Ancestry.com (www.ancestry.com) is a commercial site that maintains over 2,500 subscription-based databases and promises to add new databases daily. The site also has a lot of free content, including weekly columns and a few databases. To access the text of the databases, you must be a member (although Ancestry does put the majority of its new databases online for free for ten days and usually has a free period for all of its databases in December or January of each year). Ancestry.com also recently released its collection of census images in its Images Online subscription-based service. The first images placed online are from the 1790 Census. The Images Online service also includes the National Archives Index to Civil War Pension Applications.

GenealogyLibrary.com

GenealogyLibrary.com (`www.genealogylibrary.com`) is a subscription site maintained by Genealogy.com. It currently contains over 2,807 databases and books in its collection (and promises to add three new databases each business day). GenealogyLibrary.com also has over 283,000 digitized census images from the 1850 U.S. Census. The content of the site are periodically made available for free for a limited time, which gives you a good chance to decide whether then contents are beneficial to your research.

Browsing Comprehensive Genealogical Indexes

If you're unable to find information on your ancestor through a search engine or online database (or you want to find additional information) another resource to try is a comprehensive genealogical index. A comprehensive genealogical index is a site that contains a categorized listing of links to online resources for family history research. Comprehensive genealogical indexes can be organized in a variety of ways including by subject, alphabetically, or by resource type. No matter how the links are organized, they usually appear hierarchically — meaning that you click from category to subcategory, and so forth, until you find the link you're looking for.

Some examples of comprehensive genealogical indexes include the following:

- **Cyndi's List of Genealogy Sites on the Internet:** `www.cyndislist.com`
- **Genealogy Home Page:** `www.genealogyhomepage.com`
- **Genealogy Resources on the Internet:** `www.personal.umich.edu/~cgaunt/gen_intl.html`
- **Helm's Genealogy Toolbox:** `www.genealogytoolbox.com` (This site is more than just a list of links, so we cover it in the section "Integrating Your Search" later in this chapter.)

To give you an idea of how comprehensive genealogical indexes work, try the following example:

1. **Fire up your browser and go to Cyndi's List (`www.cyndislist.com`).**

   This launches the home page for Cyndi's List.

2. **Scroll down to the portion of the main page labeled Cyndi's List Category Index.**

Note: You have to scroll down almost one-third of the page to get to the Category Index.

3. **Select a category, such as Surnames, Family Associations & Family Newsletters.**

For example, we're looking for a page that may contain information on our ancestors. Two categories on the list may have this info: Personal Home Pages and Surnames, Family Associations & Family Newsletters. We decide to try the Surnames category.

4. **Select a subcategory.**

We can actually access the subcategories within the Surnames category in two ways. We can click the link for Surnames, Family Associations & Family Newsletters and then click another link for the letter of the alphabet that corresponds to the name we're looking for. Or, we can simply click the letter of the alphabet contained in the table beneath the Surnames, Family Associations & Family Newsletters link.

Say we're interested in finding some information on the Helm family. We select the H link and we're taken to the appropriate subcategory page. We then scroll down to the section titled Surname Specific Sites and Resources and looked for Helm resources (see Figure 3-11). We find one possible resource — although it's on the Helms, not Helm family.

5. **Click a promising link.**

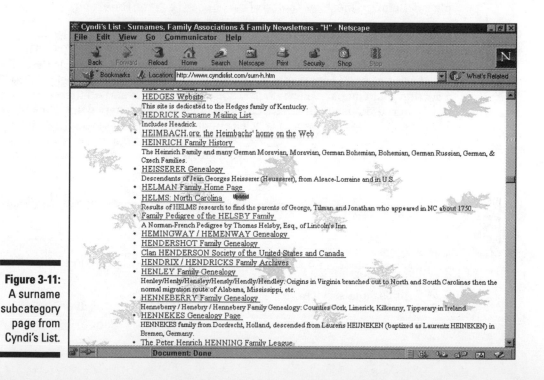

Figure 3-11: A surname subcategory page from Cyndi's List.

Of course, one drawback to comprehensive genealogical indexes is that they can be time-consuming to browse. It sometimes takes several clicks to get down to the area where you believe links that interest you may be located. After several clicks, you find that no relevant links are in that area. This may be because the maintainer of the site has not yet indexed a relevant site, or the site may be listed somewhere else in the index.

To avoid wasting time on comprehensive genealogical indexes, you many want to check to see whether the index has a search mechanism. If it does, use the search mechanism before you spend a lot of time clicking from one category to another in search of an elusive link. In the case of Cyndi's List, you can access a search interface from the home page by clicking the <u>Search It!</u> link (which is contained in the column marked Cyndi's List Category Indexes & Search Engine near the top of the home page).

Integrated Genealogical Search Sites

Okay, so we mention that search engines and comprehensive genealogical indexes can help you find information online about your ancestors. Wouldn't it be nice if you could use both resources at the same time? We're proud to say that one Web site does integrate both full-text searching of genealogical Web sites with a comprehensive genealogical index. The site is, drum roll please, Helm's Genealogy Toolbox (www.genealogytoolbox.com).

Helm's Genealogy Toolbox is one of the oldest genealogical Web sites — growing out of a list of links first placed on the Web in September 1994. The site currently contains over 86,000 links to sites of interest to genealogists, a set of eight search engines that index the full-text of online genealogical sites, a section that compares genealogical software products and utilities, over one hundred thousand queries from genealogical researchers going back to 1995, a collection of news and articles about family history research, and digitized images of microfilmed original records. All these resources are integrated together into a single site that's divided into the following categories:

- ✔ Computers
- ✔ How-to and help
- ✔ Media
- ✔ People
- ✔ Places/geographic
- ✔ Supplies and services

You can search Helm's Genealogy Toolbox a couple of different ways. You can search all the resources of the site at the same time through the Global Search or you can browse through the categories much like a comprehensive genealogical index. Here's an example search using the Global Search option:

1. **Launch your Web browser and type in the address for Helm's Genealogy Toolbox (**www.genealogytoolbox.com**).**

   The home page for the site appears. In the left column of the page is a section with a blue background called Global Search.

2. **Type your ancestor's name into the field and click the Search button.**

   The Results page returns a list of links that met your search criteria. These links include resources from the categorized list of links, the full-text search engines, queries from other researchers, and names from digitized records.

3. **Click a link that may relate to your ancestor.**

To browse links on the Genealogy Toolbox site, complete the following steps:

1. **Launch your Web browser and type in the address for Helm's Genealogy Toolbox (**www.genealogytoolbox.com**).**

   This time, scroll down to the section labeled Site Categories.

2. **Click the <u>People</u> link.**

   The resulting page contains links to surname subcategories arranged by letter of the alphabet (the letter of the alphabet corresponds to the first letter of the surname that's the subject of the Web site).

3. **Choose a link to a surname subcategory or select a link that looks interesting.**

   On some pages, you may encounter further subcategories that break down the letters of the alphabet into smaller sections. Other pages merely contain links to other Web sites.

Query for One: Seeking Answers to Your Surname Questions

Even if you can't find any surname-specific sites on your particular family, you still have hope! This hope comes in the form of queries. *Queries* are research questions that you post to a particular Web site, mailing list, or newsgroup, so that other researchers can help you solve your research problems. Often, other researchers have information that they haven't yet made available about a family, or they may have seen some information on your family even though it isn't a branch that they're actively researching.

Web queries

One of the quickest ways of reaching a wide audience with your query is through a query site on the Web. (Appendix A has some information about the Web if you need help.) For an example of a query site, try GenForum, which currently contains 5.5 million messages:

1. **Open your Web browser and go to** www.genforum.com.

2. **In the field under Forum Finder, type the surname you're looking for and click the Find button.**

   In our case, we enter **Helm**. But feel free to enter a surname that interests you. If you feel like browsing the forums, you can also select a letter beneath the word *Surnames*.

   Don't worry if your surname doesn't have a forum. The GenForum section is constantly growing and adding surnames. You may also want to search the other forums to see if the name is included in a variant spelling or if someone else mentioned the name in a passing reference in another forum (see the next section for details).

3. **After you find a forum, read a message by clicking its link.**

   As soon as your browser loads the message board page, you should see a list of bulleted messages to choose from. You can also navigate to other pages of the message board if the messages don't all fit on a single page. If you don't want to read all the messages, you have the option to see the latest messages, today's messages, and any messages posted in the last seven days. These options are available in green script at the top of the page.

4. **To post a new query, click the <u>Post New Message</u> link near the top of the message board page.**

   You should see some green text, just above the list of messages. The first one in the row is the <u>Post New Message</u> link.

   Clicking this link generates another page that contains the fields that generate your message. This page includes the Name, E-Mail, Subject, and Message fields, as shown in Figure 3-12.

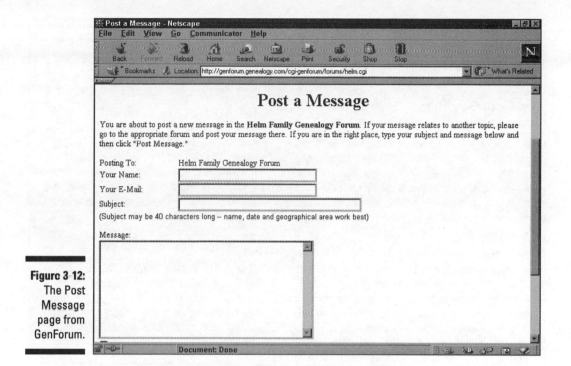

Figure 3-12:
The Post
Message
page from
GenForum.

5. **Fill out the appropriate fields and then click the Preview Message button.**

   Make sure that your message contains enough information for other researchers to determine if they can assist you. Include full names, birth and death dates and places (if known), and geographic locations where your ancestors lived (if known). For more tips on how to create effective messages, see the sidebar "Keys to an effective query" in this chapter.

   Clicking the Preview Message button is an important step because you can see how the message will look when it's posted. This option can prevent you from posting an embarrassing message.

6. **If you're satisfied with the way that the message looks, click the Post Message button.**

Some other Web sites also have large collections of queries:

✔ **GenConnect:** genconnect.rootsweb.com/index.html

✔ **FamilyHistory.com:** www.familyhistory.com

✔ **Helm's Genealogy Toolbox:** www.genealogytoolbox.com

Keys to an effective query

Have you ever asked a question of thousands of strangers around the entire world? If you haven't, then you should be aware that this is exactly what you do when you post a query.

A lot of genealogical sites on the Internet allow visitors to post questions *(queries)* about the people and places they're currently researching. Posting queries is a lot like calling the reference desk of your local library. Reference librarians can be a great help — if your questions contain enough detail for them to work with.

Keep these key things in mind when you post queries. First, make sure that your query is appropriate for the site. Several sites have specific requirements for queries, especially those sites that focus on specific geographical areas. Second, ensure that your query is formatted in a manner consistent with the site maintainer's instructions. Many query sites don't have an automated posting process, so the maintainer probably posts all the queries by hand. It helps them to have the query in a standard format and it helps those reading the query to quickly determine whether they can help the person. Here are some elements to include in your query (as long as they're consistent with the site's format):

✔ Type your surnames in all capital letters. HELM is much easier to see than Helm when reading through thousands of queries.

✔ Keep your query concise but add some concrete information. Dates of birth and death, specific locations where the person lived,

and names of any spouses, parents, or children are concise but concrete. Here's a good query example:

"HELM, George — I am looking for the parents of George Helm of Frederick County, Virginia (1723-1769). His wife was Dorothea, and he had a son named George (who was a soldier in the American Revolution and later moved to Fentress County, Tennessee). George is buried in the German Reformed Cemetery in Winchester, Virginia. I can be contacted at mhelm@tbox.com."

✔ Your query should contain the basic elements that other researchers need to determine whether they can help you. A good rule of thumb is that your query should, at a minimum, contain the answers to these questions:

Who is the person you're looking for?

What specific information do you want about the person?

Where did the person live? Where was the person born? Where did the person die?

When was the person born? When did the person die?

How can someone contact you? Include your e-mail address, but don't share your postal address or phone number in such a public forum.

Mailing list queries

When you think of mailing lists, you may have nightmares of the endless stream of *junk* mail that you receive every day as a result of some company selling your name to a mailing list. Well, fear no more. The type of mailing lists we refer to deliver mail that you actually request. They also provide a means through which you can post queries and messages about your surnames and genealogical research in general.

Mailing lists are formed by groups of people who share common interests, whether those interests are in surnames, specific geographic areas, particular topics, or ethnic groups. A list consists of the e-mail addresses of every person who joins (subscribes to) the group. When you want to send a message to the entire group, you send it to a single e-mail address that in turn forwards the message to everyone on the list. To join a mailing list, you send an e-mail to a designated address with a subscription message. You should then receive a confirmation e-mail letting you know that you're subscribed to the list and telling you where you need to send an e-mail if you want to send a message to everyone on the list.

So you know what a mailing list is, but how do you find one of interest to you? One way is to consult the comprehensive list of mailing lists found on the Genealogy Resources on the Internet site (www.rootsweb.com/ ~jfuller/gen_mail.html). The site breaks down the mailing lists into Countries other than USA, USA, Surnames, Adoption, African-Ancestored, Cemeteries/Monuments/Obituaries, Computing/Internet Resources, General Information/Discussion, Genealogical Material/Services, Jewish, Native American, Religions/Churches (other than Jewish), Software, Wars/Military, Uncategorized.

Here's how you can find and join a mailing list for your surname:

1. **Point your Web browser to** www.rootsweb.com/~jfuller/gen_mail. html **and select the first letter of a surname you're interested in under the surnames section (you have to scroll to the middle of the page to find it).**

   The letters appear near the bottom of the page. We select Hei-Hen because we're looking for a mailing list on the surname Helm. A list of surnames with mailing lists pops up.

2. **Scroll through the list and click one of the surname links on the page.**

   By scrolling through the list, you can see if your surname is represented. We scrolled through until we found our surname (see Figure 3-13) and clicked on that link. It took us to a page that had information on a mailing list pertaining to Helm.

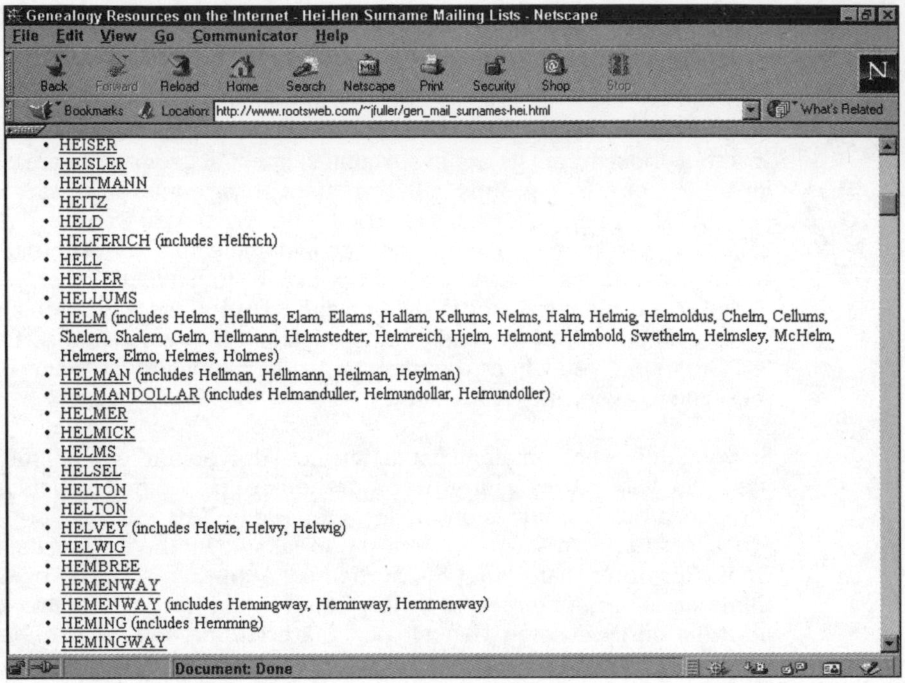

Figure 3-13:
A surname
mailing list
page from
Genealogy
Resources
on the
Internet.

Note that several mailing lists include variations of the surname as part of the scope of their discussions — the Helm list includes 28 variants. So, even if the exact spelling of your surname doesn't appear in the list, skimming some of the surnames with similar spellings is a good idea.

3. Follow the subscription instructions for your mailing list.

The instructions for the Helm mailing list tell us to send an e-mail message with the word *subscribe* as the only text in the message body to one of two addresses.

The reason for including only the word *subscribe* is to accommodate automatic processing by a computer. When you send a message to join a mailing list, chances are that the message is processed automatically without human intervention. That is, the computer automatically adds you to the mailing list when it reads the word *subscribe* in your message. If you add any other text, the computer doesn't know what to do with the message and it may not add you to the mailing list.

Typically, you can receive mailing lists in one of two ways. The first way, *mail mode,* simply forwards e-mail messages to you every time someone posts to the mailing list. Although this practice is fine for small mailing lists, you probably don't want hundreds of messages coming in individually — unless you like to have lots of e-mail sitting in your inbox. To avoid this, try the second way of receiving the mailing list — *digest mode*. Digest mode groups several messages together and then sends them out as one large message. Instead of receiving 30 messages a day, you may receive only 2 messages with the text of 15 messages in each.

4. **Start your e-mail program and subscribe to the mailing list.**

   We decide to subscribe to the digest mode of the Helm mailing list. To do this, we start our e-mail program, create a new message with only the word *subscribe* in the body, and send the message to the digest address — `helm-d-request@rootsweb.com` (see Figure 3-14). Within a couple of minutes, we receive a confirmation message welcoming us to the mailing list.

   Within the text of the confirmation messages that most mailing lists send is some valuable information that you want to hold on to for as long as you subscribe to the list — such as how to unsubscribe from the list, how to post messages to the list for others to read, and what format you should use for posting queries.

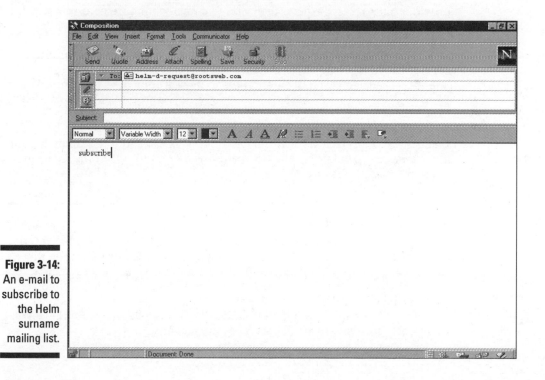

Figure 3-14: An e-mail to subscribe to the Helm surname mailing list.

5. **Read the messages without responding or posting your own messages for a while. Begin posting your own queries and responses to others' messages when you feel comfortable.**

   Reading messages but not posting your own messages is called *lurking*. You may want to lurk on the mailing list to see what other messages look like and to become familiar with the general culture of the list. After you get a feel for the structure and attitude of the messages, jump in and begin sending your own queries and messages!

Newsgroup queries

Another place where you can post queries is in a *newsgroup*. Newsgroups are similar to mailing lists in that you use e-mail to send a message that many people can read. The difference is that the message you send is not e-mailed to everyone on a list. Instead, it's stored on a news server, which in turn copies the message to other news servers. When you want to read a message on the newsgroup, you use a news reader program that connects you to a news server. To read newsgroups in this manner, your Internet service provider must receive a news feed, and you must configure your newsreader to pick up the feed.

Don't worry if you don't have access to a news feed through your Internet service provider. Some sites — such as DejaNews (`www.deja.com/usenet`) — enable you to view and post to newsgroups over the World Wide Web. You can also receive posts from newsgroups through gatewayed mailing lists.

Gatewayed means that traffic from newsgroups is relayed to a mailing list and vice versa. You can find a list of the gatewayed newsgroups in the Genealogy Resources on the Internet Web site at `www.rootsweb.com/~jfuller/gen_mail.html`.

Newsgroup hierarchies

Newsgroups are categorized in *hierarchies,* where each hierarchy has a top-level label such as `soc` or `alt`. Most genealogical traffic flows through the `soc` hierarchy (although some traffic does come through the `alt.genealogy` newsgroup). Beneath the `soc` level is a second hierarchy, which is followed by a third level, and so on. The hierarchy of most interest is `soc.genealogy`. Currently, 26 newsgroups fall under the `soc.genealogy` hierarchy. Seven of them deal directly with surnames. They are cleverly named:

✔ soc.genealogy.surnames.britain

✔ soc.genealogy.surnames.canada

✔ soc.genealogy.surnames.german

✔ soc.genealogy.surnames.global

✔ soc.genealogy.surnames.ireland

✔ soc.genealogy.surnames.misc

✔ soc.genealogy.surnames.usa

Learning the rules (formal and informal) for posting

Monitoring the newsgroup for a while (also called *lurking*) before posting a message is always a good idea. By lurking you get an idea of how the newsgroup works and what information is appropriate to post there. Believe us, a lot of people out there have used newsgroups for years and still post messages that are inappropriate for that particular newsgroup.

How do you find out what's appropriate to post? All newsgroups have *charters* that define the scope of the newsgroup. Some newsgroup *moderators* (people who help manage the newsgroup) frequently post the charters and tips on using newsgroups. Unfortunately, a lot of newsgroups don't have frequent posting of this information, so determining whether a post is appropriate may be difficult. Sometimes these discussions take on a life of their own and become distractions until the series of messages, called a *thread,* finally fizzles out. If you can't find the charter of the group, the safest thing to do is see what other people post (or you can consult the Usenet Newsgroup Charter Archive at www.faqs.org/usenet/gsearch.html). If you post an inappropriate message, hopefully someone will be kind enough to send you a simple reminder by e-mail (rather than *flame* you, or attack you online).

The soc.genealogy.surnames groups are moderated, which means that you can't post directly to them. When you send a message to a moderated newsgroup, it's first reviewed by an *automoderator*, a computer program that determines which of the surnames groups your message is posted in. Because a computer screens your message, formatting is very critical. The subject line of all queries requires a certain format, which you can find in the Frequently Asked Questions (FAQ) files located at www.rootsweb.com/ ~surnames/. Here are a few examples of acceptable subject lines:

```
Subject: HELM George / Dorothea; Frederick Co., VA,USA;
         1723-1769
Subject: HELM; VA,USA > TN,USA > IL,USA; 1723-
Subject: HELM; VA,USA>TN,USA>IL,USA; 1723-
Subject: HELM; anywhere; anytime
Subject: HELM Web Page; ENG / USA; 1723-
```

Be sure to include the correct abbreviations for the locations in your subject line. These codes determine which newsgroups the automoderator places your message in. You can find a list of the acceptable location codes on the Roots Surname List Country Abbreviations page (helpdesk.rootsweb.com/help/abbrev1.html). Also, be sure to place an e-mail address at the end of your query so that interested researchers can contact you directly.

You can search past posts to the soc.genealogy.surnames group on the World Wide Web. Go to the Web page at searches.rootsweb.com/sgsurnames.html (shown in Figure 3-15).

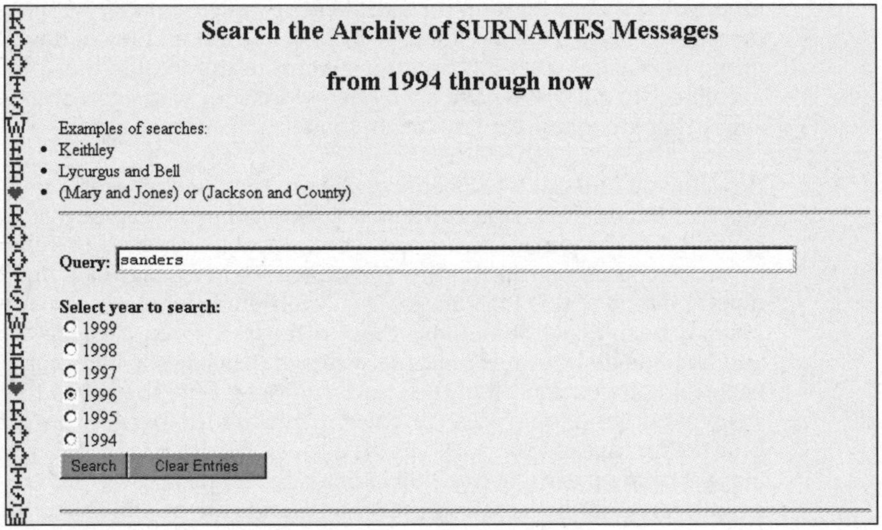

Search the Archive of SURNAMES Messages

from 1994 through now

Examples of searches:
- Keithley
- Lycurgus and Bell
- (Mary and Jones) or (Jackson and County)

Query: [sanders]

Select year to search:
- ○ 1999
- ○ 1998
- ○ 1997
- ⊙ 1996
- ○ 1995
- ○ 1994

[Search] [Clear Entries]

Figure 3-15:
The Search
the Archive
of
SURNAMES
Messages
page.

When you're at the Search the Archive of Surnames Messages page, follow these steps:

1. **Using your Web browser, go to** searches.rootsweb.com/sgsurnames.html.

   Note: For more information on using a browser, see Appendix A.

2. **Type the surname you're researching in the Query box and select the year you want to search.**

   Note that the Web site uses the words Query and Search interchangeably.

3. **Click Search.**

When you finish the preceding steps, a page called Operation Summary appears, showing you the results of your query on a specific surname. Notice that a line separates each record on the Operation Summary page. The last line of each record is labeled Select and includes a list of bracketed links that you can click to see different parts of the message in that record. To see the complete text of the message that was posted to the newsgroup, choose Full on the Select line.

Finding genealogy's most wanted

Every time you go into a post office, you see the Most Wanted pictures on the wall. The genealogical world has an online equivalent — Genealogy's Most Wanted (www.citynet.net/mostwanted/).

Genealogy's Most Wanted lets you place a query about a specific person — that is, not just a surname, but an actual individual. The query can be no more than 70 words or so, so be sure it contains enough information for someone to work with. After you submit your query, it appears in an alphabetical listing of surnames. The site contains over 22,400 listings presently.

You can also try to get your query listed as one of Genealogy's Most Wanted Top 11 Most Wanted at www.citynet.net/mostwanted/top11.html. This category lets you submit a query on a specific individual using between 200 and 500 words. You can include a photograph with a Top 11 query. Your query remains on the Top 11 list for one month.

Make sure that you follow Genealogy's Most Wanted's submission guidelines. The site has two different sets of guidelines depending on whether you're submitting a regular query or a Top 11 query.

Using E-Mail to Get Help

In the section "Query for One: Seeking Answers to Your Surname Questions" earlier in this chapter, we discuss a couple of ways to research surnames through e-mail by using queries. You can also use e-mail to directly contact other researchers of your surname. You just need to know where to find them.

Identifying potential e-mail pals by using online directories to find everyone with the surname you're researching, getting their e-mail addresses, and then mass e-mailing all of them about your research and questions is a bad idea. Although mass e-mailing everyone you can find with a particular surname generates return e-mail for you, we can almost guarantee that the responses will be hateful, not helpful. Sticking with genealogical sites (like those we identify in a moment) when looking for other researchers who are interested in the same surnames as you is the better way to go about it.

The Roots Surname List

One of the oldest of the Internet genealogy resources is the Roots Surname List. The Roots Surname List (RSL) is simply a list of surnames (and their associated dates and locations) accompanied by contact information for the person who placed the surname on the list. So if you want to contact other submitters about particular surnames, all you have to do is look at the contact information and send them e-mail messages or letters in the mail detailing your interest in the surnames.

The format for the list looks like this:

```
Helm 1723 now FrederickCo,VA>FentressCo, TN>FayetteCo,IL,USA
       mhelm
```

The line contains the surname, earliest date for which you have information on the surname, most recent date that you have for the surname, locations through which your family passed showing migration patterns (using a list of standard abbreviations), and a name tag for the submitter.

Every surname entry has a companion entry, called the *name tag*. This entry shows how to contact the submitter. The name tag contains the submitter's name, e-mail address, and an optional mailing address. The following is a name tag that could be the companion to the preceding surname example:

```
mhelm Matthew Helm, mhelm@tbox.com, P.O. Box 76, Savoy, IL,
       61874
```

You can submit surnames to the RSL through e-mail or with a form on the Web. Before you submit something for the first time, take a few minutes to read the RSL instructions (helpdesk.rootsweb.com/help/rsl6.html).

You can search the information on the RSL a couple of different ways — which is a good thing, because over 600,000 surnames are currently on the list.

✔ **The first and easiest way is to search the RSL through the Web:** You can do this by pointing your browser to rsl.rootsweb.com/cgi-bin/rslsql.cgi and filling in the surname and an optional location.

✔ **The other way to search the RSL is through e-mail:** You can search the RSL by sending an e-mail to a mail server located at rslsearch@rootsweb.com. Make sure that you place each surname you're researching on a separate line.

Surname-related e-mail resources

A number of resources are available that use e-mail as their primary communication tool. You can find a list of these at the Genealogy Resources on the Internet site (`www.rootsweb.com/~jfuller/gen_mail.html`). Among these resources are e-mail addresses of specific family associations, archives, and newsletters.

Verifying Your Information: Don't Believe Everything You Read!

We have one last piece of advice for you when you're researching — surnames or otherwise. *Don't believe everything you read.* Well, actually a pure genealogist would say, "Don't believe anything that you read." Either way, the point is the same — always verify any information that you find online with primary records (for more on primary records, see Chapter 1). If you can't prove it through a census record, vital record, or some other authoritative record, then the information simply may not be worth anything. However, just because you can't immediately prove it doesn't mean that you shouldn't hold on to the information. At some time in the future, you may run across a record that does indeed prove the accuracy of the information.

Chapter 4

Locating Your Ancestors (Geographically Speaking)

*I*n your genealogical research, finding information only about your family's surnames isn't enough. To put together a truly comprehensive genealogy, you need to know where your ancestors lived and the times in which they lived. Although you can get some of this information from other relatives and from documents that belonged to your ancestors, much of what you're looking for is available only in or from the actual areas where your ancestors lived. In this chapter, we examine some geographical resources that can help you develop the *where* and *when* in your genealogy.

Are We There Yet? (Researching Where "There" Was to Your Ancestors)

What did "there" mean for your ancestors? You have to answer this question to know where to look for genealogical information. These days, coming from a family that lived in the same general area for more than two or three generations is rather unique. If you're a member of such a family, you're a lucky person when it comes to genealogical research. However, if you're like the rest of us, you come from families that moved around at least every couple of generations, if not more often. Usually, finding out where all your ancestors lived — and when — presents a challenge. On the other hand, it's also one of the most rewarding challenges.

So, how do you find out where your ancestors lived and the approximate time frames? By examining the notes from interviews with relatives and records you've collected so far, you can get a good idea of where your ancestors lived and when.

Using documents you already have in your possession

When you attempt to geographically locate your ancestors, start by using any copies of records that you or someone else in the family has already collected. Your notes from interviews with family members, or from other resources you've found on your ancestors, most likely contain some information about locations where the family lived and hopefully the approximate time frames.

Chances are you have at least some notes with general statements, such as "Aunt Lola recalled stories about the old homestead in Fayette County, Kentucky." Of course, whether Aunt Lola recalled stories *firsthand* (those that she lived through or participated in) or her recollections were stories she heard from those before her has an effect on the time frames for which you look for records in Fayette County. Either way, these stories give you a starting point.

Likewise, most public records that you collected or someone else gave you — such as vital records, land records, military documents, and so on — provide at least two leads for you to use to track your family: the names of parents or witnesses to the event, and the date and place of the event (or at least the date and place of when and where the record was filed). Having this information points you in the right direction of where to begin looking for other records to substantiate what you believe to be true about your ancestors. Knowing a name to look for in a particular place and time gets you on your way to seeking other records.

If you have information about places where your ancestors lived, but not necessarily the time frame, you can still be reasonably successful in tracking your ancestors based on the limited information you do have. Aids are available to help you approximate time frames, such as the Period Approximation Chart (www.myroots.net/extras/tidbits3.htm). For example, say you heard stories about your great-great-grandmother being born in Red River County, Texas, but you don't know when she was born there. If you know approximately when she died and her age at death, you can use the Period Approximation Chart to calculate her approximate birth date. Of course, assuming that you know how to add and subtract, you could calculate her approximate birth year without having an aid. Knowing a birth year and death year gives you the time frame in which to look for records for her family in Red River County.

For additional information about using documents you already have and interviewing relatives to point you in the right direction, check out Ancestry.com's Library (`www.ancestry.com/library/archive.asp`).

Looking at directories and newspapers

If you have a general idea of where your family lived at a particular time, but no conclusive proof, city and county directories and newspapers may help. (Census records are quite helpful for this purpose, too. We discuss census records in Chapter 1.) Directories and newspapers can help you confirm whether your ancestors indeed lived in a particular area and, in some cases, they can provide even more information than you expect. A friend of ours has a great story — morbid as it is — illustrating just this point. He was looking through newspapers for an obituary about one of his great-uncles. He knew when his great-uncle died but could not find mention of it in the obituary section of the newspaper. As he set the newspaper down (probably in despair), he glanced to the front page only to find a very graphic description of how this local man had been killed in a freak elevator accident. And guess who that local man was? That's right, he was our friend's great-uncle! The newspaper not only confirmed for him that his great-uncle lived there, but also gave our friend a lot more information than he ever expected.

Directories

Like today's telephone books, directories contained basic information about the persons who lived in particular areas, whether the areas were towns, cities, districts, or counties. Typically, the directory identified at least the head of the household and the location of the house. Some directories also included the names and ages of everyone in the household and occupations of any members of the household who were employed.

Unfortunately, no centralized resource on the Web contains transcriptions of directories or even an index to all directories that may exist on the Internet. But don't be discouraged. Some sites can direct you to directories for particular geographic areas, but they are by no means universal. You can find a list of city directories for nearly 700 American towns and states that are available on microfilm at the City Directories at the Library of Congress Web page (`www.kinquest.com/genealogy/resources/citydir.html`). Some individuals have also posted city directories in their areas. An example of this is the San Francisco County Research Tips: City Directories page (`www.sfo.com/~timandpamwolf/sfdirect.htm`). A commercial site has also emerged that contains city directories for 99 cities from 1859 and 9 cities from 1860 to 1865. This site, City Directories of the United States Genealogical Archives Online, is found at `www.citydirectories.psmedia.com`. Another commercial effort, from Ancestry.com, is attempting to recreate the 1890 Census through city directories. For more information on this subscription-based project, see `www.ancestry.com/search/rectype/census/1890sub/upcoming.htm`. For tips on using city directories, see "City Directories," by Brian Andersson (`www.ancestry.com/library/view/news/articles/2011.asp`).

Some societies and associations have made a commitment to post on the Web the contents of directories for their areas or at least an index of what their libraries hold so that you know before you contact them whether they have something useful to you. To help you find out whether such a project exists for an area you're researching, use the location-specific search engine at GenealogyPortal.com (`www.genealogyportal.com`). This tool enables you to search the full text of several genealogical Web sites at once.

Newspapers

Unlike directories that list almost everyone in a community, newspapers are helpful only if your ancestors did something that was newsworthy — but you'd be surprised at what was considered newsworthy in the past. Your ancestor didn't necessarily have to be a politician or a criminal to get his picture and story in the paper. Just like today, obituaries, birth and marriage announcements, public records of land transactions, advertisements, and gossip sections were all relatively common in newspapers of the past.

Finding copies online of those newspapers from the past is a challenge. Most of the newspaper sites currently on the Web are for contemporary publications. Although you can read about wedding anniversaries and birthdays in England and Sweden today, you can't necessarily access online information about your ancestor's death in one of those countries in the 1800s. Many researchers are beginning to recognize the potential that the Web holds for making historical information from newspapers available worldwide. However, the lack of committed resources (time and money, primarily) prevents them from doing so as quickly as we'd like.

Here's what you're likely to find online pertaining to newspapers:

- **Indexes:** A variety of sites serve as indexes of newspapers that are available at particular libraries, archives, and universities. Most of these list the names and dates of the periodicals that are held in the newspaper or special collections. Examples of index sites include the following:

  - **The Newspapers at the National Library of Canada page:** `www.nlc-bnc.ca/services/enews.htm`

  - **The Newspaper Collections at the State Library of Victoria, Australia:** `www.slv.vic.gov.au/slv/newspapers/`

  - **New England Old Newspaper Index Project of Maine:** `www.geocities.com/Heartland/Hills/1460`

  - **The Online Newspaper Indexes Available in the Newspaper and Current Periodical Reading Room of the Library of Congress:** `lcweb.loc.gov/rr/news/npindex2.html`

✔ **Transcriptions:** A few sites contain actual transcriptions of newspaper articles, entire issues, and/or excerpts. Typically, the contents at these sites are limited to the topic and geographic interests of the person who transcribed the information and posted it for public access on the Web. Here are a couple of examples:

- **Excerpts from Old Newspapers:** `www.ida.net/users/dhanco/news.htm`

- **The Knoxville Gazette:** `www.ultranet.com/~smack/news.htm`

- **Virtual Family Records Vault: Newspapers:** `www.vfamily.com/news.htm`

✔ **Collectors' issues for sale:** Although they don't provide information directly from the newspaper online for you to use in your genealogical pursuits, these sites can help you find out about collectors' editions of newspapers and possibly even buy them online. The sites that sell old newspapers generally market their newspapers as good gift ideas for birthdays and anniversaries. For the services to be really useful to you as a genealogist, you have to know the date and place of the event you want to document (and a newspaper name helps, too), as well as be willing to pay for a copy of that paper. Here are a couple of newspaper collector sites to check out:

- **History Buff's Home Page by the Newspaper Collectors Society of America:** `www.historybuff.com`

- **Historic Newspaper Archives:** `www.historicnewspaper.com`

✔ **Online newspaper projects:** Many people are beginning to recognize the important role newspapers play in recording history and the value of putting newspaper information on the Web. To this end, we've seen an increasing number of online projects to catalog or transcribe newspapers. Some of the projects are organized on a state level, and others are for cities or particular newspapers. The Web sites for these projects explain the purpose of the project, its current status, and how to find the newspapers if they've been transcribed or digitized and placed online. Here are a couple of examples of these sites:

- **The New York State Newspaper Project (see Figure 4-1):** `www.nysl.nysed.gov/nysnp/`

- **Martin's General Store, Old Newspaper Clippings:** `www.nsn.org/wrkhome/hmca/c_indx.htm`

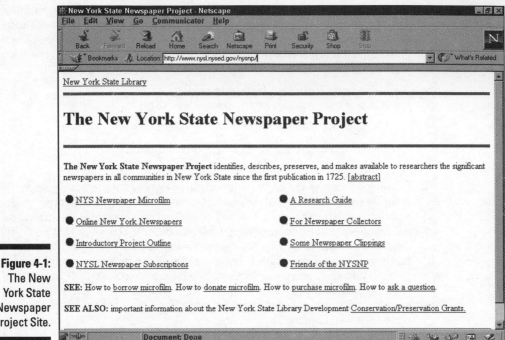

Figure 4-1:
The New
York State
Newspaper
Project Site.

Now you know what you may find online in terms of newspapers, but how do you find these sites? One option is to use a geographic category in a comprehensive genealogical site. However, most comprehensive genealogical sites may not list newspaper transcriptions if they're buried under a larger site. A better option may be to use a genealogically focused search engine or even a general Internet search engine — especially if you know the location and time frame for the newspaper.

Where Is Llandrindod, Anyway?

At some point during your research, you're bound to run across something that says an ancestor lived in a particular town or county but contains no details of where that town or county was — no state or province or other identifiers. How do you find out where that town or county was located?

A *gazetteer,* or geographical dictionary, provides information about places. By looking up the name of the town or county, you can narrow your search for your ancestor. The gazetteer identifies every known town or county by a particular name and provides varying information (depending on the gazetteer itself) about each. Typically, gazetteers provide at least the names of the state and country where the town or county is located. Many contemporary gazetteers also provide the latitude and longitude of the place.

Using an online gazetteer is easy. All online gazetteers are organized similarly and have query or search forms. Here's how to use one:

1. **Start your Web browser and head to the U.S. Geological Survey's Geographic Names Information System (GNIS) at** `mapping.usgs.gov/www/gnis/`.

   Note: For information on using a browser, see Appendix A.

2. **Scroll down to the Query the GNIS Online Data Bases section and click the <u>United States and Territories</u> link.**

   The list directly beneath the links tells you what you can expect to get from a query of the GNIS database. When you click the <u>United States and Territories</u> link, you go to the query form (see Figure 4-2).

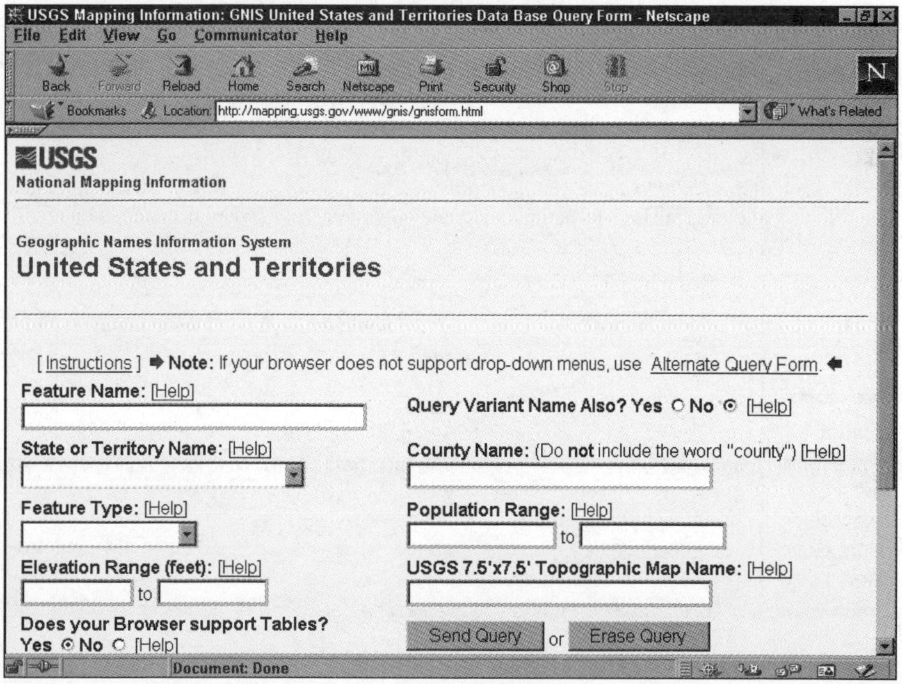

Figure 4-2:
The query form for the U.S. Geological Survey's Geographic Names Information System (GNIS).

3. **Enter any information that you have, tabbing or clicking between fields, and click the Send Query button when you're finished.**

   If you're not sure what a particular field asks for but you think you may want to enter something in it, click the Help link next to the field.

   If you know only the town name, enter the town name in the Feature Name field and leave all the other fields blank. For example, type **Carson City** in the Feature Name field; then click the Send Query button.

   GNIS executes a search of its database and returns the results to you in a list form. For Carson City, GNIS returns a number of records for you to review (see Figure 4-3). For each record, GNIS provides the feature name, state, county, type of feature (such as populated place, valley, cemetery, airport, lake, forest, and so on), latitude, longitude, and map information.

By adding the information you get from the online gazetteer to the other pieces of your puzzle, you can reduce the list of common place names to just those you think are plausible for your ancestors. By pinpointing where a place is, you can look for more records to prove whether your ancestors really lived there.

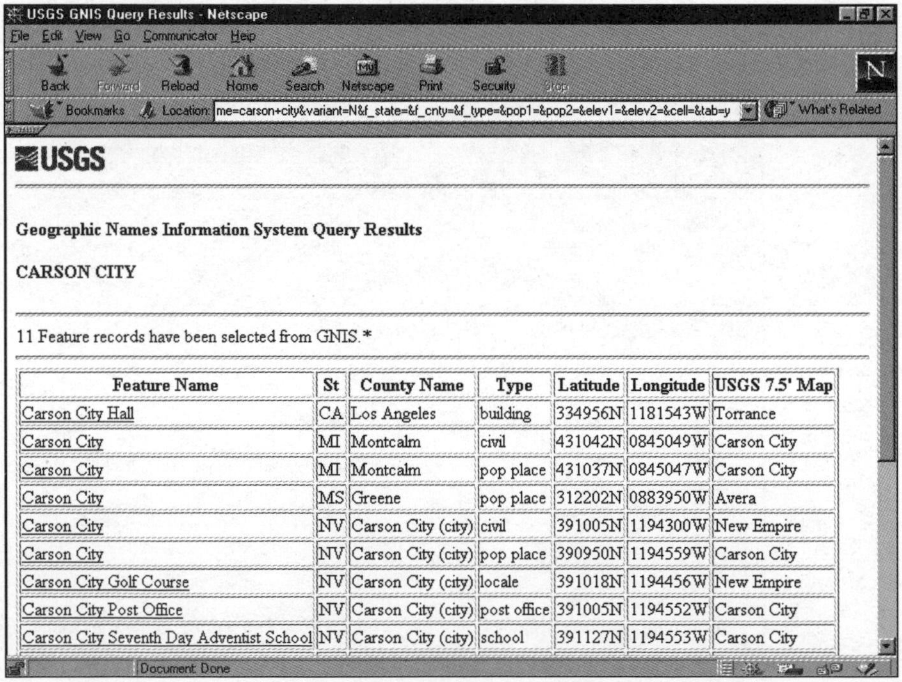

Figure 4-3: The results of a GNIS search on the name Carson City.

Geographic Names Information System Query Results

CARSON CITY

11 Feature records have been selected from GNIS.*

Feature Name	St	County Name	Type	Latitude	Longitude	USGS 7.5' Map
Carson City Hall	CA	Los Angeles	building	334956N	1181543W	Torrance
Carson City	MI	Montcalm	civil	431042N	0845049W	Carson City
Carson City	MI	Montcalm	pop place	431037N	0845047W	Carson City
Carson City	MS	Greene	pop place	312202N	0883950W	Avera
Carson City	NV	Carson City (city)	civil	391005N	1194300W	New Empire
Carson City	NV	Carson City (city)	pop place	390950N	1194559W	Carson City
Carson City Golf Course	NV	Carson City (city)	locale	391018N	1194456W	New Empire
Carson City Post Office	NV	Carson City (city)	post office	391005N	1194552W	Carson City
Carson City Seventh Day Adventist School	NV	Carson City (city)	school	391127N	1194553W	Carson City

For example, if your mother told you that your great-great-grandfather lived in a town called Carson City but didn't say where that Carson City was, you can use the information you just collected in the GNIS database query to narrow your search for places called Carson City.

From GNIS, you know that 11 Carson City places exist in the United States. By reviewing the Feature Type field, you can eliminate all the Carson City places that aren't towns or populated places. (After all, your great-great-grandfather probably didn't live in a city hall, golf course, post office, church, city square, or station.) The process of elimination narrows your search down to five Carson City places on the GNIS list.

Using other facts you collect about your great-great-grandfather (such as where he was born, where his kids were born, what kind of work he did, and so on), you may be able to determine the general area of the United States in which he lived. If you can, this narrows the list down even further. The remaining Carson City places are in Michigan, Mississippi, and Nevada — three states that aren't near each other. (However, you need to note that if great-great-grandpa was a wanderer or had an occupation that required him to travel great distances, you may not be able to rule out any of the remaining three states with Carson City places in them.)

In addition to the GNIS database, some online gazetteers identify places in the United States and other countries. Here are some for you to check out:

- **Alexandria Digital Library Gazetteer Server:** `fat-albert. alexandria.ucsb.edu:8827/gazetteer` — has a worldwide focus

- **Australian Gazetteer:** `www.ke.com.au/cgi-bin/ texhtml?form=AustGaz`

- **Canada's Geographical Names:** `geonames.nrcan.gc.ca/english/Home.html`

- **Gazetteer for Scotland:** `www.geo.ed.ac.uk/scotgaz/`

- **Gazetteer of British Place Names:** `www.abcounties.co.uk/newgaz/section0.htm`

- **U.S. Census Bureau's Gazetteer:** `www.census.gov/ cgi-bin/gazetteer`

Most gazetteers are organized on a national level and provide information about all the places (towns, cities, counties, landmarks, and so on) within that country. However, there are exceptions to every rule. Some unique gazetteers list information about places within one state or province. One such example is the Kentucky Atlas and Gazetteer (`www.uky.edu/KentuckyAtlas/`). The Kentucky Atlas and Gazetteer has information only about places within — you guessed it — Kentucky. For each place, it provides the name of the place, the type of place (civil division, school, cemetery, airport, and so on), source of information, *topoquad* (topographic map quadrangle that contains the feature), latitude, longitude, area (if applicable), population (if applicable), date of establishment, elevation, and a link to a map showing you where the place is.

Mapping Your Ancestor's Way

Maps can be an invaluable resource in your genealogical research. Not only do maps help you track your ancestors, but they also enhance your published genealogy by illustrating some of your findings.

Tracking the movements of your ancestors can be a lot of fun. Just reading about migrations in family histories, texts, and records isn't the easiest way to understand where, why, and how your ancestors moved. Charting movements on maps makes visualizing the paths your ancestors took and obstacles they may have encountered easier. Maps also make the genealogy you put together more interesting for others to read because they enable the reader to see what you're talking about in your writings. Maps help tell your ancestors' stories, so to speak.

Different types of online sites have maps that may be useful in your genealogical research:

- **Images of maps:** Several Web sites contain scanned or digitized images of historic maps. You can download or print copies of these maps, but they may not show you much in terms of how boundaries changed over time. Two such sites are Cartographic Images: Ancient, Early Medieval, Late Medieval, and Renaissance Maps (www.iag.net/~jsiebold/carto.html) and the Perry-Castañeda Library Map Collection at the University of Texas at Austin (www.lib.utexas.edu/Libs/PCL/Map_collection/Map_collection.html), which has maps for places all over the world.

- **Interactive map sites:** A few sites have interactive maps that you can use to find and zoom in on areas. After you have the view you want of the location, you can print a copy of the map to keep with your, genealogical records. Two such sites are MapQuest (www.mapquest.com), which has interactive maps for too many countries to list here (including the United States, Canada, Germany, Italy, New Zealand, and the United Kingdom), and the U.K. Street Map Page (www.streetmap.co.uk), which identifies streets in London or places in the United Kingdom. Interactive maps are especially helpful when you're trying to pinpoint the location of a cemetery or town you plan to visit for your genealogical research, but they're limited in their historical helpfulness because they typically offer only current information about places. (To see a complete list of the countries for which MapQuest has interactive atlases, click the link next to the Country field of the interactive atlas site. Use the following instructions to get to the form.)

✔ **Specialized maps:** You can view specialized maps on many Web sites. Topozone (`www.topozone.com`) has interactive topographical maps for the entire United States. For satellite maps of the United States, see Microsoft TerraServer (`terraserver.microsoft.com/default.asp`).

Here's how to use an interactive map site:

1. **Using your Web browser, go to MapQuest at** `www.mapquest.com`**.**

   Note: See Appendix A for more details on using a browser.

   MapQuest's main page comes up.

2. **Click the <u>Maps</u> link.**

   The interactive atlas form you use to submit a search appears.

3. **Enter any information you have into the form. Be sure to tab or click between the fields — if you hit the Enter key, MapQuest executes the search.**

   If you're merely looking for a town, you can skip entering information about an address/intersection, state, and zip code, but you need to specify the town and country. (Please note that MapQuest defaults to the United States. If you're looking for an address or town in a country other than the United States, make sure that the country is identified in the Country field.)

   For example, say you're looking for an old family homestead at 1600 Pennsylvania Avenue in Washington, D.C. Enter **1600 Pennsylvania Avenue** in the Address/Intersection field, **Washington** in the City field, and **DC** (with no periods) in the State field. You don't necessarily need to enter the zip code, and you can leave the country set for the United States.

4. **Click the Get Map button.**

   MapQuest brings up a map of the requested place, if it can find it. If more than one town or street fits the description for the search, MapQuest prompts you to choose among all the matches. If MapQuest can't find the requested place, it gives you a note stating this and provides a map for the closest place it could find that may match the place you requested.

   In the search for 1600 Pennsylvania Avenue, MapQuest brings up a map of Washington, D.C., with a red star on the address requested. You can use the map as it is or zoom in to see the surrounding area better by clicking the Recenter Map and Zoom In button at the bottom of the map and then clicking on the map. You can also use the zoom buttons along the right side of the map to gain perspective on where the place is located — you can choose from street level, to city, to regional, to national.

Crossing the line

Just as maps help you track your ancestors movements and where they lived, they can also help you track when your ancestors didn't really move. Boundaries for towns, districts, and even states have changed over time. Additionally, for towns and counties to change names wasn't unheard of. Knowing whether your ancestors really moved or just appeared to move because of boundary or town name changes is important when you try to locate records for them.

To determine whether a town or county changed names at some point, check a gazetteer or historical text on the area. (Gazetteers are discussed in the earlier section, "Where Is Llandrindod, Anyway?") Finding boundary changes can be a little more challenging, but resources are available to help you. For example, historical atlases illustrate land and boundary changes. You can also use online sites that have maps for the same areas over time, and a few sites deal specifically with boundary changes in particular locations. A couple of examples are the Boundaries of the United States and the Several States site (www.ac.wwu.edu/~stephan/48states.html) and the Counties of England, Scotland, and Wales Prior to the 1974 Boundary Changes site (www.genuki.org.uk/big/britain2.gif). Or you can use software designed specifically to show you boundary changes over time and to help you find places that have disappeared altogether. One such program that tracks boundary changes in Europe is called Centennia Historical Atlas. You can find information about it at its

Web site (www.clockwk.com). Another such program for boundary changes in the United States is AniMap Plus (www.goldbug.com/animap.html). A demonstration version of which is included on the CD-ROM accompanying this book. Here's a quick walk-through using the AniMap Plus demonstration to see how some counties have changed over time.

1. **Open the demonstration version of AniMap Plus that you installed from the CD-ROM that accompanies this book. (For installation instructions, see Appendix C.)**

AniMap opens to a 1683 map that shows the 12 original counties of New York. All the counties are named in the upper left corner of the map. Abbreviations of each are explained in the County Codes box, and you can see the county boundaries themselves on the map.

2. **Double-click Start Demo in the upper-left corner of the screen.**

3. **Click Next to advance to the next map of New York to see changes that took place between 1683 and 1686.**

The box in the upper-left corner briefly explains the changes that took place and which counties still existed in New York in 1686.

4. **You can advance through the maps in sequential order by clicking the Next button or you can skip to other years by double-clicking the years identified in the Go To box.**

There's No Place Like Home: Using Local Resources

A time will come (possibly early in your research) when you need information that's maintained on a local level — say a copy of a record stored in a local courthouse, confirmation that an ancestor is buried in a particular cemetery, or even just a photo of the old homestead. So how can you find and get what you need?

Finding this information is easy if you live in or near the county where the information is maintained — you decide what it is you need and where it's stored, and then go and get a copy. Getting locally held information isn't quite as easy if you live in another county, state, or country because, while you can determine what information you need and where it may be stored, finding out whether the information is truly kept where you think it is and then getting a copy is another thing. Of course, if this situation weren't such a common occurrence for genealogists, you could just make a vacation out of it — travel to the location to finish researching there and get the copy you need while sightseeing along the way. But unfortunately, needing records from distant places is a common occurrence, and most of us can't afford to pack the bags and hit the road every time we need a record or item from a faraway place, which is why it's nice to know that resources are available to help.

From geographic-specific Web sites to local genealogical and historical societies to libraries with research services to individuals who are willing to do lookups in public records, a lot of resources are available to help you locate local documents and obtain copies. Some resources are totally free, others may charge you a fee for their time, and still others will bill you only for copying or other direct costs.

Geographic-specific Web sites

Geographic-specific Web sites are those pages that contain information specifically about a particular town, county, state, country, or other locality. They typically provide information about local resources, such as genealogical and historical societies, government agencies and courthouses, cemeteries, and civic organizations. Some sites have local histories and biographies of prominent residents online. Often, they list and have links to other Web pages that have resources for the area. And sometimes, they even have a place where you can post *queries* (or questions) about the area or families from there with the hope that someone who reads your query will have some answers for you.

How can you find geographic-specific Web sites, you ask? Doing so is easy.

1. **Using your Web browser, go to the Genealogy Toolbox at** `www.genealogytoolbox.com`.

   Note: For more information on using a browser, see Appendix A.

2. **Select the <u>Places</u> link.**

   Selecting Places takes you to a list of continents, major geographical areas, and some popular countries.

3. **Click the country or geographic link that interests you.**

   Doing this brings up a list links to general sites or to states/provinces from which you can choose.

4. **Click the state or province of your choice.**

   This takes you to a page that lists all Internet sites pertaining to the state, or province you selected that are indexed in the Genealogy Toolbox. Each entry includes a brief abstract of the site and a link to that site, so you can select the sites that sound promising.

You can find several good examples of geographic-specific Web sites. One such site that conveys information about the United States is the USGenWeb Project (www.usgenweb.org). The USGenWeb Project is an all-volunteer online effort to provide a central genealogical resource for information (records and reference materials) pertaining to counties within each state. (See the sidebar "Overview of the USGenWeb Project" in this chapter for more information.) Another such site is the USGenExchange Project (www.genexchange.com/us.cfm), which is part of the Genealogy Exchange and Surname Registry. The USGenExchange is an attempt to provide raw facts in searchable databases for every state in the union. Instead of breaking the data down by county (like USGenWeb does), the USGenExchange categorizes its searchable databases by type of record/resource — indexes of information about individuals, directories, historical accounts, miscellaneous, and research resources.

The WorldGenWeb project attempts the same type of undertaking as USGenWeb, only on a global scale. For more information about WorldGenWeb (www.worldgenweb.org), see The *Genealogy Online For Dummies* Internet Directory in this book.

Genealogical and historical societies

Most genealogical and historical societies exist on a local level and attempt to preserve documents and history for the area in which they are located. Genealogical societies also have another purpose — to help their members research their ancestors whether they lived in the local area or elsewhere. (Granted, some surname-based genealogical societies, and even a couple of virtual societies, are an exception to this description of genealogical societies because they aren't specific to one particular place.) Although historical societies don't have the second purpose of aiding members researching genealogy, they are helpful to genealogists anyway. Often, if you don't live in the area from which you need a record or information, you can contact a local genealogical or historical society to get help. Help varies from look-up services in books and documents the society maintains in its library to volunteers who actually locate records for you and get copies to send you. Before you contact a local genealogical or historical society for help, be sure you know what services it offers.

Many local genealogical and historical societies have Web pages and identify exactly which services they offer to members and nonmembers online. To find a society in an area you're researching, try this:

1. **Using your Web browser, go to Genealogy Resources on the Internet: World Wide Web at** `www-personal.umich.edu/~cgaunt/ gen_intl.html.`

   Note: For more information on using a browser, see Appendix A.

2. **Scroll down (if necessary) and click a link for [Insert Place Name Here] Resources, using the location where you're looking for an association or society as the place name.**

   For example, if you're looking for a genealogical or historical society in Belgium, scroll down and click the link for Belgium Resources. This action takes you to a page that identifies and links to all sorts of genealogical sites pertaining to Belgium.

3. **Look through the list of links to see if any associations or societies exist for the area you are interested in. If so, click the link to visit the site.**

   Visit the group or society home page to see what services that group or society offers to members and nonmembers. If the group or society offers a service you need (lookup, obtaining copies of records, and so on), use whatever contact information the site provides to get in touch and request help.

Libraries and archives

Often, the holdings in local libraries and archives can be of great value to you — even if you can't physically visit the library or archive to do your research. If the library or archive has an Internet site, go online to determine whether that library or archive has the book or document you need. (Most libraries and archives that have Web pages or other Internet sites make their card catalogs or another listing of their holdings available online — and some libraries are even adding indexes or images of actual documents online.) After seeing whether a library or archive has what you need, you can contact the library or archive to borrow the book or document (if they participate in an interlibrary loan program) or to get a copy of what you need (most libraries and archives have services to copy information for people at a minimal cost).

Overview of the USGenWeb Project

The USGenWeb Project provides a central resource for genealogical information (records and reference materials) pertaining to counties within each state. USGenWeb offers state-level pages for each state within the United States that have links to pages for each county, as well as links to other online resources about the state. At the county level, the pages have links to resources about the county.

In addition to links to other Web sites with genealogical resources that are geographic-specific, most of the county-level pages have query sections in which you can post or read queries (or questions) about researching in that county. Some of the county-level pages offer other services in addition to the query section, such as a surname registry for anyone researching in the county and a look-up section that identifies people who are willing to look up information for others.

Although some states have uniform-looking county pages with the same standard resources for each county, other states don't. The content and look of USGenWeb state and county pages varies tremendously from state to state.

In addition to state- and county-level pages, the USGenWeb Project includes special projects that cross state and county lines. Some of these projects include the following:

- A project to collect and transcribe tomb-stone inscriptions so that genealogists can access the information online.

- An undertaking to transcribe all federal census data for the United States to make it available online.

- The Pension project — an attempt to transcribe pensions for all wars prior to the year 1900.

- A lineage project to provide resources for individuals researching all descendants of a particular ancestor.

- The Digital Map Library project is designed to provide free high-quality digital maps to researchers.

- The Kidz Project, a resource page for kids interested in genealogy.

The various pages and projects that make up the USGenWeb Project are designed and maintained by volunteers. If you're interested in becoming involved, visit the USGenWeb home page (www.usgenweb.org).

To find online catalogs for libraries in a particular place, follow these steps:

1. **Using your Web browser, go to WebCats: Library Catalogues on the World Wide Web at** www.lights.com/webcats/.

   Note: For more information on using a browser, see Appendix A.

2. **Click the <u>Geographical Index</u> link.**

   This brings up a Geographic Index of links sorted by area: Africa, Americas, Asia/Pacific Rim, and Europe/Middle East. The index also has links directly to some countries within those areas.

For example, you can look for the national library of Australia to see if it has any books in its collection that would be helpful for your Australian research.

3. **Scroll down the Asia/Pacific Rim area, and click the link for Australia.**

   Clicking the link for Australia takes you to a page that lists known libraries and universities in Australia that have online catalogs.

4. **Browsing through the list, you find a national library. Click the link for the National Library of Australia.**

   This action takes you to the National Library's Catalogue. The main Web page for the Catalogue explains its purpose and collection and provides specific information on how to search the site for particular publications or other works.

   From this point on, follow the site's instructions to search for books of interest and applicability to your particular research.

Professional researchers

Professional researchers are people who research your genealogy — or particular family lines — for a fee. If you're looking for someone to do all the research necessary to put together a complete family history, some do so. If you're just looking for records in a particular area to substantiate claims in your genealogy, professional researchers can usually locate the records for you and get you copies. Their services, rates, experience, and reputations vary, so be careful when selecting a professional researcher to help you. Look for someone who has quite a bit of experience in the area in which you need help. Asking for references or a list of satisfied customers isn't out of the question (that way you know who you're dealing with prior to sending the researcher money). Here's a list of questions you may want to ask when shopping around for a professional researcher:

✔ Is the researcher certified or accredited and, if so, by what organization?

✔ How many years experience does he have researching?

✔ What is his educational background?

✔ Does the researcher have any professional affiliations? In other words, does he belong to any professional genealogical organizations and, if so, which ones?

✔ What foreign languages does the researcher speak fluently?

✔ What records and resources does he have access to?

✔ What is the professional researcher's experience in the area where you need help? For example, if you need help interviewing distant relatives in a foreign country, has he conducted interviews in the past? Or if you need records pertaining to a particular ethnic or religious group, does he have experience researching those types of records?

✔ How does the researcher charge for his services — by the record, by the hour, or by the project? What methods of payment does he accept? What is the researcher's policy on refunds or dissatisfaction with his services?

✔ How many other projects is the researcher working on presently and what kinds of projects? How much time will he devote to your research project? When will he report his results?

✔ Does the researcher have references that you can contact?

One way to find professional researchers is to look for them on comprehensive genealogy sites. Another is to consult an online directory of researchers, such as the Association of Professional Genealogists (www.apgen.org/directory.html) directory or genealogyPro. Follow these steps to check the genealogy Pro directory:

1. **Using your Web browser, go to the genealogyPro site at** www.genealogyPro.com.

   Note: For more information on using a browser, see Appendix A.

2. **Select a geographic area from the list in the right column of the page.**

   At this point, you could use the search engine or browse the geographic list. For example, we're interested in finding someone to do research in England, so we look for a link to that country.

3. **Click the England and Wales link.**

   This link takes you to a page with links to particular researchers or research companies and includes a brief description of each researcher's area of concentration.

4. **Click the KBA Research link.**

   In our example, clicking the link for KBA Research takes us to a page listing the company's address, phone number, e-mail address, Web page URL, qualifications, services, and fees.

Hit the Road, Jack! (Planning Your Genealogy Travels Using the Web)

A wealth of other information is available to help you plan your travels — and it's all at your fingertips! You can surf the Web to check out hotels/motels, car-rental places, airlines, local attractions, and a host of other things related to research trips and vacations. Two sites that provide links to all sorts of travel-related information are MapQuest (www.mapquest.com) and the Yahoo! Travel section (dir.yahoo.com/recreation/travel). Each has sections for transportation, lodging, dining, and a variety of other things you need while traveling. You can even use MapQuest to plan your route if you're driving in North America (see "Mapping Your Ancestor's Way," earlier in this chapter).

Follow these steps to get driving directions from MapQuest:

1. **Using your World Wide Web browser, open the MapQuest site (**www.mapquest.com**).**

2. **Click the <u>Driving Directions</u> link.**

   This brings up the Driving Directions page, which has two columns of boxes for you to complete and some option buttons you can choose in the right column.

3. **In the first column, complete the four fields indicating where you're starting your journey.**

   You can type an actual street address in the Address field.

   Type in the city from which your journey will begin in the City field.

   Type the state from which you'll begin your trip in the State field.

4. **In the second column, complete the four fields indicating your destination (where you want to go).**

   The four destination fields are titled just like the starting fields and accept the same sort of information.

5. **Click the Get Directions button.**

   MapQuest determines the directions from your starting point to your destination. If MapQuest can't determine a route for you, it provides an explanation and recommendations for you to try your Driving Directions transaction again.

Part II
Finding the Elusive Records

The 5th Wave   By Rich Tennant

"I'm not sure I want to be claimed by a family whose home page has a link to the ZangZone."

In this part . . .

This part covers how to locate sites with hard-to-find information about groups of people and particular types of records — and figuring out how to use those sites effectively in your genealogical research. Here you find information about the following:

- ✔ Researching African-American, Native American, and European ancestors
- ✔ Finding government records online
- ✔ Finding other miscellaneous records and information on various groups

Chapter 5

Ethnic Research

• •

In This Chapter

▶ Discovering African ancestry

▶ Finding American Indian sites

▶ Identifying Hispanic roots

▶ Researching European ethnic groups

• •

Researching a particular ethnic group can often be frustrating. Even though every ethnic group has records that are unique to it, the ethnic group may have been very mobile — making records for that particular group hard to find. In some cases, records were destroyed during periods of war. Despite the difficulty in finding some of these records, ethnic research can be very rewarding. By looking for records specific to ethnic groups, you get a clearer picture of your ancestor's part in history and find unique sources of information that can add color to your family's story. This chapter examines some of the online resources available to assist you in finding ethnic-specific records.

If you're looking for a good reference resource that covers ethnic research, we recommend *The Source: A Guidebook of American Genealogy*, edited by Loretto Dennis Szucs and Sandra Hargreaves Luebking (published by Ancestry, Inc.). *The Source* is available in print, on CD-ROM (as part of the Ancestry Reference Library), or online at www.ancestry.com/search/rectype/inddbs/3259.htm.

Researching African Ancestry

A common misconception is that tracing African ancestry is impossible. In the past decade or so, much has been done to dispel that perception. If your ancestors lived in the United States, you can use many of the same research techniques and records (census schedules, vital records, and other primary resources) that genealogists of other ethnic groups consult back to 1870.

Prior to 1870, your research resources become more limited, depending on whether your ancestor was a freedman or a slave. To make that determination, you may want to interview some of your relatives. They often possess oral traditions that can point you in the right direction.

If your ancestor was a slave, try consulting the slave owners' probate records (which you can usually find in local courthouses), deed books (slave transactions were often recorded in deed books — which you also find in local courthouses), tax records, plantation records, Freedman's Bureau records, and runaway slave records. These types of records can be helpful because they identify persons by name.

Although your first inclination may be to turn to a slave schedule in the U.S. Census, such schedules are less useful in your research because the *enumerators* who collected the census information didn't record the names of slaves, nor did the government require them to do so. This fact doesn't mean that looking at slave schedules is a total waste of time; the schedules simply don't identify your ancestor by name. You need to find other resources that name your ancestor specifically.

If your ancestors served in the American Civil War, they may have service and pension records. You can begin a search for service records in an index to Civil War records of the United States Colored Troops or, if your ancestor joined a state regiment, in an Adjutant General's report. (An *Adjutant General's report* is a published account of the actions of military units from a particular state during a war; these reports are usually available at libraries or archives.) We discuss using the United States Colored Troops database in the section "United States Colored Troops database," later in this chapter.

Two other sources of records to keep in mind are the Freedmen's Bureau and the Freedmen's Savings and Trust. The Freedmen's Bureau (its full name was the Bureau of Refugees, Freedmen and Abandoned Lands) was established in 1865 to assist ex-slaves after the American Civil War (for more on the Bureau, see the article at www.nara.gov/publications/prologue/everly.html). The Freedman's Savings and Trust Company was also established in 1865 as a bank for ex-slaves (see the article at www.nara.gov/publications/prologue/everly.html for more information). Several of its contributors were members of the United States Colored Troops during the war. Although the company failed in 1874, its records are now kept at the National Archives and Records Administration, along with the records for the Freedmen's Bureau. (The National Archives and Records Administration provides information about these records and their availability on microfilm at www.nara.gov/publications/microfilm/blackstudies/blackstd.html.) For examples of Freedmen's Bureau records, see The Freedmen's Bureau Online (www.freedmensbureau.com).

For more information on using records to research your African ancestry, try the following resources:

✔ *The Source: A Guidebook of American Genealogy,* edited by Loretto Dennis Szucs and Sandra Hargreaves Luebking (published by Ancestry, Inc.). In particular, see Chapter 15, "Tracking African American Family History," written by David Thackery (available online at `search.ancestry.com/cgi-bin/sse.dll?DB=SOURCE&GS=AFRICAN+AMERICAN+&QUERY=AFRICAN+AMERICAN+&DATABASEID=3259&TITLE=THE+SOURCE%3A+A+GUIDEBOOK+OF+AMERICAN+GENEALOGY&DATABASENAME=SOURCE&SEARCHENGINE=SSE.DLL&SERVER=SEARCH&TYPE=F&ct=9825`).

✔ *Black Studies: A Select Catalog of National Archives Microfilm Publications,* available in the National Archives in Washington, D.C.

✔ *Slave Genealogy: A Research Guide with Case Studies,* written by David H. Streets (published by Heritage Books).

Mailing lists and newsgroups focusing on African research

When you look for key records that are specific to African ancestral research, it's a good idea for you to interact with other researchers who may already be knowledgeable about such resources. One place to start is the *AfriGeneas* mailing list. This mailing list focuses primarily on African genealogical research methods. On the Web page for the mailing list (`www.afrigeneas.com/`), you find the following resources (see Figure 5-1):

✔ A beginner's guide to researching genealogy.

✔ Links to census schedules and slave data on the Internet.

✔ A digital library of transcribed resources.

✔ A link to a database of African American surnames and their corresponding researchers.

Here's how you subscribe to the AfriGeneas mailing list:

1. **Start your favorite e-mail program.**

   How you start your e-mail program depends on which e-mail program you use. Generally, you can begin the program by double-clicking the program's icon or, in Windows 95 or later, by opening the program from the Start button. If you're not sure how to start your e-mail program, see the documentation that came with the program. (You also can take a look at Appendix A for more information on using e-mail.)

2. **Create a new e-mail message.**

   Usually, you create a new e-mail message by clicking an icon in your e-mail program's toolbar or by using a menu. If you don't know how to create a new e-mail message, consult the documentation that came with the program.

3. **Type** `majordomo@msstate.edu` **in the To line.**

   Make sure that you type *only* `majordomo@msstate.edu` in the To line. You subscribe to AfriGeneas at this listserv e-mail account. If you type anything more, your e-mail message won't be delivered and your attempt to subscribe fails.

4. **Make sure that your e-mail address is in the From line.**

   Most e-mail programs automatically fill in your e-mail address in the From line. In that case, just make sure that it's correct. Otherwise, type the e-mail address where you want to receive postings to the AfriGeneas mailing list.

5. **In the body of the message, type** subscribe afrigeneas **or** subscribe afrigeneas-digest.

   Use **subscribe afrigeneas-digest** if you want to receive fewer e-mail messages a day from the list. In the digest form, the listserver compiles all the messages that people post throughout the day into one e-mail. For example, if April subscribes to the mailing list in its regular format, where each posting arrives separately, she'd type **subscribe afrigeneas** in the body of her message. Again, don't type anything more than this line in the message body or you confuse the automatic program that adds you to the mailing list and it rejects your attempt to subscribe.

6. **Send the e-mail message.**

   Your e-mail program probably features a Send button that sends the message after you click it. If you don't see a Send button or a Send command in one of the drop-down menus, consult your e-mail program documentation for details on sending a message.

Another resource to turn to when starting your research is the `soc.genealogy.african` newsgroup. This newsgroup focuses on research methods for genealogists interested in their African ancestry. To access the newsgroup, you need a newsgroup reader. (For more information about newsgroups, see Appendix A.)

A third resource is the *SLAVEINFO* mailing list (`lists.rootsweb.com/index/other/Ethnic/SLAVEINFO.html` — the SLAVEINFO must be in all capital letters). This list is a forum for sharing genealogical data on slaves in the United States. To subscribe to the list, follow the same procedures that we give in the preceding numbered list, but send your subscribe message to `slaveinfo-l-request@rootsweb.com` with just the word *subscribe* in the body of the message.

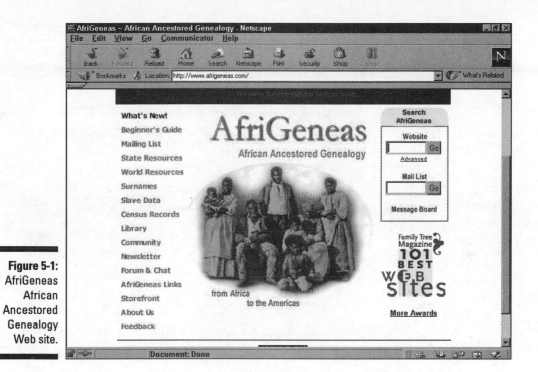

Figure 5-1:
AfriGeneas
African
Ancestored
Genealogy
Web site.

Genealogical resource pages on the Web

A number of online resources are available to assist you in finding your African ancestry in addition to the AfriGeneas Web site. One site that identifies several of these resources is Christine's Genealogy Web site located at `ccharity.com` (see Figure 5-2). Here, you find the following:

- A list of Web pages that are of interest to genealogists.
- Transcriptions of records from the Freedmen's Bureau (a government entity established to assist former slaves) arranged by state.
- Lists of ex-slaves who emigrated to Liberia from 1820 to 1843.
- Sites that contain transcribed wills that name slaves or mention them within the wills.
- Transcriptions of manumission papers (documents giving slaves their freedom).

For a brief list of resources that you can use offline, see the African and African-American Studies page (`library.jmu.edu/african/index.html`).

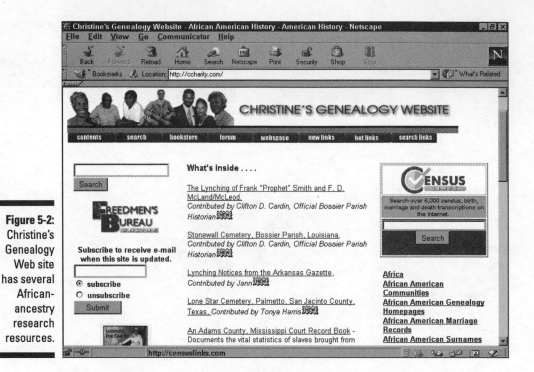

Figure 5-2:
Christine's
Genealogy
Web site
has several
African-
ancestry
research
resources.

Transcribed records pertaining to ancestors with African roots

Many genealogists recognize the benefits of making transcribed and digitized records available for other researchers. However, limited resources prohibit most of these genealogists from being able to do so. A few Web sites have transcribed records that are unique to the study of African ancestry online. Following are some examples:

- ✔ **Cemetery records:** For a transcribed list of cemeteries, see African American Cemeteries Online (`www.prairiebluff.com/aacemetery/`).

- ✔ **Freedman's Bureau records:** You can find transcribed Freedman's Bureau records at the Freedman's Bureau Online (`www.freedmensbureau.com/index.htm`).

- ✔ **Manumission papers:** For examples of manumission papers, see Christine Charity's site (`ccharity.com/contents/dcmanumissions.htm`).

- ✔ **Registers:** At the Valley of the Shadow site, you can view transcribed Registers of Free Blacks in Augusta County, Virginia (`jefferson.village.virginia.edu/vshadow2/govdoc/govdoc.html#fb`).

✔ **Slave Schedules:** You can find transcriptions of slave schedules at the African-American Census Schedules Online site at `www.afrigeneas.com/aacensus/`. (Although some of these schedules don't identify your ancestors by name, they're useful if you know the name of the slave owner.)

✔ **Wills:** Slaves were often mentioned in the disposition of wills. The Disposition of Mississippi Slaves site (`members.aol.com/MCrushshon/index.html`) offers several abstracts of wills that mention slaves by their names.

The preceding sites are a few examples of transcribed records that you can find on the Internet. To see whether online records pertaining specifically to your research exist, visit a comprehensive genealogical site and look under the appropriate category. For example, the Genealogy Toolbox's African American page (`www.genealogytoolbox.com/africanamerican.html`) identifies resources for African American research, and the site's Records page identifies all sorts of records and indexes for records that you can find online.

United States Colored Troops database

Although only a few online databases currently focus on African ancestry, one that certainly deserves mention is the United States Colored Troops (USCT) database, which is part of the larger Civil War Soldiers and Sailors (CWSS) System sponsored by the National Park Service (at `www.itd.nps.gov/cwss/`). The CWSS database contains more than 230,000 names and 180 regimental histories of USCT units (see Figure 5-3).

Follow these steps to search the USCT database:

1. **Point your Web browser to** `www.itd.nps.gov/cwss/`.

   The home page for the database appears with a list of links running down the right side of the graphic.

   Note: If you need help using your Web browser, see Appendix A.

2. **Click the <u>Soldiers</u> link.**

   This link is located at the top of the page, on the right side of the screen. Clicking it takes you to the Search by Soldier Name page, where you can type the name that you're researching.

3. **Type a surname (using all capital letters) in the Last Name text box, select Union army under the Union or Confederate drop-down menu, and then click the Submit Query button.**

   If you know the first name of the soldier you're looking for and his state, unit number, or function (such as infantry or cavalry), you can provide this information in the appropriate fields.

For example, if April is searching for someone with the surname Sanders, she types **SANDERS** in the blank text box, selects Union from the list, and then clicks the Submit Query button. The search engine looks through the database, picks up any matches to that surname, and then takes you to a page that shows the results of your search.

4. **Select a name by clicking the appropriate name link on the results page.**

The Results page contains a list of names, the side on which the person fought during the war, the function of the unit in which the soldier fought, and the unit of assignment. Click a name to see the whole record on the soldier.

For example, suppose that April is interested in learning about the soldier named Aaron Sanders. She clicks the <u>Aaron Sanders</u> link, which takes her to another page that contains the following information:

- First and last name of the soldier

- Regiment in which the soldier served

- Side on which the soldier fought during the war

- Company of assignment

- Rank at enlistment

- Rank at mustering out

- Company

- Aliases

- Notes about the soldier

- National Archives and Records Administration film number

After you identify potential ancestors by using the database, you can follow up by looking for the microfilm at the National Archives or ordering a copy of the actual military record. The USCT site explains how to find and get copies of the records at www.itd.nps.gov/cwss/tools.htm.

Special ethnic pages about African ancestry

Many Web sites include information on a particular subset of individuals of African ancestry. Here are some you may want to visit:

✔ The African-Native Genealogy home page provides details on the Estelusti, a tribe of Black Indians in Oklahoma (`members.aol.com/angelaw859/index.html`).

✔ You can find a brief article on the Free People of Color and Creoles Web site (`www.neworleansonline.com/sno21.htm`).

To find additional sites containing unique information about researching your African ancestry, visit a comprehensive genealogical site and look under the appropriate category to review a list of links to such sites or use a genealogical search engine. (For a list of comprehensive genealogical sites and search engines, see The *Genealogy Online For Dummies* Internet Directory.)

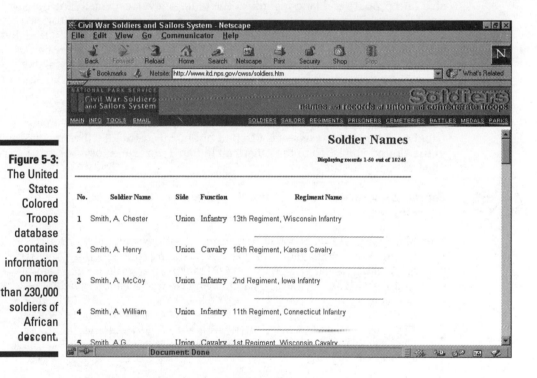

Figure 5-3:
The United States Colored Troops database contains information on more than 230,000 soldiers of African descent.

American Indian Resources

Tracing your American Indian heritage can be challenging. Your ancestor may have moved frequently and, most likely, few written records were kept. However, your task isn't impossible. With a good research strategy, you may be able to narrow down your search area and find primary resources to unlock some of the mysteries of your ancestors.

One key to your research is old family stories that have been passed down from generation to generation. Interviewing your family members is a good way to find out what tribe your ancestor belonged to and the geographic area in which that ancestor lived. After you have this information, a trip to your local library is well worth the effort to find a history of the tribe and where it migrated throughout time. From this research, you can then concentrate your search on a specific geographic area and gain a much better chance of success in finding records of genealogical value.

Fortunately, the government of the United States did compile some records on American Indians. For example, you can find annual census lists of American Indians dating from 1885 to 1940 in the National Archives. You can also find probate and land records at the federal level, especially for transactions occurring on reservations. You can also find in federal repositories school records for those who attended schools on reservations. Additionally, the Bureau of Indian Affairs has a vast collection of records on American Indians. (For more information about American Indian resources available from the National Archives and Records Administration, visit `www.nara.gov/ publications/microfilm/amerindians/indians.html`.)

You may also be able to find records on your ancestor in one of the many tribal associations in existence. (To find out how to contact tribes recognized in the United States, go to the American Indian Tribal Directory (`www. indians.org/tribes/tribes.html`.)

For more information about researching American Indian records, see the following resources:

- ✔ *The Source: A Guidebook of American Genealogy,* edited by Loretto Dennis Szucs and Sandra Hargreaves Luebking (published by Ancestry, Inc.). In particular, see Chapter 14, "Tracking Native American Family History," written by Curt B. Witcher and George J. Nixon (available online at `search.ancestry.com/cgi-bin/sse.dll?DB=SOURCE&GS= NATIVE+AMERICAN&QUERY=NATIVE+AMERICAN&DATABASEID=3259& TITLE=THE+SOURCE%3A+A+GUIDEBOOK+OF+AMERICAN+GENEALOGY& DATABASENAME=SOURCE&SEARCHENGINE=SSE.DLL&SERVER=SEARCH& TYPE=F&ct=8979`).

- ✔ *Native American Genealogical Sourcebook,* edited by Paul K. Byers and published by Gale Research.

- ✔ *Guide to Records in the National Archives of the United States Relating to American Indians,* written by Edward E. Hill and published by the National Archives and Records Services Administration.

Where to begin looking for information about American Indians

For a general look at what Internet resources are available on American Indians, see the NativeWeb site (www.nativeweb.org). NativeWeb includes a resource center with hundreds of links to other Internet sites on native peoples around the world.

If you want to know whether the United States officially recognizes a particular tribe, visit the official list at the American Indian Tribal Directory (www.indians.org/tribes/tribes.html). The list is categorized by tribe, state, and city/state.

To survey the types of records on American Indians available at the National Archives, see American Indians: A Select Catalog of NARA Microfilm Publications (www.nara.gov/publications/microfilm/amerindians/indians.html).

When you're ready to dive into research, you may want to join the INDIAN-ROOTS-L mailing list, which is devoted to discussing American Indian research methods. To subscribe to the list, type **SUB INDIAN-ROOTS-L [your first name] [your last name]** in the body of an e-mail message and send it to listserv@listserv.indiana.edu.

Another resource worth exploring is the National Archives and Records Administration's NARA Archival Information Locator (NAIL). NAIL (www.nara.gov/nara/nail.html) contains indexes to a small portion of the archive's holdings. Among the Native American collections in NAIL are the following:

- Images of the Index to the Final Rolls of the Citizens and Freedmen of the Five Civilized Tribes in Indian Territory

- Images of the Index to Applications Submitted for the Eastern Cherokee Roll of 1909 (Guion Miller Roll)

- Records of the Bureau of Indian Affairs Truxton Canon Agency

- Record of Applications under the Act of 1896 (1896 Citizenship Applications) received by the Dawes Commission

- Descriptions for records of the Cherokee Indian Agency and the Seminole Indian Agency

- Descriptions for records of the Navajo Area Office, Navajo Agency, and the Window Rock Area Office of the Bureau of Indian Affairs

✔ Some images of Cherokee, Chicasaw, Creek, and Seminole Applications for Enrollment to the Five Civilized Tribes (Dawes Commission)

✔ Images of the Kern-Clifton Roll of Cherokee Freedmen

✔ Images of the Wallace Roll of Cherokee Freedmen in Indian Territory

✔ Surveys of Indian Industry, 1922

✔ Classified Files of the Extension and Credit Office, 1931–1946

✔ Selected Documents from the Records of the Bureau of Indian Affairs, 1793–1989

✔ American Indians, 1881–1885

To search NAIL, try this:

1. **Go to** www.nara.gov/nara/nail.html.

   Note: See Appendix A for more information about using your Web browser.

2. **Click the <u>Search for Archival Holdings</u> link.**

   This link takes you to a menu of search options.

3. **Click the <u>NAIL Standard Search</u> link.**

   This brings you to the NAIL Standard Search Form page. You see a large gray box with several search options.

4. **Type the name or keyword you're looking for in the box under Enter Keywords and click the Submit Search button.**

   For example, If April is looking for a person with the name Annie Abbott, she simply types **Annie Abbott** in the blank text box and then clicks the Submit Search button. After you submit the search, you may think that the same page is returned to you. The only difference is that, if the search finds a record matching your search criteria, it is indicated in the color red next to Total Hits Retrieved. In our example, the total records in NAIL with Annie Abbott is one.

5. **Click the Display Results button to see a brief description of the record.**

   In the case of the record for Annie Abbott, the NAIL Brief Results table tells us the media type, description level, control number, title, dates, creator, and whether a digital copy of the record is available.

6. **Click the Full button to see the full record description.**

   This takes you to a screen displaying the record's control number, media, description level, record group, series, item, title, dates, access level, use restrictions, and number of items. In our example, the record tells April that the record is an enrollment of Annie Abbott, Commissioner to the Five Civilized Tribes, created by the Bureau of Indian Affairs. Annie was a member of the Cherokee tribe, a parent, and a female, and is listed on the census card number M1394. The Notes section also tells April how she can get a copy of the record.

At this point, NAIL is a working prototype and therefore still has some bugs to be worked out. However, even as a prototype, it provides access to more than 3,000 microfilm publication descriptions, more than 400,000 archival holding descriptions, and some 124,000 digital images.

For general information on how to begin researching American Indian resources, see the article "How-To Guide for Native Americans" (`members.aol.com/bbbenge/page12.html`). You can find a list of American Indian Web sites on the Native American Genealogy page (`hometown.aol.com/bbbenge/front.html`). Another page that you may want to visit is Tawodi's American Indian Genealogy site (`members.aol.com/tawodi/`). It contains a how-to guide, a list of American Indian texts online, and links to several tribal and American Indian pages.

American Indian resource pages on the Web

Genealogists would have a much easier time researching American Indian roots if some sites were dedicated to the genealogical research of specific tribes. If your ancestor's tribe passed through the state of Oklahoma, you may be in luck. Volunteers with the Oklahoma USGenWeb project developed the Twin Territories site (`www.rootsweb.com/~itgenweb/index.htm`). (For more information about USGenWeb, see Chapter 4.) The site contains a list of links to tribal genealogical pages, including the following:

- Cherokee Nation Indian Territory at `www.rootsweb.com/~itcherok/`
- Cheyenne-Arapaho Lands Indian Territory at `www.geocities.com/Heartland/Hills/1263/itcheyarapindx.html`
- Chickasaw Nation, Indian Territory 1837–1907 at `www.rootsweb.com/~itchicka/`
- Choctaw Nation, Indian Territory at `www.rootsweb.com/~itchocta/`
- Kiowa, Comanche, Apache Lands Indian Territory at `www.geocities.com/Heartland/Hills/1263/itcomancindx.html`

- Muscogee (Creek) Nation of Oklahoma at `www.rootsweb.com/~itcreek/index.htm`

- Osage Nation Genealogical Web site at `www.rootsweb.com/~itosage/`

- Quapaw Agency Lands Indian Territory at `www.rootsweb.com/~itquapaw/index.htm`

- Seminole Nation in Indian Territory at `www.rootsweb.com/~itsemino/seminoleit.htm`

- Sovereign Nation of the Kaw at `www.rootsweb.com/~itkaw/KanzaNation.html`

Transcribed American Indian records

There are some Web sites that have transcribed records that are unique to researching American Indian roots. Here are some examples:

- **The Chickasaw Historical Research Page:** This page (`www.flash.net/~kma/`) contains transcriptions of marriage records, a partial census roll of 1818, land sale records, court records, and treaty letters.

- **1851 Census of Cherokees East of the Mississippi:** This site (`members.aol.com/lredtail/siler.html`) provides a transcription of the census, including names, family numbers, ages, and relationships to head of household.

- **South Dakota Native American Genealogy page:** You can find several transcribed records at this site (at `www.geocities.com/Heartland/Plains/8430/`). These records include marriage lists, agency rolls, and links to cemetery records.

These sites are only a few examples of those providing transcribed records that you can find on the Internet. To determine whether any online records pertain specifically to your research, visit a comprehensive genealogical site and look under the appropriate category. For example, The Genealogy Toolbox's American Indian page (at `www.genealogytoolbox.com/americanindian.html`) identifies research resources, and its Records page identifies all sorts of records and indexes for records that you can find online.

Hispanic Roots

A growing number of genealogists are researching their Hispanic roots. If you have Hispanic ancestors, you can use several different types of records to pursue your genealogy, depending on when your ancestor immigrated.

If your ancestor immigrated in the nineteenth or twentieth centuries, look for vital records, military records, photographs, passports, church records, passenger lists, naturalization papers, diaries, or other items that can give you an idea of the birthplace of your ancestor. For those ancestors who immigrated before the nineteenthe century, you may want to consult Spanish colonial records after you exhaust any local records in the region where your ancestor lived.

For more information on researching Hispanic records, see the following:

- *The Source: A Guidebook of American Genealogy,* edited by Loretto Dennis Szucs and Sandra Hargreaves (published by Ancestry, Inc.). In particular, see Chapter 16, "Tracking Hispanic Family History," written by George Ryskamp. (You can view *The Source* online at search.ancestry.com/cgi-bin/sse.dll?DB=SOURCE&GS=HISPANIC+&QUERY=HISPANIC+&DATABASEID=3259&TITLE=THE+SOURCE%3A+A+GUIDEBOOK+OF+AMERICAN+GENEALOGY&DATABASENAME=SOURCE&SEARCHENGINE=SSE.DLL&SERVER=SEARCH&TYPE=F&ct=9997.)

- *Hispanic Family History Research in the L.D.S. Family History Center,* written by George R. Ryskamp (published by Hispanic Family History Research).

Where to begin searching for genealogical information on Hispanic ancestors

If you aren't sure where to begin your research, read messages that people post to the soc.genealogy.hispanic newsgroup. (For more information about newsgroups, see Appendix A.) Normally, you need a newsreader to read messages on the newsgroup; however, if you don't have a newsreader, you can read messages through a Web interface such as Deja.com (www.deja.com/usenet). If your genealogical interests lie in a specific country or ethnic subgroup, you may want to join one of the following mailing lists:

- **Basque-L:** This list discusses Basque culture and periodically includes genealogical postings. To subscribe to the mailing list, type **SUBSCRIBE BASQUE-L [your first name] [your last name]** in the body of an e-mail message and send it to listserv@cunyvm.cuny.edu.

- **Brazil:** Have ancestors from Brazil? Then subscribing to these two lists may be the thing to do. To subscribe to the BRAZIL-L mailing list, send a message to brazil-l-request@rootsweb.com with only the word *subscribe* in the body of the message. You can also subscribe to Genealogia by sending a message to majordomo@list.mps.com.br with the text *subscribe genealogia* in the body of the message.

✔ **Cuba:** This mailing list is devoted to people who have a genealogical interest in Cuba. To subscribe to the mailing list, send a message to `cuba-l-request@rootsweb.com` with only the word *subscribe* in the body of the message.

✔ **Dominican Republic:** This mailing list is for people with a genealogical interest in the Dominican Republic. Send a message to `republica-dominicana-l-request@rootsweb.com` with only the word *subscribe* in the body of the message to subscribe to the mailing list.

✔ **GEN-HISPANIC:** This is a mailing list that is gatewayed with the `soc.genealogy.hispanic` newsgroup. To subscribe to the mailing list, send a message to `gen-hispanic-l-request@rootsweb.com` with only the word *subscribe* in the body of the message.

✔ **Mexico:** This mailing list is for anyone with an interest in genealogy in Mexico. Send a message to `mexico-l-request@rootsweb.com` with only the word *subscribe* in the body of the message to subscribe to the mailing list.

✔ **Spain:** This list is devoted to people who have a genealogical interest in Spain. Send a message to `spain-l-request@ rootsweb.com` with only the word *subscribe* in the body of the message to subscribe to the list.

Hispanic resource pages on the Web

The Hispanic Genealogy Center (`www.hispanicgenealogy.com`) is a Web page that the Hispanic Genealogical Society of New York maintains to promote genealogy among Hispanic Americans. America Online also features a Hispanic forum (`users.aol.com/mrosado007/index.htm`), which includes a newsletter, surname list, and links to other Hispanic resources on the Internet. For a list of Hispanic resources by location, the Puerto Rican/Hispanic Genealogical Society maintains a page of links to genealogical resources at `www.rootsweb.com/~prhgs/` (see Figure 5-4).

Genealogia.com (`www.genealogia.com`) also has several resources for those researching their family histories, including a list of printed sources, queries, and library links, and is the home for Legado Latino, a nonprofit genealogical association. The National Society of Hispanic Genealogy (`www.hispanicgen.org`) also maintains a Web site dedicated to people researching ancestors in the Southwest area of the United States (formerly known as New Spain). For resources specific to a country or area, see the following sites:

✔ Argentina WorldGenWeb at `www.rootsweb.com/~argwgw/`

✔ Barbados at `www.rootsweb.com/~brbwgw/`

✔ Bermudian Genealogy at `www.rootsweb.com/~bmuwgw/bermuda.htm`

- Genealogía de Venezuela at `www.geocities.com/Heartland/Ranch/2443/`

- Genealogía no Brazil at `www.rootsweb.com/~brawgw/`

- Genealogical Research in South America at `www.saqnet.co.uk/users/hrhenly/latinam1.html`

- Genealogie d'Haiti et de Saint-Domingue at `www.rootsweb.com/~htiwgw/`

- Genealogy of Jamaica at `www.rootsweb.com/~jamwgw/index.htm`

- Genealogy of the Cayman Islands at `www.cayman.org/genealogy/`

- GuatemalaGenWeb at `www.rootsweb.com/~gtmwgw/`

- Honduras GenWeb at `www.rootsweb.com/~hndwgw/honduras.html`

- La Genealogia de El Salvador at `www.rootsweb.com/~slvwgw/`

- La Genealogia de Puerto Rico at `www.rootsweb.com/~prwgw/index.html`

- Mexican GenWeb Project at `www.rootsweb.com/~mcxwgw/`

- Panama GenWeb at `www.rootsweb.com/~panwgw/Panama_home.htm`

- Peru — The WorldGenWeb Project at `www.rootsweb.com/~perwgw/`

- Grenada CaribbeanGenWeb at `www.rootsweb.com/~grdwgw/`

- Saint Vincent and the Grenadines CaribbeanGenWeb at `www.rootsweb.com/~vctwgw/`

Transcribed records for Hispanic ancestors

Transcribed records are also available on sites that focus on Hispanic ancestors. Here are a few examples:

- You can view transcribed records from the 1757, 1780, 1791, 1823, and 1860 censuses of the village of Guerrero in Mexico (along with baptismal records) at `members.aol.com/gallegjj/viejo.html`.

- Selected Parish Registers from Uruguay and Argentina are available at the Genealogical Research in South America site at `www.saqnet.co.uk/users/hrhenly/latinam1.html`.

Because this is just a sampling of the transcribed records that are available online, visit a comprehensive genealogical site if you're interested in discovering whether other sites pertain more specifically to your research. For example, you can choose from a long list of ethnic groups at the Genealogy Toolbox's Ethnic/Religious Groups page (`www.genealogytoolbox.com/people.html`).

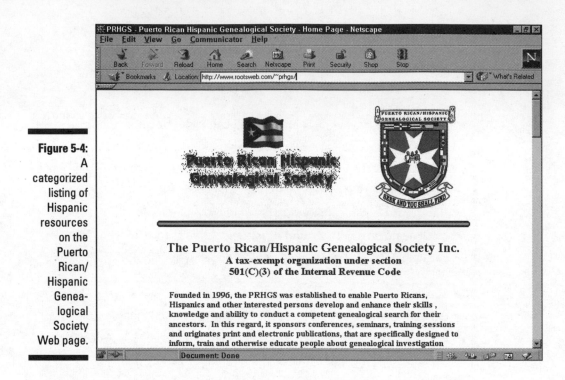

Figure 5-4: A categorized listing of Hispanic resources on the Puerto Rican/ Hispanic Genea- logical Society Web page.

European Resources

If one or more of your ancestors came from Europe, consult information on one of the continent's many ethnic groups. Your level of genealogical success with European ethnic records depends greatly on the history of the group and the areas in which they lived. Ancestors from places that weathered several wars and border changes may have fewer surviving records than those who lived in a more stable environment. Here is a sampling of European ethnic research sites:

- ✔ **Austrian:** AustriaGenWeb (`www.rootsweb.com/~autwgw/`)
- ✔ **Belarusian:** Belarusian Genealogy (`www.belarusguide.com/genealogy1/index.html`)
- ✔ **Belgian:** Genealogie in Belgie (http://`win-www.uia.ac.be/u/pavp/sdv/index.html`)
- ✔ **Bosnia-Herzegovina:** Bosnia Herzegovina Web Genealogy Project (`www.rootsweb.com/~bihwgw/`)

✔ **Bulgarian:** Bulgarian GenWeb (`www.rootsweb.com/~bgrwgw/`)

✔ **Croatian:** Croatia Genealogy Help Page (`home.att.net/~croatia/`)

✔ **Czech:** Czech Republic Genealogy (`www.rootsweb.com/~czewgw/`)

✔ **Danish:** DIS Danmark (`www.dis-danmark.dk/indexuk.htm`)

✔ **Dutch:** Genealogie en archieven in Nederland (`www.medewerker.hro.nl/SmiWT/`)

✔ **Estonian:** Estonian GenWeb (`www.fortunecity.com/meltingpot/estonia/200/genweb.html`)

✔ **Federation of East European Family History Societies (FEEFHS):** If you're looking for research guides for Eastern Europe, start here. The federation's pages (`feefhs.org`) have information on the Albanian, Armenian, Austrian, Belarusian, Bohemian, Bulgarian, Carpatho-Rusyn, Croatian, Czech, Danish, Finnish, Galician, German, Hutterite, Hungarian, Latvian, Lithuanian, Polish, Moravian, Pomeranian, Romanian, Russian, Silesian, Slavic, Slavonian, Slovak, Slovenian, Transylvanian, Ukrainian, and Volhynian ethnic groups.

✔ **Finnish:** Family History Finland (`www.open.org/~rumcd/genweb/finn.html`)

✔ **French:** Francogene (`www.francogene.com/`) focuses on genealogy of French-speaking groups, including French Canadians, Acadians, Cajuns, Belgians, and Swiss.

✔ **German:** The German Genealogy Pages (`www.genealogy.net/gene/genealogy.html`) focus on research of German, Austrian, Swiss, Alsatian, Luxemburger, and Eastern European genealogy. Also, Ahnenforschung.net (`www.ahnenforschung.net`) is a search engine dedicated to German genealogy.

✔ **Greek:** GreeceGenWeb (`mediterraneangenweb.org/greece`)

✔ **Hungarian:** HungaryGenWeb (`www.rootsweb.com/~wghungar/`)

✔ **Icelandic:** Iceland Genealogy (`www.rootsweb.com/~islwgw/`)

✔ **Irish:** Irish Ancestors (`www.ireland.com/ancestor/`) provides guides on sources of genealogical information in Ireland, a list of county heritage centers, record sources, and useful addresses.

✔ **Italian:** The Italian Genealogy Homepage (`www.italgen.com`) covers many topics including medieval genealogy, tips for researching in Italy, records repositories, common surnames, and history.

✔ **Latvian:** Latvian GenWeb (`www.rootsweb.com/~lvawgw/`)

✔ **Liechtenstein:** LiechGen (`www.rootsweb.com/~liewgw/`)

- ✔ **Lithuanian:** Lithuania GenWeb (`w3.arobas.net/~simunye/lietuva.html`)

- ✔ **Luxembourg:** Luxembourg Home Page (`www.rootsweb.com/~luxwgw/`)

- ✔ **Maltese:** MaltaGenWeb (`www.rootsweb.com/~mltwgw/`)

- ✔ **Moldava:** MoldavaGenWeb (`www.rootsweb.com/~mdawgw/`)

- ✔ **Nordic Notes on the Net:** Nordic Notes on the Net (`nordicnotes.com`) includes information on the Danish, Finnish, Icelandic, Norwegian, and Swedish ethnic groups.

- ✔ **Norwegian:** Norway Genealogy (`www.rootsweb.com/~wgnorway/`)

- ✔ **Polish:** Poland Gen Web (`www.rootsweb.com/~polwgw/polandgen.html`)

- ✔ **Portugal:** PortugalGenWeb (`mediterraneangenweb.org/portugal/`)

- ✔ **Romanian:** Romania World GenWeb (`www.rootsweb.com/~romwgw/index.html`)

- ✔ **Russian:** RussiaGenWeb (`www.rootsweb.com/~ruswgw/`)

- ✔ **Serbian:** SerbiaGenWeb (`www.rootsweb.com/~serwgw/`)

- ✔ **Slovak:** Slovak Republic Genealogy (`www.rootsweb.com/~svkwgw/`)

- ✔ **Slovenia:** Genealogy and Heraldry in Slovenia (`genealogy.ijp.si/`)

- ✔ **Spanish:** Espana GenWeb (`www.usuarios.iponet.es/fcastilla/indexegw.html`)

- ✔ **Swedish:** Sweden Genealogy (`www.rootsweb.com/~wgsweden/`)

- ✔ **Swiss:** Swiss Genealogy on the Internet (`www.eye.ch/swissgen/gener-e.htm`)

- ✔ **UK and Ireland Genealogical Information Service (GENUKI):** GENUKI (`www.genuki.org.uk`) includes details on English, Irish, Scottish, Welsh, Channel Islanders, and Manx ethnic groups.

- ✔ **Ukrainian:** Ukraine World GenWeb (`www.rootsweb.com/~ukrwgw/index.html`)

To find information on European ethnic groups, your best bet is to consult a comprehensive genealogy site. The following steps provide an example of how to conduct such a search:

1. **Go to the Genealogy Resources on the Internet site (**`www.rootsweb.com/~jfuller/internet.html`**).**

   In the first paragraph of the home page, you see a list of resources including mailing lists, Usenet newsgroups, anonymous File Transfer Protocol (FTP), Gopher, World Wide Web, Telnet, and e-mail.

2. **Click the <u>World Wide Web</u> link.**

   This link takes you to an alphabetic listing of categories of genealogical Web sites.

3. **Click a geographic location or name of an ethnic group.**

   We're interested in finding information on individuals of Dutch ancestry, so we choose the Dutch Resources link. This brings up a page with a list of Dutch-related links.

4. **Choose a link from the list that interests you.**

Asian Resources

If your ancestors came from Asia or the Pacific Rim, your success at finding records depends greatly on the history of the ancestor's ethnic group and its record-keeping procedures. Currently, little online genealogical information pertaining to these areas and peoples exists. Here's a sampling of Asian and Pacific Rim resources:

- **Dutch East Indies:** Ancestors from the former Dutch East Indies at ourworld.compuserve.com/homepages/paulvanV/eastindi.htm

- **Australia:** AustraliaGenWeb at www.rootsweb.com/~auswgw/

- **Bangladesh:** Bangladesh Genealogy at www.rootsweb.com/~bgdwgw/

- **Bhutan:** Bhutan Genealogy at www.rootsweb.com/~btnwgw/

- **China:** Chineseroots.com at www.chineseroots.com/

- **India:** Family History in India at www.ozemail.com.au/~clday/

- **Japan:** Japan GenWeb at www.rootsweb.com/~jpnwgw/

- **Lebanon:** LebanonGenWeb at www.rootsweb.com/~lbnwgw/

- **Melanesia:** MelanesiaGenWeb Project at www.rootsweb.com/~melwgw/

- **Philippines:** Philippines Genealogy Web Project at www.geocities.com/Heartland/Ranch/9121/

- **Polynesia:** PolynesiaGenWeb at www.rootsweb.com/~pyfwgw/

- **Saudi Arabia:** Saudi Arabia GenWeb at www.angelfire.com/tn/BattlePride/Saudi.html

- **South Korea:** South Korea GenWeb at www.rootsweb.com/~korwgw-s/

- **Syria:** Syria GenWeb at www.rootsweb.com/~syrwgw/

✔ **Sri Lanka:** Sri Lanka GenWeb at `www.rootsweb.com/~lkawgw/`

✔ **Taiwan:** TaiwanGenWeb at `www.rootsweb.com/~twnwgw/`

✔ **Tibet:** TibetGenWeb at `www.rootsweb.com/~tibetwgw/`

✔ **Turkey** Turkish Genealogy at `www.rootsweb.com/~turwgw/`

✔ **Vietnam:** Vietnamese Research at `www.genealogy.com/00000387.html`

✔ **Various:** Genealogical Gleanings (genealogies of the rulers of India, Burma, Cambodia, Thailand, Fiji, Tonga, Hawaii, and Malaysia) at `www.uq.net.au/~zzhsoszy/index.html`

Chapter 6

Government Records

Governments are bureaucratic institutions no matter where you live. Fortunately, you can cash in on some of the information that they've meticulously kept for hundreds of years. Records at all levels of government are immensely valuable to genealogists. During the four years that we lived in the Washington, D.C., area, we tried to take full advantage of government resources like the National Archives. In fact, we had a regularly scheduled night each week for research. Unfortunately, in moving back to the Midwest, we gave up a great deal of our ability to conveniently conduct research on government records. So we looked for ways to research them from the comfort of our own home — online.

Over the past couple of years, the amount of government records that you can find online has increased. More than just finding pointers or indexes to records, you can now find several projects that transcribe a variety of records and a few sites even place complete sets of digitized government records online. Although some records aren't being transcribed or digitized as systematically as we'd like, many resources are still available to save you lots of travel time — the trick is finding them. In this chapter, we show you what kinds of records are currently available and some of the major projects that you can use as keys for unlocking the government treasure chests of genealogical information.

Counting on the Census

Census records are one of the most valuable tools to a genealogist, at least in the United States. Many countries periodically count and gather information about their populations, although most didn't conduct nationwide censuses regularly until the 19th century.

Census records are valuable for tying a person to a place and for discovering relationships between individuals. For example, say that you have a great-great-great-grandfather by the name of Nimrod Sanders. You're not sure who his father was, but you do know that he was born in North Carolina. By using a census index, you may be able to find a Nimrod Sanders in a North Carolina census index who is listed as a child of someone else. If Nimrod's age, location, and siblings' names fit, then you may have found one more generation to add to your genealogy.

Often, a census includes information such as a person's age, sex, occupation, birthplace, and relationship to the head of the household. Sometimes, the *enumerators* (the people who conduct the census) added comments to the census record, such as a comment on the physical condition of an individual, which may give you further insight into the person's life. For additional information about the value and format of censuses, see Chapter 1.

Getting the lowdown on censuses

Several Web sites provide background information about census records in particular countries. They explain what years the census records cover, how the censuses were conducted, and what information is valuable to genealogists. Also, they give you the details on where you can find and obtain copies of these census records. Here's a list of general census information sites from various countries:

- ✓ **Australia:** Censuses in Australian Colonies (www.users.on.net/proformat/census.html)

- ✓ **Austria:** Austrian Census Returns 1869–1910 with Emphasis on Galicia (feefhs.org/ah/gal/jshea-ac.html)

- ✓ **Canada:** National Archives of Canada (www.archives.ca/exec/naweb.dll?fs&02020205&e&top&0)

- ✓ **England, Scotland, and Wales:** Genuki Census Information (www.genuki.org.uk/big/eng/census.html)

✔ **Ireland:** Irish Ancestors Census Records (www.genealogy.ie/categories/cenna/)

✔ **Norway:** Norwegian Censuses (www.rhd.uit.no/census.htm)

✔ **United States:** Availability of Census Records About Individuals (www.census.gov:80/prod/2/gen/cff/cff-9702.pdf)

To find information on census records in other countries, see the appropriate Research Helps at the FamilySearch Web site (www.familysearch.org/Eng/Search/RG/frameset_rhelps.asp). In particular, you can find information on census records for Argentina, Chile, Columbia, Ecuador, El Salvador, Guatemala, Honduras, Mexico, Nicaragua, Venezuela, Denmark, Germany, Philippines, and Sweden.

For a summary of the contents of each United States census return and advice on how to use the censuses, see *The Source: A Guidebook of American Genealogy,* edited by Loretto Dennis Szucs and Sandra Hargreaves Luebking (published by Ancestry, Inc.). Turn to Chapter 5, "Research in Census Records," written by Szucs. (You can read the book online at search.ancestry.com/cgi-bin/sse.dll?DB=SOURCE&TI=0&GS=RESEARCH+IN+CENSUS+RECORDS&QUERY=RESEARCH+IN+CENSUS+RECORDS&SUBMIT=SEARCH&DATABASEID=3259&TITLE=THE+SOURCE%3A+A+GUIDEBOOK+OF+AMERICAN+GENEALOGY&DATABASENAME=SOURCE&SEARCHENGINE=SSE.DLL&SERVER=SEARCH&TYPE=F&ct=1349.) If you run into abbreviations that you don't understand, take a look at Genealogy Record Service's "Guide to Soundex Abbreviations" page at www.genrecords.com/forms/soundexab.pdf. (Viewing this page requires installing Adobe Acrobat Reader, which is available on the CD-ROM accompanying this book.)

Finding your ancestors in census records

Imagine that you're ready to look for your ancestors in census records. You hop in the car and drive to the nearest library, archives, or Family History Center. On arrival, you find the microfilm roll for the area where you believe your ancestors lived. You then go into a dimly lit room, insert the microfilm into the reader, and begin your search. After a couple hours of rolling the microfilm, the back pain begins to set in, cramping in your hands becomes more severe, and the handwritten census documents become blurry as your eyes strain from reading each entry line by line. You come to the end of the roll and still haven't found your elusive ancestor. At this point you begin to wonder if a better way exists.

Fortunately, a better way *does* exist for a lot of census records: census indexes. *Census indexes* contain a listing of the people who are included in particular census records, along with references indicating where you can find the actual census record. Traditionally, indexes come in book form, but you can now find some of these indexes online or on CD-ROM.

Although no central World Wide Web sites contain indexes for all census records (at least not yet), some sites contain partial listings of census indexes. These sites may contain indexes for several states over several years, one index for one census year, or something in between.

So how do you find these online indexes? Well, you can check a comprehensive index site or use a search engine (both of which we discuss in Chapter 3) to find an index that interests you.

For example, say you want to find an Alan McSwain who lived in Ontario sometime around 1870. Your first step is to determine whether a census was taken in or around 1870. To do so, follow these steps:

1. **Fire up your Web browser and go to Cyndi's List of Genealogy Sites on the Internet (**www.cyndislist.com**).**

   Note: For more information about using a Web browser, take a look at Appendix A.

2. **Click the <u>Ontario</u> link (under the Canada Index category).**

   This page contains a many subcategories.

3. **Under the "Category Index for this page," click the <u>Records: Census, Cemeteries, Land, Obituaries, Personal, Taxes and Vital</u> link.**

   This takes you down this list of links that are sorted by subcategory to the Records section. You see links to several records projects online.

4. **Scroll down near the bottom of the list of Records links and click the <u>Ontario 1871 Census</u> link.**

   The link takes you to a portion of the National Archives of Canada site that features a searchable index of the 1871 Census (see Figure 6-1).

5. **In the box next to Keyword, type** mcswain **or another name that interests you and click Submit.**

   A search on the McSwain name yields two results: Alan McSwain and Mary McSwain.

6. **Click the <u>Alan McSwain</u> link to see his entry in the transcribed census record.**

   The link takes you to the entry in the record for Alan McSwain. From the record, you can see that two other entries for individuals have the surname McSwain. These individuals may be related to Alan because they have similar surnames and are from Scotland — as is Alan.

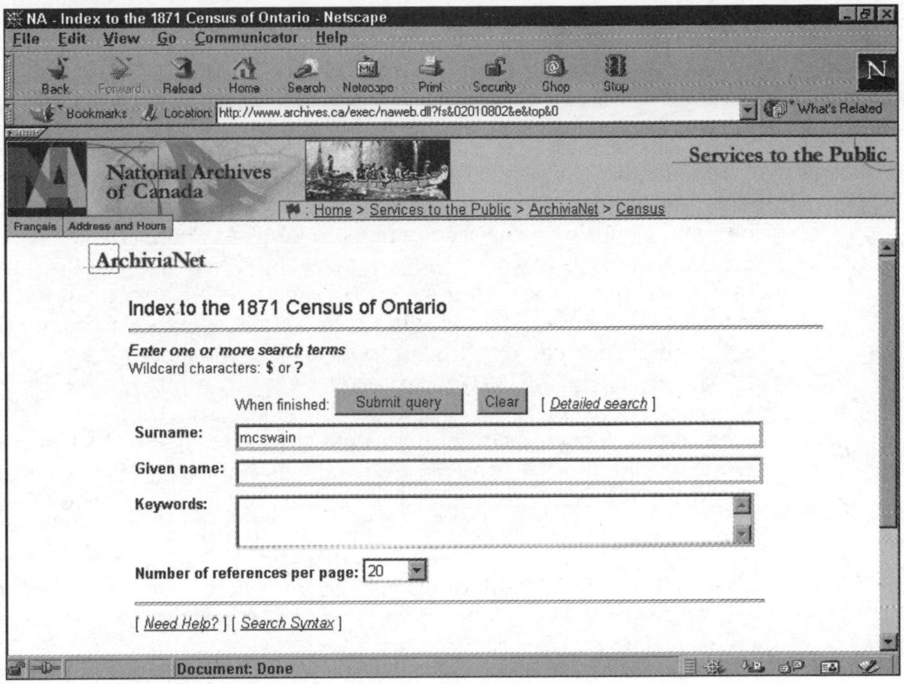

Figure 6-1:
The search
page for the
1871 Ontario
Census
Index.

This same search strategy works for a census index for any country. If you can't find an index for the census you're looking for in a comprehensive site, try using one of the large Internet search engines, such as Lycos (www. lycos.com) or AltaVista (www.altavista.com), or one of the genealogical search engines, such as GenealogyPortal.com (www.genealogyportal.com), or the Internet FamilyFinder (www.familytreemaker.com/ifftop./html). For more information about using search engines, check out Appendix A.

If you find one of your ancestors in a census index, make sure that you write down the county, township, house number, and page on which you find the ancestor. Then you can make a specific request for a copy of the census record, reducing the amount of time it takes to have it sent to you (and reducing the frustration levels of those pulling records for you). Or, of course, you can always try to find the record and make a copy of it for yourself through a site containing digitized census records or at your local library, archives, or Family History Center.

Remember that the objective of a census index is only to let you know who was included in the census return and where the record is located. Keep in mind, too, that transcribed indexes may have omissions and typographical errors and may include only the names of heads of households. If you're in doubt, you can always check a copy of the actual record.

Finding individuals in the United States census

Census indexes are a very important resource for finding individuals in the United States Census. Currently, the largest United States census index collections are found on the subscription-based Ancestry.com, GenealogyLibrary.com, and GenealogyDatabase.com sites. Ancestry.com (www.ancestry.com) and GenealogyLibrary.com (www.genealogylibrary.com) both have census indexes for the years 1790 through 1870, generated from print indexes. GenealogyDatabase.com has reindexed census entries for the years 1790, 1800, and 1870. If you don't want to pay a fee, you can find some Census indexes under the USGenWeb Archives Census Project at www.rootsweb.com/~usgenweb/census/. If you can't find an index there, try a site dedicated to providing links to online census resources, such as Census Online (www.census-online.com) or CensusLinks (www.censuslinks.com), or a geographic-specific site, such as the county-level pages in the USGenWeb Project (www.usgenweb.org).

Say you want to find Samuel Abell, who lived in St. Mary's county in 1790. Your first step is to see if an index is available for that county during the 1790 census. To do this, try the following:

1. **Fire up your Web browser and go to Census Online** (www.census-online.com)**.**

   For more information about using a Web browser, take a look at Appendix A.

2. **Click the <u>Links to Online Data</u> link in the Census Online column.**

   This page contains a number of links represented by a state or provincial abbreviation (depending on whether it's a state in the United States or province in Canada).

3. **Click the <u>MD</u> link.**

   You're presented with a page that has a blue column on the left with the names of counties for the state and a second, white column that contains the links to the census sites.

4. **Select a county from the left column (or scroll down to the appropriate county entry in the right column).**

   In this case, St. Mary's County has one link.

5. **Click <u>1790 Federal Census</u> link.**

This takes you to a file listing on the USGenWeb Census project. Clicking the index.txt file opens an index of individuals for the county. The sixteenth person on the list is Samuel Abell.

Researchers can use one additional resource to find individuals in United States records: the Family Archive CD Index.

The Family Archive CD Index (www.familytreemaker.com/cdhome.html) **is** produced by Genealogy.com. The Index contains names from census records, marriage records, Social Security records, death records, and family trees on CD-ROMs. You can use the Index to conduct a preliminary online search for individuals in census records from 1790 to 1870 and the 1890 Veterans Schedules. The Index provides the name of an individual, estimated date, location, and the name of the CD-ROM where the name appears. Here's an example:

1. **Point your Web browser to the Family Archive CD Index (**www. familytreemaker.com/cdhome.html**).**

   You see a page with a search form in the left column that enables you to search by first, middle, and last name.

   Note: Check out Appendix A for more information about using a browser.

2. **Type a name that interests you in the text boxes and click the Go button.**

   We're interested in finding census records that contain one of Matthew's ancestors, Uriah Helm, so we type **Uriah** in the First Name text box and **Helm** in the Last Name text box and click Go. This generates a Search Results page.

3. **Review the Results page that appears for the estimated date and location of the selected individual.**

   In our case, we see four entries for Uriah Helm. One entry indicates that a Uriah Helm was present in 1860 in Illinois and that you can find his information on Census CD 318 (see Figure 6-2).

After you know whether the FamilyFinder Index identifies entries that pertain to your ancestor, you can decide what route to take to get the documentation. You have a few options: You can see whether Genealogy.com or some other company has digitized that particular census so that you can get a copy of the CD-ROM or online census record in which Uriah Helm's name shows up, or you can go through the traditional means to obtain a copy of the actual census record (from microfilm) at an archives or Family History Center.

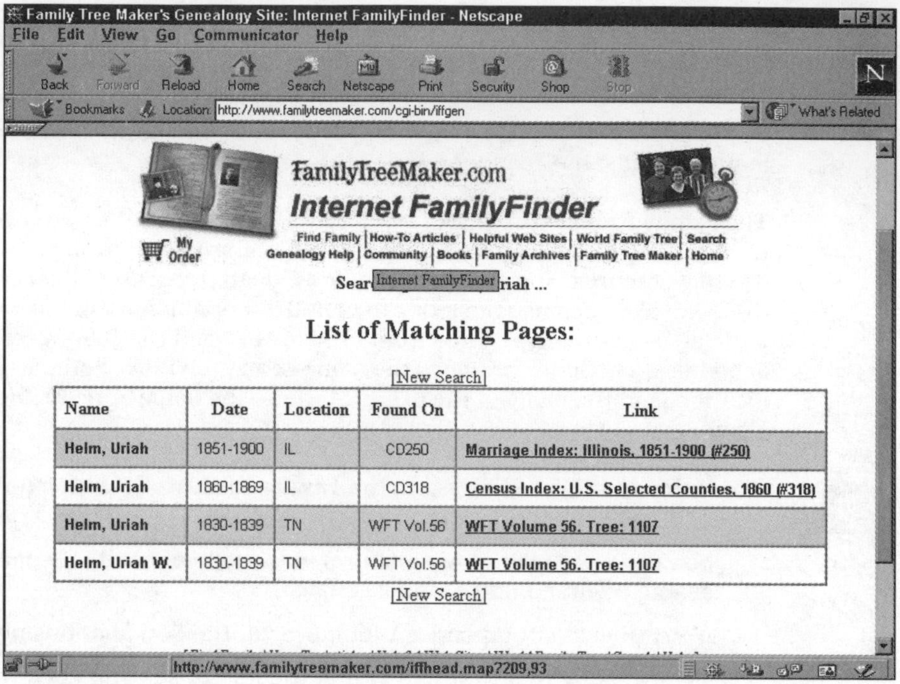

Figure 6-2:
Results of
a search
on the
FamilyFinder
Index.

Using a transcribed online census

As an online genealogist, what you want is access to all the census records on Aunt Bettie with just the click of a mouse. Unfortunately, the genealogy world isn't quite up to speed yet. Some efforts are currently underway to transcribe census records for use online. Some of these transcriptions cover only a portion of the entire census, while others feature the complete census returns for a certain area.

As with any transcribed record, you should always verify your findings with either a digitized or microfilm copy of the original record. Often, census records are difficult to read because of their age, the quality of the handwriting, and so on — so mistakes do occur in the transcription process. But these transcribed records are better than nothing at all.

Finding transcribed records on the Internet is very similar to finding census indexes. You can try one of the comprehensive genealogical sites under a geographical category or a genealogically focused search engine. For a list of comprehensive sites, see The *Genealogy Online For Dummies* Internet Directory. To see a step-by-step walk-through of a search using a comprehensive site or genealogically focused search engine, see Chapter 3.

Census records in the United States are a mainstay of genealogists, so most of the transcribed censuses that you see on the Internet come from the United States (although that doesn't mean that censuses from other countries aren't online — as we explain later in this section). Until recently, these censuses weren't transcribed in any systematic fashion. (However, there are a couple of projects undertaken by USGenWeb volunteers that are trying to change this situation. You can find the USGenWeb Archives Census Project at www. rootsweb.com/~usgenweb/census/ and the USGenWeb Census Project Archives at www.us-census.org/usgwcens.) Individuals simply transcribed those censuses in which they were interested or that were associated with a geographical area they were researching. This fact doesn't diminish the importance of these efforts; it only explains why you may see a census record for one county but not for the county right next to it.

Here's a sample search on the USGenWeb Archives Census Project site:

1. **Go to the USGenWeb Archives Census Project site** (www.rootsweb.com/~usgenweb/census/)**.**

   You see a page with a map and list of states and territories for which census transcriptions are available.

   Note: If you want more information about using a browser, flip to Appendix A.

2. **Select a state for your search by clicking the state on the map or its link in the list.**

   For our example, we're interested in finding census information on an Isaac Metcalf who lived in Baylor County, Texas, around 1880, so we select Texas. A list of available census schedules for the state appears at the top of the screen.

3. **Click a year or type of schedule that interests you.**

   We select 1880. The resulting page contains a table listing the location, roll number, status of the project, and transcriber's name.

4. **Click the status button for an available census.**

   We choose the transcription for <u>Baylor County</u> by clicking the status button marked Online, which takes us to a page of transcribed census entries where we can scroll down to an individual named Isaac Metcalf. You can also use your browser's Find in Page option to find the name you're looking for.

As the transcriptions you can use at this site are the works of volunteers, it's possible that you may find errors here and there — there may be typographical errors, some of the censuses may not be indexed, or the status of the project for a particular county may be incorrect.

The most plentiful type of transcribed census records you're likely to encounter is what we refer to as the *plain-text census,* which is a Web page or text file that's simply a transcription of the actual census record without any kind of search function. You either have to skim the page or use your Web browser's Find in Page option to find the person you're looking for. The 1870 Census for Penn Township, Stark County, Illinois (`members.aol.com/ZCyberCat/private/castleton.html`), is an example of this type of census return (see Figure 6-3). For each individual, the record includes the house number of the household, last name, first name, age, sex, race, occupation, real-estate value, personal-property value, and birthplace. This site is also typical of smaller census sites in that it focuses on the records on one county (actually, one township in one county).

Some sites contain collections of several census returns for a specific geographic area (over an extended period of time). A good example of this type of site is the Censuses of Gloucester and South Warwickshire 1851–1891 site in England (`www.silk.net/personal/gordonb/cotswold.htm`). Here, you can find several transcribed census returns for most of the subdivisions, with some providing transcribed returns for all five censuses during the time period. Each record contains at least the last name, first name, age, and occupation for the individuals identified in the census.

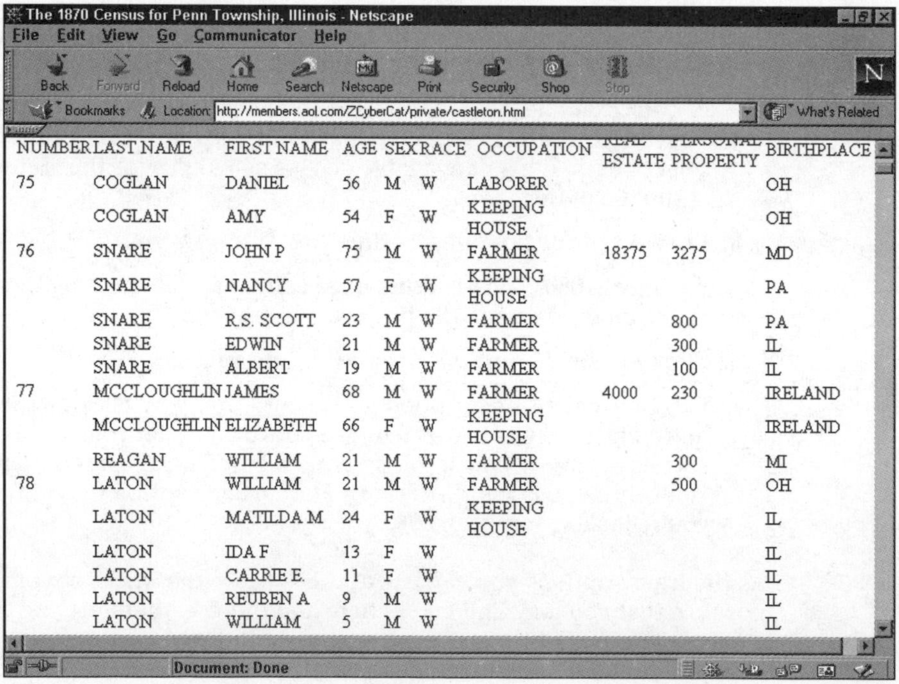

Figure 6-3: A section of the 1870 United States Census for Penn Township, Stark County, Illinois.

The 1870 Census for Penn Township, Illinois - Netscape

File Edit View Go Communicator Help

Back Forward Reload Home Search Netscape Print Security Shop Stop

Bookmarks Location: http://members.aol.com/ZCyberCat/private/castleton.html What's Related

NUMBER	LAST NAME	FIRST NAME	AGE	SEX	RACE	OCCUPATION	REAL ESTATE	PERSONAL PROPERTY	BIRTHPLACE
75	COGLAN	DANIEL	56	M	W	LABORER			OH
	COGLAN	AMY	54	F	W	KEEPING HOUSE			OH
76	SNARE	JOHN P	75	M	W	FARMER	18375	3275	MD
	SNARE	NANCY	57	F	W	KEEPING HOUSE			PA
	SNARE	R.S. SCOTT	23	M	W	FARMER		800	PA
	SNARE	EDWIN	21	M	W	FARMER		300	IL
	SNARE	ALBERT	19	M	W	FARMER		100	IL
77	MCCLOUGHLIN	JAMES	68	M	W	FARMER	4000	230	IRELAND
	MCCLOUGHLIN	ELIZABETH	66	F	W	KEEPING HOUSE			IRELAND
	REAGAN	WILLIAM	21	M	W	FARMER		300	MI
78	LATON	WILLIAM	21	M	W	FARMER		500	OH
	LATON	MATILDA M	24	F	W	KEEPING HOUSE			IL
	LATON	IDA F	13	F	W				IL
	LATON	CARRIE E.	11	F	W				IL
	LATON	REUBEN A	9	M	W				IL
	LATON	WILLIAM	5	M	W				IL

Document: Done

Another site that has a simple search engine to display census records is the Census of Norway (`digitalarkivet.uib.no/index-eng.htm`). The Census of Norway used a nationwide approach for the 1801 census. At this site, you can search for individuals who lived in each parish in Norway as of February 1, 1801. You can search by farm name, first name, or surname. Also, you can follow a link from this site to the Digital Archive, which includes the 1865 and 1900 Censuses.

Looking for more elaborate search capabilities? Point your browser to the Danish Demographic Database at `ddd.sa.dk/kiplink_en.htm`. The database is a joint project of the Danish Data Archives, Danish Emigration Archives, and Centre of Microfilming at the Danish State Archives. It contains partial census records from 1787 to 1916 — not all the paper records have been computerized. You can search for particular individuals online (by using searches by parish, district, county, birthplace, name, occupation, position in household, and year of census).

The future of census information: Digitized images

Many genealogists are no longer satisfied with using transcribed information. After all, even if you find useful information, you must take a second step to confirm the information through a copy of the primary record. In response to this demand, a few companies are now developing electronic versions of census records that you can use on your personal computer. Many of these resources are available online, as well as on CD-ROM. The following sections describe some of these currently available resources.

GenealogyDatabase.com

GenealogyDatabase.com (`www.genealogydatabase.com`), a fee-based site produced by Heritage Quest, houses digitized images of United States census population schedules from 1790 to 1920. The collection numbers more than 10 million images taken from 12,555 rolls of microfilm. These images are bitonal (black and white) and require a TIFF viewer plug-in for your Web browser. At the initial release of the site, the only years that are indexed are 1790, 1800, and 1870. In the case of the 1870 index, only selected individuals are indexed. If you're looking for individuals in other censuses, you must browse the images much like you do when using microfilm. A unique feature of the site is a sticky-note feature that enables you to annotate the census images. For example, if you have a correction or more information on a census entry, you can post a sticky note mentioning that fact. You can also use the feature to tell others that you're researching that family so that they can share information with you. The images available on GenealogyDatabase.com are also available on 12,555 CD-ROMs through Heritage Quest.

GenealogyLibrary.com

GenealogyLibrary.com (www.genealogylibrary.com) is another subscription site — this one maintained by Genealogy.com. In addition to its collection of transcribed family histories and historical texts, the site also contains 283,000 bitonal digitized images from the 1850 census (including the states of Alabama, Arkansas, California, Connecticut, Illinois, Indiana, Kentucky, Louisiana, Massachusetts, Maine, Mississippi, New Hampshire, North Carolina, New Mexico, Oregon, Pennsylvania, Rhode Island, Tennessee, Texas, Utah, Vermont, and Virginia). These images are also available on CD-ROM. Under a separate program, called the Internet Family Archives, Genealogy.com offers another fee-based service where you can purchase access to portions of the 1900 census on a per-state basis (including Maine, New Hampshire, North Carolina, and Vermont).

Helm's Genealogy Toolbox DigiSources

A new addition to Helm's Genealogy Toolbox is its DigiSources collection (digisources.genealogytoolbox.com). The collection is produced by FamilyToolbox.net and currently features 256-color grayscale images of the original and printed schedules of the 1790 census. The 1790 census images are available for free on the site. As on some of the other commercial sites, you can pan and zoom in and out of the images as well as print them (see Figure 6-4).

Images Online

Ancestry.com offers a subscription-based service that it calls Images Online (www.ancestry.com/search/io/about/main.htm), which currently contains the 1790 census. The images are 256-color grayscale, which typically makes them clearer than bitonal images. The Images Online site offers options for using a plug-in viewer, a Java applet, or just your ordinary Web browser. The company intends to place the entire census online within the course of a year.

Some noncommercial efforts also provide digitized census images. The primary source for these is the USGenWeb. Its census images are available at www.rootsweb.com/~usgenweb/cen_img.htm. The images are of various qualities and, in some cases, are difficult to read. You can't zoom into these images as you can with some of the commercial offerings. However, they're available to researchers free of charge.

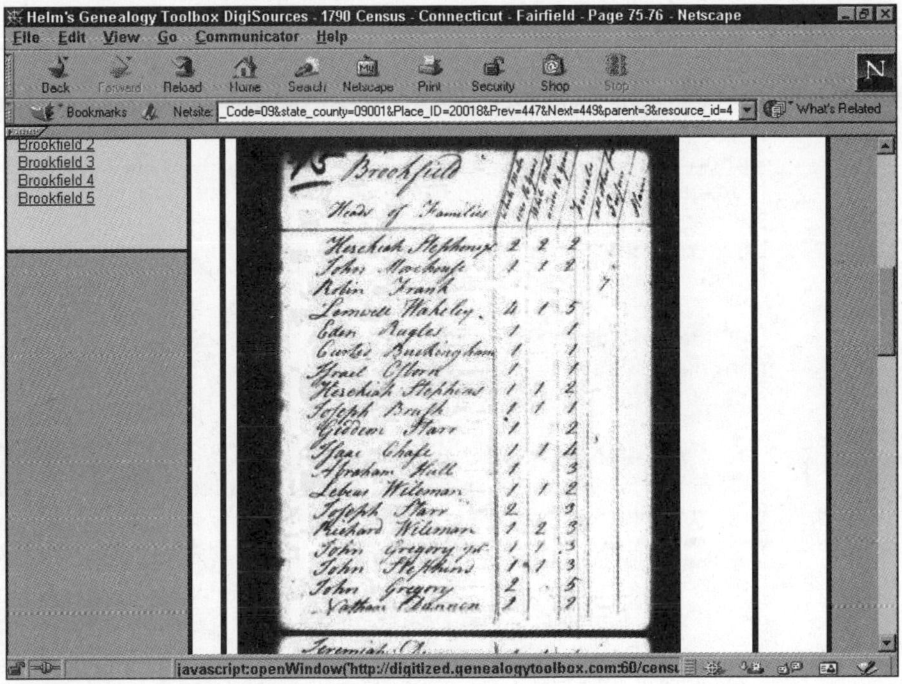

Figure 6-4:
A 1790
Census
image from
Helm's
Genealogy
Toolbox
DigiSources.

These Records Are Vital

Sometimes, it seems that with every major event in our lives comes a government record. One is generated when we are born, get married (as well as get divorced), have a child, and pass on. Vital records (also called *civil registrations*) are the collective name for records of these events. Traditionally, these records were kept at the local level. States and countries have only recently made an effort to collect and centralize their holdings of vital records. In a similar manner, the record holders have just recently begun to expand the number of vital record indexes available online. You're likely to encounter three types of vital record sites: *general information sites, vital record indexes,* and *transcribed vital records.*

Vital record information sites

If you're looking for information on how to order vital records within the United States, you can choose among a few sites. The most comprehensive site is probably Vital Records Information — United States (vitalrec.com/index. html). A page for each state lists the type of record, its cost, the address to which you should send requests, and additional remarks, such as the time period during which records were kept and to whom to make the check payable (see Figure 6-5). You also can find information on obtaining vital records for foreign or high-sea births and deaths of United States citizens.

Although the Vital Records Information site doesn't contain any online indexes or records, using it is a good way to become familiar with where each state stores its vital records. Later on, as you locate records on more ancestors, you can use this site as a quick reference for getting mailing addresses for your many records requests.

Outside the United States and Canada, vital records are called *civil registrations*. For those of you looking for these records, the following list describes some helpful sites:

- **Australia:** For Australian records, you can find an article on purchasing certificates from the General Registrar's offices at `www.cohsoft.com.au/afhc/certs.html`.

- **Canada:** For a list of addresses to request copies of civil registrations in Canada, see the National Archives of Canada page on Records of Births, Marriages, and Deaths at `www.archives.ca/exec/naweb.dll?fs&02020202&e&top&0`.

- **Denmark:** For background on and the contents of vital records in Denmark and Greenland, see the Civil Registration System in Denmark site at `www.cpr.dk/CRS_DK.htm`.

- **England:** You can find links to information on civil registrations in the Research Guidance for England Events and Time Periods page at `www.familysearch.org/Eng/Search/RG/frameset_rg.asp?Dest=E&Juris1=77`.

- **Ireland:** You can find links to information on Irish civil registrations at the Research Guidance for Ireland Events and Time Periods at `www.familysearch.org/Eng/Search/RG/frameset_rg.asp?Dest=E&Juris1=76`.

- **New Zealand:** You can find information on birth, marriage, death, and name change records at the New Zealand Births, Deaths, and Marriages Office site at `www.bdm.govt.nz/diawebsite.nsf/c3649e22547ea840cc25681e0008b39b/c26afa900922c388cc25683e007b9a3f?OpenDocument`.

- **Poland:** You can find a sample letter for requesting civil registration records from the Polish Civil Registration Office at `www.man.poznan.pl/~bielecki/cro.htm`.

- **Scotland:** If your interests lie in Scottish records, look at the Frequently Asked Questions page at `www.gro-scotland.gov.uk/grosweb/grosweb.nsf/pages/faq`, which the General Register Office for Scotland maintains. You can also find civil registration records online at the Scots Origins site (`www.origins.net`).

✔ **Slovakia:** The State Archives keeps information on births, marriages, and deaths up to the year 1900. You can find contact information for the State Archives on the Embassy of the Slovak Republic page at `www.iarelative.com/embassy.htm`.

The Research Guidance at the FamilySearch Web site (`www.familysearch.org/Eng/Search/RG/frameset_rg.asp`) includes information on civil registrations for Argentina, Brazil, Bolivia, Chile, Columbia, Costa Rica, Cuba, Dominican Republic, Ecuador, El Salvador, Guatemala, Honduras, Mexico, Nicaragua, Panama, Paraguay, Peru, Uruguay, Venezuela, Denmark, Germany, Philippines, and Sweden.

If the country you're researching isn't in the preceding list, try looking at one of the comprehensive genealogy sites (you can find a list of these in The *Genealogy Online For Dummies* Internet Directory in this book) or conduct a search on one of the genealogically focused search engines (`www.genealogyportal.com`) or general Internet search engines such as Lycos (at `www.lycos.com`) or AltaVista (at `www.altavista.com`) to see whether a similar site with vital records for the country you're interested in exists.

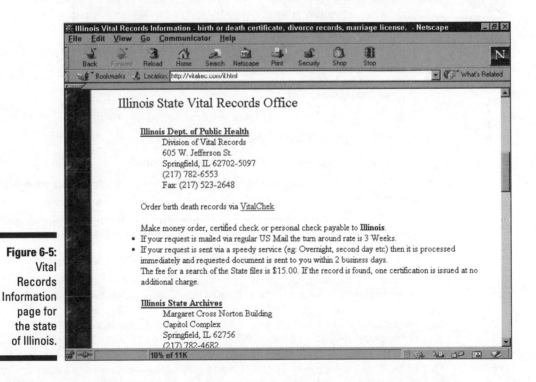

Figure 6-5: Vital Records Information page for the state of Illinois.

Don't overlook these information sites just because they don't contain primary resources. You still need to use more traditional ways of collecting records because very few transcribed or digitized records exist online. And even if you find a transcribed record online, you may want to order a copy of the original record to place in your filing system — in which case you need addresses from these sites.

Vital record indexes

Vital record indexes serve much the same purpose as census indexes: They point to the locations of original records. You can use indexes to confirm that an ancestor's vital records are available prior to submitting a request for the record. And knowing the exact location of the record can often make retrieval of the record a lot easier.

The easiest way to find vital record (and civil registration) indexes on the Internet is to search along geographical lines. Suppose that you're looking for registrations in British Columbia — you want to look under the appropriate category. As an example, here's a step-by-step search for civil registrations using the Genealogy SiteFinder:

1. **Go to the Genealogy Toolbox site (**www.genealogytoolbox.com**).**

   The home page for the Genealogy SiteFinder contains a subject directory of links on the site.

   Note: See Appendix A for how-to information about using a browser.

2. **Click the <u>Places</u> link in the subject directory.**

   You see a list of links to continents and countries.

3. **Scroll down to the country that interests you and click the appropriate link.**

   In this case, you're looking for civil registrations in British Columbia, so you scroll down to the Canada entry and click the <u>British Columbia</u> link.

4. **Click a link to go to a site featuring civil registrations (vital records).**

   You click the <u>Vital Events Indexes</u> link on the British Columbia page, which takes you to a site that the British Columbia Archives maintains, containing indexes to birth, marriage, and death registrations. Depending on the county you selected in Step 3, you may need to go through additional steps to find the information you're looking for.

The site that we mention in the preceding steps includes a query page for the marriage index that enables you to search for the groom's surname, groom's given name, bride's surname, bride's given name, year or year range for the marriage, month, date, event place, registration number, British Columbia

Archives microfilm number, or GSU microfilm number (see Figure 6-6). The results of the search provide you with the bride's name and groom's name, event date, event place, registration number, British Columbia Archives microfilm number, and GSU microfilm number. You can use this information to order a copy of the appropriate original document.

Another approach to finding vital statistics (civil registrations) is to go to the USGenWeb (www.usgenweb.org) or WorldGenWeb (www.worldgenweb.org) site for the appropriate state or country. For example, we want to find a death certificate for Matthew's great-grandfather, William Henry Abell of Larue County, Kentucky. To do so, we go through the following steps:

1. **Go to the USGenWeb site (**www.usgenweb.org**).**

   You see a page with two columns on it.

   Note: See Appendix A for more details about using browsers.

2. **Click the link entitled <u>The Projects State Pages</u> and then click the Text Only State List.**

   This link takes us to a page with a list of states and the URLs associated with each state page.

3. **Click a state that interests you.**

   In our case, we select Kentucky because we're looking for someone who died in the state of Kentucky.

   As a shortcut, you can always access any USGenWeb state page by typing www.usgenweb.org and the two letter postal code for the state. For example, for Kentucky, you can type www.usgenweb.org/ky.

4. **At the USGenWeb state page for the state that you choose, look for a link to vital records information or research links.**

   We choose the <u>Vitals</u> link under the Kentucky Research Sources heading on the Kentucky USGenWeb. This takes you to a page with search interfaces for the Kentucky Death Index and Marriage Index.

5. **Scroll down to the appropriate section and type the name that you want to search in the text box and then click Submit Query.**

   Sticking with the example, we go to the Kentucky Death Index for 1911–2000 section, type **Abell** and **William H.**, and click Submit Query. We then wait for the results to return.

6. **Scan the results of your query.**

   In our case, the results page contains two individuals named William H. Abell. One died in Larue County and the other in Jefferson County. The location seems right for the William from Larue County. We check the death date, September 7, 1955, and the age, 82, both of which are consistent with what we've heard from interviews with family members. The database also supplies us with the record volume number and certificate number, which we can use to obtain a copy of the certificate.

A few new projects are currently transcribing civil registrations. The FreeBMD (freebmd.rootsweb.com) project's goal is to place an index of civil registrations in England and Wales from 1837 to 1900 online. Currently, over three million records exist in the database. You can search the database on type of record, surname, first name, spouse surname, spouse first name, start date, end date, volume, page, districts, and counties. Results of the search include type of record, surname, first name, age, district, volume, page, and contributor name. A companion to the FreeBMD site is the FreeREG site (freereg. rootsweb.com). This site focuses on baptism, marriage, and burial records transcribed from parish and nonconformist church registers. The International Internet Genealogical Society Births, Deaths and Marriages Exchange (www.iigs.org/global_village/bdm/) is also creating indexes of civil registrations for the United Kingdom, New Zealand, Australia, Papua New Guinea, Belgium, Luxembourg, Netherlands, and Ireland.

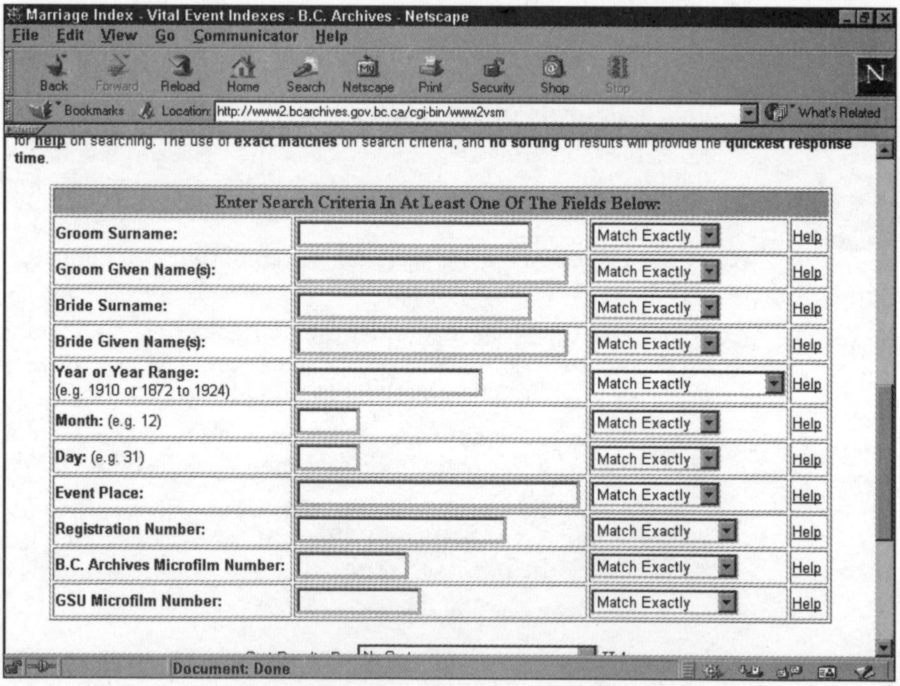

Figure 6-6: Search form for the British Columbia Archives Marriage Index.

Transcribed vital records

If you aren't lucky enough to have a copy of your great-grandfather's marriage certificate, you need a way to discover the information that the document contains. The best way to find this information is to order a copy of the certificate from the appropriate government source. (For more information on this strategy, see "Vital record information sites," earlier in this chapter.) But before you spend the money to get a copy, you want to find out whether the record is really of interest to you — this is where transcribed vital records come in handy.

Transcribed records can come in several forms. A researcher may have transcribed a series of records of a particular county, or a state may have established a database of records. Either way, these sites can be helpful in determining whether the record you're looking for is useful.

A good place to begin searching for transcribed vital records is a comprehensive genealogy site. For example, the following is a step-by-step search for a transcribed record for a Jacob Gardner, who was married in Indiana around 1850.

1. **Go to the Genealogy Resources on the Internet site (**www.rootsweb.com/~jfuller/internet.html**).**

   In the first paragraph on the page that you access, notice the list of resources including mailing lists, Usenet newsgroups, anonymous file transfer protocol (FTP), gopher, World Wide Web, Telnet, and e-mail.

2. **Click the World Wide Web link.**

   This link takes you to an alphabetic listing of categories of genealogical Web sites.

3. **Click a geographic location where you believe a transcribed vital record may be located.**

   We're looking for a record in the state of Indiana, so we click the Indiana Resources link.

4. **Click a link from the list that contains transcribed vital records.**

   In our case, the Marriage Index — Through 1850 link looks promising. We click the link and go to the page maintained by the Indiana State Library.

   Note: If you select a link other than the one we chose here, follow the directions on the site to access the transcribed records.

5. **For this search, click the part of the alphabet corresponding to the first letter of either the bride's or groom's surname.**

   We're looking for Jacob Gardner, so we choose the E-F-G link, which loads a page containing six text boxes. These boxes ask you to type the name of the bride or groom, the spouse's name, the county, and the date.

6. **Type the surname of either the bride or groom in the appropriate text box and click the Search button.**

   We type the surname **Gardner** and first name **Jacob** for the groom. We leave the rest blank because we don't know the spouse's name or the actual date of the marriage. We then wait for the results to return.

7. **Examine the results to see whether the record is useful to you.**

   The results page gives us one marriage record of Jacob Gardner and Harriet Simmons married in Jefferson County, Indiana, on November 2, 1848. Using some groundwork that we already have on the family, we then check to see whether this Jacob Gardner is the same Jacob Gardner who is our ancestor. If he is, then we now have his wife's maiden name.

Commercial online databases are another source for transcribed vital records. For example, you can find the following transcribed records among the subscription databases at Ancestry.com (www.ancestry.com):

✔ Accomack County, Virginia Births, 1874–1877

✔ Floyd County, Virginia Deaths, 1883–1896

✔ Indiana Marriages to 1850

✔ Leavenworth, Kansas Funeral Home Records, 1942–1954

✔ New York Births and Baptisms, Southeast Region, 1660–1916

Investigating Immigration and Naturalization Records

You may have heard the old stories about your great-great-grandparents who left their homeland in search of a new life. Some of these stories may include details about where they were born and how they arrived at their new home. Although these are great stories, as a genealogist you want to verify this information with documentation.

Often the document you're looking for is an immigration or naturalization record. *Immigration records* are documents that show when a person moved to a particular country to reside; *naturalization records* are documents showing that a person became a citizen of a particular country without being born in that country. Sometimes these documents can prove difficult to find, especially if you don't know where to begin looking. Unless you have some evidence in your attic or have a reliable family account of the immigration, you may need a record or something else to point you in the right direction. Census records are one useful set of records. (For more information about census records, see "Counting on the Census," earlier in this chapter.) Depending on the year your ancestors immigrated, census records may contain the location of birth and tell you the year of immigration and the year of naturalization of your immigrant ancestor.

Emigration records — documents that reflect when a person moved out of a particular country to take up residence elsewhere — are also useful to researchers. You find these records in the country your ancestor left, and they can often help when you can't find immigration or naturalization records in the new country.

Locating immigration, emigration, and naturalization records online can be difficult. The common types of records that genealogists use to locate immigrants — passenger lists, immigration papers, emigration records — are just now becoming available on the Internet. A good starting point for determining an ancestor's homeland is to look at census records. (For more information about census records, see "Counting on the Census," earlier in this chapter.) Because a great deal of early immigration and naturalization processing occurred at the local level, census records may give you an indication of where to look for immigration records.

Some examples of online records include the following:

- ✔ **Immigration/Naturalization Records:** McLean County, Illinois, Immigration Records (www.mclean.gov/cc/imgrecs/imgrecs.html)

- ✔ **Passenger Lists:** Mayflower Passenger List (members.aol.com/calebj/passengers2.html)

If you don't have a lot of details on when your ancestor may have immigrated but have a general idea of the time or place of immigration, you may want to consider looking for information on a comprehensive genealogical index. (See The *Genealogy Online For Dummies* Internet Directory for a list of comprehensive genealogy indexes.) As you look at comprehensive genealogy sites, you're likely to find these types of records categorized under immigration, naturalization, or passenger lists or by geographical area. If you know more details, try using a genealogically focused search engine or a general Internet search engine.

As an example, suppose that you have a family legend that Martin Saunders immigrated to America on a ship called *Planter* sometime in the first part of the seventeenth century. The following steps show you how to search for a passenger list to confirm the legend:

1. **Go to the Google search engine (**www.google.com**).**

   The home page for Google is simple, showing only a field for your search terms and a few links.

2. **Type your search terms into the Search field and click the Google Search button.**

   For this example, you type **martin saunders planter**.

3. **Click a promising link from the list of results.**

   The second link on the Results page reads <u>Passengers of the Planter, sailed April, 1635</u>. In the abstract that you access by clicking the link, you see that a Martin Saunders, age 40, sailed on the *Planter*.

Another source for passenger lists is the Immigrant Ships Transcribers Guild passenger list transcription project (istg.rootsweb.com). Currently the transcriptions made by the Guild are divided into three volumes, including information on 2,946 ships. The passenger lists are organized by date, ship's name, port of departure, port of arrival, surname and captain's name. You can also search the site to find the person or ship that interests you.

Looking for some background information on immigration and naturalization within the United States? Take a look at the National Archives and Records Administration page on Naturalization Records (www.nara.gov/genealogy/natural.html) or the Immigration and Naturalization Service's History, Genealogy, and Education page (www.ins.gov/graphics/aboutins/history/index.htm).

You can also check out Chapter 13, "Immigration: Finding Important Immigrant Origins," written by Kory L. Meyerink and Loretto Dennis Szucs, in *The Source: A Guidebook of American Genealogy,* edited by Szucs and Sandra Hargreaves Luebking (published by Ancestry, Inc.). You can read this chapter online at search.ancestry.com/cgi-bin/sse.dll?DB=SOURCE&TI=0&GS=FINDING+IMPORTANT+IMMIGRANT+ORIGINS&QUERY=FINDING+IMPORTANT+IMMIGRANT+ORIGINS&DATABASEID=3259&TITLE=THE+SOURCE%3A+A+GUIDEBOOK+OF+AMERICAN+GENEALOGY&DATABASENAME=SOURCE&SEARCHENGINE=SSE.DLL&SERVER=SEARCH&TYPE=F&ct=7598.

For general information on Canadian immigration records, see the National Archives of Canada pages on immigration records (www.archives.ca/exec/naweb.dll?fs&02020204&e&top&0) and on citizenship (www.archives.ca/exec/naweb.dll?fs&02020203&e&citizen&0). To search Canadian passenger lists, see the InGeneas site at www.ingeneas.com.

Land Lovers

Land records are among the most plentiful sources of information on your ancestors. Although a census occurs only once every ten years, land transactions may have taken place two or three times a year, depending on how much land your ancestor possessed. These records don't always contain a great deal of demographic information, but they do place your ancestor in a time and location, and sometimes in a historical context as well. For example, you may discover that your ancestors were granted military bounty lands. This discovery may tell you where and when your ancestors acquired the land, as well as what war they fought in. You may also find out how litigious your ancestors were by the number of lawsuits they filed or had filed against them as a result of land claims.

Getting a foundation in the history of land records prior to conducting a lot of research is probably a good idea. Here are some sites with general information on land records:

- **Canada:** Land Records in Ontario (`wwnet.com/~treesrch/ontland.html`)

- **Denmark:** Denmark Research Outline (`www.familysearch.org/Eng/Search/RG/frameset_rg.asp?Dest=G1&Aid=&Gid=&Lid=&Sid=&Did=&Juris1=&Event=&Year=&Gloss=&Sub=&Tab=&Entry=&Guide=Denmark.ASP`)

- **England:** GENUKI Land and Property (`www.genuki.org.uk/big/eng/#Land`)

- **Germany:** Germany Research Outline (`www.familysearch.org/Eng/Search/RG/frameset_rg.asp?Dest=G1&Aid=&Gid=&Lid=&Sid=&Did=&Juris1=&Event=&Year=&Gloss=&Sub=&Tab=&Entry=&Guide=Germany.ASP`)

- **Ireland:** Irish Ancestors — Land Records (`scripts.ireland.com/ancestor/browse/records/land/intro.html`)

- **Latin America:** Latin America Research Outline (`www.familysearch.org/Eng/Search/RG/frameset_rg.asp?Dest=G1&Aid=&Gid=&Lid=&Sid=&Did=&Juris1=&Event=&Year=&Gloss=&Sub=&Tab=&Entry=&Guide=Latin_America.ASP`)

- **Norway:** Norway Research Outline (`www.familysearch.org/Eng/Search/RG/frameset_rg.asp?Dest=G1&Aid=&Gid=&Lid=&Sid=&Did=&Juris1=&Event=&Year=&Gloss=&Sub=&Tab=&Entry=&Guide=Norway.ASP`)

- **Philippines:** Philippine Research Outline (`www.familysearch.org/Eng/Search/RG/frameset_rg.asp?Dest=G1&Aid=&Gid=&Lid=&Sid=&Did=&Juris1=&Event=&Year=&Gloss=&Sub=&Tab=&Entry=&Guide=Philippines.ASP`)

- **Scotland:** GENUKI Land and Property (`www.genuki.org.uk/big/sct/#Land`)

- **United States:** Land Records Reference (`www.ultranet.com/~deeds/landref.htm`) and Chapter 8, "Research in Land and Tax Records," by Sandra Hargreaves Luebking, in *The Source: A Guidebook of American Genealogy,* edited by Loretto Dennis Szucs and Luebking (published by Ancestry, Inc.). You can read this book online at `search.ancestry.com/cgi-bin/sse.dll?DB=SOURCE&TI=0&GS=RESEARCH+IN+LAND+AND+TAX+RECORDS&QUERY=RESEARCH+IN+LAND+AND+TAX+RECORDS&DATABASEID=3259&TITLE=THE+SOURCE%3A+A+GUIDEBOOK+OF+AMERICAN+GENEALOGY&DATABASENAME=SOURCE&SEARCHENGINE=SSE.DLL&SERVER=SEARCH&TYPE=F&ct=4098.`

Of course, these are just a few examples of some sites offering background information about land transactions in those particular countries. To see if a similar site exists for a country you're interested in (or if you're looking for any kind of land record), visit a comprehensive genealogical site and look under that location, as well as under a directory heading or category for land records (if you see one).

One exciting site relating to land records in the United States is the Bureau of Land Management, Eastern States, General Land Office Official Land Patents Records Site (`www.glorecords.blm.gov`). This site enables you to search the more than two million Federal land title records for the Eastern States Office issued between 1820 and 1908. Recently the database was expanded to include serial patent records issued after 1908, but this is still an ongoing project.

Follow these steps to search the records on this site:

1. **Go to the Land Patents Records Site (`www.glorecords.blm.gov`).**

   Note: For more information about using a browser, see Appendix A.

2. **In the left column, click the Search Land Patents button and, on the following page, enter your Zip code in the appropriate space and click the Continue button.**

   This brings you to a page displaying a form that you can fill out to search the patents. Matthew's interest, for example, is in finding land that one of his ancestors, Jacob Helm, owned in Illinois.

3. **Select the state that you're interested in from the State drop-down list.**

   We select Illinois.

4. **Type a first name and last name in the text boxes and then click the Search button.**

   We type **Helm** in the Patentee Last Name text box and **Jacob** in the First Name text box and then click the Search button. This brings us to a page listing one result for Jacob Helm. The table tells us the name of the patentee, state, issue date, document number, and accession number, and provides a button that we can click for details on the entry.

5. **Click the Details button.**

   The Land Patent Details page loads with the Patent Description showing. From this information, we can obtain the document number of the purchase, how many acres, how and when the land was purchased, and which land office recorded the transaction. Most databases stop here, but this site offers more as you can see from the four tabs — Patent Description (what you're currently viewing), Legal Land Description, Document Image, and Certified Copy.

6. **Click the Document Image tab to view a digitized copy of the patent.**

   We can choose one of four ways to view the document including a small GIF image, large GIF image, TIFF image, and PDF document. We can then save the copy of the document on our computer.

In addition to the methods that we mention so far in this section, you may want to check out geographical-related resources, such as the USGenWeb project (www.usgenweb.org) or the WorldGenWeb project (www.worldgenweb.org). These sites break down resources by location (country, state, and/or county, depending on which you use). For more information about USGenWeb, see Chapter 4 or The *Genealogy Online For Dummies* Internet Directory that we include with this book; for more information about WorldGenWeb, see the directory as well. Of course, if your attempts to find land records and information through comprehensive sites and geographical-related sites don't prove as fruitful as you'd like, you can always turn to a search engine such as AltaVista (www.altavista.com). See Appendix A for more information about using search engines.

Military Tales

You've probably heard the family stories about how your great-great-grandfather fought in a particular war. Or you may have a weapon that he used or uniform that he wore. Either way, you probably want to find more information about the part that he played in history.

Military records come in various forms, such as unit rosters, muster records, service records, and pension applications. You can piece together quite a story for a family history book when you use military records along with other resources, such as regimental histories. For example, one of Matthew's ancestors, George Helm, served in the American Revolution. His pension record shows that he served in Captain Shepherd's company of Colonel Rawlings' Rifle regiment in the Maryland line from 1776 to 1779 and that he was taken as a prisoner of war for seven weeks at Fort Washington. To find out just what George was doing, we can check a regimental history or pick up a history book that discusses the campaigns in the vicinity of Fort Washington. Although Matthew could have relied on George's account alone, he lucked out by finding George's testimony of his activities over the three-year period in a pension record. Matthew confirmed these details in a history book to verify that George's memory hadn't failed him — after all, George was giving testimony almost 50 years after the war.

Online military records appear in several different forms, depending on where and when the individual served. Following are just a few online resources describing military records:

- **Australia:** Australian Archives Fact Sheet page on military service (`www.naa.gov.au/fsheets/fs63.html`)

- **Canada:** Military and Civilian Personnel Records page on the National Archives of Canada site (`www.archives.ca/exec/naweb.dll?fs&020203&e&top&0`)

- **United Kingdom:** Public Records Office leaflets (`www.pro.gov.uk/leaflets/riindex.htm#Army`)

- **United States:** The National Archives and Records Administration's page on military service records (`www.nara.gov/publications/microfilm/military/`), the National Personnel Records Center (`www.nara.gov/regional/mpr.html`), and Chapter 9, "Research in Military Records," written by Johni Cerny, Lloyd DeWitt Bockstruck, and David Thackery, in *The Source: A Guidebook of American Genealogy,* edited by Loretto Dennis Szucs and Sandra Hargreaves Luebking (published by Ancestry, Inc.). You can read the chapter online at `search.ancestry.com/cgi-bin/sse.dll?DB=SOURCE&TI=0&GS=RESEARCH+IN+MILITARY+RECORDS&QUERY=RESEARCH+IN+MILITARY+RECORDS&DATABASEID=3259&TITLE=THE+SOURCE%3A+A+GUIDEBOOK+OF+AMERICAN+GENEALOGY&DATABASENAME=SOURCE&SEARCHENGINE=SSE.DLL&SERVER=SEARCH&TYPE=F&ct=4658`.

As we mention at the beginning of this section, military records come in various forms. Here are examples of the online version of these types:

- **Casualty Lists:** Canadian Books of Remembrance (`collections.ic.gc.ca/books/remember.htm`)

- **Cemetery Records:** Confederate Graves at Brice's Crossroads (`sunset.backbone.olemiss.edu/~cmprice/cavalry/brice_cem.html`)

✔ **Draft Registrations:** Civilian Draft Registration Database (`userdb.rootsweb.com/ww1/draft/search.cgi`)

✔ **Military Census:** Cumberland, Providence County, Rhode Island, 1777 Military Census (`ftp://ftp.rootsweb.com/pub/usgenweb/ri/providen/military/militry1.txt`)

✔ **Muster/Recruitment Records:** National Archives of Canada, Canadian Expeditionary Force Database (`www.archives.ca/exec/naweb.dll?fs&020106&e&top&0`)

✔ **Pension Records:** 1835 Federal Pension List for Virginia (`www.rootsweb.com/~usgenweb/va/vapensio.htm`)

✔ **Regimental Histories:** Duke of Cornwall's Light Infantry (`www.lightinfantry.org/dcli.htm`)

✔ **Service Records:** Civil War Soldiers and Sailors System (`www.itd.nps.gov/cwss`)

✔ **Unit Rosters:** Ohio Historical Society Military Rosters Searchable Database (`www.ohiohistory.org/resource/database/rosters.html`)

If you're looking for military records for countries outside the United States, consult one of the comprehensive genealogy sites or conduct a search using a general Internet search engine. (You can find sites for both of these types in The *Genealogy Online For Dummies* Internet Directory.)

The following is an example of a search using one of the general search engines, AltaVista:

1. **Go to the AltaVista search engine** (`www.altavista.com`).

2. **Type your query in the box and click the Search button.**

   Say you're interested in finding a regimental history of the Royal Welsh Fusilier Regiment that was assigned to America during the American Revolution, so you type **welsh fusiliers**, a simple query that results in 27,346 documents.

3. **Click a link that interests you.**

   You can click your browser's Back button to return to the search engine results page if a particular link proves unfruitful.

   Select the first link. The link takes you to The Royal Welsh Fusiliers in America home page — a page for the re-enactment company. (It's possible that clicking the first link takes you to a different site as the number and order of sites available through general search engines change frequently.)

4. **Look for a link to regimental history.**

   In our case, the page has a link to a brief history of the regiment.

If you're researching United States military units, you may want to consult the United States Internet Genealogical Society Military Collection site (`www.usigs.org/library/military/index.htm`). This site has links to other sites all across the United States that contain some form of military records. The sites are categorized by major war.

Most online military sites cover one specific war or historical period. In fact, a great deal of the available military sites are about the American Civil War. If you're unable to find information on the particular war or unit in a comprehensive genealogy site or general Internet search engine, you may want to try a search on the Yahoo! site (`www.yahoo.com`) under the appropriate country or historical heading.

Taxation with Notation

Some of the oldest records available for research are tax records. Tax records come in a variety of forms, including property, inheritance, and church taxation records. Most of the early tax records that you encounter were most likely collected at a local level (that is, at the county or parish level). However, many local tax records have since been turned over to state or county archives. Some of these archives now make tax records available on microfilm, as do Family History Centers. (If you have a Family History Center in your area, you may be able to save yourself a trip, call, or letter to the state archives by checking with the Family History Center to see whether it keeps copies of tax records on hand for the area in which you're interested.) And a few maintainers of tax records — including archives and Family History Centers — are starting to make information about their holdings available online. Generally, what you find online are either indexes or transcriptions of these microfilm records.

Here are just a few examples of the types of online resources that you can find pertaining to tax records:

- **General Information:** Chapter 8, "Research in Land and Tax Records," by Sandra Hargreaves Luebking, in *The Source: A Guidebook of American Genealogy,* edited by Luebking and Loretto Dennis Szucs (published by Ancestry, Inc.); you can read it online at `search.ancestry.com/cgibin/sse.dll?DB=SOURCE&TI=0&GS=RESEARCH+IN+LAND+AND+TAX+RECORDS&QUERY=RESEARCH+IN+LAND+AND+TAX+RECORDS&DATABASEID=3259&TITLE=THE+SOURCE%3A+A+GUIDEBOOK+OF+AMERICAN+GENEALOGY&DATABASENAME=SOURCE&SEARCHENGINE=SSE.DLL&SERVER=SEARCH&TYPE=F&ct=4098`.

- **Tax List:** Edmonson County, Kentucky, Tax List For The Year 1825 (`www.tlcgen.com/edmonson.htm`)

- **Transcribed Tax Record Book:** Woodruff County, Arkansas 1867 Tax Records (`steveandcamella.com/1867_8.htm`)

To identify sites that contain tax records for countries other than the United States, visit a comprehensive genealogical site or the appropriate WorldGenWeb site (www.worldgenweb.com). For more information about WorldGenWeb, see The *Genealogy Online For Dummies* Internet Directory.

If you're locating records in the United States, try a USGenWeb site for the state or county. Here's what to do:

1. **Go to the USGenWeb site (**www.usgenweb.org**).**

   You see a page with two columns on it.

   Note: See Appendix A for more details about using Web browsers.

2. **Click The Projects State Pages link and click the Text Only State List link.**

   This link takes you to a page with a list of states and the URLs associated with each state page.

3. **Click a state that interests you.**

   In our case, we select the Pennsylvania link because we're looking for tax records in Lancaster County.

   As a shortcut, you can always get to any USGenWeb state page by typing www.usgenweb.org and the two letter postal code for the state. For example, for Pennsylvania, we can type www.usgenweb.org/pa.

4. **From the USGenWeb state page (for the state that you choose), find a link to tax records or other research links.**

   On the Pennsylvania counties page, we click the Lancaster link to get to the Lancaster County GenWeb site. We then click the Courthouse Records link (because tax records were often kept in county courthouses), which leads us to another link called Tax and Census Lists. Clicking this link takes us to another page with a listing of tax lists for the county.

The state and county Web sites in the USGenWeb Project vary immensely. Some have more information available than the Pennsylvania and Lancaster County pages, while others have less. The amount of information that's available at a particular USGenWeb site affects the number of links that you have to click through to find what you're looking for. Don't be afraid to take a little time to explore the sites for states and counties in which your ancestors lived and become familiar with them.

Chapter 7

Records Off the Beaten Path

● ●

In This Chapter

▶ Seeking information through religious group records

▶ Finding information through fraternal orders

▶ Using photographs as a research aid

▶ Checking out genealogy and adoption records

● ●

*M*any people who are familiar with genealogy know to use census records, vital records, tax lists, and wills to find information on their ancestors. These records tend to take historical "snapshots" of an individual's life at particular points in time. But as a genealogist, you want to know more than just when your ancestors paid their taxes — you want to know something about them as people.

For example, one time April was looking through some pictures, and she came across a photograph of her great-great-grandfather. He was dressed in a uniform with a sash and sword and was holding a plumed hat. As far as April knew, her great-great-grandfather hadn't been in the military, so she decided to dig for some information about the uniform. Although part of the picture was blurry, she could make out three crosses on the uniform. One was on his sleeve, the second was on the buckle of his belt, and the third was a different kind of cross that was attached to his sash. April suspected that the symbols were Masonic. She visited a few Masonic sites on the World Wide Web and found that the crosses indicated that her great-great-grandfather had been a member of the Order of the Temple within the Masonic organization. Of course, she would never have known that he was a member of the organization had she depended solely upon the usual group of records used by genealogists.

This chapter looks at some examples of unique or hard-to-find records that can be quite useful in family history research. These records include those kept by religious groups and fraternal orders, photographs, and adoption records.

Religious Group Records

In the past, several countries required attendance at church services or the payment of taxes to an ecclesiastical authority. Although your ancestors may not have appreciated these laws at the time, the records that were kept to ensure their compliance can benefit you as a genealogist. In fact, before governments started recording births, marriages, and deaths, churches kept the official records of these events. For those places where no such laws were in effect, you can use a variety of records that were kept by church authorities or congregations to develop a sketch of the everyday life of your ancestor.

Some of the common records that you may encounter include baptismal records, parish registers, marriage records, death or burial records, tithes, welfare rolls, meeting minutes, and congregation photographs. Each type of record may include several different bits of information. For example, a baptismal record may include the date of birth, date of baptism, parents' names, and location where the parents lived.

Several sites provide general information and links to all sorts of resources that pertain to specific religions and sects. Here are a few examples:

- **Anabaptists:** The Hall of Church History — The Anabaptists site (`www.gty.org/~phil/anabapt.htm`) has an introduction to the beliefs of the Anabaptists and links to Anabaptist resources on the Internet.

- **Catholic:** The Local Catholic Church History & Genealogy Research Guide (`home.att.net/~Local_Catholic/`) includes links to information on diocese and genealogy categorized by location.

- **Church of Scotland:** The Scots Origins site (`www.origins.net`) features searchable indexes of births/baptisms and banns/marriages from the Old Parish Registers dating from 1553 to 1854.

- **Huguenot:** The Huguenot Resources — Olive Tree Genealogy site (`www.rootsweb.com/~ote/hugres.htm`) lists books and societies available to those researching French Protestants that fled to Switzerland, Germany, England, America, and South Africa.

- **Hutterite:** The Hutterite Genealogy HomePage (`feefhs.org/hut/frg-hut.html`) gives an introduction and links to resources for this sect found in Austria, Bohemia, Moravia, Slovakia, Hungary, Romania, Canada, the United States, and the Ukraine.

- **Jewish:** JewishGen (`www.jewishgen.org`) has information about the JewishGen organization and frequently asked questions about Jewish genealogy, as well as indices of other Internet resources, including searchable databases, special interest groups, and JewishGen family home pages.

- ✔ **Lutheran:** The Lutheran Roots Genealogy Exchange (`www.aal.org/ LutheransOnline/Gene_Ex`) has a registry of researchers looking for information about Lutheran ancestors and a message board to which you can post questions about your research.

- ✔ **Mennonite:** The Mennonite Research Corner (`www.ristenbatt.com/ genealogy/mennonit.htm`) features general information about Mennonites and a collection of online resources for researchers.

- ✔ **Methodist:** The Methodist Archives and Research Centre (`rylibweb.man. ac.uk/data1/dg/text/method.html`) contains information on its collections and a guide to using the archives for family history research (under "Guides and Catalogues").

- ✔ **Moravian Church:** The Moravian Church home page (`www.moravian. org`) includes information on one of the oldest Protestant denominations. You can also find links to various Moravian resources on the Internet.

- ✔ **Quaker:** The Quaker Corner (`www.rootsweb.com/~quakers`) contains a query board, a list of research resources, and links to other Quaker pages on the World Wide Web.

- ✔ **United Church of Canada Archives:** The United Church Archives page (`vicu.utoronto.ca/archives/archives.htm`) has information on the holdings of the archives and a page on genealogical research. The archives contain records for the Presbyterian Church (Canada), Methodist Church (Canada), Congregational Union of Canada, Local Union Churches, and the Evangelical United Brethren Church.

A few church organizations have online descriptions of their archives' holdings. The Center for Mennonite Brethren Studies in Fresno, California (`www.fresno.edu/cmbs/geneal.htm`) and the Catholic Archives of Texas (`www.onr.com/user/cat`) identify the specific resources available at their locations, including databases, original records, rare books and periodicals, and old photographs.

Of course, at some point you may want to find sites with indices or actual records online. Finding religious records on the Internet can be quite challenging. We recommend that you start by using one of the larger comprehensive genealogy sites listed in The *Genealogy Online For Dummies* Internet Directory found in this book or some of the specialty religious sites, or by looking at sites that are referenced on personal genealogy pages. To find religious sites, try this:

1. **Open your Web browser and go to the Genealogy Toolbox** (`www.genealogytoolbox.com`).

   Note: If you need a refresher on operating a browser, see Appendix A.

2. **Click the People category, and select Ethnic/Religious Groups.**

3. **Under Ethnic/Religious Groups, select the religious group that interests you.**

   For example, we're interested in finding out information on Quakers, so we click the <u>Quakers</u> link.

4. **Click a link on the religious group's page to visit related pages on the Internet.**

   After you select a religious group, you see links to sites on the Web about that group. You may want to read the abstracts to determine whether the site may contain the information that you're looking for.

If you're curious about what types of information for religious groups are available on the Internet, here are a few examples:

✔ **Baptism/Marriage Records:** The Illinois GenExchange Baptismal Registry (`www.genexchange.com/baptismregco.cfm?state=ny&county=newyork`) places transcribed records from a variety of areas online.

✔ **Cemetery Records:** The Quaker Burying Ground Cemetery, Galesville, Anne Arundel County, Maryland site (`www.interment.net/data/us/md/anne_arundel/quaker.htm`), which is part of the Cemetery Records Online site, provides transcribed burial information, including the person's name and dates of birth and death, as well as some other information. (See Figure 7-1.)

Figure 7-1:
The Quaker Burying Ground Cemetery site provides information taken from gravestones in Galesville, Anne Arundel County, Maryland.

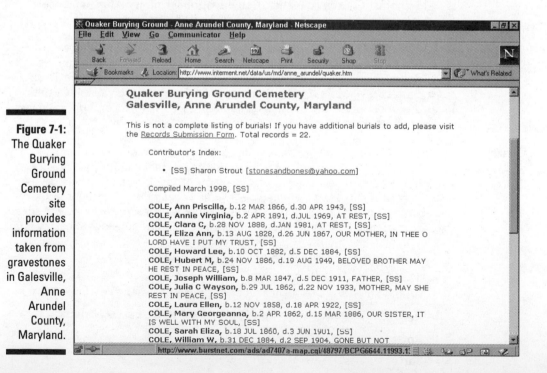

✔ **Parish Directories:** The Holy Trinity Church, Boston, Massachusetts site (`homepages.rootsweb.com/~mvreid/bgrc/htc.html`) has a searchable 1895 parish directory, an ongoing project to identify and post information about church members who served in the Civil War, and a list of church members who served in World War I.

Of course, in addition to some sites that focus specifically on one type of record, you may run across sites like the Genline Project (`www.genline.se/`), which collects digitized copies of all sorts of records pertaining to a particular church. The goal of the Genline Project is to place all digital copies of Swedish church records online.

Fraternal Orders

Were any of your ancestors members of fraternal orders or service clubs? Many such organizations are out there, and chances are, you have at least one ancestor who was a member of an order or club. Although most of the more commonly known organizations are for men, affiliated organizations for women exist, too. Here are a few general information sites on fraternal orders and service clubs:

✔ **DeMolay:** DeMolay International (`www.DeMolay.org`)

✔ **Elks:** Benevolent Protective Order of the Elks (`www.elks.org`)

✔ **Freemasonry:** e-m@son (`www.freemasonry.org`) and A Page About Freemasonry (`web.mit.edu/dryfoo/www/Masons/index.html`)

✔ **Job's Daughters:** International Order of Job's Daughters (`www.iojd.org`)

✔ **Kiwanis International:** Kiwanis International (`www.kiwanis.org`)

✔ **Knights of Columbus:** Knights of Columbus (`www.kofc.org/`)

✔ **Lions Clubs:** LionNet (`www.lionnet.com`)

✔ **Moose:** Moose International (`www.mooseintl.org`)

✔ **Odd Fellows:** Independent Order of Odd Fellows (`128.125.109.137/IOOF.shtml`)

✔ **Optimist International:** Optimist International (`www.optimist.org`)

✔ **Order of the Eastern Star:** Grand Chapter Order of the Eastern Star (`www.indianamasons.org/easternstar.htm`)

✔ **Rainbow for Girls:** International Order of the Rainbow for Girls (`www.iorg.org`)

✔ **Rebekahs:** Rebekahs (`128.125.109.137/IOOF/Rebekahs.html`)

✔ **Rotary International:** Rotary International (`www.rotary.org`)

✔ **Shriners:** The Shrine of North America home page (`www.shriners.com`)

Most of the online sites related to fraternal orders provide historical information about the clubs and current membership rules. Although the sites may not provide you with actual records (membership lists and meeting minutes), they do give you an overview of what the club is about and an idea of what your ancestor did as a member. The sites also provide you with the names and addresses of local chapters — you can contact them to see if they have original resources available for public use or if they can send you copies of anything pertaining to your ancestor.

An important thing to note is that having information about a fraternal order doesn't necessarily make a particular site the organization's official site. This is particularly true for international organizations. You may find Web pages for different chapters of a particular club in several different countries, and although each site may have some general club information in common, they are likely to have varying types of information specific to that chapter of the organization.

If you're looking for sites containing information on fraternal organizations, you may want to try some of the comprehensive genealogy sites. If you can't find sufficient information there, try one of the general Internet search engines. You can find a list of both types of sites in The *Genealogy Online For Dummies* Internet Directory in this book. To find information on fraternal orders through a general Internet search engine, try this:

1. **Open your Web browser and go to the AltaVista search engine page (**www.altavista.com**) or substitute the address of your favorite search engine.**

   Note: For more information on using browsers and search engines, check out Appendix A.

2. **Type the name of a fraternal organization in the Search box and click the Search button.**

   We're interested in finding information about the Knights of Columbus, so we type that phrase in the Search box.

3. **Click a link that interests you from the search results page.**

   After you click the Search button, you see a page with the results of your search. Each result has the site's title and a brief abstract taken directly from the page. You can use these to determine whether the site contains information that you're interested in before visiting it.

A Photo Is Worth a Thousand Words

In Chapter 1, we discuss the value of photographs in your genealogical research (if you don't want to look back to Chapter 1 — just believe that we think that photos are very valuable). But a lot of us don't have photographs of our family beyond two or three generations, though it sure would be great to find at least an electronic copy of a picture of your great-great-grandfathers. Actually, a picture of your great-great-grandfather may exist. Another researcher may have posted it on a personal site or the photograph may be part of a collection belonging to a certain organization. You may also be interested in pictures of places where your ancestors lived. Being able to describe how a certain town, estate, or farm looked at the time your ancestor lived there adds color to your family history.

You can find various types of photographic sites on the Internet that can assist you with your research. Some of these sites explain the photographic process and the many types of photographs that have been used throughout history, some sites contain collections of photographs from a certain geographic area or time period in history, and some sites contain photographs of the ancestors of a particular family. Here are some examples:

✔ **General Information:** City Gallery (www.city-gallery.com) has a brief explanation of the types of photography used during the nineteenth century, a photography query page, and a gallery of photographs from one studio of the period (see Figure 7-2).

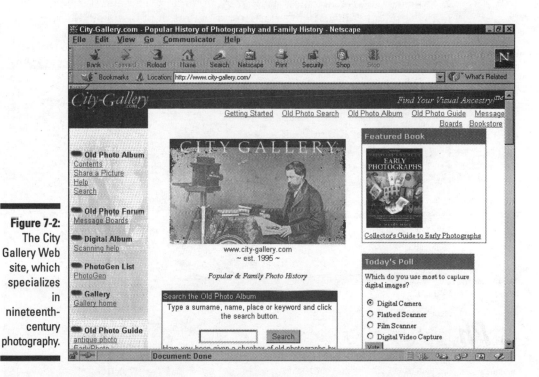

Figure 7-2:
The City Gallery Web site, which specializes in nineteenth-century photography.

✔ **Photograph Collections:** Images of the American West (`www.treasurenet.com/images/americanwest/`), Images of the Civil War (`www.treasurenet.com/images/civilwar/`), and American Memory: Photographs, Prints, and Drawings (`lcweb2.loc.gov/cgi-bin/query/S?ammem/collections:@field(FLD003+@band(origf+Photograph)):heading=Original+Format%3a+Photos+&+Prints`) all contain several digitized photographs.

✔ **Photograph Identification:** Lost Leaves (`www.lostleavesphotos.com/`) has a collection of photographs with more of a focus on genealogy. Designed and maintained by the Arizona Genealogy Computer Interest Group, this site posts old photos that have been donated to the group with the hope that someone may recognize the people and claim the photos. The site also posts information about the photos, including any names written on them, the photographer's name, approximate time frame in which the picture was taken, and anything pertaining to where the photos were taken or found (see Figure 7-3).

✔ **Personal Photographs:** The Harrison Genealogy Repository site (`moon.ouhsc.edu/rbonner/photos/harrphot.htm`) is an example of a personal Web site with a photo gallery. The gallery includes the likenesses of several famous Harrisons, including Benjamin Harrison V, President William Henry Harrison, and President Benjamin Harrison.

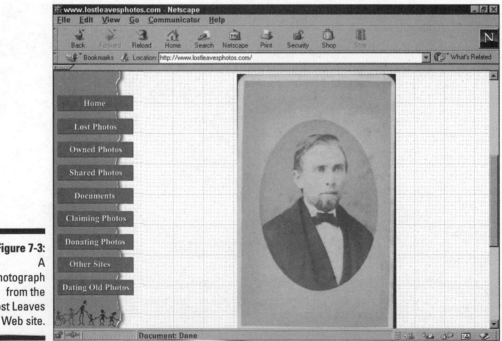

Figure 7-3:
A photograph from the Lost Leaves Web site.

To find photographic sites, you may want to visit one of the comprehensive genealogy sites or general Internet search engines mentioned in The *Genealogy Online For Dummies* Internet Directory in this book.

Adoption Records

Adoption records are of interest to a lot of genealogists, including those who were adopted themselves, those who gave up children for adoption, and those who have ancestors who were adopted.

If you fall into the first two groups (you were adopted or gave up a child for adoption), some online resources may help you. Most of the adoption-related sites are intended to help individuals find members of their birth family. The online resources include registries, reference materials, advice and discussion groups, and information on legislation pertaining to adoption. Registries enable you to post information about yourself and your adoption with the hope that a member of your birth family may see the posting and contact you. (Likewise, if you're the birth parent of an adoptee, you can post a message with the hope that the adoptee sees it and responds.)

Unfortunately, you won't find online sites that contain actual adoption records — for legal reasons, generally. Instead, you need to rely on registries and other resources that point you toward more substantial information about adoption. If you have a successful reunion with your birth parent(s) by registering with an online site, then hopefully you can obtain information about their parents, grandparents, and so on — so that you know where to begin your genealogical pursuit of that family line.

Here are some online sites that have adoption registries, reference materials, advice and discussions, and/or legislative information:

- **Adoptees Internet Mailing List:** www.aiml.org
- **AdoptioNetwork:** www.adoption.org
- **AdoptionSearch:** www.adoptionsearch.com
- **Australia Adoption Registry:** www.geocities.com/HotSprings/4427/AUS.html
- **Reclaiming My Roots Registry Database:** www.geocities.com/Heartland/Hills/2638/

If you're interested in adoption records because you have ancestors who were adopted, you may have a more difficult time finding information. We have yet to discover any sites specifically designed to aid in research for adopted ancestors. In fact, you may have to rely on the regular genealogical resources — particularly query pages and discussion groups — and the kindness and knowledge of other researchers to find information about your adopted ancestors.

If you're searching for general types of adoption resources, using a general Internet directory like Yahoo! may be the best course of action. To find resources using Yahoo!, try this:

1. **Open your Web browser and go to Yahoo! (**www.yahoo.com**).**

   Note: If you need a refresher on operating a Web browser, see Appendix A.

2. **Click the <u>Society And Culture</u> link, and click the <u>Families</u> link.**

   A second way to find items in Yahoo! (this may be a lot faster): You can type a search term in the box near the top of the screen and have Yahoo! search for the topic. For example, you can type **Adoption** in the box and click the Search button, which produces a results page that has links to take you directly to the appropriate page in Yahoo! containing adoption links.

3. **Under the Families category, click the <u>Adoption@</u> link.**

   This takes you directly to the adoption page — even though it's a couple of levels down in the directory's hierarchy.

4. **Click a link to another subdirectory in Yahoo! or a link to an Internet site containing information that interests you.**

   Descriptions follow most of the links in Yahoo! to give you an idea of what kind of information is on the sites. Figure 7-4 shows an example of a Yahoo! page.

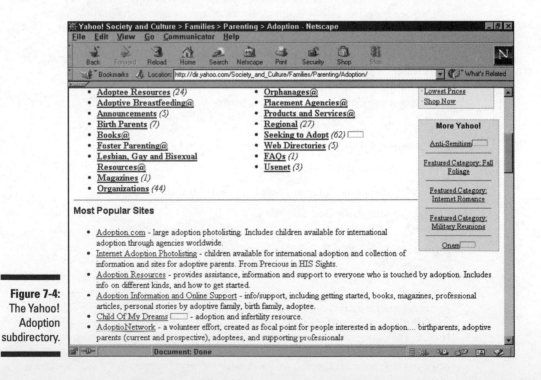

Figure 7-4:
The Yahoo!
Adoption
subdirectory.

Part III
Keeping Your Ancestors in Line: Organizing and Presenting Your Findings

The 5th Wave   By Rich Tennant

"Well, she now claims she's a descendant of the royal Egyptian line of cats, but I'm not buying that just yet."

In this part . . .

Find out how to organize what you find in your research and preserve it for the future. The chapters in this part cover some traditional methods of organization in the genealogical field, how to safely preserve documents and photos, and how to use your computer and genealogical software to store information. We also explore various computer components and peripherals that you may find handy.

Chapter 8

Fine-Tuning Your Organizational and Preservation Skills

In This Chapter

▶ Constructing good record-keeping

▶ Using a numbering system

▶ Discovering some preservation methods

After you collect all this great genealogical data, your findings don't do you much good if you can't find any of them when you need them. You don't want to run all over your house trying to pull together all the scraps of paper — notes from your research at the library in your desk, letters from relatives in your mail-to-be-sorted basket, photocopies of some Pedigree charts mixed in with your magazines. You may forget where you placed a particular document and miss something important because your documents aren't organized and kept in a centralized location.

This chapter examines ways of organizing and preserving genealogical information and documents using traditional storage methods and preservation techniques.

Getting a Firm Foundation in Traditional Methods of Genealogical Organization

No finer tradition exists in genealogy than that of collecting tons of paper and photographs. Until now, you've probably used whatever means possible to take notes while talking with relatives about your ancestors or looking up information in the local library — from notebook paper, to receipts you have in your pocket or purse, to stick-on notes. You may have used your camera to take pictures of headstones in the cemetery where some of your ancestors are buried or the old family homestead that's now abandoned and barely standing. And you've probably collected some original source documents — like the certified copy of your mother's birth certificate that grandma gave you, the family Bible from Aunt Lola, and the old photograph of your great-great-grandfather as a child that you found while digging through the attic. Now what are you supposed to do with all these things? Organize, organize, organize!

Even if you decide to use genealogical software to track your research progress, you always have paper records and photographs you want to keep. The following sections offer some tips to help you become well organized (genealogically, anyway).

Establishing good organizational skills

You probably already discovered that taking notes on little scraps of paper works adequately at first, but the more notes you take, the harder time you have sorting through them and making sense of the information on each. To avoid this situation, establish some good note-taking and organizational skills early by being consistent in how you take notes. Write the date, time, and place that you research and the names of the family members that you interview at the top of your notes. This information can help you later on when you return to your notes to look for a particular fact or when you try to make sense out of conflicting information.

You want to be as detailed as possible when taking notes on particular events, persons, books, and so forth — include the who, what, where, when, why, and how. And most important, always cite the source of your information, keeping the following guidelines in mind:

- ✔ **Person:** Include that person's full name, relationship to you (if any), the information, contact data (address, phone number, e-mail address), and the date and time that you and this person communicated.

- ✔ **Record:** Include the name or type of record, record number, book number (if applicable), the name and location of the record-keeping agency, and any other pertinent information.

- ✔ **Book or magazine:** Include all bibliographic information.

- ✔ **Microfilm or microfiche:** Include all bibliographic information and note the document media (microfilm roll, microfiche), document number, and repository name.

- ✔ **Web site or other Internet resource:** Include the name of the copyright holder for the site (or name of the site's creator and maintainer if no copyright notice appears on it), name of the site, address or uniform resource locator (URL) of the site, the date the information was posted or copyrighted, and any notes with traditional contact information for the site's copyright holder or creator.

It's a good idea to print a copy of the Web page or other Internet resource that contains information about your research interest to keep in your paper files. Some Web sites have a tendency to disappear over time, so it's best to get documentation of the site while it exists.

If you need some help citing sources, check out *Evidence: Citation and Analysis for the Family Historian,* written by Elizabeth Shown Mills and published by Genealogical Publishing Company.

Understanding genealogical charts and forms

Many charts and forms can help you organize your research and make your findings easier to understand for those you share them with. Some examples include Pedigree charts that show the relationships between family members, descendant charts that list every person who descends from a particular ancestor, and census forms that contain the data for particular years. Some of these charts and forms are available from companies such as Everton Publishers (www.everton.com). The sooner you become familiar with the most common types of charts and how to read them, the sooner you can interpret a lot of the information you receive from other genealogists. Chapter 1 examines some of these charts and forms in greater detail, and we discuss some forms you can generate using your computer in Chapter 9.

Assigning unique numbers to family members

If you have ancestors who share the same name, or if you've collected a lot of information on several generations of ancestors, you may have trouble distinguishing one person from another. To avoid confusion and the problems that can arise from it, you may want to use a commonly accepted numbering system to keep everyone straight.

The ahnentafel (Sosa-Stradonitz) system

One well-known numbering system is called *ahnentafel,* which means "ancestor" *(ahnen)* and "table" *(tafel)* in German. You may also hear the ahnentafel system referred to as the *Sosa-Stradonitz* system of numbering because it was first used by a Spanish genealogist named Jerome de Sosa in 1676, and was popularized in 1896 by Stephan Kekule von Stradonitz.

The ahnentafel system is a method of numbering that shows a mathematical relationship between parents and children. Ahnentafel numbering follows this progression:

1. **The child is assigned a particular number: y**

   Of course, we recognize that *y* isn't really a number — it's a letter. However, in our mathematical (or algebraic, to be more specific) example, *y* represents a unique number for that particular person.

2. **The father of that child is assigned the number that is double the child's number: 2y**

3. **The mother of that child is assigned a number that is double the child's number plus one: 2y + 1**

4. **The father's father is assigned the number that is double the father's number: 2(2y)**

   The father's mother is assigned the number that is double the father's number plus one: 2(2y) + 1

5. **The mother's father is assigned a number that is double the mother's number: 2(2y + 1)**

   The mother's mother is assigned a number that is double the mother's number plus one: 2(2y + 1) + 1

6. **Continue this pattern through the line of ancestors.**

The mathematical relationship works the same way going forward through the generations — a child's number is one-half the father's number and one-half (minus any remainder) the mother's number.

In a list form, the ahnentafel for April's grandfather looks like the following list (see Figure 8-1 for the chart):

1 John Duff Sanders, b. 10 Mar 1914 in Benjamin, Knox Co., TX; d. 15 Mar 1996 in Seymour, Baylor Co., TX; ma. 24 Dec 1939 in Sherman, Grayson Co., TX.

2 John Sanders, b. 19 Oct 1872 in Cotton Plant, Tippah Co., MS; d. 2 Mar 1962 in Morton, Cochran Co., TX; ma. 28 Sep 1902 in Boxelder, Red River Co., TX.

3 Nannie Elizabeth Clifton, b. 1 Apr 1878 in Okolona, MS; d. 27 Apr 1936 in Morton, Cochran Co., TX.

4 Harris Sanders, b. 27 Mar 1824 in Montgomery Co., NC; d. 21 Feb 1917 in Tippah Co., MS; ma. 26 June 1853.

5 Emeline Crump, b. 20 Oct 1836; d. 21 Feb 1920 in Tippah Co., MS.

6 William Clifton, b. 5 Mar 1845 in SC; d. 9 Feb 1923 in Boxelder, Red River Co., TX; ma. 5 Nov 1872 in Birmingham, AL.

7 Martha Jane Looney, b. 8 Mar 1844; d. Boxelder, Red River Co., TX.

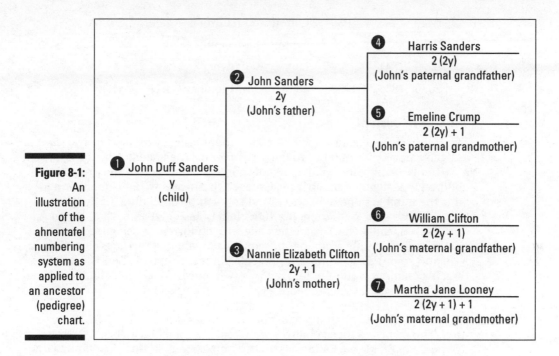

Figure 8-1:
An
illustration
of the
ahnentafel
numbering
system as
applied to
an ancestor
(pedigree)
chart.

John Duff Sanders is number one because he's the base individual for the ahnentafel. His father (John Sanders) is number two (because 2 x 1 = 2), and his mother (Nannie Elizabeth Clifton) is number three (2 x 1 + 1 = 3). His father's father (Harris Sanders) is four (2 x 2 = 4) and his father's mother (Emeline Crump) is five (2 x 2 + 1 = 5). John Sanders' number (2) is one-half his father's number (4 ÷ 2 = 2), or one-half minus any remainder of his mother's number (5 ÷ 2 = 2.5; 2.5 minus remainder of .5 = 2) — well . . . you get the idea.

As you can imagine, after a while you begin to tire from all these calculations — especially if you do them for ten or more generations of people. So, if your genealogy software supports it, we highly recommend that you run an ahnentafel report from it — saving you a lot of time and trouble. (We discuss software packages and some of their capabilities in The *Genealogy Online For Dummies* Internet Directory in this book.)

The tiny tafel system

Some people confuse ahnentafel with *tiny tafel,* which is a compact way to show the relationships within a family database. Tiny tafel provides only the Soundex code for a surname, and the dates and locations where that surname may be found according to the database. (For more on Soundex codes and how they're determined, check out Chapter 1.) Computer programs sometimes use tiny tafels to match the same individual in two different genealogy databases. The following example shows a tiny tafel:

C413	1845	1936	Clifton\South Carolina/Cochran Co. TX
C651	1836	1920	Crump/Mississippi
L500	1844		Looney/Red River Co. TX
S536	1824	1996	Sanders\Montgomery Co. NC/Baylor Co. TX

The Henry system

The *Henry* system is another well-known numbering system. This system assigns a particular number to the *progenitor,* or the ancestor farthest back in a particular family line (that you know about). Then each of the progenitor's children is assigned a number in sequence that starts with his number and adds the numbers one, two, three, and so forth through nine. (If the progenitor had more than 9 children, the 10th child is assigned an X, the 11th an A, the 12th a B, and so on.) Then the children's children are assigned the parent's number plus a number in sequence (again one through nine, then X, A, B, and so on). For example, if progenitor number one (1) had 12 children, then his children would be 11, 12, 13, . . . 1X, and 1A. The 11th child's children would be assigned the numbers 1A1, 1A2, 1A3, and so forth.

For example, suppose that one of your ancestors, John Jones, had 12 children. The names of these children were Joseph, Ann, Mary, Jacob, Arthur, Charles, James, Maria, Esther, Harriett, Thomas, and Sophia. Joseph had one child named Gertrude and Thomas had three children named Lawrence, Joshua, and David. Under the standard Henry system, the children's children are numbered like this:

1   John Jones

    11   Joseph Jones

        111   Gertrude Jones

    12   Ann Jones

    13   Mary Jones

    14   Jacob Jones

    15   Arthur Jones

    16   Charles Jones

    17   James Jones

    18   Maria Jones

    19   Esther Jones

1X	Harriett Jones	
1A	Thomas Jones	
	1A1	Lawrence Jones
	1A2	Joshua Jones
	1A3	David Jones
1B	Sophia Jones	

By no means are these systems the only genealogical numbering systems in existence. Ahnentafel and Henry are just two of the easier systems to learn. Several others have been designed to display genealogies in book form. If you're curious about some of these systems, take a look at `www.saintclair.org/numbers/` where you can find descriptions of each major numbering system.

If you decide to use a numbering system, you can place the corresponding unique number for each individual on the file that you set up for that person in your paper record-keeping system, as well as in your genealogical software.

Making copies of source documents

You don't want to carry original records with you when you're out and about researching. The chances of misplacing or forgetting a document are too great. You have a few options:

- ✔ You can enter the information into a database and take a notebook computer with you.
- ✔ You can copy data from your desktop computer to a palmtop.
- ✔ You can print out your data.
- ✔ You can make photocopies of data that you must have with you for your research.
- ✔ You can scan the documents and store them on your laptop or notebook computer. (We talk more about using computers for your notes in Chapter 9.)

Then use your notes and copies out in the field. Place the original documents in the safest place you can think of that is available to you — a lockbox, fire-proof file cabinet or safe, or a safe-deposit box.

Deciding on a storage method

How are you going to store all that information? A filing system is in order! You can set up a good filing system in many ways, and no one system is right or wrong. Just use one that's comfortable for you.

If you're at a loss as to how to start a system, here's one we like: We prefer to have both electronic and physical components to our filing system. To establish an electronic system, enter your ancestors in your database. Most genealogical programs enable you to enter numbers for each individual. (We cover how to use a database in Chapter 9.) Use the numbers that you create in the electronic system on file folders for paper documents that you collect on each individual. Although we like to scan all of our paper documents, sometimes we get behind, so we set up temporary folders in which we can store the documents until we can scan them. After we scan documents, we transfer them to permanent folders that we keep in a fireproof container. You may consider saving your scanned images to a notebook computer's hard drive, a Zip disk, or a writable CD-ROM so that you can easily transport the images when you go on research trips. Remember to make backup copies of all your electronic documents as a safety precaution.

Preserving Your Treasured Family Documents

Time is going to take its toll on every document in your possession. The longer you want your records and pictures to last, the better care you need to take of them now. The following sections discuss some tips for preserving your family treasures so that you can pass them down to future generations in the best possible shape.

Storing vital records under the right conditions

Place birth certificates, marriage licenses, and other records between acid-free paper in albums. Keep these albums in a dark, dry, and temperature-consistent place. Ideally, store these documents in a place that is 65 to 70 degrees Fahrenheit year-round, with a relative humidity of less than 50 percent. You may consider placing these albums in a steel file cabinet. Also, try to avoid using ink, staples, paper clips, glue, and tape around your documents (unless you use archival products designed for document repair).

For your precious documents (original birth certificates and family papers), rent a safe-deposit box or find another form of off-site storage. Of course, one of the best methods of preservation is to make electronic copies of your documents using a scanner. Then keep disk back-ups at a fire-safe, off-site location (again, a safe-deposit box is a good choice).

Protecting your photographs

Fight the urge to put all your photos of every ancestor on display, because light can damage them over time. Keep your most-prized pictures in a dark, dry, and temperature-consistent place. If you use a photo album for storage, make sure that it has acid-free paper or chemically-safe plastic pockets, and that you affix the pictures to the pages using a safe adhesive. Other storage options include acid-free storage boxes and steel file cabinets. Store the photographs in a place around 65 to 70 degrees Fahrenheit year-round, with a relative humidity of less than 50 percent. Avoid prolonged exposure of photographs to direct sunlight and fluorescent lights. And, by all means, have negatives made of those rare family photos and store them in clearly-marked, acid-free envelopes (the kind without gumming or glue!).

You can preserve photographs a couple of other ways. First, you can convert photographs of an earlier time to a newer and safer kind of film. A local photograph shop that specializes in preservation can do this for you. Because color photographs fade more quickly than their black-and-white counterparts, you may want to make black-and-white negatives of your color photographs. Also, as with documents, you can always preserve your photographs electronically by scanning them into your computer or by having a photo CD made by your photographic developer.

Here are a few Web sites that provide more detailed tips on preserving your family treasures:

> ✔ **Just Black and White's Tips for Preserving Your Photographs and Documents** by David Mishkin: `www.maine.com/photos/tip.htm`
>
> ✔ **Guidelines For Preserving Your Photographic Heritage** by Ralph McKnight: `www.geocities.com/Heartland/6662/photopre.htm`
>
> ✔ **Document and Photo Preservation FAQ** by Linda Beyea: `genweb.net/~gen-cds/faq.html`

Additionally, a couple of these sites list some sources for chemically safe storage products (albums, paper, boxes, adhesives, and so forth) for your photos and records.

Even though you want to preserve everything to the best of your ability, don't be afraid to pull out your albums to show visiting relatives and friends if you want to do so. On the other hand, don't be embarrassed to ask these guests to use caution when looking through your albums. Depending on the age and rarity of some of your documents, you may even want to ask guests to wear latex gloves when handling the albums so that the oil from their hands doesn't get all over your treasures. Upon realizing how important these treasures are to you, most guests won't mind using caution.

Chapter 9

Using Your Computer to Store and Organize Information

After you organize your paper records and photographs, put your computer to work storing and manipulating your family history. Although some genealogists argue otherwise, we think that a computer may be your best friend when it comes to storing, organizing, and publishing your genealogical information.

With your computer, you can use genealogical software to store information on thousands of individuals, access CD-ROMs containing indexes to valuable genealogical records, scan images to preserve your family heritage, and share information with researchers throughout the world via the Internet. This chapter examines genealogical database software and what it can do for you.

Finding and Running Genealogical Software

Several different kinds of software programs are available that enable you to track your ancestors easily and successfully. You can store facts and stories about them, attach files containing scanned photographs of them with their biographical information, and generate numerous reports at the click of a button. Some programs even enable you to store audio and video recordings. (This capability is especially wonderful if you want to put together a multimedia presentation on your genealogy to share at a reunion or conference.)

Most of the genealogical software programs available from major software companies have many features and system requirements in common. Look closely at the specific system requirements on the box of the software that you choose to ensure that you make the most out of your computer and software.

In general, the following list is what we recommend as the minimum requirements for your computer system to adequately run most genealogical software. However, keep in mind that if you want additional accessories for your computer to assist your genealogical effort (such as scanners, other software, and so forth), or if you want to store electronic images, you may need to have a higher-end system — that is, a faster microprocessor, more random access memory (RAM), and more hard drive space.

If you have a PC, you need at least the following:

- ✔ A Pentium processor
- ✔ Windows 95, 98, or 2000
- ✔ A CD-ROM drive
- ✔ 500 megabytes of free hard drive space
- ✔ 64 megabytes of RAM
- ✔ VGA display with at least 256 colors
- ✔ A Microsoft-compatible mouse

If you have a Macintosh computer, you need at least the following:

- ✔ A PowerPC processor
- ✔ System 7.6 or higher
- ✔ A CD-ROM drive
- ✔ 500 megabytes of free hard drive space
- ✔ 64 megabytes of RAM

Finding a Research Mate (Of the Software Variety)

You probably think that you already have the perfect research mate — that special person you drag to every library, cemetery, and courthouse to do your research, right? Wrong! The research mate we're referring to comes in a little box, with CD-ROMs or floppy disks, and you load it onto your computer and then let it perform all sorts of amazing tasks for you.

Several software programs can store and manipulate your genealogical information. They all have some standard features in common; for instance, most serve as databases for family facts and stories, have reporting functions to generate already-completed charts and forms, and have export capabilities so that you can share your data with others. Each software program has a few unique features that make it stand out from the others, such as the capability to take information out of the software and generate online reports at the click of a button. Here's a list of the features you want to look for when evaluating different software packages:

✔ **How easy is the software to use?** Is it graphics-friendly so that you can see how and where to enter particular facts about an ancestor?

✔ **Does the software generate the reports that you need?** For instance, if you're partial to Family Group Sheets, does this software support them?

✔ **Does the software allow you to export and/or import a GEDCOM file?** *GEDCOM* is a file format that's widely used for genealogical research. For more info about GEDCOM, see the "GEDCOM: The genealogist's standard" sidebar later in this chapter.

✔ **How many names can this software hold?** Make sure that the software can hold an adequate number of names (and the accompanying data) to accommodate all the ancestors about whom you have information. Keep in mind that your genealogy continues to grow over time.

✔ **Can your current computer system support this software?** If the requirements of the software cause your computer to crash every time you use it, you won't get very far in your genealogical research.

✔ **Does this software provide fields for citing your sources and keeping notes?** Including information about the sources you use to gather your data — with the actual facts, if possible — is a sound genealogical practice. For more info about the importance of citing sources and how to do so, take a look at Chapter 11.

Entering Information into Family Tree Maker

To help you get a better idea of how software can help you organize your records and research, and to help you figure out what features to look for in particular software packages, this section examines the basics of using Family Tree Maker from Genealogy.com (formerly part of Broderbund Software), one of the more popular genealogy software programs.

You can load a basic version of the software onto your computer from the CD-ROM accompanying this book. (For installation instructions, see Appendix C.)

When you first open Family Tree Maker, you see a blank Family Page with the cursor already set in the *Husband* field. This page is the starting point for inserting information about yourself and your family. If the first person for whom you are entering information is female, tab down to the *Wife* field to begin. Figure 9-1 shows a Family Page within Family Tree Maker.

We walk you through some of the basic functions of Family Tree Maker to show you generally how a genealogical database works. If you're looking for more detailed information about using this particular software, we've written a book designed specifically for you and we highly recommend it. It's called *Family Tree Maker For Dummies* and is available from fine bookstores everywhere.

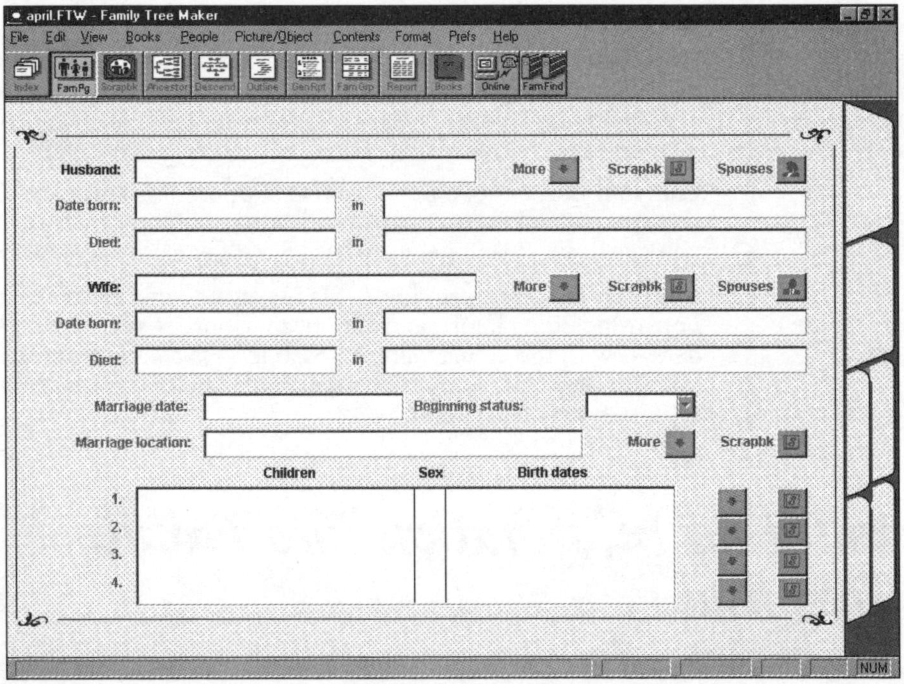

Figure 9-1:
A blank
Family Page
in Family
Tree Maker.

Completing the Family Page

Usually, it's easiest to enter information about yourself, your spouse, and children, and then work backward through your parents, grandparents, great-grandparents, and so forth. After you complete your direct lines back as far as you can, come back and enter Family Page information about siblings, nieces and nephews, cousins, and other relatives. Always enter as much information as you can for each of the fields on the Family Pages. This may save you from coming back to complete the page later. Follow these steps to fill in the Family Page:

1. **Enter your name.**

   Using the appropriate field *(Husband* or *Wife)* based on your gender or family role, enter your name in this order: first name, middle name, and last name (use your maiden name if you're female). Even if you're not married, use one of these two fields for your own information and just leave the spouse field blank.

   After you enter your name, Family Tree Maker automatically creates a Family Page for your parents. When you need to enter more detailed information about your parents, you can click the appropriate tab on the right side of the screen to access their Family Page.

2. **Enter your date of birth in the Date Born field, and enter your place of birth in the In field.**

   Press the Tab key to move among the fields on the page. Notice that some fields (Date Born, Died, and Location) are disabled when you first begin. As soon as you type your name, these fields become active.

   In the Date Born field, enter your birth date, including month, day, and full four-digit year. The software has a default format for dates, so you can spell out the date (January 15, 1965) or abbreviate it with numerals (01/15/1965). The system automatically converts the date to the spelled out format (January 15, 1965) unless you change the default format.

   Note: Uh-oh. Some people will say we just gave you wrong instructions about the way to enter dates! Diehard genealogists and former military personnel tell you that the order should be day, month, and then year instead (for example, 15 January 1965) — another perfectly acceptable method for dating, and one that is quite often international. Even though we're likely to get a lashing for saying this, over the past couple of years, we've seen both methods (month, day, year and day, month, year) used just about equally, so we recommend that you use whichever method feels most comfortable to you.

GEDCOM: The genealogist's standard

As you probably already discovered, genealogy is full of acronyms. One such acronym that you hear and see over and over again is *GEDCOM (GEnealogical Data COMmunication)*. Over the past ten years or so, GEDCOM has become the standard for individuals and software manufacturers for exporting and importing information to or from genealogical databases. Simply put, GEDCOM is a file format intended to make data transferable between different software programs so that people can share their family information easily.

The Church of Jesus Christ of Latter-day Saints first developed and introduced GEDCOM in 1987. The first two versions of GEDCOM were released for public discussion only and not meant to serve as the standard. With the introduction of Version 5.x and later, however, GEDCOM was accepted as the standard.

Having a standard for formatting files is beneficial to you as a researcher because it enables you to share the information that you collect with others who are interested in some or all of your ancestors. It also enables you to import GEDCOM files from other researchers who have information about family lines and ancestors in whom you're interested. And you don't even have to use the same software as the other researchers! You can use Reunion for Macintosh and someone with whom you want to share information can use Family Tree Maker;

having GEDCOM as the standard in both software programs enables each of you to create and exchange GEDCOM files.

To convert the data in your genealogical database to a GEDCOM file, follow the instructions provided in your software's manual or Help menu. You can create the GEDCOM file relatively easily; most software programs guide you through the process with a series of dialog boxes.

In addition to creating GEDCOM files to exchange one-on-one with other researchers, you can generate GEDCOM files to submit to larger cooperatives that make the data from many GEDCOM files available to thousands of researchers worldwide via the World Wide Web and e-mail. Here are a couple of cooperatives that you may want to check out:

✔ **GenServ:** www.genserv.com

✔ **The WorldConnect Project at RootsWeb:** worldconnect.rootsweb.com

You can also convert your GEDCOM file to HTML so that you can place the data directly on the World Wide Web for others to access. Software utilities are available (such as GED2HTML) that make it a snap for you to convert your GEDCOM file to HTML. (For more information on generating Web pages using GED2HTML, see Chapter 12.)

If you inadvertently use only two numerals for the year, the software prompts you to use a four-digit year. For example, if you enter 01/15/65 into a Died field, a dialog box appears, asking you to choose a complete year for the date — 1965, 1865, 1765, and so forth. Additionally, if you aren't sure about the exact date of an event, Family Tree Maker enables you to use abbreviations for *circa* (or about). However, the software automatically defaults to Abt in the field when you enter one of the codes. For example, if you enter **cir. 01/15/1965**, the software converts it to Abt January 15, 1965. (Again, if you prefer Cir to Abt, you can change the default settings.)

Tab to the next field and enter your place of birth. Always include as much information as possible in every field, including the town, county or parish, state, and country of your birth.

3. **Enter information about your spouse. If you don't have any spouse information to enter, go to Step 5.**

   Enter your spouse's name in the appropriate Husband or Wife field. After the date and place of birth fields are active, tab down and enter your spouse's information in the Date Born and In fields just like you did for yourself.

   After you enter your spouse's name, Family Tree Maker automatically creates a Family Page for the spouse's parents. When you need to enter more detailed information about your in-laws, you can click the appropriate tab on the right-hand side of the screen to get to their Family Page.

4. **Enter your marriage information in the Marriage Date, Beginning Status, and Marriage Location fields.**

   Like the birth and death fields, the Marriage Date and Marriage Location fields are disabled until you enter names in both the Husband and Wife fields. After the fields become active and you finish entering the basic information about you and your spouse, tab down to the Marriage Date field and enter the date of your wedding. In the Marriage Location field, enter the town, county/parish, state, and country where you were married. If, for some reason, the Beginning Status field reflects the wrong marital status after you complete the date and place fields for marriage, use the drop-down menu to change the status. For example, if the status field still shows that you're single after you enter your marriage date and place, you can use the drop-down menu to change the status field to Married.

   The Beginning Status field reflects the relationship status between the persons whose information is contained in the Husband and Wife fields. The Beginning Status field starts out blank until both fields have information, and then it assumes Married. If the Beginning Status field reflects the wrong status for the relationship of the two people, use the drop-down menu to change the status. Your choices are Single, Married, Friends, Partners, Private, Unknown, and Other. Also, the Beginning Status field controls titles for some of the other fields on the Family Page. If you select Friends or Partners for the relationship status of the two people, Family Tree Maker automatically changes Husband and Wife to Friend or Partner and Marriage Date and Marriage Location to Meeting Date and Meeting Location.

5. **Enter information about your children (if applicable) in the table at the bottom of the page. If you don't have any information to enter, skip this step.**

When you record information about your children, the software can be a little deceiving. At first glance, you may think that you can enter information about only one to four children, but this is not the case. To get to a fifth or subsequent child field, press Enter after recording the previous child's date of birth; the software brings up a fifth or subsequent line for you to use. (You can also use the scroll bar to get to additional lines — the scroll bar appears when you enter the fourth child's information.)

For each child, enter the child's full name, sex, and date of birth in the appropriate columns. As you begin entering the child's name, Family Tree Maker assumes that the child has the same last name as the father on this Family Page. If this is not the case, simply delete the last name that Family Tree Maker provides and type in the correct surname for the child.

After you enter a child's information, Family Tree Maker automatically creates a Family Page for that child. When you're ready to enter more detailed information about your children (such as their places of birth, marriage information, and so forth), click the appropriate child's tab on the right side of the screen to get to his or her Family Page. Or you can use the View drop-down menu to find the Index of Individuals, from which you can choose the child by name.

As you enter information about people, cite your data sources. Most genealogical software programs, including Family Tree Maker, allow you to enter source information. For specific instructions on how to enter info in your particular software, see the Help file or user's manual that comes with the software. In Family Tree Maker, you need to complete two processes in order to adequately cite sources. First, you need to create a master source by completing the window that you can access by selecting Edit⇨Edit Master Sources. After you've created a master source, you select View⇨Source, and complete the fields in the Source Citation box that pops up. For example, if you were citing a source for information about your birth, you would first create a master source for your birth certificate providing as much information as possible in the fields of the Master Source window and clicking OK. Then you would bring up the Source Citation box and complete its fields, including the field that references the Master Source. After you cite a source for a particular fact, notice that a little "s" appears next to the field on the Family Page.

Another feature of Family Tree Maker that you should know about — called Fastfields — tries to help you enter name and location information. (You may have already encountered this feature in your first Family Page.) Sometimes, this feature saves you time, but if the word that you're typing differs slightly from what you entered before, this feature can frustrate you. As soon as the software recognizes that you're repeating characters in the same order as in a previous field, a dialog box appears with the name or location so that you can just press Enter to accept that name or location. For example, say you have several ancestors who were born in Larue County, Kentucky. After you type **Larue County, Kentucky** or **Larue Co., Kentucky** for one ancestor, then anytime you begin typing it for additional ancestors, the software recognizes it and gives you the option to use the same phrase.

Another feature of Family Tree Maker is that all the fields have instructional boxes that pop up after the mouse's pointer has been on the field for a couple of seconds (see Figure 9-2). The instructional boxes are very helpful if you aren't sure exactly what information to include in the field.

Working with the supplemental pages

On the Family Page, you find icons for some interesting features. You see three icons next to the Husband and Wife fields and two icons next to the Marriage Location field. These icons lead you to supplemental pages for information about these particular people or events.

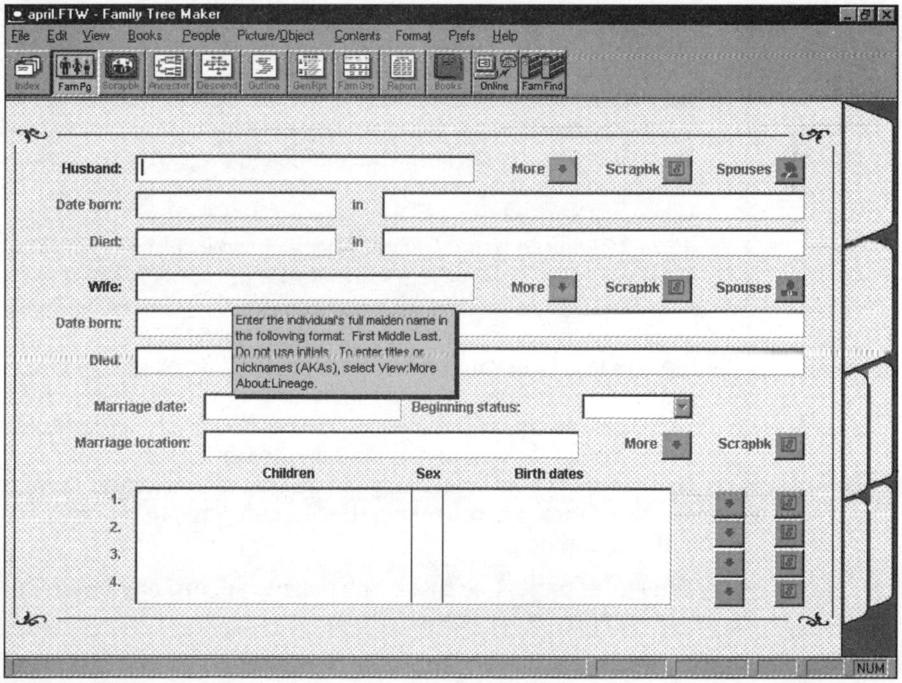

Figure 9-2:
An example
of an
instructional
box.

The More icon takes you to a section where you can select pages with forms for recording particular types of information about yourself or your relatives, including Facts, Address, Medical, Lineage, and Notes. The following list explains how to use each page:

- ✔ **The Facts page:** Use this page to record facts about an ancestor. The page provides three fields for each fact — a Fact field (where you select a title for the event from a pull-down menu or type in your own fact title), a Date field (optional), and a Comment/Location field. There's also a Pref'd box where you can indicate which fact is preferred if you have multiple facts that are similar in nature. Use this Facts page to record information such as the places and dates of an ancestor's christening, burial, or even where your ancestor lived during particular census years. Some people also use this page to record events such as gradua-tion, Bar Mitzvah, or employment dates.

- ✔ **The Address page:** Use this page to enter the current or last-known address and phone number of the relative. You can use this information in another feature of the software to generate letters or address labels for those with whom you correspond by mail.

- ✔ **The Medical page:** Use this page to enter the individual's height, weight, cause of death, and other medical notes.

- ✔ **The Lineage page:** Use this page to record a number of items, such as any titles (Dr., Rev., Jr., Sr., Col., etc.) the person has, "also known as" information (such as nicknames or aliases), and your filing system refer-ence number. There's a box you can check if you want to exclude infor-mation about this person from any calendars you generate using Family Tree Maker. If the person whose Lineage page you're completing is female, there's a field for you to select the format in which her married name will appear in trees and reports — whether to provide her name as "First Maiden Married," "First Middle Married," or "First Middle Maiden." Also, you can record the nature of this person's relationship with the individuals who are identified as the person's father and mother, as well as select whether to include the relationship in any trees or kinship reports you generate using the software. For example, you can record whether the individual was the natural-born child, stepchild, foster child, and so on, of the ancestor identified as the individual's father. And if the individual was considered an illegitimate child of the ancestor or disowned for some reason, you can select to exclude them from any trees or reports by checking the Exclude This Relationship from Trees and Kinship box.

- ✔ **The Notes page:** Use this blank page to record any personal notes and stories about a particular ancestor.

Clicking the Scrapbook icon takes you to a section where you can link your software to photographs, sound files, and movies (called *objects*) about this particular ancestor that you've stored on your computer. To insert an object, choose Insert from the Picture/Object menu and follow the instructional boxes. (You can also get to the scrapbook section at any time by clicking the Scrapbook button in the bar at the top of the page.)

If your ancestor was married more than once, click the Spouses icon to include information about the additional spouses. You can create "new" spouses and record other spousal information, as well as designate which spouse should be the "preferred" one for your database. The preferred spouse will automatically appear on the Family page and other reports with your ancestor.

Entering information for your other ancestors

After you enter all the information you have for your first person (most likely yourself), use the tabs that run down the right side of the screen to go to the Family Page for your parents and enter all the information you have about them. After you're done with them, use the tabs to get to the Family Pages for your grandparents and so on as you progress backward through your ancestors. Later, come back and add your siblings, aunts, uncles, and other relatives.

Sharing Your Genealogical Success with Others

After you organize all your paper documents and enter as much information as possible into your genealogical software, you can share what you've gathered and organized with others, or you can generate notes to take with you on research trips. (If you haven't organized your information yet, Chapter 8 can help you.)

Your genealogical software can help you by generating printed reports reflecting the information that you collected and entered. Most genealogical software packages have several standard reports or charts in common, including a Pedigree chart (also called an Ancestor chart), Descendant chart, Outline of Descendants, Family Group Sheet, and Kinship report.

In this section, we examine the different types of reports and explain how to generate them using Family Tree Maker. For more information about entering information into and using this program, please review the preceding section.

Pedigree charts (Or Ancestor Trees)

Family Tree Maker calls its Pedigree chart an Ancestor Tree. Flowing horizontally across a page, it identifies a primary person by that person's name, date and place of birth, date and place of marriage, and date and place of death. The chart uses lines to show the relationship to the person's father and mother, then each of their parents, then their parents, and so on until the chart runs off the page. See Figure 9-3 for an example of an Ancestor Tree generated using Family Tree Maker.

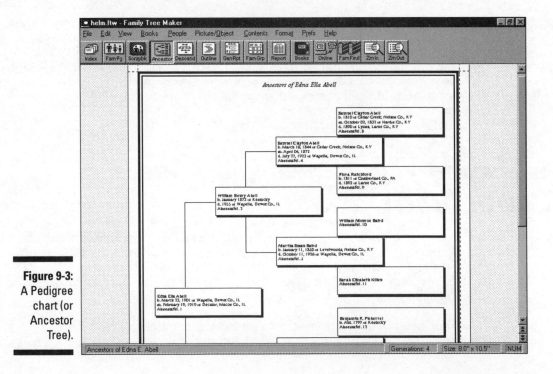

Figure 9-3:
A Pedigree
chart (or
Ancestor
Tree).

Descendant charts

A *Descendant* chart contains information about an ancestor and spouse (or spouses if more than one exists), their children and their spouses, grandchildren and spouses, and so on down the family line. (Family Tree Maker calls this type of chart a Descendant Tree.) A Descendant chart usually flows vertically on a page, rather than running horizontally across the page like a Pedigree chart (Ancestor Tree). See Figure 9-4 for an example of a Descendant Tree generated by Family Tree Maker.

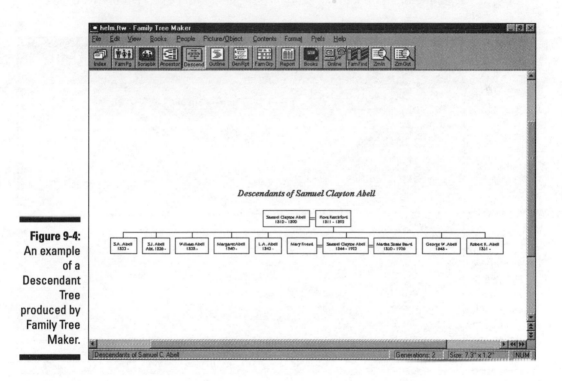

Figure 9-4:
An example
of a
Descendant
Tree
produced by
Family Tree
Maker.

Outline reports

A family *Outline* is a list of the descendants of a particular ancestor. (Family Tree Maker calls it an Outline Descendant Tree.) The first numbered line contains the name (and sometimes the years for birth and death) of the primary ancestor. The next line shows a spouse, followed by the next numbered line, which contains the name of the ancestor and spouse's first child. If that child is married and has children, the child's spouse follows, as do the names and information on each of the child and spouse's children. See Figure 9-5 for an example of an Outline Descendant Tree generated using Family Tree Maker.

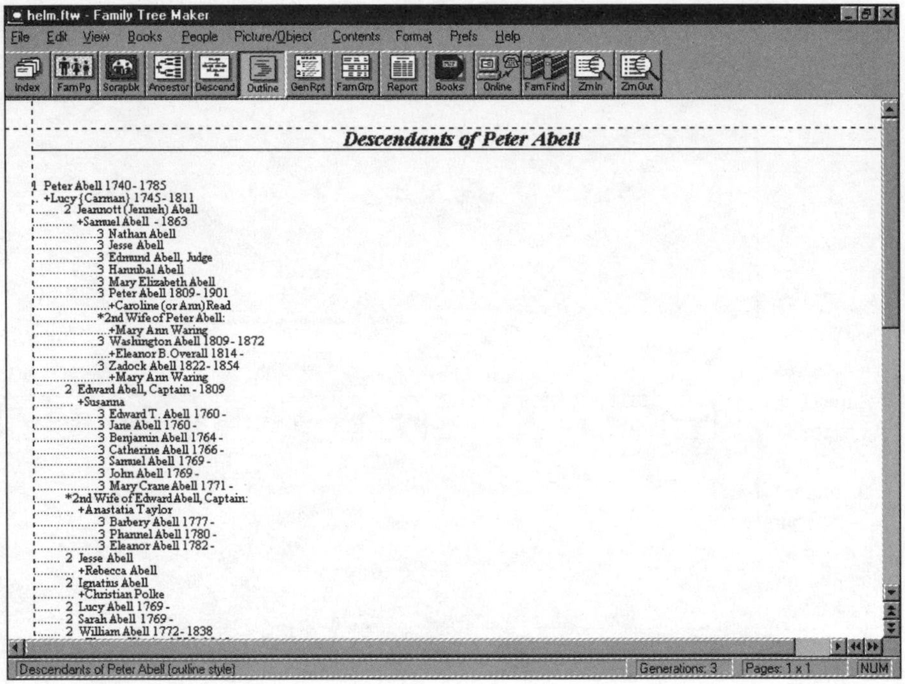

Figure 9-5: An Outline Descendant Tree in Family Tree Maker.

Family Group Sheets

A *Family Group Sheet* is a summary of vital information about a particular family. At the top of the page, it shows the *Husband,* followed by the *Wife,* and then any children of the couple, as well as biographical information (such as dates and places of birth, marriage, and death). However, information on the children's spouses and children isn't included on this Family Group Sheet; you can generate a separate Family Group Sheet for each child's family (if applicable). See Figure 9-6 for an example of a Family Group Sheet generated by Family Tree Maker.

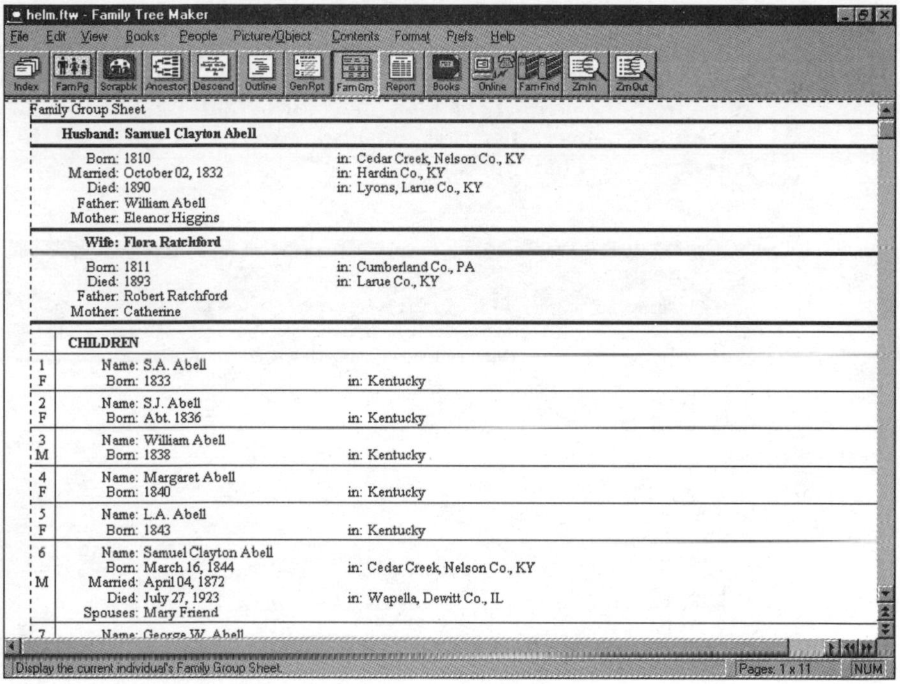

Figure 9-6:
A Family Group Sheet in Family Tree Maker.

Kinship reports

A *Kinship report* is a list of family members and how they relate directly to one particular person. This report includes the name of the family member, the person's relationship to the primary ancestor, and the Civil and Canon Codes reflecting the degree of relationship between the two people. See Figure 9-7 for an example of a Kinship report generated by Family Tree Maker.

Civil and Canon Codes explain the bloodline relationship in legal terms — in other words, they identify how many *degrees of separation* (or steps) are between two people who are related by blood. Civil law counts each step between two relatives as a degree, so two people who are first cousins have a degree of separation equal to four, which is the total of two steps between one cousin and the common grandparent and two steps between the other cousin and the common grandparent. Canon law counts only the number of steps from the nearest common ancestor of both relatives, so the degree of separation between two first cousins is two. Two steps separate the grand-parent from each of the cousins.

Figure 9-7:
An example
of a Kinship
report in
Family Tree
Maker.

```
● helm.ftw - Family Tree Maker                                                   _ 8 X
 File   Edit   View   Books   People   Picture/Object   Contents   Format   Prefs   Help
 [Index][FamPg][Scrapbk][Ancestor][Descend][Outline][GenRpt][FamGrp][Report][Books][Online][FamFind][ZmIn][ZmOut]
        Type name:
```

Kinship of Samuel Clayton Abell

Name	Relationship with Samuel Abell	Civil	Canon
(Carman), Lucy	Grandmother	II	2
(Gardiner), Susannah	4th great-grandmother	VI	6
Abell	Sister	II	1
Abell, Abner	1st cousin twice removed	VI	4
	2nd cousin twice removed	VIII	5
Abell, Albert	2nd cousin once removed	VII	4
Abell, Alberta	3rd cousin	VIII	4
Abell, Alfred	2nd cousin	VI	3
Abell, Aloysius	1st cousin once removed	V	3
Abell, Althea	Great-grandaunt	V	4
Abell, Ann	4th cousin once removed	XI	6
Abell, Ann	3rd cousin twice removed	X	6
Abell, Ann	1st cousin once removed	V	3
Abell, Ann	Wife of the 1st cousin once removed		
Abell, Ann	2nd cousin once removed	VII	4
Abell, Anna Briscoe	3rd cousin twice removed	X	6
Abell, Anna Gibson	1st cousin once removed	V	3
	3rd cousin	VIII	4
Abell, Arthur	1st cousin twice removed	VI	4
Abell, Austin	2nd cousin	VI	3
Abell, Barbery	1st cousin	IV	2
Abell, Becca	Wife of the 1st cousin twice removed		
Abell, Belinda	2nd cousin once removed	VII	4
Abell, Benedict Joseph	2nd cousin	VI	3
Abell, Benito	3rd cousin	VIII	4
Abell, Benito, Jr.	3rd cousin once removed	IX	5

```
 Kinship of Samuel C. Abell. Type last name first to find a specific individual.       All Ind's    Pages: 1 x 11
```

Generating charts and reports using Family Tree Maker

See the "Completing the Family Page" section earlier in this chapter for details on how to fill out a Family Page entry for each of your family members. When you have at least a few Family Pages completed, follow these steps to create any of the five charts/reports that we discuss in the preceding paragraphs:

1. **Open Family Tree Maker.**

2. **Under the View drop-down menu, select the Index of Individuals.**

   This action brings up a box that lists all the individuals entered in your database in alphabetical order.

3. **Scroll through the index and select the person for whom you want to generate a chart/report by double-clicking the name or highlighting the name and clicking OK.**

   This takes you to the Family Page for the person that you selected.

   For example, if Matthew wants to produce a Pedigree chart for his ancestor Samuel Abell, he highlights Samuel Abell in the index and clicks OK.

4. **Place your cursor in the person's name field.**

   Move your cursor into the Husband, Wife, or Children field to select the exact person on whom you want to generate a chart/report.

   Matthew places the cursor in the Husband field, which reflects the name Samuel Abell.

5. **Click the appropriate button in the toolbar at the top of the Family Tree Maker screen, or choose View⇨[Type of tree or report].**

   You can find buttons for Ancestor Trees, Descendant Trees, Outline Descendant Trees, and Family Group Sheets. Or if you use the drop-down menu, the charts/reports appear as Ancestor Tree, Descendant Tree, Outline Descendant Tree, Kinship Report, and Family Group Sheet. (You can generate other reports using Family Tree Maker, but these are the most common types and the five types that we discuss in this chapter. For information about other types of charts and reports, as well as other Family Tree Maker features, we recommend the book *Family Tree Maker For Dummies.*)

   Family Tree Maker generates the requested chart/report for the person that you selected.

   Matthew clicks the button that says Ancestor Tree or uses the View drop-down menu to select Ancestor Tree. Family Tree Maker automatically generates a Pedigree chart for Samuel Abell. (To see what this Pedigree chart looks like, refer to Figure 9-3.)

6. **Look at the chart on the screen, copy it to your word processor to save it, or print it out to share with others.**

   For more information about moving reports into your word processor, see Chapter 11.

Formatting and customizing charts and reports

Keep in mind that you can control exactly what to include in each of these charts or reports — by telling Family Tree Maker how many generations to include, to exclude particular ancestors, to change the types of information to include, or to customize the appearance (borders and fonts). Here are some quick references to help you when manipulating the content of these reports in Family Tree Maker:

- ✔ **To control the number of generations included on the chart or report:** Choose Contents⇨# of Generations to Show.
- ✔ **To change the format:** Choose Format⇨Tree Format (or Report Format if you're working with a report).
- ✔ **To change boxes, lines, and borders:** Choose Format⇨ Box, Line, & Border Styles.
- ✔ **To change the fonts:** Choose Format⇨Text Font, Style, & Size.

Other genealogical software programs enable you to manipulate your charts and reports in a similar manner. When you use other programs, simply take a look at the manual or Help files, or follow the tutorial (if it has one) for precise guidance when creating charts and reports.

Hammers, Screwdrivers, and Other Hardware: Is Your Computer Equipped?

As you grow more accustomed to using the information that you store in your computer, you may want to consider other hardware and peripheral equipment that you may need or want to add to your system in order to enhance your genealogy research and the reports that you generate. You may want to start including electronic images of some of the photographs and original documents that you have in your paper filing system. You may think about adding audio of your grandmother reminiscing, or video of your grandchild greeting people at the family reunion. As you find additional documents, you may want to add images of them to your main database as well. So what kind of computer hardware or other equipment do you need in order to include images and other enhancements with your genealogical information?

You should consider several pieces of equipment as you prepare to enhance your genealogy with audio and video. The first four are basics: sound cards, video-capture boards, scanners, and digital cameras. Others include ZIP, JAZ, and CLIK! drives and disks, and the BUZ multimedia producer — or what we like to call "the Iomega suite of nifty gadgets we think are cool." The writable CD-ROM drive is also becoming popular.

Sound cards

A *sound card* is an internal device that is a standard feature on most computers today. It allows you to hear any audio that comes on software (particularly games) or audio files that you download off the Internet. In most cases, the card also enables you to record your own audio from your stereo, radio, video camera, or microphone. However, you must have software that supports recordings. If your sound card is capable of recording and you have adequate software, you simply plug the sound source into the microphone jack or sound-in jack on the back of your computer, set your software to record, and go for it. After you make the recording, you can import it into your genealogical software if your genealogical software supports audio.

Video-capture boards

Similar to a sound card, a *video-capture board* enables you to grab images from your video camera or VCR. You can use moving images or still pictures, depending on the type of your video-capture board and the accompanying software. Video-capture boards aren't usually a standard feature on computers. They have varying system requirements depending on the manufacturer and the software that's included. Be sure that your computer system can handle a particular video-capture board and software before making your purchase.

Scanners

Scanners are one of the most popular computer peripherals for genealogists. Everyone wants to include some family photos with their genealogy or preserve precious documents electronically. And with the cost of scanners decreasing and the availability of bundled software that allows you to use a scanner as a scanner, fax machine, and copier, adding a scanner to your equipment collection can make your genealogical research more colorful and more efficient without making a big dent in your wallet.

A variety of scanners are available. The most common types are snapshot, sheet-fed, and flatbed. Although they're harder to find, a few hand-held scanners are still around. You can find color scanners and scanners that capture images only in black and white. The system requirements for scanners vary greatly, so read the packaging of the scanner that you're considering very carefully. Additionally, each scanner requires software to make it work, so carefully read the software's system requirements and capabilities as well. Here's a quick rundown of the major types of scanners:

- **Snapshot scanners:** Useful for creating electronic images of photographs that measure 5 x 7 inches or smaller because they're designed to work primarily with that size of photograph. Snapshot scanners are compact and come in external and internal varieties. You feed the photograph into the scanner, and then the scanner captures an image before sending the photo back out. Some snapshot scanners have a removable top that you can use as a hand-held scanner in order to capture images larger than 5 x 7 inches. One caution with snapshot scanners: You may not want to use these with old, fragile photographs. The scanner can damage the photograph as it's fed through the scanner.

- **Sheet-fed scanners:** Typically a little wider than a regular sheet of paper (8.5 inches across). They're still rather compact as far as scanners go, but all are external. You feed the photograph or document into the feeder on the scanner, and the scanner captures an image as the document goes through. Like some snapshot scanners, some sheet-fed scanners have a removable top that you can use as a hand-held scanner in order to capture images larger than 8.5 inches across. Use caution when using these scanners with fragile photographs.

- **Flatbed scanners:** These scanners used to be large and bulky but are now more compact. You lift the top of the scanner and place your document or photograph on the bed, close the lid, and tell the scanner (through software) to capture the image. Flatbed scanners are somewhat safer for photographs than other types of scanners because photos are laid on the scanner's glass rather than fed through the device.

- **Hand-held scanners:** Great for genealogy because of their relatively low cost and flexibility. You can use them not only for scanning photographs and paper documents but also for scanning books. Hand-held scanners are external and compact. They're the perfect size to carry with you when you go on-site for your genealogical research. You scan photos and other objects by holding the scanner and slowly moving it over the object while holding down a button. Although hand-held scanners are convenient, the quality of the scanned image depends greatly on how steady your hand is, how good the lighting is where you're scanning, and the original size of the document.

Digital cameras

Over the past couple of years, digital cameras have increasingly captured the interest of genealogists. Being able to take all your photographs with a camera that downloads the images directly to your computer — where they can be easily imported into your genealogical database — is definitely exciting. Some digital cameras even come with a document setting these days, so you don't need both a scanner and a digital camera.

Depending on the model, you store the digital pictures within the memory of the camera, on compact flash cards, or on a 3½-inch disk. With the models that store the images internally, you must take the extra step to download the images to your computer through a serial cable. For the models that save the images to a floppy disk, you can simply insert the disk into your computer and copy the files to your database.

As with every other computer peripheral, if you're considering purchasing a digital camera, carefully read the package and software requirements to make sure that your computer system can support the equipment.

The Iomega suite of handy gadgets

Iomega makes a variety of tools for storing data and putting together multi-media presentations. If you want to see the company's entire line of products, take a gander at www.iomega.com. We think four Iomega tools are particularly enticing to genealogists: ZIP drives, JAZ drives, CLIK! drives, and the BUZ multimedia producer.

A ZIP drive is a portable peripheral that enables you to store anywhere from 100 to 250 MB of data on each disk. (The storage space depends on the model of drive and disk that you use.) A whole family of ZIP drives is on the market, and you're bound to find one that meets your needs, whether you choose the high-end ZIP 250, the multi-platform USB ZIP, the ZIPPlus (which works with parallel or SCSI ports), or the regular ZIP (which works with parallel ports).

If the ZIP drive isn't small enough to fit your portability needs, then maybe the CLIK! drive is for you. CLIK! is a tiny portable drive that enables you to store up to 40 MB of data on its disks. You can find several varieties of CLIK! drives: You can get a CLIK! drive for your computer (also for your laptop or notebook and your hand-held PC), for your digital camera, or for both your computer and your digital camera.

JAZ drives are good for large-scale storage. Depending on the model, you can store either one or two gigabytes of data on a single JAZ cartridge. Although they're more expensive than ZIP drives and CLIK! drives, JAZ drives are good for genealogists with large collections of digitized files and multimedia. They are also handy for backing up computer hard drives.

For your multimedia needs, check out the BUZ tool. It's a small box that acts as a go-between for your computer, stereo, video camera, and VCR. BUZ enables you to add and manipulate audio, video, and digitized photos to your genealogy.

Traveling with Your Genealogical Tools

Whether you go to a family reunion, travel a couple hundred miles to research in a particular county or province, or give a presentation at a conference, chances are you may eventually want to take your show on the road. If you're just testing the waters to see whether buying a computer for genealogical purposes is worth your time and money, you may want to consider getting a laptop or notebook computer instead of a desktop system. Portable computers give you the flexibility to take your genealogical database with you wherever you go, as well as some presentation possibilities that desktop systems don't allow because of their size.

Portable databases

As you get more involved in genealogy and begin to take research trips, you may find having your database with you to be useful. Of course, you can always print out the contents of your database, but who wants to carry around thousands of pages? One alternative is to carry a notebook computer with you. Notebooks have become popular recently, especially because they've become more affordable and more powerful. Most notebook computers have capabilities similar to their desktop counterparts, but in a more convenient package.

Another group of research assistants are gaining prominence on the market — *palmtops*. Palmtops are hand-sized computers that can contain some of the same programs housed on desktop computers. You can transfer information from a palmtop to your desktop or laptop PC. Some first-generation palmtops run on a scaled-down version of Microsoft Windows (called Windows CE) and have special versions of software designed to run on the smaller machines. Others have more storage capacity and run under full operating systems, such as Windows 98. You can even have a scaled-down version of your genealogical database on your palmtop. For example, Pocket Family

Researcher (www.dwalker.demon.co.uk/pocketfamilyresearcher.htm) allows you to view and edit GEDCOM files on palmtops that run Windows CE or Palm PC operating systems. Unfortunately, due to palmtop memory constraints, you can't house your database of 10,000 individuals. The program has a limit of 1000 individuals — and you probably won't even be able to input this number of people if you have a small amount of memory.

Storage on the run

If you already own a desktop system and aren't in the market to buy a notebook or palmtop, don't worry! You have other means for transporting your data and reports without spending the money on another computer.

Your database may grow too large to fit on a regular 3½-inch floppy disk. However, CD-ROMs, ZIP disks, and CLIK! disks hold a lot more data and can easily accommodate your genealogical database. Buying a CD-ROM writer or ZIP drive is a lot cheaper than buying a laptop computer. Of course, the drawback to using a disk to transport your data is that you need a computer on the other end that can handle the disk and information contained on it. So before you take a CD-ROM with all your family information to that reunion at Aunt Lola's, make sure that Aunt Lola's computer has a CD-ROM drive and any necessary software to open the contents of your disk. Of course, another option is to upload your information to the Internet so that you can access it from any computer that's connected to the Internet.

One other portability issue is having a means for getting information from a computer source away from home to your computer. Most public libraries and Family History Centers have genealogical information on computers that you can access. You can use a 3½-inch floppy disk to download information that you find on computers and CD-ROMs at these research facilities. Popping a floppy disk into the computer at the library to download a few lines of information about an ancestor is much easier than hand-writing everything, and a lot cheaper than paying for each individual printout!

The Genealogy Online For Dummies Internet Directory

The 5th Wave   By Rich Tennant

©RICHTENNANT

"Hold your horses. It takes time to locate the ancestors for someone of your background."

In this directory . . .

*L*ook no further for an overview of the types of sites that you can find online. This directory lists sites and abstracts of what you find at each site. We've also provided some descriptive narratives telling you why these types of sites are useful to you. Among our examples are all sorts of search engines (genealogically focused and otherwise), comprehensive genealogical sites, and resources that are surname-related, government-sponsored, geographic-specific, or commercial in nature. More specifically, this directory has information to help you find the following:

- ✔ Comprehensive genealogical Web sites
- ✔ Search engines
- ✔ Surname-related Web pages
- ✔ Hard-to-find records
- ✔ Booksellers and publishers
- ✔ Professional researchers
- ✔ Software information

About Those Micons

For each site, we provide the name of the site, the URL (Web address), and a brief description of what you can find there. Also, the mini icons (micons, as we like to call 'em) tell you at first glance what kinds of resources the site offers. Here's a list of the micons and what each one means:

Queries: At this site, you can post genealogical questions pertaining to surnames, geographic locations, or research in general, or read and respond to queries left by other researchers.

Online database: This site includes an online database of genealogical information. By online database, we mean a collection of data that may include any of the following: information known about a family or surname, indexes, and other such collections of information.

Online records: Here you find transcribed and/or digitized records with genealogical value. The information at this site is either in the form of transcriptions from actual records (such as vital records, military personnel files, census returns, and so on) or digitized (scanned) copies of actual records.

FAQs: This site includes a section with Frequently Asked Questions and their answers about a particular aspect of genealogical research.

Searchable: This site has a search engine you can use to look for keywords and/or surnames.

Index: This site includes a section listing genealogical resources (including other genealogical sites, types of records, and information from actual records).

GEDCOM: This software supports GEDCOM, the standard for sharing data between genealogical programs.

Post to Web: This software enables you to take information from the database and post it directly to the Web.

On the CD: A version of this software is included on the CD-ROM that accompanies this book.

Book: This software has features that enable you to put together your own genealogical book containing charts, forms, photographs, and reports that you generate using the data you enter into that software.

Online ordering: Here you can place orders for genealogical books or supplies online.

Multimedia: This software supports the use of photographs, sound, or video in your genealogy.

Download: You can download software at the URL indicated.

Charge for Services: The Web site creator charges for some services at this site or described at this site.

Booksellers and Publishers

Sometimes, finding a specific book about a particular surname, geographic location, or event in history can be difficult. After all, not all local bookstores or libraries have the best collections of genealogical books and supplies. In fact, most of the bookstores that we've been to carry somewhere around 10 to 20 titles on genealogy, and that's about it.

When you're unable to find that certain book you're looking for in the local bookstore or library, online bookstores and publishers come in handy. These online resources identify books and other products that they publish and/or sell, and most of them tell you how you can order from them. (Even if you can't order online from them, their Web sites tell you how you can order by mail or phone.) Following is a list of some online bookstores and publishers that specialize in genealogy-related materials. If you want to see a more extensive listing of genealogy bookstores, visit a comprehensive genealogy Web site. (See the next section for more information about comprehensive sites.)

Ancestry.com

www.ancestry.com

Ancestry.com is best known as the publisher of *The Source: A Guidebook of American Genealogy*, and the two magazines *Ancestry* and *Genealogical Computing*. Its Web site contains information about books and electronic products that are available for online purchase. It also has several value-added resources for genealogists, including searchable databases like the online Social Security Death Index and the World Tree, as well as informational columns by well-known genealogists. Although a decent number of Ancestry. com's online services are free, some of its online services are restricted to subscribers. The Web site provides detailed information about what's restricted to subscribers and how to subscribe.

Everton Publishers

www.everton.com

Everton Publishers publishes the popular *Everton's Genealogical Helper* magazine, as well as genealogical books and research aids. Its Web site provides detailed information about *Everton's Genealogical Helper* and has an Online Search section that you can join to use several online databases that are available at the site. Additionally, some free resources are included: forms you can download, information about beginning your research, a list of available genealogical workshops, and a couple of free databases. And, of course, there's secure online shopping on the site so you can order what you need from Everton Publishers — books, CD-ROMs, software, and other products.

Frontier Press Bookstore

www.frontierpress.com/frontier.cgi

Frontier Press Bookstore specializes in providing genealogical and historical books, CD-ROMs, and audio tapes. The Frontier Web site has an online catalog that you can browse by subject, as well as listings of new publications that are available and a bargain basement where you can find special deals. After you determine which books you'd like, you can order by e-mail, mail, phone, or fax.

Genealogical Publishing Company

www.genealogybookshop.com

Genealogical Publishing Company is a large publisher of genealogical books. Its Web site provides a catalog of books that are published by and available from Genealogical Publishing Company, as well as a listing of releases on CD-ROM. You can search the site using keywords, or browse through the many categories of offerings, then order a product in which you're interested (you can order online, by fax, mail, e-mail, or phone).

GlobalGenealogy.com, Inc.

www.globalgenealogy.com

GlobalGenealogy.com is the Internet-based shopping experience for all things genealogical. The site offers books, software, CD-ROMs, maps, microfilm, and archival supplies (items for preservation of documents and photos) for purchase online. The online store has a sister-operation that's a physical store in Milton, Ontario — called the Global Genealogy Shoppe. Global Heritage Press (GlobalHeritagePress.com) is the publishing arm of Global Genealogy Supply and prints genealogical and historical books. Global Genealogy Supply also offers a free online newsletter for genealogical research in Canada, called *The Global Gazette* (GlobalGazette.net).

Heritage Books, Inc.

www.heritagebooks.com

$

Heritage Books, Inc., publishes genealogical and historical books and CD-ROMs, as well as Web-based information. Its Web site has an online library to which you can subscribe, as well as some free resources. It also has general information about the company, online book and CD-ROM catalogs, and a list of links to other resources you may be looking for that Heritage does not carry (like photo restoration, out-of-print books, and software). You can also subscribe to a monthly online newsletter announcing special deals from Heritage Books, research tips, and news of interest to genealogists. When you find a book or CD-ROM you want, you can order online, or follow the detailed instructions about how to order by mail, fax, phone, or e-mail.

Heritage Quest

www.heritagequest.com

Heritage Quest publishes Heritage Quest magazine and a variety of resources on CD-ROM. It also offers many items — books, charts and forms, maps, CD-ROMs, software, and other genealogical products — for sale online. In addition to information about titles for sale, Heritage Quest's Web site includes the Genealogy Bulletin (an online newsletter), Genealogy 101 (an Internet-based tutorial to genealogy), a query section where you can post messages, and a list of upcoming genealogical events in the United States.

The Institute of Heraldic and Genealogical Studies Family History Bookshop

www.ihgs.ac.uk/institute/bookshop.html

The Institute of Heraldic and Genealogical Studies Family History Bookshop is physically located in England. It has books that are geographic-specific in nature (covering England, Scotland, Wales, and Ireland), as well as heraldic titles and books specifically for beginners to genealogy as well as for advanced researchers. Its Web site includes a list of publications and their prices that are available from the Family History Bookshop. The Bookshop also offers research aids including maps, charts, and pamphlets, along with visual-aid kits to use in teaching others about genealogy.

iUniverse.com's Family Tree Press

www.iuniverse.com/publish/family_tree/
    family_tree.asp

iUniverse.com is an economical, on-demand publisher of all sorts of books. Its Family Tree Press imprint specializes in publishing genealogies, family histories, and other historical works related to family-history research. This Web site provides detailed information about how you can publish your own book, what it will look like, and its costs.

Comprehensive Sites

A comprehensive genealogical site is one that identifies a large number of other sites of interest to genealogists, which contain information on surnames, families, locations, or a variety of other subjects. Most comprehensive sites have the names and URLs categorized (or indexed) in some manner — usually the sites are broken down into categories. Some people refer to these comprehensive sites as large genealogical *indexes* or *listings*.

Most comprehensive sites are relatively easy to navigate because they categorize and cross-index their links to other genealogical sites. As long as you know the topic that you're looking for, you can glance through the listing and see if anything is available. For example, if you're looking for American Revolutionary War records for the state of Massachusetts, you can visit a comprehensive site and look in its sections pertaining to the American Revolution, military records, and the state of Massachusetts.

Some comprehensive sites make searching even easier through the use of a search engine. Rather than clicking through the hierarchy of categories and subcategories to find a list of links pertaining to the topic in which you're interested, you can enter a keyword into a form and let the search engine do the work for you. Typically, the search engine returns the results in the form of a list of possible matches to your keyword, and you can pick from that abbreviated list any sites you wish to visit.

Here are a few of the comprehensive genealogical sites you can find online, along with descriptions of their features.

Cyndi's List of Genealogy Sites on the Internet

www.cyndislist.com/

This popular site, by Cyndi Howells, has over 67,000 links indexed and cross-indexed by topic in more than 120 categories. The categories are based on ethnic groups, religious groups, geographic locations, products (such as books and software), types of records, learning resources (like beginner information, how-to, and writing a family history), and other interests (for example, adoption, reunions, royalty, and travel).

Genealogy Home Page

www.genealogyhomepage.com

The Genealogy Home Page was the very first comprehensive genealogical site. It classifies Internet genealogical sites in 15 areas, including Genealogy Help and Guides, Internet Genealogy Guides, Religious Genealogy Resources, and Upcoming Genealogy Events. Two unique aspects to Genealogy Home Page are the FTP site and "What's New" sections. The Genealogy Anonymous FTP Site is a collection of downloadable freeware, shareware, archived ROOTS-L files, and other FTP files. And in the "What's New" and "What's Really New in WWW Genealogy Pages" sections, you can find frequently updated lists of new sites on the Web or sites that are newly listed in the Genealogy Home Page.

Genealogy Resources on the Internet

www-personal.umich.edu/~cgaunt/gen_int1.html

Christine Gaunt and John Fuller work together to bring you Genealogy Resources on the Internet. This comprehensive site identifies online resources by type of resource. It includes sections on mailing lists, USENET newsgroups, anonymous FTP, Gopher, World Wide Web, Telnet, and e-mail. The Web resources are sorted by various topics including geographic-specific, ethnic, and descriptive. Several sections not only identify and link to resources, but also explain in detail what the resource is and how to use it.

Helm's Genealogy Toolbox

www.genealogytoolbox.com

Helm's Genealogy Toolbox started simply as a list of links on Matthew's first Web page in the fall of 1994 and became the second comprehensive genealogical index when he moved the links to their own site in early 1995 — at that time, there were 134 links. Now the index is part of a larger, integrated site (still known as Helm's Genealogy Toolbox) and contains over 86,000 categorized links. The links are divided into six top-level categories: People, Places, Computers, How-To and Help, Media, and Supplies and Services. The index is completely searchable (along with the other parts of the site) using the Global Search function.

Elusive Records

Some unique records and resources can be of great value to you in your genealogical pursuits. Some records pertain to a particular group of people; others are commonly thought of records that are just hard to find because of past disasters (fire, war, and government changes). Here are some examples of sites that fit the bill.

Adoptee and Genealogy Page

www.kichline.com/carrie/page3.html

Part of Carrie's Crazy Quilt Web site, the Adoptee and Genealogy Page identifies online resources for persons researching their adoptions and the genealogies of their birth parents.

Adoptee Searcher's Handbook

www.ouareau.com/adoptee/

This is a how-to site that explains the where and how of researching adoptions, particularly in Canada. It identifies resources that are available online to help in your research, including general adoption Web sites, registries and support groups, searchable databases, church archives, and libraries and newspapers. This site also has information about researching adoptions in the United States, United Kingdom, Australia, and New Zealand.

Cemeteries in and around Gunning Shire, New South Wales

www.pcug.org.au/~gchallin/cemeteries/top.htm

Graeme Challinor has visited and catalogued the graves and memorials at cemeteries in and around Gunning Shire in New South Wales, Australia. For each cemetery that he visited, he includes the exact coordinates (longitude and latitude), the size of the cemetery, miscellaneous information about the cemetery or its surroundings, an area diagram, and transcriptions of the inscriptions on every gravestone in the cemetery. In all, he provides information on 24 cemeteries.

Ghosts of the Gold Rush

www.gold-rush.org/ghost-01.htm

This site's fun and interesting for everyone — even those without ancestors who were part of the Klondike Gold Rush! In addition to a chapter-by-chapter history of the Gold Rush (appropriately called the Klondike Gold Rush) and stories about

"Klondike stampeders," this site has a searchable database of information about individuals involved in the Gold Rush. The Pan for Gold Database contains information from many sources and was put together by the Dawson City Museum. You can search by surname or part of a name, and the database provides a list of resources about individuals who have that name. The list identifies the source of the information, tags each column of information provided, and then includes a transcription of the original information. Some entries have codes attached to them to indicate file sources, microfilm numbers, mining claims, and some census information including ethnicity, occupation, social status and religion.

Illinois State Archives: Chicago City Council Proceedings Files, 1833-1871

www.sos.state.il.us/depts/archives/
data_chi.html

The Illinois State Archives, in conjunction with the University of Illinois at Chicago, provide an online index of the more than 35,000 files that document the Chicago City Council Proceedings between 1833 and 1871. These files, which were thought to have been lost in the Great Fire in 1871 until they were rediscovered in 1983, contain the working papers and documents of the city council. You can search this index by subject term or by date. For each record identified in the index, there's a file title, calendar and/or fiscal year for the file, file number, and filing month and date. If you find the index for a file in which you're interested, you can then use the control number to write to the Illinois Regional Archives Depository to get a copy.

If your ancestors were members of a particular ethnic group, you probably want to find online sites that have records and information pertaining specifically to that group. Although not as prevalent as surname-related and geographic-specific Web sites, some ethnic resources are now available to help you. Here are a few sites geared toward particular ethnic groups.

AfriGeneas

www.afrigeneas.com/

The AfriGeneas Web site is closely associated with and complements the AfriGeneas mailing list, which was created as a place to discuss family history research and promote genealogy, particularly as it pertains to African ancestry. The Web site has several resources, including a beginner's guide, lists of resources based on location, and slave data. There is also a forum/chat area and information about the AfriGeneas mailing list and how to subscribe.

American Indian Tribal Directory

www.indians.org./index.html

Under the Resource Library Tribal Directory link, the American Indian Tribal Directory lists all the American Indian tribes recognized by the United States government. The list is sorted by geographic area of the country.

Christine's Genealogy Website

ccharity.com

Christine's Genealogy Website is a collection of online resources for African American genealogical research. It contains transcriptions of documents, indexes to records, historical information, and links to many other resources. You can read through the index of online resources, or you can search the site using keywords or names.

National Archives and Records Administration: American Indians

www.nara.gov/publications/microfilm/
   amerindians

The National Archives and Records Administration (NARA) provides an online copy of "American Indians: A Select Catalog of NARA Microfilm Publications." It identifies records and other resources that are available from NARA pertaining to American Indians. NARA provides background information about each of the government agencies for which it holds records and gives detailed information about each of the types of records that are available on microfilm for the agencies. Some of the agencies include the Bureau of Indian Affairs, the Geological Survey, and the Fish and Wildlife Service. Some of the records include various correspondence, field reports, orders and circulars, fiscal records, special censuses, records relating to treaties, territorial papers, appointment papers, court cases, and military records. The site also explains how and where you can get copies of the microfilms of these records.

National Archives and Records Administration: Black Studies

www.nara.gov/publications/microfilm/
   blackstudies/blackstd.html

This is an online copy of the National Archives and Records Administration (NARA) guide called "Black Studies: A Select Catalog of NARA Microfilm Publications." It identifies records and other resources that are available from NARA pertaining to African Americans. NARA provides background information about each of the government agencies for which it holds records and gives detailed information about each of the types of records that are available on microfilm for the agencies. Some of the agencies include the Congress, General Accounting Office, Department of State, and the Bureau of Refugees, Freedmen, and Abandoned Lands. Some of the records include various correspondence, military service records,

reports of operations, reports about abandoned and confiscated lands, personnel records, labor contracts, school reports, census records, and public health records. The site also explains how and where you can get copies of the microfilms of these records.

Civil War Soldiers & Sailors System

www.itd.nps.gov/cwss/

This well-designed and interesting Web site contains a searchable database of more than 230,000 names of soldiers and sailors who served during the Civil War. (The database also includes the names of soldiers who served in the United States Colored Troops.) To use the database, click the link for the category in which you wish you search: Soldiers, Sailors, Regiments, Cemeteries, Battles, Prisoners, Medals of Honor, or National Parks. The site then walks you through how to search that particular area of the database and returns a list of results based on your search terms.

NativeWeb

www.nativeweb.org

NativeWeb is a cooperative effort to provide a community on the Internet for aboriginal or native persons of the world. Click the Start Here link to get to the main Resource Center, which lists the categories of information at the site.

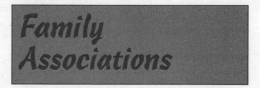

Family Associations

Sometimes, distinguishing between one-name studies and family association sites is difficult because their content is usually similar (see "One-Name Studies," later in this directory). However, generally every family association has an underlying organization, whereas one-name studies do not have such an organization. Formal family associations may focus on a surname as a whole or on a particular branch and, as a result, the association's Web site focuses on the same. Similarly, projects that the family association is undertaking (such as writing a book or putting together a comprehensive database of information from all members) may carry over to the Web site. The most distinguishable characteristic is that the Web site may require you to be a member of the family association before you can fully participate at the site or access some of the information online.

Harrington Genealogy Association

www.harringtons.org

The Harrington Genealogy Association's Web site provides information about all its resources and membership. The Association focuses on collecting data on all Harringtons and those with variations of that surname, and it has a collective database made up of GEDCOM files. The main communication tools are the HarrGene mailing list and a bulletin board, where you can participate in discussions or post queries about any Harrington family. It also includes sections on identifying current researchers, ongoing projects, and some of the Harrington branches worldwide.

MacDermot Clan Homepage

www.macdermot.com

The MacDermot Clan Homepage provides online family trees and a notice board where you can post messages about your genealogical research on a MacDermot or variations of that surname. Also, the site has all sorts of membership information, including how to join and some of the

benefits that are limited to members. Some of these benefits are an online registry of all members and their e-mail addresses and receipt of the official clan journal.

Peacock Family Association of the South

www.peacockfamily.org/

Regardless of its name, membership in this family association is open to anyone who's interested in the surname Peacock. The Web site identifies resources available from the association, including information about reunions and membership, photographs of some ancestors and from past reunions, GEDCOM files pertaining to Peacocks, and various downloadable files.

The Rutledge Family Association

www.rootsweb.com/~rutledge

Here, you can find information about membership in the Rutledge Family Association, and instructions for meeting others in the Rutledge Chat room to discuss your genealogical research. Also, you can find pages with Frequently Asked Questions, a glossary, online Family Group Sheets submitted by other Rutledge researchers, a list of association members and their e-mail addresses, and queries.

Watkins Family History Society

iinet.net.au/~davwat/wfhs/index.html

The Watkins Family History Society collects and organizes genealogical information on all Watkins worldwide. Its Web site has a register where you can identify yourself as a researcher of the Watkins surname, as well as provide details about the particular Watkins line you are looking for and collecting information on. You can also search the Web site to see who else may be researching the same Watkins family line. You can post general messages or queries on a message board, and you can also read what others have posted. You can join a mailing list in order to participate in further discussions on the Watkins surname. Additionally, the Web site explains how to join the society and what some of the benefits of membership are, including a searchable database of Watkins worldwide from which information is taken for the membership newsletter.

Genealogically Focused Search Engines

Some genealogy-specific search engines employ technology similar to the general search engines. The overall number of links that they cover is significantly less than general search engines. However, they do enable you to have a more focused search by limiting the number of sites they index that aren't directly related to genealogy.

GenPageFinder

www.ancestry.com/search/rectype/ directories/gpf/main.htm

Ancestry.com offers the newest genealogically focused search engine, called GenPageFinder. It returns results from the entire Internet and Ancestry.com's own free, and pay, databases.

GenealogyPortal.com

www.genealogyportal.com

A joint project by The Genealogy Home Page and Helm's Genealogy Toolbox, GenealogyPortal.com features eight

different genealogically focused search engines. Each search engine focuses on a particular subject area including archives and libraries, guides to research, historical sites, location-specific research, names and personal sites, primary records, research supplies, and software and utilities.

Internet FamilyFinder

www.genealogy.com/genealogy/ ifftop.html

Part of Genealogy.com's Web site, the Internet FamilyFinder is a surname-focused search engine. You can search for sites on the Internet, the GenealogyLibrary.com Web site (fee-based), Family Tree Maker user home pages, or commercial CD-ROMs offered by Genealogy.com from the same interface.

General Search Engines

You've probably been hearing about the Big Guys (the major search engines, that is) ever since you first thought about going online. *Search engines* are programs that search large indexes of information gathered by robots (sometimes called *spiders*) that are sent out to catalog resources on the Internet. Typically, the search engine has an interface form where you can enter keywords to search for in the index. The engine then searches its index and returns its findings to you online with links directly to the pages where the search engine's robot identified the keywords.

Although we don't recommend starting your online genealogical research using one of the major search engines (see Chapter 3 for the reasons), if you hit a brick wall in your research, a general search engine may be the only place left to go for some leads. Maybe the comprehensive sites didn't identify enough resources pertaining to a particular religious or ethnic group, and the searchable genealogical pages had only surname information. Where do you turn? To the Big Guys, of course.

Because a search on one name or word likely will result in thousands — even hundreds of thousands — of results, follow the particular engine's instructions for narrowing your search. Typically, this means using more than one word in your search and avoiding really common words altogether. (For example, you don't want to include *the, a,* and *of* in your search, or you get an unmanageable number of results if the search engine doesn't automatically ignore those words.) Reviewing the information that the search engine site provides online is a good idea and a quick way to learn new methods of narrowing your searches.

AltaVista

www.altavista.com

Using the main search box on AltaVista searches its index of Internet sites. Check out the Help section, or customize your settings, to narrow your search results. Or if you prefer not to search, you can use the directory of AltaVista categories to click through and find links of interest. And if you'd like to focus your search on information from or about a particular country, or in a language other than English, check out the links to AltaVista Around the World near the bottom of the page.

Excite

www.excite.com

Excite has a directory of subjects from which you can choose to look for sites of interest to you. Like the other search engines with directories, you click the subject of interest that takes you to a submenu

where you can select a more specific topic to get down to links to actual sites on that topic. Or you can use the search engine to look for particular keywords in Excite's databases of Web sites. Excite also offers links to Excite Global search engines at the bottom of the main page. The Excite Global search engines focus your searches for information from or about a particular country and/or provide the results of your search in a language other than English.

Go.com

www.go.com

Go.com's search interface is at the top of its main page, and it has directories of links you can follow in various sections on the page, including PlayFinder, Everyday Life, and Look It Up. When you use the search engine, you can choose to search All information in the index, just images, or just audio/video clips. To narrow your searches for genealogical purposes, try using the Power Search interface, which you can get to by clicking the link below the Search field. Also, if you're interested in reading results in a language other than English, you can use one of Go.com's six online translators for which there is a link under the Everyday Life section of the main page.

Google

www.google.com

The Google search engine is a no-nonsense sort of site. Its main page is simple — you notice the search interface field, two buttons from which to choose, the total number of Web sites that Google has indexed, and a few links to other parts of the Google site. Simply enter your search term in the field, and click Google Search. (Of course, if you're optimistic that Google will find the perfect site that you're looking for, you may choose to select the I'm

Feeling Lucky button instead.) To narrow your search, check out the Advanced Search function and follow the instructions. If you prefer to use the search engine's directory of links instead, click the link near the bottom of the screen that says Try our Web Directory.

HotBot

www.hotbot.com

In addition to a search engine, the HotBot site has a directory from which you can choose topics of interest to click your way down to Web sites about those topics. The HotBot search engine enables you to search indexes of its database including information on all identified Web sites, Usenet newsgroups, top new sites, businesses, people, e-mail addresses, classified advertisements, domain names, stocks, discussion groups, and shareware. Use the Help section to learn how to search more precisely on HotBot.

Lycos

www.lycos.com

Lycos has a list of topics in which it categorizes sites that have been identified by its robot, and a search engine that looks through the entire Lycos database of identified Web sites. The guide is divided into common topics such as entertainment, home and family, society and beliefs, and travel. You can click through the subjects and their submenus to locate sites of interest, or you can use the search engine to look for keywords. You may want to check out the Advanced Search feature to narrow your searches. And although this main Lycos page is in English, Lycos offers its pages in several other languages (you can select the language you want from the list at the bottom of the page).

WebCrawler

www.webcrawler.com

In addition to its search interface, WebCrawler has a menu of *channels* (or subjects) you can use to find information on a particular topic. Just like other directory structures, you can click a particular channel (such as computers and Internet, entertainment, or kids and family) to get to a submenu where you can select more specific topics, or go to links to actual sites. Or you can use the search engine to look for particular keywords in the WebCrawler database. You can find search tips under the Help section that explain how to narrow your results. WebCrawler offers you links to Excite Global search engines at the bottom of the page. These Global search engines focus on searches for information in specific countries and in languages other than English.

Government Resources

If you're like us, you probably groan and grumble about paying taxes and sometimes even wonder what exactly the government is using your good tax dollars for. Maybe you're lucky and all you have to do is go down to your local library or courthouse where you find efficient operations and friendly government employees who give you the assurance that your tax dollars are being well spent. With the increasing popularity of the Internet, it is now a little easier for some of us to see our tax dollars at work — helping spread useful information along the superhighway. Here are some sites — either created by government entities or containing government-related information and records — that contain helpful information for genealogists.

Ancestry.com: Social Security Death Index

www.ancestry.com/search/rectype/vital/ssdi/main.htm

The United States government (through the Social Security Administration) assigns a unique nine-digit number to everyone who lives and works in the United States. The purpose of this number is to track who's eligible for Social Security benefits (sort of a supplemental retirement income) after they reach a certain age.

Whenever a claim for death benefits is filed with the Social Security Administration, the government adds the person's name and some other information to the Master Death Index. If your ancestors lived and worked in the United States, the Social Security Death Index can be useful in your genealogical pursuits, and Ancestry's online interface to search the index makes it easy to check and see if your ancestors are included.

To search the database of over 64 million names, go to the search site, enter your ancestor's name, and click Search. (Only the last name is required, but knowing the first name can be helpful.) Also, to narrow the search, you may want to complete any of the other fields on the form for which you have information. After you complete the form and click Search, Ancestry gives you a list of persons matching your search. Besides the person's name, the list includes the Social Security number, date born, date died, residence, zip code to which the person's last Social Security benefit was sent, state in which the person's Social Security card was issued, and date that the card was issued.

Archives of Mechelen (Belgium)

www.mechelen.be/archief/

This site provides general information about the hours and holdings of the Archives of Mechelen. Some of the records held by the Archives include birth, death, marriage, population, and parish registries, property records, tax lists, and a registry of abandoned children.

National Archives of Australia

www.naa.gov.au

The mission of the Australian Archives is to preserve Commonwealth records and make them accessible to the public. Some of the Archives' services include public reference, an archival library, and maintaining personnel records of those Australians who served in World War I. The Web site provides information about the Archives' collections, publications, and exhibitions.

Other Australian Sites to Check Out

State Records: New South Wales
www.records.nsw.gov.au

Queensland Government State Archives
www.archives.qld.gov.au

State Records of South Australia
www.archives.sa.gov.au

Archives Office of Tasmania
www.tased.edu.au/archives

Public Record Office of Victoria
www.prov.vic.gov.au/welcome.htm

Library and Information Service of Western Australia
www.liswa.wa.gov.au

Northern Territory Archives Service
www.nt.gov.au/nta

Bureau of Land Management, Eastern States, General Land Office, Official Land Patents Records Site

www.glorecords.blm.gov

The Bureau of Land Management, General Land Office site contains a searchable database and digitized Federal land patent records for the states of Alabama, Arkansas, Florida, Illinois, Indiana, Louisiana, Michigan, Minnesota, Mississippi, Missouri, Ohio, and Wisconsin. Simply click the Search Land Patents link in the upper left corner of the main page, provide your zip code, and follow the instructions to complete the online form to search the land patents database. (If you need additional help, there's a Search Tips page that you can access from a link at the bottom of the search form.) The system returns a list of potential matches to your search criteria from which you can choose to see more details and a digitized copy of the land record.

Canadian Archival Resources on the Internet

www.usask.ca/archives/menu.html

Canadian Archival Resources on the Internet provides just that — an index of archives in Canada that have Web sites. In addition to some basic information about the types of archives, this site has links to each of the archival resources identified. The various archives are categorized as provincial, university, municipal, religious, medical, and other. They're also cross-categorized by region (western, central, eastern, and national).

Danish State Archives

www.sa.dk

The Danish State Archives home page is, as you would expect, in Danish. It provides general information about the Archives, its publications, and its film center.

General Register Office (Northern Ireland)

www.nics.gov.uk/nisra/gro

The General Register Office (GRO) maintains statutory registers of vital events — births, deaths, and marriages. Although the registers themselves aren't available for public use, you can order

copies of certificates that contain information from the registers. This site explains in detail exactly what is available, how to order copies of certificates, what you must include when requesting certificates, and the costs for doing so.

General Register Office (Scotland)

www.open.gov.uk/gros/groshome.htm

The General Register Office (GRO) is the government agency responsible for registering births, deaths, marriages, divorces, and adoptions in Scotland. It's also responsible for conducting censuses of Scotland's population. The GRO's Web site is well organized and easy to use. It has helpful Frequently Asked Questions (FAQs), an alphabetical index identifying records and how to use them, annual reports and statistical information about the GRO, and services that the GRO offers (including researching on behalf of genealogists who can't visit the GRO and evening visits for genealogical groups). To find fully searchable indexes of Scottish birth and marriage records (1553 to 1899), death records (1855 to 1924), and the 1891 Census, see Origins.net's Scots Origins site at `www.origins.net/GRO/`. You're charged on a pay-per-view basis to search the indexes.

Library of Congress

www.loc.gov

Although not officially recognized as the national library of the United States, this is what the Library of Congress has become since its inception in 1800. The Library now holds approximately 15 million books, 39 million manuscripts, 13 million photographs, 4 million maps, 3.5 million pieces of music, and half a million motion pictures. The Library of Congress Web site explains its many research tools, including searchable Library of Congress catalogs; country studies and area handbooks; a database with information pertaining to U.S. military personnel who were killed, missing in action, or imprisoned in Southeast Asia during the Vietnam conflict; and U.S. Copyright Office records from 1978 to the present. Of special interest is the American Memory: Historical Collections section. Part of the Library of Congress National Digital Library Program, American Memory provides digitized and transcribed historical documents that you can view on the Internet. The collection is divided into these categories: photos and prints, written materials, motion pictures, maps, and sound recordings.

National Archives and Records Administration: United States

www.nara.gov/genealogy/genindex.html

The mission of the National Archives and Records Administration (NARA) is to provide access to evidence documenting the rights of American citizens, actions of federal officials, and the national experience. Among the resources at NARA's Web site are a couple of sections of special interest to genealogists. The Genealogy Page provides information about records held by NARA pertaining directly to individuals — including census returns, military service records, and passenger lists. The section explains how to use NARA and its resources in your genealogical research. You may also find interesting the section containing information about historical records for government agencies, particularly if events surrounding or prompted by one of these agencies had a direct impact on your ancestors and/or the area in which they lived. NARA has regional facilities across the United States that contain microfilmed copies of the records of interest to genealogists. Their Web sites (which provide their hours and locations and identify resources held by the branch) can be found at the following addresses:

Northeast Region: Boston
www.nara.gov/regional/boston.html

Northeast Region: Pittsfield, Massachusetts
www.nara.gov/regional/pittsfie.html

Northeast Region: New York City
www.nara.gov/regional/newyork.html

Mid Atlantic Region: Center City Philadelphia
www.nara.gov/regional/philacc.html

Mid Atlantic Region: Northeast Philadelphia
www.nara.gov/regional/philane.html

Southeast Region: Atlanta
www.nara.gov/regional/atlanta.html

Great Lakes Region: Chicago
www.nara.gov/regional/chicago.html

Great Lakes Region: Dayton
www.nara.gov/regional/dayton.html

Central Plains Region: Kansas City
www.nara.gov/regional/kansas.html

Southwest Region: Fort Worth
www.nara.gov/regional/ftworth.html

Rocky Mountain Region: Denver
www.nara.gov/regional/denver.html

Pacific Region: Laguna Niguel, California
www.nara.gov/regional/laguna.html

Pacific Region: San Francisco (San Bruno)
www.nara.gov/regional/sanfranc.html

Pacific Alaska Region: Seattle
www.nara.gov/regional/seattle.html

Pacific Alaska Region: Anchorage
www.nara.gov/regional/anchorag.html

National Personnel Records Center: St. Louis
www.nara.gov/regional/stlouis.html

National Archives of Canada

www.archives.ca

The National Archives of Canada Web site states the agency's purpose is to preserve the memory of the nation and government of Canada and enhance a sense of national identity. The site provides information about researching on location and contains detailed descriptions of the types of records that the Archives holds. Among the many resources are civil registrations of births, marriages, and deaths dating from the 19th century, passenger manifests from 1865, immigration documents for people who arrived in Canada from U.S.

borders, some naturalization records dating from 1828 to 1850, and petitions for land. Of particular interest to those with ancestors who served in the military is an online index of about 620,000 personnel folders for the citizens who enlisted in the Canadian Expeditionary Force (CEF) during World War I. The personnel folders contain various documents including attestation and enlistment papers, medical records, discipline and pay records, and discharge papers. You can search the index online; if your search is successful, you can order copies of the documents from the personnel folder. The Web site explains how to do all of this.

National Archives of Ireland

www.kst.dit.ie/nat-arch

The National Archives of Ireland Web site contains information to help you prepare to research in the Archives. It includes instructions for using the census returns, primary valuation (also known as Griffith's valuation — these are records pertaining to leased properties), and tithe applotment books (information collected in order to determine how much a person was required to tithe to the Church of Ireland). You can also find detailed information about the availability of birth, marriage, and death records, as well as wills.

Public Record Office (United Kingdom)

www.pro.gov.uk

Founded in 1838, the Public Records Office (PRO) serves as the national archives for England, Wales, and the United Kingdom. It preserves the records of the government and the courts, and makes those records accessible to the public. Among the resources that are explained at the PRO's Web site is information specifically for genealogists. You can find general information about the Family Records Centre (address, hours, holdings), its publications, paid research services that are available, and referrals to other agencies and

organizations that may help you with your research. Additionally, a helpful section called Family Fact Sheets provides detailed information about researching a particular type of ancestor in the United Kingdom — such as one who served as a soldier, sailor, police, or one who was an immigrant or ship passenger.

Public Record Office of Northern Ireland

proni.nics.gov.uk

FAQs

The Public Record Office of Northern Ireland (PRONI) is the official depository for records of government agencies, courts, and other public offices, as well as for records contributed by businesses, institutions, churches, and individuals. The PRONI's Web site provides general information about the office, its resources and how to use them, publications, and exhibitions and events.

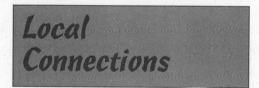

Local Connections

Most of the information about your ancestors was recorded at a local level — in the towns, counties, parishes, or states where they lived. Online sites can help you whether you live near to or far from the areas where your relatives hailed. Look for sites that have a local flavor to them. They contain information and, in some cases, records that are specific to a geographical area. Here are some examples.

Australasian-Genealogy Web Resources: Australasia

home.vicnet.net.au/~AGWeb/agweb.htm

The Australasian-Genealogy Web (AGWeb) links together and provides access to regional genealogical resources. In addition to providing links to sites that are members of the network, AGWeb links to nonmember sites that have information pertaining to Australia. Of special interest to genealogists researching ancestors from the area is its section on Categories and Records that contains transcribed files that you can view online or download for use. The categories include aborigines; civil registration; convicts; directories and almanacs; land records; local government records; manuscripts, letters, and diaries; news-papers; occupational records; passenger arrivals and departures; family histories and biographies; local histories; research directories and indices; shipping; and genealogy-related. Not all the categories have files associated with them at this time, so check back periodically to see what's been added.

CanadaGenWeb Project

www.rootsweb.com/~canwgw

The CanadaGenWeb Project helps researchers find the enormous amount of Canadian information available through the Internet. It is modeled after the USGenWeb project and has links to each of the main pages for the provinces/territories of Canada. Each territorial page has links for county/district pages, which provide links to resources for those areas. Additionally, the CanadaGenWeb page has a historical timeline of Canada and some facts and trivia about the country.

CaribbeanGenWeb

www.rootsweb.com/~caribgw

CaribbeanGenWeb has Web sites set up or planned for each island in order to provide information about (and links to) genealogical resources on the Internet that pertain to that particular island. Additionally, the

main CaribbeanGenWeb page provides links to some resources that pertain to the Caribbean in general.

EuropeGenWeb

www.rootsweb.com/~ceneurgw

www.rootsweb.com/~easeurgw

www.rootsweb.com/~sthamgw/
    medgw.html

EuropeGenWeb is actually three sites, including the CenEuroGenWeb Project (www.rootsweb.com/~ceneurgw/), EastEuropeGenWeb (www.rootsweb.com/~easeurgw/), and MediterraneanGenWeb (www.rootsweb.com/~sthamgw/medgw.html). Each section provides information about and links to the WorldGenWeb pages for countries that are located in that particular area. Each WorldGenWeb page for such countries then provides information and links to genealogical resources on the Internet that pertain to that country, as well as links to any state/county/province pages that fall under the particular country.

GENUKI: UK + Ireland Genealogy

www.genuki.org.uk

GENUKI is a service that's intended to be a "virtual reference library" of primary historical and genealogical information in the United Kingdom and Ireland. And it's just that! The creators of GENUKI provide a comprehensive information service that covers all aspects of genealogy in the United Kingdom and Ireland, yet remains coherent and easy to use. Its structure is a four-level hierarchy corresponding to locality — from the British Isles as a whole down to each country within, to each county, to each parish. Its links are to sites that contain actual primary information, indices of such information, or transcriptions or electronic images of actual records. Some of the subjects covered in GENUKI are archives and libraries, cemeteries, census, church records, civil registrations, colonization, heraldry, military, probate records, and taxation.

International Internet Genealogical Society

www.iigs.org

This site is available in 11 languages. The International Internet Genealogical Society (IIGS) helps the genealogical community find new and better ways to preserve and present records and information on the Internet to share with others. This site explains in detail the services and resources that are available from IIGS. Two ongoing projects include an IIGS University, which holds online classes about genealogical research, and an Internet Relay Chat, where genealogists can go to discuss research and ideas.

MidEastGenWeb

www.rootsweb.com/~mdeastgw/

MidEastGenWeb provides information about and links to the WorldGenWeb pages for countries that are located in the Middle East. Each WorldGenWeb page for such countries then provides information and links to genealogical resources on the Internet that pertain to that country, as well as links to any state/county/province pages that fall under the particular country.

Perry-Castañeda Library Map Collection

www.lib.utexas.edu/Libs/PCL/ Map_collection/Map_collection.html

The Perry-Castañeda Library Map Collection at the University of Texas at

Austin has online copies of various continent, country, state/territory/province, and county outline maps. This main Web page provides links to pages for several continents and countries, as well as outline county maps for the state of Texas. It also has historical maps and city maps.

SouthAmGenWeb

www.rootsweb.com/~sthamgw

SouthAmGenWeb provides information about and links to the WorldGenWeb pages for countries that are located in South America. Each WorldGenWeb page for such countries then provides information and links to genealogical resources on the Internet that pertain to that country, as well as links to any state/county/province pages that fall under the particular country.

United States Internet Genealogical Society

www.usigs.org/index.htm

The United States Internet Genealogical Society (USIGS) is just that — an online genealogical society. Its Web site provides a history of the fairly new organization and explains its current projects.

USGenWeb

www.usgenweb.org

The USGenWeb Project provides Web sites for every county in every state in the United States. Each Web site is tasked with identifying genealogical resources that are available on the Internet for its particular county. This main site provides links to all the state pages, which, in turn, provide links to existing county pages. It also contains information about the USGenWeb's Archives project (where it now stores FTP files for each state) and explains how you can become involved in the USGenWeb.

World Factbook Master Home Page

www.odci.gov/cia/publications/factbook/
index.html

The Central Intelligence Agency's World Factbook site provides information on every country and ocean in the world. The country pages are organized regionally, and all are accessible from this main page. Each country page includes a map and the geographical location of the country, as well as detailed information about the country's flag, geography, people, government, economy, transportation, communication, and defense. The pages for the oceans contain a map and geographical location, as well as information about the ocean's geography, economy, and transportation.

WorldGenWeb Project

www.worldgenweb.org

The goal of the WorldGenWeb Project is to have a Web site for every country in the world that would contain information about and links to genealogical resources on the Internet. Although many of the countries have pages, many more still need volunteers.

One-Name Studies

Unlike personal Web pages, which provide you with detailed information about an individual's research and particular branch of a family, one-name studies give you a wide range of information on one particular surname. Usually the information presented at these sites is not constrained by geographic boundaries — in other words, the site may have information about the surname in several different countries. One-name studies typically have information

that includes histories of the surname (including its origins), variations in spelling, heraldry associated with the name, and databases and queries submitted by researchers worldwide.

Beard/Baird Genealogy

www.outfitters.com/~chelle/chelle.htm

Beard/Baird Genealogy contains a collection of information and links to other resources on the Beard and Baird surnames, and variations. The site has a discussion group, a genealogy forum where you can post and read queries pertaining to Beards/Bairds, several online biographies, historical information about some Beards/Bairds and places named for them, and lots of other goodies.

Chicken Family Histories

ourworld.compuserve.com/homepages/
Chicken_Matthews/homepage.htm

Chicken Family Histories is "intended to be a focus for ALL Chickens and their descendants across the world." The Master Coop tells you about the origins of the Chicken surname, and the Chicken Scratchings section has information about some better-known Chickens. Geoff Matthews, the site's creator, also provides a narrative genealogy on his Matthews-Chicken ancestors and the surnames of some of his other ancestors. The various poultry graphics and play-on-words at this site make it fun to visit even if you're not a "Chicken-chaser!"

The Gyllenhaal Family Tree Project

www.gyllenhaal.org/

This is an international effort to collect and share as much information as possible on the Gyllenhaal surname. Most of the current information on the site relates to descendants in Sweden and North

America. A growing GEDCOM file is available for viewing at the site, as well as information on the surname and Coats of Arms. You can also find online biographies and photographs of some Gyllenhaals, and transcriptions (in Swedish and English) of the letter ennobling Nils Gunnarsson Gyllenhaal in 1672.

Kelton Family HomePage

rampages.onramp.net/~ekelton/
index.html

The Kelton Family HomePage is intended to serve as a repository for any information pertaining to families with the surname Kelton. It has an exchange section where you can post questions and general information about your Kelton ancestors, along with your e-mail address so that others may contact you directly. Additionally, it has sections with histories about some Kelton families, family registers, stories about some famous Keltons and contemporary naming patterns, and links to other sites of interest to those researching the Kelton name. This site is easy to navigate and has online forms you can use to submit any information you have on Kelton ancestors.

Thompson One Name Study

www.geocities.com/Athens/2249

The Thompson One Name Study site focuses on collecting and making available for users information about all Thompsons (and variations of the surname). The site includes some downloadable records for some Thompsons from the United Kingdom, as well as information about the origins of the surname, Coats of Arms, the one-name study project in general, and researchers of the Thompsons. You can also find several online histories of various Thompsons.

Walsh Family Genealogy

homepages.rootsweb.com/~walsh/

Walsh Family Genealogy is a site dedicated to sharing information about the Walsh surname and families worldwide. You can register as a researcher and identify the Walsh ancestors you're researching, post messages and queries about your research, and join the Walsh-L mailing list to participate in discussions. The site also has sections with some online Walsh family trees, searchable indices and lists of information (cemetery, marriage, passenger lists, and land records), and information about the origins of the surname and Coats of Arms.

Personal Web Sites

Personal Web sites usually provide information about an individual's or family's specific research interests, and they're the most common type of surname-related sites you will find. Generally, a personal Web site has information about a particular branch of a family. The format and presentation of this information can vary greatly. Some personal Web pages merely list the surnames that the site maintainer is researching; others contain the GEDCOM file of the site maintainer. And others have narrative histories about the family and areas in which they lived.

Given that thousands and thousands of personal Web pages exist, we had a difficult time narrowing our choices for this directory. A lot of good personal pages contain detailed and useful information. We chose these sites because they each provide a variety of information about the maintainer's interests and research, they are well-organized and easy to use, and they show that the maintainer cares a lot about genealogical research and sharing information with others.

The Ashworth Family Page

www.murrah.com/gen/ashworth.htm

The Ashworth Family Page provides a narrative about the descendants of James Ashworth of Craven County, South Carolina. Included in the narrative are the surnames of some other families that married into the Ashworths, information about the Ashworths' role in the American Revolution, and their moves to South Carolina, Louisiana, and Texas. The controversy surrounding the Ashworths' race provides for very interesting reading at this site. You can find excellent explanations of and references to other sites with more information about Melungeons, Lumbee Indians, and Redbones.

Chenoweth Family Site

chenowethsite.com/

This site has extensive resources on the Chenoweth family, including an online database of the descendants of John Chenoweth and Mary Calvert, and some descendant reports, too. You can find background information on the genealogy itself and the Coat of Arms, discussions about disputes among researchers over information that is presented online, and explanations of areas in which Jon Egge (the site creator) is looking for information. The site also has sections with specific information about Chenoweths who served in the Civil War and other wars. You can find snail mail (regular mail) and e-mail addresses for other researchers interested in Chenoweths. We found it quite nice to see that there's a section that graciously cites the sources of the information contained on the Web site.

Jeff Alvey Genealogy and Other Good Stuff

www.fred.net/jefalvey

Jeff Alvey shares an index of the persons contained in his genealogical database, as well as historical information about various Alveys and the origins of the surname. Two unique resources at this site are an informative section about heraldry and an index of names that appear in the book, *The Chronicles of Newgate,* which has information about inmates and others associated with the Newgate prison in London.

The Mabry Family

homepages.rootsweb.com/~mabry/

Don Collins, the creator of the Mabry Family Web site, shares with you lots of information about the Mabry (and various spellings) family in America. The site has a list of descendants of Francis Maybury and Elizabeth Gilliam, who were married in Virginia in 1685. It also has information about various Mabrys who fought in the American Revolution and Civil War, a chronology of events in which Mabrys were involved, information about the Mabry Family newsletter, and several online photographs of Mabrys. You can also find a list of various spellings of the surname and a history of the Mabry Mill in Virginia, as well as several resources to help you research your Mabry family — including queries, a list of books, and a schedule of family reunions.

McCutchan

www.mccutchan.org

In addition to a historical narrative about the migration of McCutchans from Scotland to Ireland to the United States, the McCutchan genealogy Web site contains information about the various spellings of the surname and one of the family tartans. The site also includes descendant charts for Samuel McCutchen and some of the other family lines that Bill McCutchan, the site's creator, is researching. Additionally, the site features an online photo album, a guest book where you can post messages (including messages with information about the McCutchan line you are researching), and links to other sites of interest to those researching the McCutchan surname.

Mike Schwitzgebel's Genealogy Pages

homepages.rootsweb.com/~mschwitz/

In addition to sharing a GED2HTML copy of his GEDCOM file, Mike Schwitzgebel has an online photo album and information about the origins of his surname and a Coat of Arms. He also identifies the main goals of his current research for you to review to see if you have any information that may help him and other researchers — they are listed under the Most Wanted section of his site. We were impressed with Mike's open and gracious acknowledgments of the work by other researchers from whom he's received information about the Schwitzgebels. This is an excellent example of citing one's sources and giving credit where credit is due.

Nafzger Genealogy Home Page

sailfish.exis.net/~tjnoff

Jay Noffsinger, the site's maintainer, shares some of his Nafzger (and related surnames) genealogy with you in the form of online versions of his two books, an online photo album, and reports containing information from his genealogical database. He also provides a guest book where you can register and indicate the Nafzger line that you're researching.

Professional Researchers

At some time, you may need to hire a professional researcher to pursue your genealogy of a particular family line. Maybe you have exhausted all your leads on that

family line, or you no longer have the time to devote to research, or the records you need are in a distant land and you have neither the time nor the money to travel there just to look for paper. A lot of research services are available — some from reputable companies, others from individuals who just want to help others.

The following is a list of just a few professional research services that are available in different parts of the world. Chapter 4 provides more information about finding and choosing professional researchers.

Adelaide proformat

www.users.on.net/proformat/jaunay.html

$

Adelaide proformat was formed in 1994. Although Adelaide proformat specializes in helping Australians with their genealogical research and researching Australian resources for those who do not live there or cannot travel there to do their own research, it also offers research services in the United Kingdom, Europe, and North America. Adelaide proformat offers services consulting and researching, looking for documents, preparing family histories, and drawing family trees.

Family Tree Genealogical and Probate Research Bureau Ltd.

www.familytree.hu

$

Family Tree Genealogical and Probate Research Bureau Ltd. was formed in Hungary in 1988. Its researchers work in Hungary, Slovakia, Austria (Burgenland), Transylvania (part of Romania), Croatia, Slovenia, former Yugoslavia (Banat), and the Ukraine (Sub-Carpathia). In addition to explaining how it researches, the Family Tree Web site explains how historical Hungary varies from contemporary Hungary and how that affects genealogical research in the area; the site also provides details about Jewish genealogy and probate searches in the area. Family Tree also offers a service called Root Tours, where it arranges for you (and a group if you'd like) to tour the countries in the former Austro-Hungarian Empire and conduct your own genealogical research.

Lineages, Inc.

www.lineages.com/store/searches.asp

$

Lineages, Inc., was founded in 1983 to provide genealogical research services and products nationwide in the United States. The Lineages Web site provides detailed information about using the organization's research services, including what you can expect upon hiring it to the costs of its services. One of the things you can expect if you do hire Lineages to conduct some research for you is an extensive report explaining how it researched your ancestors, copies of records it used, and ancestry charts and family group sheets reflecting your line of descent.

Molander's Genealogy Service

www.algonet.se/~family

$

Molander's Genealogy Service helps you trace your family in Sweden and/or Norway. Molander's services include conducting look-ups in church records and other written sources, as well as at archives in the area, and supplying to you detailed information about the community in which your ancestors lived and the people with whom they associated. Although Molander's Web site provides basic information about its services, you have to contact Molander's directly by mail or phone (at the address and phone number provided on the Web site) for more information and the costs of its services.

Scottish Family Research

www.linnet.co.uk/linnet/tour/67015.htm

$

Scottish Family Research uses base information that you provide (birth, marriage, or death details about a Scottish ancestor) and researches many genealogical sources in Scotland to put together a report for you. The service includes using civil registrations, census returns, and old parish registers. The Scottish Family Research home page provides detailed information about the services, what information about your ancestor is initially required, costs of the services, and what you can expect to get in the report.

Threshold Concepts, Inc.

www.xmission.com/~tconcept/
  genhome.htm

$

Threshold Concepts, Inc., specializes in research services in Salt Lake City, Utah, and Washington, D.C. Its Web site explains what research services it offers, as well as its other services: restoring and preserving photographs and documents, and preparing and publishing family histories, among others. Threshold's Web site includes the costs for each of its services.

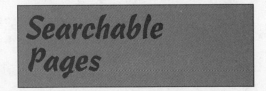

Searchable Pages

Searchable genealogical pages are just what they sound like — Web sites where you can search for a particular keyword by using a search engine or by following a hierarchical menu through the site to the information you are looking for. Generally, searchable pages are relatively easy to navigate because they have a search field that is readily apparent, or they have clear instructions for using the hierarchy. Most searchable pages are surname-related or contain queries (about surnames, particular families, or geographic areas). Here are a few that you may want to examine.

Gendex

www.gendex.com/gendex

Gendex is a site with a server that indexes hundreds of Web pages containing genealogical data. The index contains some 12 million names and brief biographical information about those persons for whom information is available. The biographical information includes dates and places of birth and death. The entries also include contact information for the individuals who registered the Web sites from which the data was obtained, and links to the actual sites. You can use the Gendex search engine to search the database by surname, or you can click through the alphabet to find surnames. Access to use Gendex is available on two levels: unregistered users (free access) and registered users (pay for use). Registered users are given priority access for searching Gendex, search filters that enable them to customize their searches, and the ability to modify how the data resulting from a search is displayed on their computers.

SurnameWeb

www.surnameweb.org

SurnameWeb is intended to serve as a central collection point for information about Internet resources pertaining to surnames worldwide. It contains an index of sites that are set up as Surname Resource Centers, which are basically one-name study sites devoted to particular surnames. You will also find an extensive index of surnames found across the Web on various types of sites (personal Web pages, family histories, geographic-specific sites, and so forth). You can search the listing of sites using SurnameWeb's search

engine, which is easily accessible from the main page. Or you can browse the entire site by clicking on the directory-type links to various parts.

Over the past couple of years, we've seen huge expansion in the area of genealogical software — from commercial databases, to mapping programs, to freeware and software that lets you manipulate your GEDCOM. Whether you want to buy your first genealogical organization program, upgrade to a program that is more powerful, or make some sort of enhancement to your genealogical files, you're probably interested in what software is available and what it has to offer you. Here's a list of genealogical software databases and a few specialty-type programs you may want to check out.

Ancestors and Descendants

www.aia-and.com

Ancestors and Descendants is available for Windows 3.1 and above, MS-DOS, and OS/2. It produces over 100 reports, including family group sheets, pedigree charts, and source lists.

Ancestral Quest

www.ancquest.com

Ancestral Quest is available for Windows 3.1 or higher. It produces ahnentafel reports, family group sheets, pedigree charts, and wall charts. The CD-ROM version includes the Hammond Maps of the World, Konica Picture Show, and a genealogy resources list.

Brother's Keeper

ourworld.compuserve.com/homepages/
Brothers_Keeper

Brother's Keeper is available for Windows 3.1 or higher and MS-DOS. Reports include ahnentafel, pedigree charts, family group sheets, and a timeline. Each database can contain up to 1,000,000 individuals. Versions come in English, French, Norwegian, Danish, Swedish, German, and Dutch.

Create Family Trees Quick and Easy

www.individualsoftware.com/consumer/
conqnetree.htm

Create Family Trees Quick and Easy is available for Windows 95 or higher. Reports include Ancestor charts, descendant charts, and family group sheets.

Cumberland Family Tree

www.cf-software.com

Cumberland Family Tree is available for Windows 95 or higher. Thirty-one types of reports are available, including ahnentafel, pedigree charts, family group sheets, and descendant charts. Each database can hold 1,000,000 individuals. Reports can be generated in Danish, Dutch, Finnish, French, German, Italian, Norwegian, Portuguese, Spanish, and Swedish.

EZITREE

www.ram.net.au/users/ezitree

EZITREE is available for Windows 95 or higher. Reports include ancestor charts, descendant charts, and family group

sheets. The number of individuals allowed per database is 99,999.

Family Explorer

www.Commercial.Com/kinware/
software.html

Family Explorer is available for Windows 95/NT or Windows 98. Reports include ahnentafel, register, lineage, and custom.

Family History System

fhs.tallahassee.net

Family History System is available for MS-DOS. Reports include ahnentafel, descendant, box charts, and tiny tafel. The number of individuals allowed in a database is 32,000.

Family Matters

members.aol.com/matterware/index.html

Family Matters is available for Windows 95 or higher. Reports include pedigree and descendant charts. The software has Soundex, relationship, and birth/age calculators.

Family Origins

www.formalsoft.com/

Family Origins is available for Windows 3.1 and above. Reports include pedigree charts, family group sheets, descendant charts, kinship, and wall charts. You can have an unlimited number of names in each database. It includes a family reunion planner, cemetery records form, research log, place finder, databases of the royal houses of Europe, and source manager.

Family Reunion

www.famware.com

Family Reunion is available for Windows 95. Reports include ahnentafel, pedigree, descendant, family group sheets, and life span lists.

Family Tree Maker

www.familytreemaker.com

Family Tree Maker is available for Windows 95 or higher and Macintosh platforms. Reports include ancestor, descendant, kinship, calendar, and family group sheets. The number of individuals allowed per database is 2,000,000.

Gene

www.ics.uci.edu/~eppstein/gene

Gene is available for the Macintosh platform. Reports include ancestor, calendar, and relationship charts.

Genealogical Information Manager

www.gimsoft.com/

Genealogical Information Manager is available for MS-DOS. Reports include family group sheets, pedigree, and descendant charts. The software also enables you to split the database.

Genius

www.gensol.com.au/genius.htm

Genius is available on the Windows 3.1 (and higher) platform. Reports include descendant, pedigree, individual information sheet, and family group sheets. You can have 10,000 individuals per database. The software includes built-in backup and restore.

Généatique

www.cdip.com/geneatiq.htm

Généatique is designed for Windows 95 or higher. Reports include ancestor and descendant charts. The program only comes in French.

Generations Family Tree, Beginner's Edition

www.sierrahome.com/software/catalog/
   familytree/

Generations Deluxe Edition runs on Windows 95 or higher. You can produce a variety of reports, including ancestor and descendant charts. In addition to the Beginner's Edition, several other suites of the Generations Family Tree software exist. Each has unique features and additional material included with the software. The URL given here provides information about each suite or edition.

Heredis

www.heredis.com

Heredis is available for Windows 95/98/NT. Available reports include ahnentafel, descendant, pedigree, and anniversary lists. Currently, the program is only available in French.

Heritage

www.eskimo.com/~grandine/
  heritage.html

Heritage is available for the Macintosh
platform. You can generate three types of
ancestor and descendant charts, as well as
family group sheets.

KinQuest

www5.interaccess.com/orelleweb/
  kinquest.htm

Kinquest is available for MS-DOS. Reports
include ahnentafel and family group
sheets. You can store two billion names in
each database.

Kith and Kin

www.spansoft.org/

The basic version of Kith and Kin is available for Windows 3.1, and a Kith and Kin
Pro version is available for Windows 95/98.
Reports include ancestor, descendant, and
census reports.

Legacy

www.legacyfamilytree.com

Legacy is available for Windows 95 or
higher. Reports include ancestor, ahnentafel,
descendant, pedigree, family group sheets,
calendar, timeline, and individual.

LifeLines

www.genealogy.org/~ttw/lines/lines.html

LifeLines is designed for UNIX and related
systems. Reports include register, pedigree,
family group sheets, and tiny tafels.

The Master Genealogist

www.whollygenes.com

The Master Genealogist is available for
Windows 95 and higher. Reports include
ahnentafel, descendant, family group
sheets, individual, register, and custom.

My Family History

www.blackfire.com.au/

My Family History is available for Windows
3.1 and higher. Reports include descendant, family group sheets, pedigree, and
individual summary. The number of individuals per database is limited to 3,000.

Oedipus II

web.inter.nl.net/hcc/L.G.Lamain/
  odp95.htm

Oedipus II is available for Windows 95 and
higher. Reports include ancestor, descendant, and family group sheets. The software is in Dutch.

Personal Roots

www.expertsoftware.com/
  personal_roots_deluxe.htm

Personal Roots Deluxe is available for
Windows 3.1 or higher. Reports include
ancestor, descendant, pedigree, family
group sheets, and custom reports.

Reunion

www.leisterpro.com

Reunion is available for the Mac. Reports
include pedigree, family group sheets, register, timeline, and ahnentafel.

Windows into PAF

**ourworld.compuserve.com/homepages/
phoenix/WIPafhom.htm**

Windows into PAF is available for Windows
3.1. Reports include pedigree, family group
sheets, ahnentafel, and descendant.

Miscellaneous Utilities

DeedMapper

www.ultranet.com/~deeds/factsht.htm

Direct Line Software produces
DeedMapper, which is a program that
enables you to transfer information from
land records to maps that you can see and
use on your computer.

GED2HTML

www.gendex.com/ged2html

GED2HTML is Gene Stark's popular program for converting your GEDCOM file into
an HTML file that you can post on the Web.

GED2WWW

www.lesandchris.com/ged2www/

GED2WWW is Leslie Howard's freeware to
convert GEDCOM files to HTML so that you
can post your information on the Web.

GEDClean

www.raynorshyn.com/gedclean

GEDClean is Tom Raynor's shareware
that helps you strip your GEDCOM file of

information on living persons or particular
other information that you specify.

Gedpage

**www.frontiernet.net/~rjacob/
gedpage.htm**

Gedpage converts your GEDCOM files to
HTML for posting on the Web. Rob Jacob
wrote this program that provides output in
the form of family group sheets. The software is available for Windows and
Macintosh.

GenBrowser

**www.pratt.lib.md.us/~bharding/
rippleeffect/GenBrowser/
GenBrowser.html**

Ripple Effect developed and sells
GenBrowser, a software program that
searches for and downloads to your computer GEDCOM files that it finds online and
that meet specifications you enter.
GenBrowser converts HTML pages that
were generated from GEDCOM files back
into GEDCOM for your use.

Genelines

**www.progenysoftware.com/
genelines.html**

Genelines is a utility that creates historical
bar charts from the data contained in your
Personal Ancestral File database, Family
Tree Maker database, or a GEDCOM file. It
produces five types of charts including the
individual geneline, comparative geneline,
Pedigree, direct descendant, and family
group.

JavaGED

www.sc3.net/JavaGEDHome.html

➘

JavaGED converts GEDCOM files into JavaScript and HTML for posting on the Web. It was developed by Chris Shearer Cooper and is available as shareware.

Sparrowhawk

www.bradandkathy.com/genealogy/ sparrowhawk.html

➘

Sparrowhawk is Bradley Mohr's GEDCOM to HTML converter for the Macintosh.

Surname-Related Resources

You're probably wondering how to find sites that pertain to the specific surnames in which you're interested. Wonder no more! Here are some sites that index surname resources with explanations of what each resource has to offer. And if these sites don't pan out for you, we have a couple of other suggestions. First, run a search on the surname that you're researching at a genealogically focused search engine. (See the "Genealogically Focused Search Engines" section earlier in this directory.) Second, take a look back at some comprehensive genealogical sites — some of which are identified, appropriately enough, in the "Comprehensive Sites" section in this directory.

The Guild of One-Name Studies

www.one-name.org

The Guild of One-Name Studies site is literally a guild of groups and online sites that have registered as repositories for information pertaining to particular surnames. The site's Register of One-Name Studies is searchable here. Additionally, you will find general information about the Guild and how to join.

Online Genealogical Database Index

www.gentree.com/gentree.html

The Online Genealogical Database Index provides brief information about and links to genealogical databases on the Web. Most of the databases were created using GEDCOM files that have been converted to HTML. The index itself is organized alphabetically by the main surname of the database and does not include a complete listing of all surnames in the database.

Yourfamily.com

www.yourfamily.com

Among other services, Yourfamily.com provides a free, searchable index of family home pages. By entering the surname you want to search and clicking the Find Your Family button, the search engine produces a list of links to pages that may meet your name specification. You can then look through the list and any accompanying comments about the sites to pick home pages to visit. Additionally, if you have a family home page that you want to register with Yourfamily.com, this is the place to do it.

Part IV
Share and Share Alike

The 5th Wave   By Rich Tennant

"Well, shoot! This eggplant chart is just as confusing as the butternut squash chart and the gourd chart. Can't you make a family chart like everyone else?"

In this part . . .

Discover how to maximize your online research by effectively using as many resources as possible. You may discover the value of sharing your information. This part addresses sharing information with others using reports, GEDCOMs, and Web pages that you create yourself, as well as how to coordinate research efforts. Along the way, you also find out a little history about GEDCOM and the best way to respect others' privacy and copyrights.

Chapter 10

Coordinating Your Attack: Getting Help from Other Researchers

In This Chapter

▶ Finding friends to help you

▶ Joining research groups

▶ Discovering genealogical societies

Y ou can think of genealogical research as a long journey. You may begin the journey by yourself, but before long, you discover that the journey goes a lot faster when someone else is along for the ride. In your genealogical journey, these travel partners may appear in the form of a single individual researching the same family, or a research group searching for several branches of a family in which you're interested, or a genealogical society that coordinates the efforts of several individuals researching different families.

In the next few pages, we explore ways of finding (and keeping) research partners, as well as ways that rescarch groups and genealogical societies can help you meet your research goals.

Putting All Your Eggs in One Basket: Relying Only on Your Research

Don't put all your eggs in one basket — so the old saying goes. A variation of this adage applies to genealogical research — don't try to do all the research yourself. As you'll discover, an awful lot of people out there are researching, and it would be a shame for you not to take advantage of the work that they have done and vice versa.

We can't emphasize enough the benefits of sharing genealogical data. Sharing is the foundation on which the genealogical community is built. For example, when Matthew began researching his genealogy, he went to the National Archives, Library of Congress, and several regional libraries and archives. Along the way, he found a few books that made a passing mention of some of his ancestors and he discovered some original records that helped him put some pieces together. When he shared his information online, he then discovered how many people were working on his surname. During the month following the posting of his Web site, he received messages from 40 other Helm researchers — one of whom lived in Slovenia! Although not all of these researchers were working on Matthew's specific branch (only two of the 40 were directly related), he received valuable information on some of the areas that other researchers were working on. Matthew may never have known that some of these researchers existed had he not taken the first step to share his information.

By knowing what other researchers are pursuing, you can coordinate with them to share not only information you've already collected, but also to work together toward your common goal. Maybe you live closer to a source for court records relating to your ancestor than a distant cousin with whom you're communicating online, but the cousin lives near a family grave site that you'd like to have a photo of. Rather than duplicating efforts to collect the court records and photographs, you can make arrangements for each of you to get the desired items that are closest to you and then exchange copies of them over the Internet or through traditional mail.

The Shotgun Approach

You're probably wondering how to find individuals to share your information with. Well, you could start by going through telephone books and calling everyone with the surname that you're researching. But given how some people feel about telemarketers, we don't recommend this as a strategy.

Similar to this telemarketing strategy is sending mass e-mails to anyone that you find with your surname through one of the online white pages sites. We refer to this mass e-mail strategy as the *shotgun approach*. Although you may find one or two people who answer you in a positive way, a lot of people may find your unsolicited e-mail irritating. Instead of bearing the wrath of hundreds of people, go to a site focusing on genealogy to find the names of researchers who are interested in your surname — this is a much better way to go about finding others with the same interests as you.

Also, please note that we aren't saying that e-mail directories don't have a function in genealogy (see Appendix A for details on how to use an e-mail directory). E-mail directories can be a good place to find an e-mail address that you've lost or an address of a relative who may be interested in your e-mail. You can also use e-mail directories to see the distribution of your surname in the United States and throughout the world (see Figure 10-1).

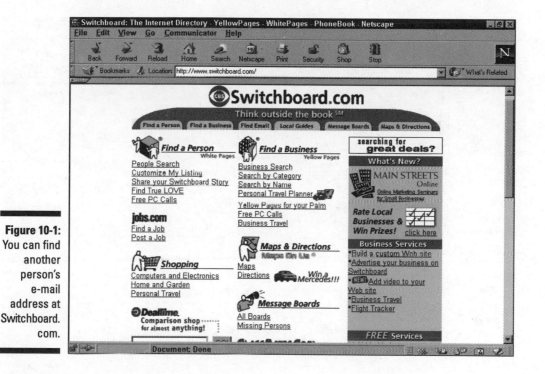

Figure 10-1: You can find another person's e-mail address at Switchboard.com.

Making Friends (And Keeping Them) Online

The best place to begin your search for others doing similar research is the Roots Surname List (see Figure 10-2). The Roots Surname List (`rsl.rootsweb.com/cgi-bin/rslsql.cgi`) is one of the oldest genealogy resources on the Internet and consists of a list of individuals, the surnames that they're researching, and the geographic locations where those surnames are found. (For more info on using the Roots Surname List, see Chapter 3.) Other places to find fellow researchers include query pages on the World Wide Web, newsgroups, and mailing lists (if you need a refresher on using these or other surname resources, you can find more information in Chapter 3 and Appendix A). After you identify some potential online friends, send them e-mail messages introducing yourself and briefly explaining your purpose for contacting them and the ancestors that you're researching.

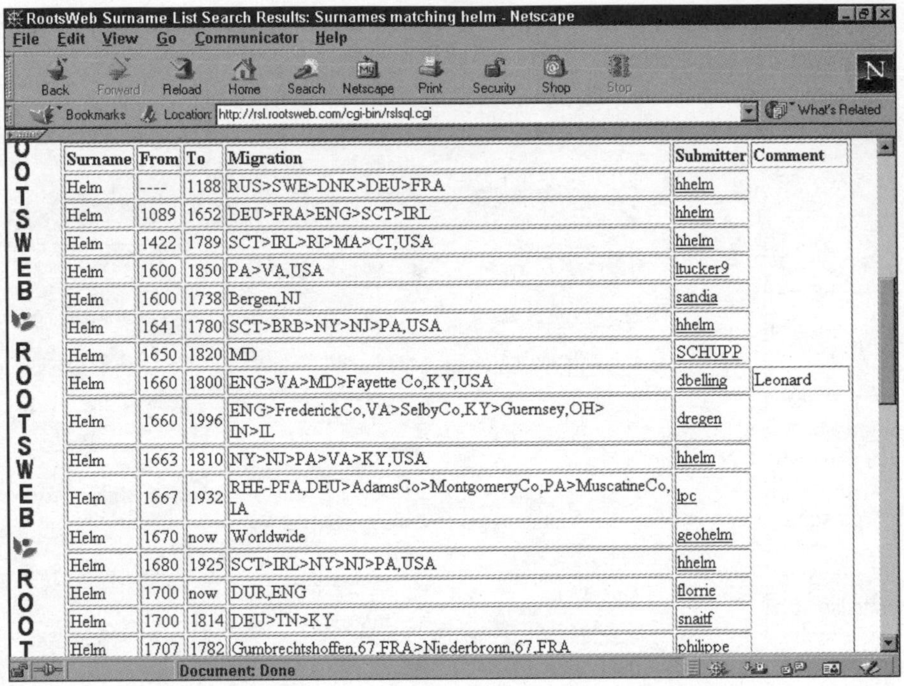

Surname	From	To	Migration	Submitter	Comment
Helm	----	1188	RUS>SWE>DNK>DEU>FRA	hhelm	
Helm	1089	1652	DEU>FRA>ENG>SCT>IRL	hhelm	
Helm	1422	1789	SCT>IRL>RI>MA>CT,USA	hhelm	
Helm	1600	1850	PA>VA,USA	ltucker9	
Helm	1600	1738	Bergen,NJ	sandia	
Helm	1641	1780	SCT>BRB>NY>NJ>PA,USA	hhelm	
Helm	1650	1820	MD	SCHUPP	
Helm	1660	1800	ENG>VA>MD>Fayette Co,KY,USA	dbelling	Leonard
Helm	1660	1996	ENG>FrederickCo,VA>SelbyCo,KY>Guernsey,OH>IN>IL	dregen	
Helm	1663	1810	NY>NJ>PA>VA>KY,USA	hhelm	
Helm	1667	1932	RHE-PFA,DEU>AdamsCo>MontgomeryCo,PA>MuscatineCo,IA	lpc	
Helm	1670	now	Worldwide	geohelm	
Helm	1680	1925	SCT>IRL>NY>NJ>PA,USA	hhelm	
Helm	1700	now	DUR,ENG	florrie	
Helm	1700	1814	DEU>TN>KY	snaitf	
Helm	1707	1782	Gumbrechtshoffen,67,FRA>Niederbronn,67,FRA	philippe	

Figure 10-2: Entries for the surname "Helm" on the Roots Surname List.

Before we send you out to contact people, however, we want to give you a few pieces of advice:

- **When sending messages to a *Web* site maintainer, make sure that the maintainer can use or respond to information on the surname that you're researching:** Sometimes, site maintainers keep information on their sites for other people. If so, they usually have separate contact addresses for those individuals. Other sites may be more general in nature where the site maintainers have information on several surnames that they personally don't research. Usually, these maintainers have notices on their sites stating that they don't entertain research questions.

✔ **Make your messages brief and to the point:** E-mail messages that run five or six pages can overwhelm some people. If the person you send the message to is interested in your information, you can send a more-detailed message at a future date.

✔ **Ensure that your message has enough detail for the recipients to decide whether the information relates to their research:** Include names, dates, and places as appropriate.

✔ **Use net etiquette, or *netiquette,* when you create your messages:** Remember, e-mail can be an impersonal medium. Although you may mean one thing, someone who doesn't know you may mistakenly misinterpret your message. (For more on netiquette, see the "Netiquette: Communicating politely on the Internet" sidebar.)

✔ **Don't disclose personal information that could violate a person's privacy:** Information such as address, birth dates, and Social Security numbers for living persons is considered private and should not be freely shared with other researchers.

✔ **Get permission before forwarding messages from other researchers:** Sometimes a researcher may provide information that they do not want made available to the general public. Asking permission before forwarding a message to a third party eliminates any potential problems with violating the trust of your fellow researchers.

If you need more information on using e-mail, refer to Appendix A.

Netiquette: Communicating politely on the Internet

Part of becoming a member of the online genealogy community is learning to communicate effectively and politely on the Internet. Online communication is often hampered by the fact that you can't see the people with whom you're corresponding — and you can't hear the intonation of their voices to determine what emotions they're expressing. To avoid misunderstandings, follow some simple guidelines — called *netiquette* — when writing messages:

✔ Don't send a message that you wouldn't want posted on a bulletin board at work. You should expect that every e-mail you send is potentially public.

✔ Make sure that you don't violate any copyright laws by sending large portions of written/published works through e-mail. (For more information on copyrights, see Chapter 12.)

✔ If you receive a *flame* (a heated message usually sent to provoke a response), try to ignore it. Usually, no good comes from responding to a flame.

(continued)

(continued)

✔ Be careful when you respond to messages. Instead of replying to an individual, you may be replying to an entire group of people. Checking the To line before you hit the Send button is always a good idea.

✔ Use mixed case when writing e-mail messages. USING ALL UPPERCASE LETTERS INDICATES SHOUTING! The exception to this is when you send a query and place your surnames in all uppercase letters, such as George HELM.

✔ If you participate in a mailing list or newsgroup, and you reply with a message that interests only one person, then consider sending that person a message individually rather than e-mailing the list as a whole.

✔ When joking, use smileys or type **<grins>** or **<g>**. A *smiley* is an *emoticon* that looks like

:-). (Turn the book on its right side if you can't see the face.) *Emoticons* are graphics created by combinations of keys on the keyboard to express an emotion within an e-mail. Here are a few emoticons that you may run into:

:-) Happy, smiling

;-) Wink, ironic

:-> Sarcastic

8-) Wearing glasses

:-(Sad, unhappy

:-< Disappointed

:-o Frightened, surprised

:-() Mustache

Forming Research Groups

If your relatives are tired of hearing about your genealogy research trips or the information that you found on great-uncle William, but you'd like to share your triumphs with someone, then you may be ready to join a research group. *Research groups* consist of any number of people who coordinate their research and share resources to achieve success. These groups may conduct research based on a surname, family branch, or geographic location. Individuals who live geographically close to each other may make up a research group, or the group may consist of people who have never personally met each other. Research groups may have a variety of goals and may have a formal or an informal structure. They are quite flexible organizationally and depend entirely on the membership of the group.

A good example of an informal research group is one that Matthew discovered shortly after he posted his first Web page. An individual who was researching one of his surnames on the East Coast of the United States contacted him. After exchanging a couple of e-mails, Matthew learned that this individual was part of a small research group studying the origins of several different branches of the Helm surname. Each member of the group contributes the results of his or her personal research and provides any information that he or she has found, which may be of use to other members of the group. As a whole, the group has sponsored research by professional genealogists in other countries. Several more researchers have joined the group recently (as more researchers are discovered on the Internet), and everyone communicates regularly through e-mail.

You can find an example of a more formal approach to research groups at the Dawson Family History Project page (`ntfp.globalserve.net/dawson/`). The mission of this group is to become the definitive source for all genealogical and historical information chronicling the Dawson family from the days of William the Conqueror to the present. The site is constructed to help Dawson researchers collaborate with each other and is divided into three principal areas: researchers, reunions and family associations, and library. The reunions and family associations section contains, as you would expect, address and contact information on associations and reunions. The library has a bibliography of works on the surname. Central to the site's mission, however, is the researchers area. Here you can see the members of each of the nine research groups that are arranged geographically. Groups exist for Australia, Canada, Northern Ireland, Scotland, Wales, England, New Zealand, the Republic of Ireland, and the United States. Under each research group, you find the names of researchers (including e-mail addresses); date ranges that they're interested in; provinces, states, or counties of research; and the researchers' Web addresses (see Figure 10-3).

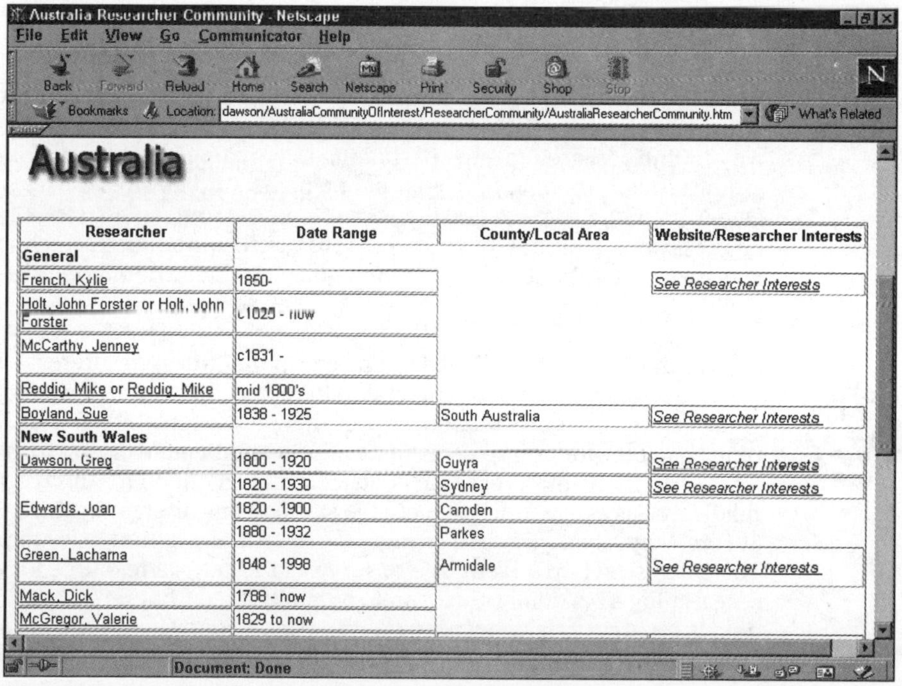
Australia Researcher Community - Netscape
File Edit View Go Communicator Help
Back Forward Reload Home Search Netscape Print Security Shop Stop
Bookmarks Location: dawson/AustraliaCommunityOfInterest/ResearcherCommunity/AustraliaResearcherCommunity.htm
What's Related
Australia
Researcher | Date Range | County/Local Area | Website/Researcher Interests
General
French, Kylie | 1850- | | See Researcher Interests
Holt, John Forster or Holt, John Forster | c1820 - now
McCarthy, Jenney | c1831 -
Reddig, Mike or Reddig, Mike | mid 1800's
Boyland, Sue | 1838 - 1925 | South Australia | See Researcher Interests
New South Wales
Dawson, Greg | 1800 - 1920 | Guyra | See Researcher Interests
Edwards, Joan | 1820 - 1930 | Sydney | See Researcher Interests
1820 - 1900 | Camden
1880 - 1932 | Parkes
Green, Lacharna | 1848 - 1998 | Armidale | See Researcher Interests
Mack, Dick | 1788 - now
McGregor, Valerie | 1829 to now
Document: Done

Figure 10-3: A list of the Australian research group at the Dawson Family History Project site.

To find research groups, your best bet is to visit a comprehensive genealogical Web site or a site that specializes in surnames, such as SurnameWeb (www.surnameweb.com). The following steps show you how to find groups pertaining to a surname on the site:

1. **Launch your Web browser and go to the SurnameWeb site** (www.surnameweb.com).

   After the page loads, you see a column on the left with letters of the alphabet at the top.

2. **Choose the letter of the alphabet that's the first letter of the surname that you're researching.**

   For example, say the surname that you're researching begins with the letter *P*. Find the link to the letter *P* and click it. This action brings up a Web page with the *P* Index.

3. **Click a link for the appropriate first three letters of the name that you're researching.**

   We want to find sites relating to the surname *Pollard,* so we choose the Pol link. This action loads a page with the Pol Index, which has a list of links of surnames beginning with *Pol* that have entries on the site.

4. **Select a surname from the list of surname links.**

   We click the link for the Pollard surname, which presents us with links to various surname-based resources about that surname.

In addition to using comprehensive genealogy sites and specialized surname sites, you can use other strategies to identify possible research groups. One way to find research groups pertaining to surnames is to visit a one-name studies index. You can find a list of one-name studies sites at the Guild of One-Name Studies page (www.one-name.org). You can also look to existing larger groups that may have specific research components, such as genealogical societies. (The following section goes into more detail on genealogical societies.)

If you can't find an established online group that fits your interests, why not start one yourself? If you're interested in researching a particular topic, the chances are very good that others out there are interested as well. Maybe the time has come for you to coordinate efforts and begin working with others toward your common research goals. Starting an online research group can be relatively easy — just post a message stating your interest in starting a group at some key locations, such as message boards, newsgroups, or mailing lists. You can also set up a Web page to serve as the central resource for anyone researching a particular topic, area, or family. (See Chapters 12 and 14 for details on how to design your own Web page.) Soon (hopefully!) others will come to visit your site, and you can begin to coordinate your efforts with them.

Becoming a Solid Member of (Genealogical) Society

Genealogical societies can be great places to learn research methods and to coordinate your research. Several different types of societies exist. They range from the more traditional geographical or surname-based societies to new *cyber-societies* (societies that exist only on the Internet) that are redefining the way that people think about genealogical societies.

Geographical societies

Chapter 4 introduces geographical-based *genealogical societies* as groups that can help you discover resources in a particular area in which your ancestors lived or as groups in your hometown that can help you discover how to research effectively. However, local genealogical societies can provide another service to their members. These societies often coordinate local research efforts of the members in the form of projects. To locate geographical societies, consult a comprehensive genealogy site (see The *Genealogy Online For Dummies* Internet Directory) or the site of a genealogical society federation like the Federation of Genealogical Societies Society Hall (www.familyhistory.com/societyhall/), Federation of Family History Societies (www.ffhs.org.uk), and the Federation of East European Family History Societies (www.feefhs.org).

These projects can take many forms. For example, the Illinois State Genealogical Society (www.tbox.com/isgs) is working on several projects, including creating a database of county marriage records, updating a list of Illinois pioneers, and forming a list of all cemeteries in the state (see Figure 10-4).

Smaller groups of members sometimes work on projects in addition to the official society's projects. For example, you may belong to a county genealogical society and decide to join with a few members to write a history on the pioneers of a particular township within the county. If each member of the team shares the fruits of his or her research, you can cover three or four times more ground than you can by yourself.

Illinois State Genealogical Society - Projects - Macon County Cemeteries - Netscape

File   Edit   View   Go   Communicator   Help

Back   Forward   Reload   Home   Search   Netscape   Print   Security   Shop   Stop

Bookmarks   Netsite: http://www.tbox.com/isgs/ilcemetery-mz/macon.html   What's Related

ILLINOIS STATE GENEALOGICAL SOCIETY

CEMETERY LOCATION PROJECT

C=Church R=Reading V=Illinois Veterans SEC=Section TWP=Township

R=Range Mer=Meridan Stat=Status["AC=Active IN=Inactive DE=Despoiled"]

Macon County (22K)

NAME	ALIAS	C	R	V	QTRQTR	QTRSECT	SEC	TWP	R	MER	STAT	TOWNSH
Abrams	Abrams			Y	*	NE	19	16N	01E	3	IN	Blue Mound
Bethel		C		Y	*	NW	28	15N	01E	3	AC	Pleasant View
Blue Mound	Brown			Y	*	NW	34	16N	01E	3	AC	Blue Mound
Boiling Springs		C		Y	*	NE	32	17N	02E	3	AC	Hickory Poin
Brick	Garver	C		Y	*	NW	28	17N	03E	3	AC	Whitmore
Brown	Blue Mound			Y	*	NW	34	16N	01E	3	AC	Blue Mound
Brown				Y		NW	24	18N	03E	3	IN	Friends Cree
Brush College	Wyckles			Y	*	SE	07	16N	03E	3	AC	Decatur
Calvary	Catholic	C		Y	*	NE	16	16N	02E	3	AC	Decatur
Catholic	Calvary	C		Y	*	NE	16	16N	02E	3	AC	Decatur
Center Ridge	Wrights Grove/Ridge			Y	*	SW	06	18N	02E	3	AC	Maroa

Document: Done

Figure 10-4:
The Illinois State Genealogical Society Cemetery Location Project.

Family and surname associations

GENEALOGY LINGO

Family associations also frequently sponsor projects that coordinate the efforts of several researchers. These projects may focus on the family or surname in a specific geographic area or point in time, or they may attempt to collect information about every individual possessing the surname throughout time and then place the information in a shared database.

You can find family and surname associations through comprehensive genealogy sites (listed in The *Genealogy Online For Dummies* Internet Directory), general Internet search engines (also listed in this book's directory section), or sites specializing in associations.

If a family or surname association isn't currently working on a project that interests you, by all means suggest a project that does interest you (as long as the project is relevant to the association as a whole).

Chapter 11

Sharing Your Wealth Online

• •

In This Chapter

▶ Marketing your research

▶ Storing your information online

▶ Exporting your work from your genealogical database

▶ Citing electronic resources

• •

After you hit a certain point in your research, you may want to find ways to share the valuable information that you discovered — after all, sharing information is one of the foundations of the genealogical community. When you share information, you often get a lot of information in return from other researchers. For example, shortly after we began the Helm/Helms Family Research Web page, several other Helm researchers throughout the world contacted us. We discovered that several Helm lines existed that we didn't even know about. Plus, we received valuable information on our own line from references that other researchers discovered during their research.

In this chapter, we focus on methods that you can use to share information (except for placing your information on the World Wide Web, which we cover in Chapter 12) and ways to let other researchers know that you have information to share.

Why Would Anyone Want Your Stuff?

"Why would anyone want my stuff?" seems like a logical first question when you stop and think about making the many tidbits and treasures that you collected available to others. Who would want a copy of that old, ratty-looking photograph you have of great-great-grandma as a girl sitting in a pile of dirt on an Illinois farm? Nobody else wanted it in the first place, and that's probably how you ended up with it, right? The picture has sentimental value only to you. Wrong! Some of great-great-grandma's other descendants may be looking for information about her. They, too, would love to see a picture of her when she was a little girl — even better, they'd love to have their own electronic copy of that picture!

As you develop more and more online contact with other genealogists, you may find a lot of people who are interested in exchanging information. Some may be interested in your research findings because you share common ancestors, and others may be interested because they're researching in the same geographical area where your ancestors were from. Aren't these the reasons that you're interested in seeing other researchers' stuff? Sharing your information is likely to encourage others to share theirs with you. Exchanging information with others may enable you to fill in some gaps in your own research efforts. Even if the research findings that you receive from others don't directly answer questions about your ancestors, they may give you clues about where to find more information to fill in the blanks.

Also, just because you haven't traced your genealogy back to the Middle Ages doesn't mean that your information isn't valuable. Although you need to be careful about sharing information on living persons, you should feel free to share any facts that you do know about deceased ancestors. Just as you may not know your genealogy any further than your great-grandfather, someone else may be in the same boat — and with the same person! Meeting up with that fellow researcher can lead to a mutual research relationship that can produce a lot more information in a shorter amount of time.

Spreading the Word on What You Have

So you're at the point where you recognize the value in sharing your genealogical information online. If you're not, reread the preceding section! How do you begin to let people know what you have? Well, the first thing to do is to come up with a marketing plan for your information — much like a business does when it decides to sell a product.

Masterminding a surname marketing plan

A *surname marketing plan* is simply a checklist of places and people to contact to effectively inform the right individuals about the information that you have to contribute to the genealogy community. As you devise your plan, ask yourself the following questions:

- ✔ **What surname sites are interested in my information?** To find surname sites, see Chapter 3.

- ✔ **What geographical sites are interested in my information?** For geographical sites, see Chapter 4.

- ✔ **What association sites (both family and geographical) are interested in my information?** See Chapters 3 and 4 for association sites.

> ✓ **What general sites (such as query sites and GEDCOM collections) are interested in my information?** See Chapters 3 and 4 for some examples of these sites.

You may want to use all available Internet resources to let people know about your information, including mailing lists, newsgroups, and Web sites.

For example, April has information on a McSwain family. She knows that they lived in Madison, Estill, Jessamine, and Nicholas counties in Kentucky. To identify sites where she may be able to post this information, she looked for one-name study pages on the surname McSwain, personal pages that have connections to the McSwain family, and any mailing lists dedicated to discussing the family. She also tried to find sites for each of the four counties in Kentucky that the McSwains resided in. Then she searched for family societies or county genealogical or historical societies in Kentucky that look for information on their past inhabitants. Finally, she looked for general query sites and GEDCOM repositories that may accept her information.

Contacting your target audience

After you write down the names and addresses of sites that probably attract an audience that you want to target, you need to notify them. Create a brief but detailed e-mail message to make your announcement. When you submit your message, look at the format required by each resource that you're contacting. For example, the soc.genealogy.surnames newsgroups have a specific format for subject lines (for examples, see Chapter 3). Some *query sites* (places where you can post genealogical questions to get help from other researchers) also have specific formats, so you may need to modify your message for each of these sites. (For more information about query sites and posting queries, see Chapter 3.)

Here's a sample message to give you some ideas:

```
MCSWAIN, 1810-1910, KY, USA
I have information on the family of William McSwain of
Kentucky. William was born in 1802, married Elizabeth Hisle
in March 1827, and had the following children:
Thomas, Mary, Joseph, Sarah, Susan, Margaret, Elizabeth,
Nancy, and James.
```

Most people understand that you're willing to share information on the family if you post something to a site, so you probably don't need to say that within your message. Remember, people are more likely to read your message if it has a short, descriptive subject line, is short and to the point, and contains enough information for the readers to determine whether your information can help them (or whether they have information that can assist you).

Exporting Your Information

Suppose you contact others who are interested in your information. What's the best way to share your information with them? Certainly, you can type everything up, print it, and send it to them. Or you can export a copy of your genealogy database file that the recipients can then import into their databases and then run as many reports as they want — and save a few trees in the process.

GEDCOM files

Most genealogical databases subscribe to a common standard for exporting their information called *Genealogical Data Communication,* or GEDCOM. (Beware that some genealogical databases deviate from the standard a little — making things somewhat confusing.) A GEDCOM file is a text file that contains your genealogical information with a set of tags that tells the genealogical database importing the information where to place it within its structure. For a little history and more information about GEDCOM, see Chapter 8. Figure 11-1 shows an example of a GEDCOM file.

```
Helm1.ged - WordPad
File  Edit  View  Insert  Format  Help

0 @I09040 INDI
1 NAME Samuel Clayton /Abell/, Jr.
1 SEX M
1 BIRT
2 DATE 16 Mar 1844
2 PLAC Cedar Creek, Nelson Co., KY
1 DEAT
2 DATE 27 Jul 1923
2 PLAC Wapella, Dewitt Co., IL
1 CHR
2 DATE 1850
2 PLAC Census - Larue Co., KY
1 BURI
2 DATE 1860
2 PLAC Census - Larue Co., KY (listed as Clayton)
1 BAPM
2 DATE 1870
2 PLAC Census - Larue Co., KY
1 CONF
2 DATE 1880
2 PLAC Census - Larue Co., KY
1 FAMS @F03970
1 FAMS @F02910
1 FAMC @F02920
1 NOTE Records of Samuel's Civil War Service contained in the Compiled Service
2 CONT Records of Volunteer Union Soldiers Who Servied in Organizations from
2 CONT Kentucky.  Samuel enlisted as a private in Co. F, 37th Kentucky Infantry
2 CONT at 16 years of age on August 3, 1863 (not consisted with birth date).
2 CONT Recorded as present for duty on October 31, 1863; November and December
2 CONT 1863; Januaryand February 1864; March and April 1864; May and June 1864;
2 CONT and July and August 1864.  Mustered out as a corporal on December 29,
2 CONT 1864 in Louisville, KY.  One author mentioned that Samuel's grandfather
For Help, press F1                                                    NUM
```

Figure 11-1: A typical GEDCOM file displayed in WordPad.

So why is GEDCOM important? It saves you a lot of time and energy in the process of sharing information. The next time someone asks you to send them some information, you can export your genealogy data into a GEDCOM file and send it to them instead of typing it up or saving your entire database.

Making a GEDCOM file using Family Tree Maker, a program on the CD-ROM that accompanies this book, is easy. (For installation instructions, see Appendix C.) To export information from Family Tree Maker to GEDCOM, try this:

1. **Open Family Tree Maker.**

   Usually, you can open your software by double-clicking the icon for that program or by going to the Programs menu from the Start button (in Windows 95 or 98) and selecting the particular program.

2. **Use the default database that appears, or choose File⇨Open Family File to open another database.**

3. **After you open the database for which you want to create a GEDCOM file, choose File⇨Copy/Export Family File.**

   The New Family File dialog box appears. This dialog box enables you to enter a name for the file and choose the format to save the file in (GEDCOM).

4. **Type the new name for your GEDCOM file in the File Name field, move your cursor to the Save as Type field and select GEDCOM (*.GED) as the format, and then click Save.**

   The Export to GEDCOM dialog box appears, as shown in Figure 11-2. This dialog box enables you to set up the GEDCOM file in a specific format.

5. **In the Destination field, choose the destination software program to which you want to export the file.**

   If you don't know which program the other person with whom you're sharing the GEDCOM uses, leave the setting on its default of Family Tree Maker.

6. **In the GEDCOM field, choose the version of GEDCOM to which you're exporting.**

   Most genealogical software is compatible with the most recent version of GEDCOM, so you're usually safe to keep the default setting. If you know that the person to whom you're sending your GEDCOM uses older software that supports an older version of GEDCOM, you can change the output settings to accommodate that person.

7. **In the Character Set field, choose ANSI (which is the default).**

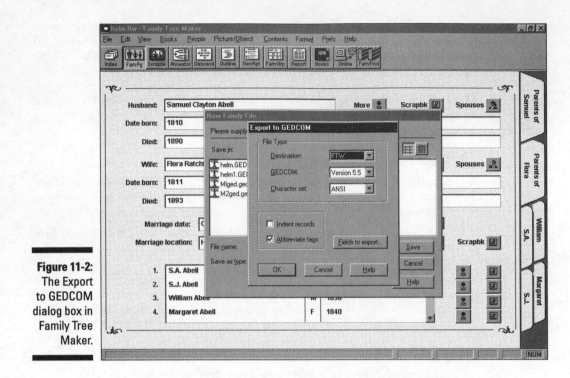

Figure 11-2:
The Export
to GEDCOM
dialog box in
Family Tree
Maker.

8. **If you have a preference for how the GEDCOM output is formatted, check or uncheck the Indent Records and Abbreviate Tags check boxes.**

   You can choose to have the records indented on your GEDCOM output instead of having all the coded lines in a straight list, flushed left in the file (refer to Figure 11-1 for an example of the flush-left GEDCOM). Indenting the records makes reading through the GEDCOM a little easier when you open it in a word processor. Family Tree Maker indents lines based on the number code for the line. For example, all 1s are flush left, 2s are indented once, and 3s are indented twice.

   Likewise, you can have the GEDCOM tags abbreviated rather than written in their entirety. For example, the tag *Header* would be *Head* and *Address* would be *Addr*.

9. **Click the Fields to Export button to select which fields to export to your GEDCOM output file, if you want to export only selected fields.**

   The default settings don't include all the fields of information that are possible in a GEDCOM, so tell the software to include particular fields or all fields if you want to include certain notes or other information.

10. **After you complete all the required boxes and are satisfied with the options that you selected, click OK.**

    When you click OK, a bar appears across the screen showing the progress of the export, with the message "Exporting Individuals" listed above it.

XML: GEDCOM's successor?

Although GEDCOM was originally designed to help researchers exchange information with each other while using various genealogical software, it isn't necessarily the best way to present information on the World Wide Web. Currently, an effort is underway to create a better way to display and identify genealogical information on the Web. Eventually, this could become the successor to GEDCOM.

One of the possible successors to GEDCOM is *eXtensible Markup Language*, more commonly recognized by the acronym, *XML*. XML is similar to HyperText Markup Language (HTML) in that it uses tags to describe information. However,

the purpose of XML is different than HTML. HTML was designed to tell a Web browser, such as Netscape or Internet Explorer, how to arrange text and graphics on a page. XML is designed not only to display information, but also to describe the information.

An early version of XML for the genealogical community was *GedML* constructed by Michael Kay. GedML uses XML tags to describe genealogical data on the Web, much like GEDCOM does for genealogical software. Here's an example of information provided in a GEDCOM file and its GedML equivalent:

GEDCOM:

```
0 @I0904@ INDI
1 NAME Samuel Clayton /ABELL/
1 SEX M
1 BIRT
2 DATE 16 Mar 1844
2 PLAC Nelson County, KY
1 FAMS @F0397@
```

GedML:

```
<INDI ID="I0904">
<NAME> Samuel Clayton
    <S>ABELL</S></NAME>
<SEX>M</SEX>
<EVEN EV='BIRT'>
<DATE>16 Mar 1844</DATE>
<PLAC> Nelson County, KY</PLAC>
    </EVEN>
<FAMS REF="F397"/>
</INDI>
```

XML, whether it's GedML or some other XML structure, promises an enhancement of the searchability of genealogical documents on the Web. Right now, it's difficult for genealogically focused search engines to identify what's genealogical in nature and what's not (for more on genealogically focused search engines, see Chapter 3). Also, tags allow search engines to determine whether a particular data element is a name or a place.

XML also provides an efficient way to link genealogical data between Web sites, gives

users more control over how particular text is displayed (such as notes), and allows genealogists to place information directly on the Web without using a program to convert databases or GEDCOM files to HTML.

For more information on GedML, see `users.iclway.co.uk/mhkay/gedml`. For more on the genealogical community's efforts to find a successor to GEDCOM, see the Technology Committee reports of GENTECH at `www.gentech.org`.

After the GEDCOM file's created on your hard drive, you can open it in a word processor (such as WordPad) and review it to ensure that the information is formatted the way you want it. Also, reviewing the file in a word processor is a good idea so you can ensure that you included no information on living persons. After you're satisfied with the file, you can cut and paste it into an e-mail message or send it as an attachment using your e-mail program.

Reports

GEDCOM is a great option when two individuals have genealogical software that supports the standard. But what about all the people who are new to genealogy and haven't invested in software yet? How do you send them information that they can use? One option is to generate reports through your genealogical software and export them into your word processor, and then print copies to mail or attach copies to e-mail messages.

Chapter 9 gives step-by-step instructions for entering all your detailed family information into Family Tree Maker (a basic version of this genealogical software is included on the CD-ROM accompanying this book). The process for exporting a report should be similar for most genealogical software. The following steps show you specifically how to export a report from Family Tree Maker to a word processor:

1. **Open Family Tree Maker.**

   Usually, you can open your software by double-clicking the icon for that program or by going to the Programs menu from the Start button (in Windows 95 and 98) and selecting the particular program.

   Note: If you aren't sure how to open your word processor, consult the user's manual that came with the software.

2. **Choose View⇨Index of Individuals.**

   This action brings up a box that lists all the individuals entered in your database in alphabetical order.

3. **Scroll through the index and select the person for whom you want to generate a chart/report by double-clicking the name or highlighting the name and clicking OK.**

   This action takes you to the Family Page for the person that you select.

   For example, if Matthew wants to generate a report for his ancestor Samuel Abell IV, he highlights Samuel's name in the index and clicks OK.

4. **Place your cursor in the person's name field.**

   Move your cursor into the Husband, Wife, or Children field to select the exact person that you want to generate a chart/report on.

   Likewise, Matthew moves the cursor into the name field for Samuel Abell IV.

5. **Click the appropriate button for the chart/report that you want (in the button bar at the top of the Family Tree Maker screen), or choose View⇨[Type of tree or report].**

   Buttons in the button bar correspond to Ancestor Tree, Descendant Tree, Outline Descendant Tree, and Family Group Sheet. Or, if you're using the drop-down menu, the charts/reports appear as Ancestor Tree, Descendant Tree, Outline Descendant Tree, Kinship Report, and Family Group Sheet. (You can generate other reports using Family Tree Maker, but these are the most common types and the five that we discuss in this chapter.)

   Family Tree Maker generates the requested chart/report for the person that you select.

   For our example, if Matthew wants to generate an outline of Samuel Abell's descendants, he clicks the Outline button or uses the View menu to choose an Outline Descendant Tree. Family Tree Maker then generates an Outline chart on-screen.

6. **Choose Edit⇨Copy Outline Descendant Tree.**

   This places a copy of the report on the Windows clipboard, which enables you to paste it into any Windows application that supports cutting and pasting information.

   Matthew copies the Outline Descendant Tree to the clipboard.

7. **Open WordPad (or any other word processor), and choose Edit⇨ Paste.**

   This action places the Outline Descendant report into your word processor. You can now edit the report just as if you had typed the report into the program itself (see Figure 11-3).

   After he pastes the Samuel Abell Outline chart into WordPad, Matthew can review and edit it to ensure that it has all the information that he wants to include when sharing it with others. He can also double-check the chart to ensure that it doesn't include any information on living persons.

When your Outline report is in a word-processing file, you can activate your favorite e-mail program and send the file to the individual who requested information. If the report is long, you can include it with your e-mail as an attachment. If the report is short, you can simply cut and paste it into the text of your e-mail message.

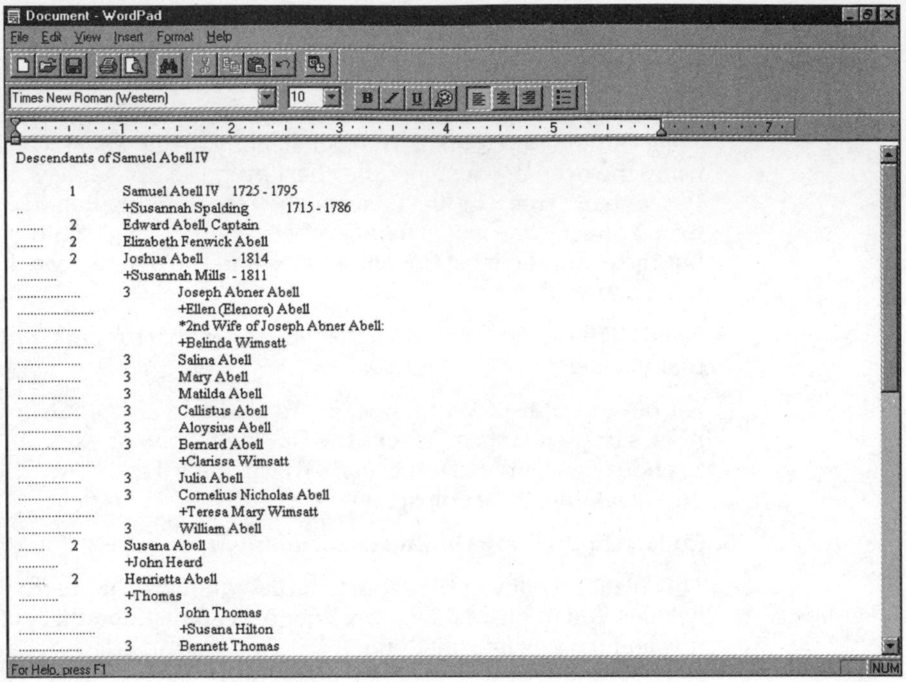

Figure 11-3: A Family Tree Maker Outline Descendant Tree inserted into WordPad.

If You Post It, They Will Come

Instead of sending information to several different individuals, consider placing your information at a site where people can access it at their convenience. One option is to post your information on a Web site (see Chapter 12 for more information). But you have some other options if you're not ready to take the Web-designing plunge.

One option is to find others who are working on the same surnames or geographical areas and who already have Web pages, and ask them to post your information on their sites. Don't be offended if they decline — most Internet accounts have specific storage limits, and they may not have room for your information.

A second option is to submit your information to a general site that collects GEDCOM files. Examples of these sites include:

✔ **Ancestry World Tree:** www.ancestry.com/share/awt/main.htm

✔ **GenServ:** www.genserv.com

✔ **My-GED.com:** www.my-ged.com

✔ **WorldConnect:** worldconnect.rootsweb.com

If you use one of the genealogical programs produced by larger software companies, then you have a third option, which is really a variation of the first option (creating a Web page): You can submit reports directly to the Internet by taking advantage of space offered by the software company. Versions 3.4 and later of Family Tree Maker offer this option and allow you to submit reports directly to its Web site for users of the software at no charge (see Figure 11-4).

The basic edition of Family Tree Maker that appears on this book's CD-ROM offers the capability to upload reports from the software to Family Tree Maker's Web site. To do so, go to the Family Page for the person for whom you want to share a family tree and place the cursor in the appropriate name field. Then select Internet⇨Publish Family Tree to Internet, and follow the instructions in the resulting dialog boxes. As you complete the steps to upload your family tree to the Family Tree Maker Web site, you are asked if you'd like to contribute your information to the World Family Tree. The World Family Tree is a collection of individuals' Family Tree Maker files that is periodically produced for sale on CD-ROM. For more information about the World Family Tree, we recommend you visit Genealogy.com's Web site (www.genealogy.com).

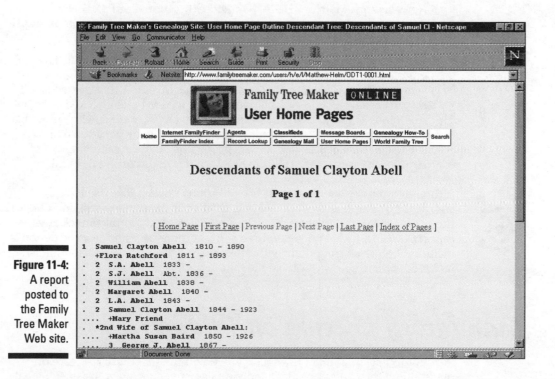

Figure 11-4:
A report posted to the Family Tree Maker Web site.

Citing Your Sources

We can't stress enough the importance of citing your sources when sharing information — online or through traditional means. Including references that reflect where you obtained your information is just as important when you share information as it is when you research the information. Not only does referencing provide the other person with leads to possible additional information, but it also provides you a place to return and double-check your facts if someone challenges the information. Sometimes, after exchanging information with another researcher, you both notice that you have conflicting information about a particular ancestor. Knowing where to turn to double-check the facts and hopefully find out whose information is correct can save you time and embarrassment.

Here are some examples of ways to cite online sources of information:

- **E-mail messages:** Matthew Helm, [<mhelm@tbox.com> or P.O. Box 76, Savoy, Illinois 61874]. "Looking for George Helm," Message to April Helm, 12 January 2001. [Message cites vital records in Helm's possession.]

- **Newsgroups:** Matthew Helm, [<mhelm@tbox.com> or P.O. Box 76, Savoy, Illinois 61874]. "Computing in Genealogy" in soc.genealogy.computing, 12 January 2001.

- **Web sites:** Matthew Helm, [<mhelm@tbox.com> or P.O. Box 76, Savoy, Illinois 61874]. "Helm's Genealogy Toolbox."<genealogy.tbox.com> January 2001. [This site contains numerous links to other genealogical resources on the Internet. On January 12, located and checked links on Abell family, found two that were promising.] (Of course, with a note like the preceding one in brackets, you expect that your next two citations are the two Web sites that looked promising, and for each site you should provide notes stating exactly what you did or did not find.)

Although most genealogical software programs now enable you to store source information and citations along with your data, many still don't export the source information automatically. For that reason, double-check any reports or GEDCOMs you generate to see whether your source information is included before sharing them with other researchers. If the information isn't included, create a new GEDCOM file that includes sources.

Mandatory Lecture on Privacy

We couldn't sleep at night if we didn't give you the mandatory lecture on maintaining the privacy of living individuals when sharing your genealogical information.

In the rush to get genealogical information posted on the Internet, people sometimes forget that portions of the information in their databases, and thus in their GEDCOM files, are considered private. We've heard horror stories about Social Security numbers of living individuals ending up in GEDCOM files that are available on the Internet. We've also heard of people who didn't know that their biological parents weren't married (to each other, anyway) and found out through an online database, and so forth. Private detectives and other people who search for information on living persons frequently use genealogical databases to track people. For these reasons, some states and countries have made it illegal to share information about living persons on the Internet without first getting each person's permission to do so. To avoid an invasion of privacy and any legal problems that could arise from you sharing your information, you should always clean out (exclude) any information on living individuals from your GEDCOM file before you give it to anyone.

More and more genealogists are now aware of the privacy implications of online genealogy. As a result, some have designed programs to clean out information on living individuals from GEDCOM files. One such piece of freeware, GEDClean, is available on the CD-ROM that accompanies this book, as well as from www.raynorshyn.com/gedclean/Compare.html. Even if you use software to clean a file, make sure that you double-check the data in the file to ensure that the software catches everything and that you don't share any information on living people.

Chapter 12

From Your Computer to the World

So you've loaded your genealogical database with information about your relatives and ancestors, and you've shared data with others by e-mail. Now you're ready to create and post your own Web site. In this chapter, we explore where you can post a simple site and how to do so. This chapter gives you the basics on creating a Web site.

If you're looking for more detailed information about creating a full-blown and fancy Web site, or about beginning and advanced HTML programming, then you're looking in the wrong place. Genealogy is the focus of this book — not Web-site creation or HTML programming. This chapter covers the very basics to get you started. For more information about HTML, we recommend that you check out these other ...*For Dummies* books (all published by IDG Books Worldwide, Inc.): *Creating Web Pages For Dummies*, 5th Edition, by Bud Smith and Arthur Bebak; *The Internet For Dummies*, 7th Edition, by John R. Levine, Carol Baroudi, and Margaret Levine Young; and *HTML 4 For Dummies*, by Ed Tittel and Stephen Nelson James.

Home Sweet Home

Before you can build your home page, you need to find a home (or a host, if you prefer) for it. Although you can design your home page on your own computer using a word processor, others won't be able to see it until you put the page on a Web server on the Internet. A *Web server* is a computer that's connected directly to the Internet that serves up Web pages when you request them using your computer's Web browser.

Commercial Internet service providers

If you subscribe to a commercial Internet service provider (ISP) like America Online, AT&T WorldNet, or WebTV, or if you subscribe to a local provider, then you may already have a home for your Web pages — whether you realize it or not. Most commercial ISPs include in their memberships a specific space allocation for user home pages, as well as some tools to help you build your site. Check your membership agreement to see whether you have space, and follow the ISP's instructions for creating your Web site using the service's page builder or editor, or for getting your Web pages after you create them independently from your computer to the ISP's server. (If you didn't keep a copy of your membership agreement, don't fret! Most ISPs have an informational Web page that you can get to from your ISP's main page; the informational page reviews membership benefits.) You may as well take advantage of this service if you're already paying for it.

If your particular membership level doesn't include Web space, but the ISP has other membership levels that do, then hold off on bumping up your membership level. You can take advantage of some free Web-hosting services that may save you money. Keep reading . . .

Free Web-hosting services

Several Web sites give you free space for your home page provided that you agree to their rules and restrictions. We can safely bet that you won't have any problems using one of these freebies, because the terms (such as no pornography, nudity, or explicit language allowed) are genealogist-friendly. Using that picture of Uncle Bob in his birthday suit on New Year's Eve would be in poor taste, anyway.

If you go the free Web space route, remember that the companies that provide the space must pay their bills. Often, they are able to make space available free to individuals by charging advertisers for banners and other advertisements. In such cases, the Web hosts reserve the right to require that you leave these advertisements right there on your home page. If you don't like the idea of an advertisement on your home page, or if you have strong objections to one of the companies that advertises with the site that gives you free space, then you should find a fee-based Web space for your home page.

For a list of places where you can get a free Web page, check out Yahoo! Free Web Pages (`dir.yahoo.com/Business_and_Economy/Business_to_ Business/Communications_and_Networking/Internet_and_World_Wide_ Web/Network_Service_Providers/Hosting/Web_Site_Hosting/Free_ Web_Pages/`). We don't have enough room in this book to provide information about each of the companies or services listed at Yahoo!'s site (after all, this is a book about genealogy — not Web pages), so we focus on a couple of services that have been around for awhile.

Tripod

```
www.tripod.lycos.com
```

Tripod provides 50MB of free space for your Web pages and 25MB of storage space for other files, as well as access to tools to help you build your Web pages. You also get chat-room access, an online guest book for your page, and a free e-mail account.

To join Tripod, click the Sign Up Now for 50 MB of Free Space! link and complete the online form. Lycos (Tripod's parent company) and Tripod ask you to provide a member name and password, as well as your name, e-mail address, birth date, zip code, and the country in which you live. Click the Sign Me Up! button. A secondary registration page appears, and Tripod asks you to verify your e-mail address and offers you some newsletters, affiliate participation (which allows you to earn money with your Web site by selling items from Tripod affiliates), participation in a banner exchange program, and file-sharing. After you complete the second registration page, click the Complete Sign-Up button.

After you submit the registration form, Tripod takes you to the Get Started Here page, where you can begin to build your Web site using various tools.

Yahoo! GeoCities

```
http://edit.yahoo.com/config/login?.src=geo&.done=http%3a//
            geocities.yahoo.com/join/freehp.html
```

GeoCities provides 15MB of free space, a free e-mail account, wizards to help you build your Web pages, and a file manager. You can choose to participate in a banner advertisement exchange or an affiliate program that enables you to earn money using your Web site. If you're a new user to Yahoo! GeoCities, click the Sign Me Up! link and complete the resulting form. You're asked to provide an ID or member name and password, as well as your birth date, e-mail address, country of residence, zip code, gender, and occupation and industry. You also have the opportunity to sign up for mailings. After you complete the form, click the Submit This Form button. Yahoo! GeoCities gives you a confirmation Web page where you can click the Continue to Yahoo! GeoCities link. This Web page shows you how to create your site using the available tools.

User pages from software companies

Some software companies offer free Web sites to customers who use their products. A few of the genealogical software manufacturers allow software users to upload Web pages created with the software directly to their servers. One example is Family Tree Maker. If you use Family Tree Maker (versions 3.4 or greater for Windows, or 3.02 for Macintosh), you can create a user home page with the software and upload it to the Family Tree Maker site. Chapter 11 briefly covers uploading your family tree to the Family Tree Maker Web site. If you use a different program, we recommend that you check the user's manual that comes with your software for more information about creating and posting Web pages using your genealogical software.

Do You Speak HTML?

Hypertext Markup Language (or HTML) is the language of the World Wide Web. HTML is a code in which text documents are written so that Web browsers can read and interpret those documents, converting them into graphical images and text that you can see through the browser. HTML is a relatively easy language to learn, and many genealogists who post Web pages are self-taught. If you prefer not to read about it and teach yourself by experimenting, however, classes and some other resources are available to teach you HTML and code documents. Check with a local community college for structured classes, local genealogical societies for any workshops focusing on designing and posting Web pages, or the World Wide Web itself for online courses. Chapter 14 provides you with a few sites that you can use to find online courses and other tools to help you build your Web site.

For more information about the World Wide Web and Web browsers, take a look at Appendix A.

Here are a couple of things to remember about HTML:

- ✔ You write HTML as a text document using a text editor, an HTML editor, or a word processor, and you save it as a text document (with the file-name extension of `htm` or `html`).
- ✔ You use a Web browser to interpret HTML documents as graphical and text pages on the Internet.

What does HTML look like?

To get an idea of what HTML looks like — both as the text document and as the converted graphical image — take a look at some extremely simple HTML tags that April created for a Web page called Leapin' Lizard's Genealogy Page. Figure 12-1 shows the Web page that's created by the tags.

Here's what the HTML codes (also called tags) look like:

```
<HTML>

<HEAD>
<TITLE>Leapin' Lizard's Genealogy Page</TITLE>
</HEAD>
<BODY BGCOLOR = "White" ALINK = "Blue" VLINK = "Gray">
<H1><FONT COLOR = "Green"><CENTER>Leapin' Lizard's Genealogy
        Page</CENTER></FONT></H1>
Welcome to Leapin' Lizard's Genealogy Page. I'm so glad you
        stopped by.<P>
I've been researching my family history for almost a year.
        These are the surnames I'm looking for information
        about:
<UL>
<LI>Reptilius
<LI>Watermonger
<LI>Swampman
</UL><P>
I love my Genealogy Online For Dummies book and I'm a big fan
        of the entire
<A HREF = "http://www.dummies.com">...For Dummies</A> series
        of books by IDG Books.
</BODY>
</HTML>
```

The tags are placed within angle brackets, like this: <BODY>. These tags tell the browser how to interpret the text that follows and whether to actually show that text on the Web page. Just as you need to tell the browser when to begin interpreting text in a certain manner, you also need to tell it when to stop. This ending command consists of an open bracket, a front slash, the tag word, and a close bracket, like this: </BODY>.

For example:

```
<TITLE>Leapin' Lizard's Genealogy Page</TITLE>
```

In this line, the <TITLE> tag tells the browser where to begin treating text as a title and </TITLE> also tells it where to end that treatment. Think of HTML tags as on and off commands where < > indicates *on* and </ > indicates *off*.

Some basic tags for writing your own HTML

If you've been reading along systematically in this chapter, you know that just preceding this section is an example of what HTML codes or tags look like. But what are the tags themselves? HTML involves too many tags to do justice here when the main point is to create and post a basic genealogical Web page. We really only have space here to cover just a few of the many tags.

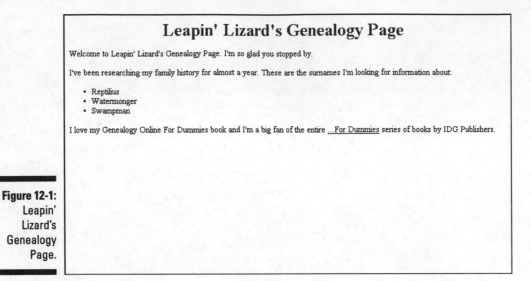

Leapin' Lizard's Genealogy Page

Welcome to Leapin' Lizard's Genealogy Page. I'm so glad you stopped by.

I've been researching my family history for almost a year. These are the surnames I'm looking for information about:

- Reptilius
- Watermonger
- Swampman

I love my Genealogy Online For Dummies book and I'm a big fan of the entire ...For Dummies series of books by IDG Publishers.

Figure 12-1:
Leapin'
Lizard's
Genealogy
Page.

If you're interested in more advanced HTML programming, Chapter 14 provides a couple of Web sites to visit. For an even more detailed read, check out *HTML 4 For Dummies,* by Ed Tittel and Stephen Nelson James (published by IDG Books Worldwide, Inc.). Or if you're looking for more information than we can offer here but not quite as much detail as a straight-HTML book offers, then we recommend that you check out *Creating Web Pages For Dummies,* 5th Edition, by Bud Smith and Arthur Bebak.

Take a look at Table 12-1 for some basic tags and their functions. For each of the tags identified, the off (or ending) command would be the same word in brackets preceded by a / (slash symbol). (We explore a few exceptions to the off command rule in Table 12-2.) You must turn off tags in the reverse order that you turned them on. For example, if you use the tags <HTML><HEAD>, then you close them with </HEAD></HTML>.

Table 12-1 explains what some common HTML tags tell Web browsers to do.

Table 12-1	Tag, You're It!	
Tag	*What It Means*	*What It Tells the Browser*
<HTML>	HTML	This text document is written in HTML and should be interpreted as such.
<HEAD>	Head element	The following text is the header of the document. (This is where you put the title and any descriptive information.)

Tag	What It Means	What It Tells the Browser
`<TITLE>`	Title	The following text is the title of the Web page. (It appears in the title bar at the top of your browser.)
`<BODY>`	Body	The body or main part of the document. (Here, you put all pertinent information that you want to appear on your Web page.)
`<H1>`	Heading	Denotes a heading for the page or section of text and the size that it should be. (Headings come in six levels: `<H1>`, `<H2>`, `<H3>`, `<H4>`, `<H5>`, and `<H6>`. `<H1>` is the largest print and `<H6>` is the smallest.)
`<CENTER>`	Center	Center the following text on the page or within a table cell or column.
`<B>`	Bold	Bold the following text.
`<I>`	Italicize	Italicize the following text.
`<U>`	Underline	Underline the following text.
`<A HREF="URL">`	A hypertext link	The following text is a link to another reference page/site and should take people there when they click it. (The URL for the other site goes in the quotation marks; the off command for this code is simply `</A>`.)
`<FONT COLOR= "(color)">`	Font color	The following text should be a particular color. (The color, written in either code or plain English, goes in the quotation marks; the off command is `</FONT>`.)
`<FONT SIZE= "(number)">`	Font size	The following text should be a particular size. (The size goes in the quotation marks; the off command is `</FONT>`.)
`<FONT FACE= "(font name)">`	Font face	The following text should be printed in a particular font or typeface. (The font or typeface name goes in the quotation marks; the off command is `</FONT>`.)

(continued)

Table 12-1 *(continued)*

Tag	What It Means	What It Tells the Browser
<OL>	Ordered list	The following is a numbered list. (Use this code with <LI>, identified in Table 12-2. The off command is </OL>.)
<UL>	Unordered list	The following is going to be a bulleted list. (Use this code with <LI>, identified in Table 12-2. The off command is </UL>.)

You don't necessarily have to close all HTML tags. Table 12-2 shows codes that are exceptions to the off command rule. You don't have to use a </> code to tell the browser when to stop interpreting something.

Table 12-2   **Closing-Tag Exceptions**

Tag	What It Means	What It Tells the Browser
<P>	Paragraph break	Skip a line and begin a new paragraph.
 	Line break	End a line here, then go to the next line to begin the next command or line of text.
<LI>	List item	This is a new item to identify on its own line in a list.
<IMG SRC "image URL">	Image source	Picks up a graphical image from a URL to insert here. (The URL or address of the graphical file goes between the quotation marks.)
<HR>	Horizontal rule	Puts a horizontal line across the page here to divide up the page.
<BODYBGCOLOR= "(color)">	Body background	The background color of the document should be a particular color. (The color, written in either code or plain English, goes in the quotation marks.)

Tag	What It Means	What It Tells the Browser
`<ALINK COLOR= "(color)">`	Active link color	Colors each link on the page a certain color until it's visited by people who load the page into their browsers. (The color, written in either code or plain English, goes in the quotation marks.)
`<VLINK COLOR= "(color)">`	Visited link color	The color that each link on the page becomes after the person clicked through to the link and then returns to the page. (The color, written in either code or plain English, goes in the quotation marks.)

You probably noticed that we use all uppercase letters in our coding, but that's just our own preference. You can use lowercase, uppercase, or a combination of both when programming in HTML. We prefer all uppercase so that we can more easily identify where the codes are when we need to edit an HTML document. We also like to skip lines between commands so that we can more easily look through the HTML document to see how we coded it.

Writing some HTML

Using the basic codes we provide in the preceding section, you can design and write a simple but functional Web site based on the Leapin' Lizard's Genealogy Page. To make the process easier, you can use your word processor to copy the codes for Leapin' Lizard's page as they appear, simply substituting your own information where Leapin' Lizard's personal information appears. After you finish, save the file in plain-text format with an HTML extension (.htm or .html). Save the file to your hard drive or a floppy disk. (When you're ready to make your real home page, save the file to your hard drive and then upload it to the Web server that will host your site. Although you may be able to save your page directly to the Web server, be sure to keep a backup copy of the file on your own machine or a floppy disk.)

Want to see what the page looks like through a browser's eyes? Try this:

1. **Launch your Web browser.**

   Usually, you can open the browser by double-clicking its icon or by using the Start menu (in Windows 95 and higher) to get to your programs. You don't necessarily have to be online to look at your Web page, so don't worry about going through all the steps for signing onto your Internet service provider account. Just open the browser.

2. **Use your browser's Open Page command to open the document.**

   Most browsers have an Open Page command in the File menu. When you click Open Page, a dialog box appears, asking you which file you want to open. Type the name of the file where you saved your HTML document (or use the Browse feature to search for your document) and hit Enter or click the OK button.

Does anything look funny — like everything past a certain point is all bolded, italicized, or in a huge font? If so, go back and double-check your coding to make sure that you turned off all the codes. To refresh your memory about turning off codes, see "What does HTML look like?" earlier in this chapter, and read everything from there to here.

Using an HTML editor

An *HTML editor* is a program that walks you through HTML programming so that you don't have to learn all the codes and remember to turn them on and off. Some editors use text that you've already written in your word processor, while others have you type text directly into the editor. To tell the editor how particular text should appear on a Web page (such as the format it should take — title, body of text, a list, and so on), you click an icon or drop-down menu option, and the editor applies the necessary codes.

The CD-ROM that accompanies this book has a couple of HTML editors on it that you can experiment with:

- ✔ HTML Web Weaver Lite (for Macintosh)
- ✔ HomeSite and HotDog (for PCs)

Using tutorials or online HTML editors

Some of the sites that host Web pages for free have online HTML editors and tutorials that you can use (also for free) if you sign up for a Web site with them. Likewise, many of the commercial Internet service providers, such as America OnLine, Compuserve, and WebTV, have HTML editors in the form of wizards or templates that help you design your Web pages. The tutorials and editors walk you through designing your Web page, prompting you to select items that you want on your page and even reminding you to save your page at appropriate times. Then they write the actual HTML tags for your page. Follow the instructions for using the editor that are provided by the free hosting service or Internet service provider.

A Little Help from Some Genealogical Software Utilities

After figuring out how to write some HTML or to use HTML editors to code documents for you, you're ready to design your home page. To do this, you need to decide exactly what you want your home page to contain. In Chapter 11, we look at how to share GEDCOM data online without using the World Wide Web. Of course, you'd probably like to share your GEDCOM file on your own home page. In this section, we explain how to get your GEDCOM file ready for sharing on the Web and how to format it without manually converting your GEDCOM to HTML. For more information about GEDCOM, see Chapter 9.

First and foremost, make sure that your GEDCOM file is ready to share with others. By this, we mean that it's free from any information that could land you in the doghouse with any of your relatives — close or distant! (For more about ensuring that your GEDCOM file has no information about living individuals, head to Chapter 11. You can also take a look at this chapter's sidebars, "Privacy" and "Copyrights.")

Some genealogical software programs enable you to indicate whether you want information on each relative included in reports and GEDCOMs. Other programs don't allow you to do this. You can imagine what a hassle it is to sort through a GEDCOM file line by line, deleting information on living relatives when you have several hundred individuals (or more!) in your database. To alleviate the necessity of this task, one of our fellow genealogists developed a helpful little program called *GEDClean*.

GEDClean is a freeware utility that searches through your GEDCOM file and removes any information about living persons for you. The utility then saves the cleaned GEDCOM for you to use with other genealogical utilities designed to help you put your information on the Web. We include GEDClean on the CD-ROM that accompanies this book. Here's how to use the utility:

1. **Install and open the GEDClean program by following the instructions in Appendix C.**

   A yellow window pops up with the three steps for GEDClean.

2. **Click Step 1: Select the Name of Your GEDCOM File.**

   You see a dialog box asking you to specify the GEDCOM file that you want to use GEDClean on.

3. **Choose the GEDCOM file that you created in Chapter 10 or another GEDCOM that you have readily available. Click OK.**

   This step brings you back to the yellow window, and the name and directory path of your GEDCOM file should appear under Step 1.

4. **Click Step 2: Select Individuals to Exclude from Your GEDCOM File.**

   You see a dialog box asking what you want to do to exclude living individuals from your GEDCOM. You can use an existing file that identifies all living persons whose data is in your GEDCOM file. You can have GEDClean scan your GEDCOM file looking for anyone with a specific note that indicates that they are alive. Or you can have GEDClean scan your entire GEDCOM file and look for anyone who may possibly be alive.

   Unless you have an existing file that states who should be excluded, or you've somehow marked your GEDCOM file to reflect living individuals, you should choose Option 3 and have GEDClean scan the whole GEDCOM looking for people who may be alive.

5. **Click Option 3: Analyze GEDCOM and then click OK.**

   For each person that GEDClean finds with no vital information (primarily birth date or death date), you get an Unknown Status window asking what you want to do with that person.

6. **If GEDClean prompts you with an Unknown Status window, type either** living **(details are excluded in the cleaned GEDCOM) or** not living **(details are included).**

   Be forewarned that if you have a lot of people in your database and thus in your GEDCOM file, the process of responding to each window for Unknown Status can be a little time-consuming. However, making sure that you exclude information on any living relatives is well worth the effort!

7. **Click Step 3: Clean the GEDCOM File.**

   GEDClean runs through the GEDCOM file and removes information on those people that you indicated as alive. The utility then saves your original GEDCOM file under a new name (with the extension .old) and saves the cleaned GEDCOM file under your original GEDCOM filename.

8. **Choose File⇨Exit to exit GEDClean.**

When you have a GEDCOM file that is free of information about all living persons, you're ready to prepare your GEDCOM file for the Web. You can choose from several programs to help you convert your GEDCOM to HTML. (We identify a few of these programs — and their Web addresses — in The *Genealogy Online For Dummies* Internet Directory in this book.) GED2HTML may be the most commonly known GEDCOM-to-HTML converter available, and guess what — we include it on the CD-ROM that accompanies this book. Here's how to use it with your cleaned GEDCOM file:

1. **Open the GED2HTML program that appears on the CD-ROM that accompanies this book.**

   Follow the instructions in Appendix C for installing and opening GED2HTML. A dialog box asks you to enter the location of your GEDCOM file. (You can browse if you can't remember the path name for the GEDCOM file.)

2. **Type the path for your GEDCOM file (for example c:\my documents\ helm.ged). Click OK.**

   GED2HTML runs a program using your GEDCOM file. You can watch it going through the file in a black window that appears.

3. **After the program is done, press Enter to close the program window.**

   This action brings you to a yellow window. The name and directory path of your GEDCOM file should appear under Step 1.

   GED2HTML saves the output HTML files in a folder appropriately called HTML in the same directory where the GED2HTML program is saved.

4. **Open your Web browser.**

   Usually you can open the browser by double-clicking its icon or by using the Start menu (in Windows 95 or higher) to get to your programs.

5. **Use your browser's Open Page command to open any of the HTML output files.**

   Most browsers have an Open Page command in the File menu. When you choose Open Page, a dialog box appears, asking you which file you want to open. Use the browse feature to go to the directory where GED2HTML put your HTML output. Select an HTML document to look at.

   After seeing what your output looks like and reviewing it to make sure that it doesn't contain any information that shouldn't be posted, you're ready to add it to your Web site (or link to it as its own Web page).

6. **Follow any instructions from your Web host, and upload your GED2HTML files to your Web server. Put any links to those files on your home page so you can share your GEDCOM information online.**

   For example, GED2HTML saved an HTML-coded index of all of the people in your GEDCOM to a file called `persons.html`. After uploading or copying this file to your Web host's server, you can use a link command `<A HREF = "[directory path]/persons.html">` from your main home page to this index of persons to share it on the Web.

Uncle Ed for All to See: Displaying Your Photos Online

Although the content of genealogical Web pages with lots of textual information about ancestors or geographic areas may be very helpful, all-text pages won't attract the attention of your visitors. We get tired of sorting through and reading narratives on Web sites; we like to see things that personalize a Web site and are fun to look at. Graphics, icons, and photographs are ideal for this purpose. A couple of nice-looking, strategically placed photos of ancestors make a site feel like a home.

Privacy

Sometimes, we genealogists get so caught up in dealing with the records of deceased persons that we forget that much of the information that we've collected and put in our databases pertains to living individuals. In our haste to share our information with others online, we create our GEDCOM files and reports and then ship them off to recipients without thinking twice about whether we may offend someone or invade his or her privacy by including personal information. We need to be more careful.

Why shouldn't you include everything that you know about your relatives?

✔ **You may invade someone's right to privacy:** Your relatives may not want you to share personal information about them with others, and they may not have given you permission to do so.

✔ **Genealogists aren't the only people who visit genealogical Internet sites:** For example, private detectives are known to lurk about, watching for information that may help their cases. Estranged spouses may visit sites looking for a way to track down their former partners. Also, people with less-than-honorable intentions may visit a genealogical Web site looking for potential scam or abuse victims. And some information, such as your mother's maiden name, may help the unscrupulous carry out fraud.

Your safest bet when sharing genealogical information is to include only the data that pertains to people who have long been deceased — unless you have written consent from living persons to share information about them. By *long been deceased,* we mean deceased for more than ten years — although the time frame could be longer depending on the sensitivity of the information. You may also want to keep in mind that the U.S. Government standard dictates that no record covered under the Privacy Act is released until it's at least 72 years old.

If you have some photographs that have been scanned and saved as .jpg or .gif images, you can post them on your Web site. Just make sure that a copy of the .jpg or .gif file is uploaded to your Web host's server in a directory that you can point to with HTML codes on your home page. By using the <IMG SRC = " "> code, you can tell browsers where to go to pick up that image or photograph. (Be sure to type the filename for that image exactly as it appears on your hard drive or other resource.)

Just as you should be careful about posting factual information about living relatives, be careful about posting photos of them. If you want to use an image that has living relatives in it, get their permission before doing so. Some people are very sensitive about having their pictures posted on the Web. Also, use common sense and taste in selecting pictures for your page. Although a photo of little Susie at age 3 wearing a lampshade and dancing around in a tutu may be cute, a photo of Uncle Ed at age 63 doing the same thing may not be so endearing!

Copyrights

Copyright is the controlling right that a person or corporation has over the duplication and distribution of a work that the person or corporation created. Although facts themselves can't be copyrighted, works in which facts are contained can be. Although the fact that your grandma was born on January 1, 1900, can't be copyrighted by anyone, a report that contains this information and was created by Aunt Lola may be. If you intend to include a significant portion of Aunt Lola's report in your own report, you need to secure permission from her to use the information.

With regard to copyright and the Internet, remember that just because you found some information on a Web site (or other Internet resource) does not mean that it's not copyrighted. If the Web site contains original material along with facts, it is copyrighted to the person who created it — regardless of whether or not the site has a copyright notice on it!

To protect yourself from infringing on someone's copyright and possibly ending up in a legal battle, you should do the following:

- Never copy another person's Web page, e-mail, or other Internet creation (such as graphics) without his or her written consent.

- Never assume that a resource is not copyrighted.

- Never print an article, story, report, or other material to share with your family, friends, genealogical or historical society, class, or anyone else without the creator's written consent.

- Always cite sources of the information in your genealogy and on your Web pages.

- Always link to other Web pages rather than copying their content on your own Web site.

If you don't understand what copyright is or you have questions about it, be sure to check out the U.S. Copyright Office's Home Page at `lcweb.loc.gov/copyright/`. Two U.S. Copyright Office pages of particular interest at the site are Copyright Basics and Frequently Asked Questions (FAQs).

Part V
The Part of Tens

The 5th Wave   By Rich Tennant

"THAT'S A LOVELY SCANNED IMAGE OF YOUR SISTER'S PORTRAIT. NOW TAKE IT OFF THE BODY OF THAT PIT VIPER BEFORE SHE COMES IN THE ROOM."

In this part . . .

Ah, The Part of Tens — a staple of the *For Dummies* books. Use these chapters as quick references when you're looking for the following:

- Online databases to search for records and information
- Some things to ponder when designing your own genealogical Web pages
- Places to visit when you're getting started in your genealogical pursuits
- Tips for making the most of your research

Chapter 13

Ten Handy Databases

In This Chapter

▶ Discovering online databases with useful data

▶ Finding databases that can provide research hints

Throughout the book, we talk about different online databases that are available. Here's a list of some databases that we think you may find useful in your research. Each database contains a brief description of the data that it contains and how you may use it to further your research goals.

Social Security Death Index

ssdi.genealogy.rootsweb.com/cgi-bin/ssdi.cgi

The Social Security Death Index is a listing of individuals whose deaths were reported to the Social Security Administration since 1962. Currently, this database contains over 64 million records and is updated monthly. The information that is available here includes name, birth date, death date, last residence, last benefit, Social Security number, and the state of issue of Social Security card. With this information, you can request a copy of the Social Security card application, which is easy to do because the site generates the proper letter for you. This database is a good resource when you try to fill in the gaps of missing information on individuals after the 1920 census.

The Source: A Guidebook of American Genealogy

www.ancestry.com/search/rectype/inddbs/3259.htm

If you're looking for some online guidance to research your family history, *The Source* should be one of your first stops. This database contains the electronic version of the popular book, *The Source: A Guidebook of American Genealogy,* edited by Loretto Dennis Szucs and Sandra Hargreaves Luebking. You can find topics like census records, church records, tax and land records, African-American research, American-Indian research, finding twentieth century ancestors, and locating urban ancestors. Using the book through the database interface is tedious, but the information provided in the text is well worth it.

FamilySearch: Family History Library Catalog

www.familysearch.org/eng/Library/FHLC/frameset_fhlc.asp

In Chapter 3, we highlight several features of the FamilySearch site. One that we don't talk about is the Family History Library Catalog. This catalog lists over three million microfilms and 300,000 books in the Family History Library collection. This is a good resource for finding family histories that are already completed on branches of your family. You can search the catalog by author, microfilm/fiche, place, surname, and call number.

National Archives and Records Administration Archival Information Locator

www.nara.gov/nara/nail.html

To do research in the United States, it's a good idea to know what federal records can help your search. The National Archives and Records Administration Archival Information Locator (NAIL) database houses descriptions of 3,000 microfilm publications and 400,446 archival holdings, and contains 124,000 digital images. You can search through a standard or expert-search interface or you can search just on digital images or physical holdings. You also have the option of searching through descriptions of all microfilm publications.

Bureau of Land Management, General Land Office Records

www.glorecords.blm.gov

This site contains the images of over two million land records issued between 1820 and 1908. Over the next few years, serial patents issued after 1908 until the mid-1960s will also be added. Keep in mind that this site has information on only the first transfer of land title from the federal government to an individual. If that individual sold that land to someone else, it's not shown in this database. You can view the land patent images here in a variety of ways including GIF images, TIFF images, and Adobe Acrobat (PDF) files.

World War 1 Civilian Draft Registration

userdb.rootsweb.com/ww1/draft/search.cgi

The World War I Civilian Draft Registration database contains information on individuals born between 1872 and 1900. Currently, this database contains 1.2 million names representing about 15 percent of the counties within the United States. The results of the search provide the last name, first name, birth data, and ethnic group. Another version of the same information is found on the Ancestry.com site at www.ancestry.com/search/rectype/inddbs/3172a.htm.

Alexandria Digital Library Gazetteer Server

Fat-albert.alexandria.ucsb.edu:8827/gazetteer/

Looking for a particular place in the world? The Alexandria Digital Library Gazetteer contains over four million features throughout the world. You can search by place name and define what feature type that you're looking for (for example — buildings, cities, drainage basins, landmarks, parks, and rivers). You can also limit the area searched by clicking a map to define the search area.

HyperHistory Online

```
www.hyperhistory.com/online_n2/History_n2/a.html
```

Although it's not a genealogical database per se, HyperHistory Online contains some interesting resources for genealogists who want to see what historical events occurred during their ancestors' lives. The site contains over 2,000 maps, charts, and articles recounting 3,000 years of world history. It's divided into four topical areas including People, History, Events, and Maps. The People area contains lifelines of individuals from 1000 B.C. to 1996 A.D. Historical timelines are available from before 1000 B.C. to 1998 A.D. The Event index covers significant occurrences in science, culture, and politics between 1791 A.D. and 1999 A.D. The Map section contains several maps covering ancient times to the twentieth century.

National Union Catalog of Manuscript Collections

```
lcweb.loc.gov/coll/nucmc/
```

Sometimes, it's difficult to find materials in archives and manuscript repositories, because their catalogs are not always readily available. These institutions often have family histories and Bibles, journals, personal papers, and political papers. The purpose of the National Union Catalog of Manuscript Collections (NUCMC), which is maintained by the Library of Congress, is to provide you with access to a listing of collections of archives and repositories that don't have their own publicly-accessible catalogs. You can search the catalog using an easy-search or an advanced-search form. Each entry contains the item title, description, notes, subject categories, and the location of the item (the institution housing the item).

Topozone

```
www.topozone.com
```

Location, and the terrain surrounding it, often played an important role in the lives of our ancestors. Although we may not be able to see maps of the terrain as it existed a hundred years ago, we can see modern-day topographic maps produced by the United States Geological Survey for the entire United States. To find a map, just type a place name in the search field (or you can search by latitude or longitude), select a state (if known) and you're off to the races. The Results page of the search lists the place name, county, state, type of feature, elevation, USGS quad, latitude, and longitude. Clicking the place name brings up the appropriate topographical map. You can view maps at different scales (if available) and in different image sizes (small, medium, and large).

Chapter 14

Ten Things to Remember When You Design Your Genealogical Web Site

You've probably seen them: Web sites that look like the maintainers simply plugged their surnames in specified spots and maybe changed the background color of the page. Such pages don't contain much information of value to anyone — it's simply a list of surnames with no context and maybe a list of links to some of the better-known genealogical Web sites. Clones! That's what they are. You don't want your genealogical Web site to look just like everyone else's, and neither do you want it to contain almost exactly the same information. You want yours to be unique and useful to other genealogists so that a lot of people visit your site — and recommend it to others. So what can you do to avoid the genealogical Web site rut that many genealogists find themselves in? Here we offer a few ideas and places to get help.

Be Unique — Don't Copy Other Web Sites

Please, please, please tell us that you want to set your home page apart from all other genealogical Web sites! You don't really have to be told not to copy other sites, right? But when you design your site, the pressure's on, and coming up with ideas for textual and graphic content can be pretty hard sometimes. We understand that this pressure can make it awfully tempting for you to take ideas from other Web sites that you like. Although you can certainly look to other sites for ideas on formatting and types of content, don't copy them! Web sites are copyrighted by the person(s) who created them — even if they don't contain a copyright notice — and you can get in trouble for copying them. (See Chapter 12 for more information about copyrights.)

The other reason you shouldn't copy other Web sites is that you want your page to attract as many visitors as possible and, in order to do this, you need to offer something unique that makes it worth people's time to stop by. After all, if your site has the same old information as another site that already exists, people have no need to visit your page. For example, because several comprehensive genealogical sites already exist (see Chapter 15), posting a Web site that merely has links to other genealogical pages doesn't make much sense. Likewise, if you're thinking about making a one-name study site on a surname for which four or five one-name study sites already exist, you may want to focus your home page on another surname you're researching.

Be creative. Look around and see what other genealogical Web sites offer and then seek to fill the void — pick a unique topic, name, or location that doesn't have much coverage (or better yet, one that doesn't have any coverage at all). If you really want to post a surname site, think about making a site for your surname in a particular state or country. Or think about posting some transcribed records that would benefit genealogists who are researching ancestors from a particular county.

Include the Surnames That You're Researching and Provide Your Contact Information

If the purpose of your Web site is not only to share your collection of genealogical information but to get information from others as well, then be sure to include a list of the names that you're researching on your home page. And don't be stingy with information. We encourage you to share at least a little information about your ancestors with those surnames. Just a list of surnames alone isn't going to be very helpful to visitors to your site. An online version of the information contained in your GEDCOM (which you create using GED2HTML or another similar program — see Chapter 12 for more info) will do because it includes an index of surnames that people can look through and also has information about your ancestors with those surnames. Also be sure to include your name and e-mail address so that people know how to get in touch with you to share data.

If you're comfortable doing so, you can include your address and phone number on your Web site so those who don't have e-mail access can contact you. Or, if you're not comfortable providing such personal information but you want other researchers to be able to contact you, you may want to consider getting a post office box that you can post on your Web site and use for receiving genealogy-related mail.

Use Caution When Applying Colors and Graphics

Choose your colors and graphics wisely! Although using some color and graphics (including photographs) helps your Web site stand out and makes it more personal, be careful about using too much color or too many graphics. By too much color, we mean backgrounds that are so bright that you blind your visitors, or backgrounds that drown out the colors of your links. You want your site to be appealing to others as well as to you, so before using neon pink or lime green, stop and think about how others may react.

The more graphics you use and the larger they are, the longer a computer takes to load them. (And animated graphics are even worse! Not only do they take a long time to load, but they can make your visitors dizzy and disoriented if you have several graphics moving in different directions at the same time.) Graphics files aren't the only factor that affects how quickly computers load files: the amount of bandwidth of your Internet connection and the amount of space available on your hard drive also affect download time. Waiting for a page to load that has more graphics than useful text content is frustrating. You can pretty much bet that people won't wait around, so concentrate on making your page as user-friendly as possible from the beginning. Use graphics tastefully and sparingly.

If you have a large amount of family photos that you really want to share, put each on its own page and then provide links to the photo pages from your home page. This way, visitors who aren't interested in seeing any of the photos don't have to wait for the images to load on their computers just to view the other contents of your site, and visitors who are only interested in a particular image don't have to wait for all the other photos to load.

The "Where to Go for Help" section later in this chapter identifies some online resources that lead you to sites with colors and graphics that you can download and use on your Web site.

To shrink the size of the graphics on your Web site, try using a graphics optimizer such as NetMechanic GIFBot available at www.netmechanic.com/accelerate.htm.

Be Careful What You Post

Be careful and thoughtful when designing your Web site. Don't post any information that could hurt or offend someone. Respect the privacy of others and post information only on people who have been deceased for many years. (Twenty-five years is a good conservative figure to use when in doubt.) Even then, be cautious about telling old family stories that may affect people who are still alive. (For more information about privacy, see Chapters 11 and 12.)

Always Cite Your Sources

We can't stress this enough! Always cite your sources when you put genealogical narrative on your Web site, or when you post information from records that you've collected or people you've interviewed. That way, people who visit your page and get data from it know exactly where you got the information and can follow up on it if they need or want to. (Also, by citing your sources, you keep yourself out of trouble because others may have provided the information to you and they deserve the credit for the research.)

Not All Web Browsers Are Created Equal

World Wide Web browsers interpret HTML documents differently depending on who created the software. Also, some Web browsers have HTML tags that are specific to the browser. So, although you may create a Web site that looks great using Microsoft Internet Explorer, it may look off-center or somewhat different when using Netscape Navigator. (And it looks a lot different in Lynx, which is a text-only browser.) Because of this problem, try not to use tags that are specific to any one browser when you create your Web site. And, whenever possible, test your page in several browsers before posting it for public access. Better yet, use a testing service that allows the "experts" to look at your page and give you feedback. The Yahoo! HTML Validation and Checkers page at `dir.yahoo.com/Computers_and_Internet/Data_Formats/HTML/Validation_and_Checkers/` provides a decent list of programs that check your Web site and notifies you about broken links. To find out more about browsers, see Appendix A.

Check and Recheck Your Links

If you include links on your home page to other Web sites that you've designed or sites maintained by someone else, double-check the links when you post your pages. Make sure that the links work properly so that visitors to your site don't have problems navigating around sites that you recommend or that support your home page. A lot of genealogical Web sites tend to be transient — the maintainers move them for one reason or another, or take them down entirely — so you should also check back periodically (once a month or so) to make sure that the links still work.

If you have a lot of links on your Web site and you don't have the time to check every single one yourself (which is a common scenario), look to the Yahoo! HTML Validation and Checkers page at `dir.yahoo.com/Computers_ and_Internet/Data_Formats/HTML/Validation_and_Checkers/`. It links to a list of programs that check your Web site and notify you about broken links.

Market Your Genealogical Web Site

After you put together your Web site and post it on your provider's server, you need to let people know that it exists so they can stop by and visit your site. How do you do this? You can follow some of the same tips in Chapter 3 for marketing the research that you've done on your surnames (using mailing lists if the site deals with particular surnames or geographic areas).

You can use a one-stop URL Registration site at the Genealogy Toolbox (`registration.genealogytoolbox.com`) to register your Web site with several comprehensive genealogical Web sites that receive a lot of traffic from people looking for genealogy-related pages.

Also, most of the major search engines have links to pages within their sites that enable you to submit your URL. Of course, in the interest of saving time, you can visit SiteOwner.com (`www.siteowner.com`), which offers a variety of announcement services, including one that allows you to submit your Web site information to several search engines for free.

Helping Others Is Its Own Reward

Don't go overboard promoting your home page on the actual home page for the sake of receiving awards from other sites, magazines, societies, or other sources. Post your genealogical home page with the intent of helping other genealogists and encouraging a sharing genealogical community — not to get a pat on the back. If you use the majority of your page to advertise your awards and beg people to vote for your site in popularity contests, you lose a lot of valuable space where you can post information that's useful to genealogists. Your bragging may turn visitors away — which defeats your purpose for self-promotion in the first place.

Now, we're not saying that you shouldn't acknowledge the awards that your site receives if it has good and sound genealogical content. We recognize that it's good business to give a little traffic back to the sites, magazines, societies, or other sources that send visitors your way by awarding your page some honor. We're simply saying that you can acknowledge the honors you receive in a tasteful and humble manner. You don't have to plaster all the graphics for every single award across the top of your page. Rather, you can set up a separate Web page for awards and provide a link from your home page so that those who are interested in seeing your honors can go to that page.

Where to Go for Help

Chapter 12 tells you how to create a simple Web site and discusses some HTML editors that are available from Web hosts. But these resources may not even begin to cover all the wonderful things that you intend to do with your Web site. Maybe you want to learn more about how to do fancier things with your Web site. If this is the case, you should check out community colleges in your area or workshops offered by local libraries or genealogical societies. Community colleges and workshops often offer classes or sessions on how to make a Web site, walking you through the basics of HTML — what the tags are, how to use them, and how to post a Web site.

If the thought of attending a structured class gives you hives or even just makes you roll your eyes, you can learn more about HTML and Web-site design in other ways. You can teach yourself; several books and online sites are out there to help you. Two such books are *HTML 4 For Dummies,* by Ed Tittel and Stephen James and *Creating Web Pages For Dummies,* by Bud Smith and Arthur Bebak, published by the good people at IDG Books Worldwide, Inc. The following online sites have links to many resources for writing HTML, in addition to resources that have colors, backgrounds, graphics, and other Web-site enhancements that you can download:

- **Yahoo!'s World Wide Web: Page Creation:** www.dir.yahoo.com

- **ZDNet's Developer:** www.zdnet.com/devhead/

- **Netscape Netcenter: Web Building:** www.netscape.com/computing/webbuilding

Chapter 15

Ten Sites for Genealogy Beginners

Do census records make you feel senseless? Panicked at the idea of using the Soundex? Just plain confused about where to start? These ten sites may relieve some of the anxiety you feel toward researching your genealogy.

Ancestors

`www2.kbyu.byu.edu/ancestors`

Ancestors — a unique multi-part television series about genealogy — has a companion Web site that contains several resources for beginners. The first *Ancestors* series premiered in 1997, and the second series was released in 2000.

The companion Web site has information on various types of records and sources that you collect as a genealogist, tips from other researchers, and a resource guide with locations of genealogy resources in each state. If you're interested in watching the two series, you can find a television schedule for the second series and information about ordering copies of the first series on video.

Ancestry.com

`www.ancestry.com`

Known initially for its publications, Ancestry.com has become famous in the online genealogical community. Ancestry.com features searchable databases (some are free, but most are available for a fee), articles and columns, an electronic copy of *The Source: A Guidebook of American Genealogy* (a popular genealogical reference book), online lessons, forms you can download, and all sorts of genealogical products available for purchase.

Most of the over 2,500 online databases are available only to subscribers, but the Social Security Death Index is free to all. This database is helpful if you're looking for an ancestor in United States who lived in the twentieth century. Ancestry.com also makes databases available for free for ten days when they are first introduced site. The topics and contents of these databases vary.

Genealogy.com

www.genealogy.com

The Genealogy.com site contains a variety of resources for beginners and advanced researchers alike. Using its Internet FamilyFinder, you can look for ancestors that you're researching in resources containing over 470 million names. Other resources at the site include GenealogyLibrary.com, Family Tree Maker user home pages and message boards, and information about Family Tree Maker software and commercial genealogy CDs. (For more information about Internet FamilyFinder, see Chapter 3).

The Family Explorer section walks you through the initial steps of researching your genealogy. You can also find searchable directories of phone numbers and e-mail addresses, articles on various genealogical topics, online classes, a reference library, GenForum message boards, and a searchable Social Security Death Index (SSDI) database.

Genealogy Toolbox

www.genealogytoolbox.com

Of course, we have to include our own Web site in the list. Its intent is to help beginning and advanced genealogists research online. The Genealogy Toolbox is the home of the following:

- **DigiSources:** Digitized images of actual records that you can use for primary research. For example, the 1790 U.S. Federal Census is currently available (both original and printed schedules).

- **GenealogyPortal.com:** A mega-search engine (a joint project between The Genealogy Home Page and the Genealogy Toolbox) dedicated to genealogical Web sites.

- **Journal of Online Genealogy:** A free, monthly e-zine (available only on the Web) with articles about all facets of online research.

- **Query Central:** A site where you can post queries about all the surnames you research.

- **GenealogySoftware Toolbox:** A site that provides all sorts of information about all the software (commercial, shareware, and freeware) we can find.

- **Genealogy BookZone:** A list of genealogical books available for purchase online and reviews of some of the books.

- **GenealogyNews.com:** A site with links to news articles of interest to the genealogical community.

- **Registration Central:** A one-stop site where you can register your Web page with several of the larger comprehensive genealogical sites.

GEN-NEWBIE-L

www.rootsweb.com/~newbie

This is the home page for the GEN-NEWBIE-L mailing list. This mailing list is a forum for individuals who are new to computers and genealogy to discuss a variety of topics in a comfortable environment.

To subscribe to the GEN-NEWBIE-L mailing list, follow these steps:

1. **Open your favorite e-mail program and start a new e-mail message.**

2. **Type** `Gen-Newbie-L-request@rootsweb.com` **in the Address line.**

3. **Leave the Subject line blank and type only the word** `subscribe` **in the body of your message.**

4. **Send your e-mail message.**

Soon, you receive a confirmation message with additional details on unsubscribing from the mailing list and other administrative items. If you have questions about the mailing list, consult the home page for help. For more information about using e-mail, see Appendix A.

Global Genealogy Supply

www.globalgenealogy.com

Global Genealogy Supply is a company in Canada that sells all sorts of genealogical products, including books, software, CD-ROMs, and maps. The Web site not only has information about its products, but also has the Global Gazette (an online magazine devoted to genealogical research), which you can find directly at `globalgazette.net/backtop.htm`.

National Genealogical Society

www.ngsgenealogy.org

The National Genealogical Society has more than 17,000 members nation-wide. At its Web site, you can find information on the society's home-study genealogy course, starting your genealogy research, and conferences. The site also has information about membership, news and events, information about its library, and a bookstore.

The Present Meets the Past: Genealogy Instruction for Beginners, Teenagers, and Kids

home.earthlink.net/~howardorjeff/instruct.htm

This site offers basic information for starting your genealogical research. Sections of the site include instructions on where to begin, a list of questions to ask relatives, where to go for information, and what you need in your "research kit." Of special interest are two sections for children and teenagers who want to begin researching their family trees. Each section identifies projects for children and teenagers to complete. The site has links to some other unique sites, as well as some blank forms you can print and use in your genealogical notebooks and files.

ROOTS-L

www.rootsweb.com/roots-l

This is the home page for the ROOTS-L mailing list. If you're looking for an all-purpose mailing list on genealogy, ROOTS-L may be for you. ROOTS-L is the oldest and largest genealogical mailing list, with more than 10,000 subscribers. List members discuss all types of genealogical issues. On the mailing list's companion Web page, you can find subscription information, help files, a searchable archive of past ROOTS-L messages, and a brief history of the list.

To subscribe to the list, follow these steps:

1. **Open your favorite e-mail program and start a new e-mail message.**

2. **Type** `ROOTS-L-request@rootsweb.com` **in the Address line.**

3. **Leave the Subject line blank and type only the word** `subscribe` **in the body of your message.**

4. **Send your e-mail message.**

Soon, you receive a confirmation message with additional details on un-subscribing from the mailing list and other administrative items. (Check out Appendix A for more on using e-mail.)

You may want to consider subscribing to the digest mode of the ROOTS-L mailing list. Because it's one of the largest lists, your e-mail inbox may quickly fill up if you receive every message that's posted to the list separately. *Digest mode* enables you to receive a single message with the text of several messages embedded within it periodically throughout the day. So instead of receiving some 50 to 200 messages per day, you may receive only five. For more information on subscribing to digest mode, see the ROOTS-L home page.

Getting Started in Genealogy and Family History

`www.genuki.org.uk/gs/`

The GENUKI (U.K. and Ireland Genealogy) Web site provides a list of helpful hints for starting out in genealogical research. The extensive list covers these elements: deciding the aim of your research, using Family History Centers, joining a society, tracing immigrants, and organizing your information. You also find a list of reference materials — should you want to read more about the topics GENUKI discusses.

Chapter 16

Ten Tips for Genealogical Smooth Sailing

In This Chapter
▶ Enhancing your genealogical research
▶ Avoiding pitfalls

*Y*ou want to make optimal use of your time when researching your genealogy — online and offline. Being time-efficient means planning well and keeping organized notes so that bad leads don't distract you. Making the most of your time also means staying motivated when and if a bad lead does distract you. Your genealogy research is worth continuing. This chapter offers some tips to help you plan, organize, and execute your research.

Start with What You Know

Sure, this concept seems basic, but it's worth repeating: When you begin researching your genealogy, start with what you know — information about yourself and your immediate family. Then work your way back in time using information from relatives and records that you obtain copies of. Putting together the puzzle is much easier if you have some pieces first. If you start directly with your great-great-grandpa and all you know about him is his name, you're going to get frustrated very early in the process — especially if great-great-grandpa has a relatively common name like John Sanders or William Martin! Can you imagine trying to track down records on all the John Sanders or William Martins that turn up in one year's census? (We believe in thoroughly covering the basics, so if you want to hear this again, go to Chapter 1.)

Get Organized

The better organized you are, the more success you're likely to have with your research efforts. If you know ahead of time where you stand in researching your family lines, you can identify rather quickly which records or other materials you need to find about a particular surname, location, or time frame. This strategy enables you to get right down to the nitty-gritty of researching instead of spending the first hour or two of your research rehashing where you left off last time.

To help yourself get organized, keep a research log recording when and where you searched for information. For example, if you ran an Alta Vista search on the surname McSwain on December 31, 2000, and found three pages that you wanted to visit, record that in your research log. Also record when you visited those three pages and whether they provided any useful information to you. That way, next time you're online researching your McSwain ancestors, you know that you already ran an Alta Vista search and visited the particular resulting pages, so you don't need to do it again. (Of course, you may want to check back in the future and run the search again to see whether any new McSwain-related sites turn up. And again, your research log can come in handy because it can remind you of whether you've already visited some of the resulting sites.)

You can print a copy of a research log at the Church of Jesus Christ of Latter-day Saints site (www.lds.org/images/howdoibeg/Research_Log.html). Although this particular log is intended for offline research, you can modify it for your online pursuits — substituting the URL of a site you visit for the Location/Call Numbers section of the form. Or you can find a research table (which is basically a research log by another name) at the Family Tree Maker Online site (www.familytreemaker.com/00000002.html). A couple of other options are to create your own research log with a plain old notebook or a spreadsheet on your handy-dandy computer, or to use an already-prepared form that comes with your genealogical database (if available).

Always Get Proof

Don't trust everything you hear from other people, or read in their books, reports, Web pages, or any other written documents. Always be a little skeptical about secondhand information and seek to get your own proof of an event. We're not saying that if your Aunt Bettie gives you a copy of great-grandma's birth certificate that you still need to get your own copy from the original source. However, if Aunt Bettie merely tells you that great-grandma was born in Hardin County, Kentucky, and that she knows this because great-grandma said so, you do need to get a copy of great-grandma's birth certificate or some other primary record that verifies this fact.

If you assume that everything you hear or read is true, you're likely to get frequently distracted by bad leads. You could end up tracing an entire branch of a family that you're not even related to. And just think of all the lost time that you could have spent working on your family line!

Always Cite Your Sources

We can't say this enough — always cite your sources. In other chapters (Chapter 14, for example), we explore why citing your sources when sharing your genealogical information with others is a smart thing to do. We also touch on the importance of citing sources for your own research — so important, in fact, that we reiterate the point here. Make sure that you know where, when, and how you obtained a particular piece of information about your ancestors just in case you ever need to verify the information or get another copy of the record. Doing so saves you a lot of grief. It also brings you greater respect from others for your efforts.

Focus, Focus, Focus

If you're trying to remember all your ancestors in all your family lines and research them all at the same time, you're bound to get confused and burnt out! Focus on one or two branches at a time. Even better — focus on one or two people within a branch at a time. By maintaining a tight focus, you can still find information on other relatives in that branch of the family and collect records and data that pertain to them — but you're able to do so without driving yourself crazy.

Share Your Information

One of the best ways to facilitate getting genealogical information from others is to share some information first. Although most genealogists are rather generous people to begin with, some still believe in protecting their discoveries like closely-guarded treasures — it's "every man for himself" in their minds. However, after they realize that you want to give information as well as receive it, some of them lighten up and are much more willing to share with you. By sharing information, you can save each other time and energy, as well as begin to coordinate your research in a manner that benefits both of you.

Sharing information is one area where the Internet has proven to be an invaluable resource for genealogists. It provides easy access for unconditional and conditional sharing of information among genealogists. Those of you who are willing to share your knowledge can go online and post information to your heart's content. And in return, simply ask the researchers who benefit from your site to share interesting information with you. And for those of you who are a little more apprehensive about sharing your knowledge, you can post messages describing what you're looking for and state that you're willing to share what you have with anyone who can help you.

You have several different ways to share your information online. We cover many of these methods in various chapters of this book. You can share in one-on-one e-mail messages, mailing lists, newsgroups, and Web pages — just to name a few.

Join a Society or Research Group

You've probably heard the phrase "Two heads are better than one," right? Well, this theory holds true for genealogy. Joining a society or a research group enables you to combine research efforts with others who are interested in a particular surname or geographic location, so that together you save time and energy obtaining documents that benefit everyone. A society or research group also provides you with a support group to which you can turn when you begin to get discouraged or whenever you want to share a triumph.

You can find genealogical societies and research groups in several ways. Check out your favorite comprehensive genealogical site (see The *Genealogy Online For Dummies* Internet Directory in this book for a list) and look under both the category that lists societies and the place category for the location where you live. Or, if you're interested in finding a society in the United States, take a look at the Federation of Genealogical Societies home page at www.fgs.org (which identifies member societies by location) or the USGenWeb Project at www.usgenweb.org (which links to state pages that identify resources for the state and its counties).

If you're interested in finding a society in a country other than the United States, check out the WorldGenWeb site at www.worldgenweb.org to link to any resource pages for the region that you're researching. These resource pages should include at least general information about societies in the area.

Attend a Conference or Workshop

Conferences and workshops that are hosted by genealogical societies can be a great resource for you. They can help you get organized, learn how to research a particular place or look for specific records, and motivate you to keep plugging along with your research even if you have days when you feel like you haven't accomplished a thing. Conferences and workshops also enable you to meet other researchers with whom you have something in common, whether it's researching a specific surname or geographic location, or just research in general. Being in the company of someone with whom you can share your genealogical successes and failures is always nice.

Typically, conferences and workshops offer sessions that instruct you on various traditional researching topics like the following:

- ✔ Using local libraries and archives
- ✔ Finding and using land records
- ✔ Obtaining vital records
- ✔ Converting Soundex codes and using the census
- ✔ Publishing a genealogical report or book

More and more workshops offer computer-based sessions like the following:

- ✔ Using genealogical software
- ✔ Designing and posting your own genealogical Web page
- ✔ Joining online societies and mailing lists
- ✔ Presenting overviews of the Internet's genealogical offerings
- ✔ Using a computer in general

You can use your trusty computer and Internet connection to find genealogical and historical conferences and workshops in your area. Family Tree Maker's Upcoming Events site (`www.familytreemaker.com/othrevnt.html`) provides information about large conferences coming up within the next couple of months. Global Genealogical Supply also has a Genealogy Conferences and Workshops page (`globalgazette.net/events/events.htm`). You can also use these sites to get the word out about a conference or workshop that you're helping to plan!

Attend a Family Reunion

Family reunions enable you to visit relatives that you haven't seen in a long time and to meet new relatives you never would have known! Reunions are a wonderful opportunity to build your genealogical base by just chatting with relatives about old family stories, ancestors, and the like. Although a reunion doesn't feel like a formal interview, it can give you much of the same information that you would receive if you sat down and formally interviewed each of the people in attendance. Taking along a tape recorder or video camera is a good idea because you don't have to worry about writing down everything your relatives say right at that moment — you can just sit back and enjoy talking with your family. Plus, your genealogy records are greatly enhanced by audio or video. (Just make sure that when you're going to tape a conversation, you have the permission of the relatives that you plan to record.)

Family reunions also offer you the opportunity to share what you know about the family and exchange genealogical records and reports. If you know ahead of time that several of your relatives are also into genealogical research, you can better plan with them what records, pictures, reports, and other resources to bring. If you're not sure that any of your relatives are into genealogical research, we recommend that you take a notebook with some printed reports and maybe a narrative family history or genealogy (if you've already put one together). Remember, your work doesn't have to be complete (in fact, it probably won't be) or perfect in grammar for others to enjoy seeing what you've collected.

If you'd like more information about how family reunions can motivate you and help you in your research, take a look at Family Tree Maker Online's Family Reunions articles (`www.familytreemaker.com/issue1.html`). To find out about family reunions, watch the family association and one-name study Web sites of the surnames that you're researching. Typically, this type of Web site has sections set up for reunion announcements. Also, see the Reunions Magazine site (`www.reunionsmag.com`).

Planning a reunion can often be a challenging experience. Fortunately, software is available to help you with all the details. Family Reunion Organizer by Formalsoft is just such a program. You can find a demo copy of the software on the CD accompanying this book, or at the software's Web site (`family-reunion.com/organizer/`).

Don't Give Up

You're going to have days where you spend hours at the library or archives or on the Internet with no research success whatsoever (or so you may think). Don't let those days get you down, and certainly don't give up! Instead of thinking about what you didn't learn about your ancestors on such days, think in terms of what you did learn — that your ancestors were not in that record for that particular place at that particular time. By checking that record, you eliminated one more item on your to-do list. So the next time you get ready to research, you know exactly where *not* to look for more information.

Appendix A

Going Online

• •

*B*efore we talk about what you need to go online and how to do it, we want to explain what we mean by *online*. We use the term *online* to refer to gaining access to and using the Internet. So what is the Internet?

The *Internet* is a system of computer networks joined together by high-speed data lines called *backbones*. The Internet began as a smaller system of regional networks, called ARPANET, sponsored and used by the United States military in the 1960s. Over time, other government agencies and colleges and universities that were conducting research for the government were added to the network. Eventually, the Internet sprang forward and became accessible to the average person through Internet service providers (which we talk about later in this appendix in the "Getting an Internet Service Provider" section).

This appendix covers the computer equipment that you need to access the Internet, finding an Internet service provider to provide the access, and the types of resources that you find on the Internet after you're on it. Of course, the primary focus of this book is genealogy online — not the Internet and computer use in general — so we just touch on the types of Internet resources available. In some cases, we do provide examples and details to help you when you come across some common situations in your online genealogical research (situations like sending e-mail, joining mailing lists, and using newsgroups). And because we don't want to leave you in a lurch if you're trying to learn all you can about every Internet resource, we include some references to other books that may interest you if you want to know more about something in particular.

Is Your Computer Ready to Go Online?

If your computer is relatively new, it most likely came loaded with the hardware and software that you need to access and effectively get around on the Internet. However, if you purchased your computer several years ago, you may have to add a piece of hardware or software in order to access and use the Internet. In general, you need to have a base system that meets the same requirements to run genealogical software (see Chapter 9 for more information), plus a modem and some communications software.

Modem on up

A *modem* is a piece of equipment that enables your computer to talk to other computers through a telephone line. A modem can be internal (meaning inside your computer) or external (meaning you plug it into your computer). A modem transmits information to and from your computer at a speed that's measured by the total number of characters, or *bits,* that it can send or receive per second. The higher the number of bits — the faster the modem. Most Internet service providers recommend that you have a modem with a minimum speed of 28,800 bits per second (bps). (For more on Internet service providers, move ahead to the section "Getting an Internet Service Provider," later in this appendix.)

To use a modem to access the Internet and talk with other computers, you need communications software that tells the modem what to do and also interprets information coming back to your computer. The exact kind of software that you need depends on your modem and your Internet service provider (ISP). Check with your ISP to determine exactly what you need and how to get it, and then double-check the owner's manual for your modem to ensure that the software is compatible with your modem. Most commercial ISPs (like America Online, Prodigy, AT&T WorldNet, and CompuServe) give you free copies of the software that you need to access and use any of the many online resources they offer.

Don't forget a telephone line

In addition to having a computer equipped with a modem, you need a telephone line to access the Internet. Using a jack-to-phone telephone cord, connect your modem to the wall jack so that the modem can use the telephone line to dial out and communicate with other computers. (Generally, you can find the modular plug to hook the phone cord into your modem on the back of your external modem or on the back of your computer if you have an internal modem.) Your modem calls your Internet service provider and gains access to the Internet for you.

You don't necessarily have to have a second telephone line in your house to access the Internet. You can use your regular line and phone number. However, you may want to think about a few things:

✔ If you subscribe to a call-waiting service, be aware that call waiting can interrupt an online session, which can be very frustrating. When a call-waiting call rings through, your computer gets very confused, and the consequences can be far from fun. The computer does anything from trying to answer the second line to disconnecting from your online service to shutting down completely. So if you have call waiting, we recommend that you follow your communications software instructions or your phone company's instructions for blocking it while you're online.

✔ If you spend long periods of time online (which is extremely easy to do when you get into genealogical research and dialogues with other researchers), you may want to remind your relatives and friends that your computer sometimes uses that phone line to access the Internet. Letting them know that the line will be tied up saves them frustration and worry if they're trying to reach you and continually get a busy signal.

✔ If you have several phones hooked up on the line, remember to tell others in the household you're going to be online. When someone picks up an extension in the home, it can cut off your Internet connection.

WebTV: An alternative to a computer

If you haven't yet purchased a computer or laptop, and are still weighing your needs for one, you may consider getting *WebTV* instead. WebTV is a cheaper method for accessing the Internet (particularly e-mail, newsgroups, and the World Wide Web), but the trade-off is the limitations of the equipment and your overall access. To use WebTV, you must have a WebTV console (a small computer with limited functions) that hooks directly into your television set. Makes sense, right? The consoles are relatively inexpensive pieces of equipment and you can find them at any electronics store. The console comes with a remote control that you can use for all functions, but we strongly recommend that you invest in the optional keyboard (for an additional cost, of course) so that you don't tax your patience and cramp your fingers trying to use only the remote control to send e-mail messages! In addition to having your own television and the WebTV console, you need to have a telephone line nearby so WebTV can dial out. (For more information about using telephone lines to access Internet service providers (ISPs), see the preceding section.)

WebTV is its own Internet service provider, so you don't need to look around for an ISP. The first time you set up the WebTV system, the console knows to dial the WebTV network and you merely need to follow the on-screen instructions. Each time you want to use WebTV after that, all you have to do is turn on the console and it begins calling in. Your main WebTV account page pops up, and you have access to your e-mail and other Internet functions.

If you're looking for more information about WebTV, you might want to check out *WebTV For Dummies,* 2nd Edition, by Brad Hill (published by IDG Books Worldwide, Inc.).

Getting an Internet Service Provider

When you're looking for an Internet service provider (ISP), you can choose among several types of access:

✔ Work or school

✔ Direct connection

✔ Commercial online service providers (local, national, or international)

✔ Freenets

Some services are free, while others charge a monthly fee to give you access to more resources and even some specialized resources. So how do you choose? Review all the available options in your area and determine which one offers the most of what you need.

Access from work or school

If you work for an office or attend a school that has an Internet connection, you may already have access to some or all of the resources available on the Internet, particularly e-mail and the World Wide Web. Whether you're allowed to use that access for personal, genealogical research depends on your company or school, of course. Many offices have reasonable policies against using company equipment and time for personal purposes, so be sure that you know your company's policy before embarking on your genealogical pursuits online at work. If you work in an office that doesn't permit personal use of the Internet, you're in the same boat as the majority of the population and you need to get Internet access from your home.

Direct connection to the Internet

Traditionally, direct connection to the Internet was just that — an Internet line came directly into your home, and your computer was hooked directly into it. Because the line coming into your home was dedicated just to the Internet, you didn't need to worry about keeping a phone line available or a modem to use that phone line. Typically, if you had a direct connection, you had a computer that was running at all times and may have been acting as a *server* (a computer that makes information on its drives available for access by other computers). This server ran programs that knew where to route visitors to your computer, and also let you onto the Internet to look at other sites and use other resources. For most online genealogists, however, the expense and technical knowledge that it took to maintain a dedicated Internet line at home made having one unrealistic.

Today, you have several options for direct connections to the Internet within the home. The options that are available depend on what services are offered in your particular area. Increasingly, three types of connections are making their way into homes: cable, Digital Subscriber Line, and satellite connections.

Cable connections are offered by cable television and some telecommunication companies. These connections use cable that's similar to cable TV. The cable hooks into a cable modem which, in turn, is connected to your computer. This connection is "always on" — meaning that you do not have use a phone line to dial into an ISP. The quality of the cable connection depends on how many people in your area are online at the same time as you. In some ways, cable modems are the modern equivalent of the old telephone "party lines."

A *Digital Subscriber Line (DSL)* is an Internet-access service that's usually offered by telephone companies. These lines use the capacity of traditional phone lines to connect to the Internet. The speed of these lines depends on how far you're located from the central telephone office. The farther away you are, the slower your connection. Unlike cable connections, the capacity of DSL lines isn't shared by multiple people.

The newest technology that enables you to have a direct connection is accessing the Internet through a *satellite*. A few companies are currently testing Internet connections using satellite dishes, which are similar to the digital dishes some people use to receive television channels. Although this technology is not fully implemented yet, these connections are expected to be close to cable modem speed and will probably suffer from the same kind of traffic constraints.

Commercial Internet service providers

Chances are, names like America Online, Prodigy, AT&T WorldNet, and CompuServe pop into your mind when we say *commercial Internet service providers*. Although these are four of the better-known providers, many more are available, and taking a look around to find the service that best meets your needs is worth your time. Commercial Internet service providers are companies or organizations that provide subscribers dial-up access to the Internet. They can be international, national, or local in scope. Commercial ISPs offer varying services, but typically all provide e-mail and Internet access. Most of the major providers also have special interest groups and forums that members can participate in, as well as access to newsgroups.

Many now offer space where you can post your own Web site. (For more information about designing and posting Web sites, see Chapters 12 and 14.)

Just because your aunt, brother, or best friend uses a particular commercial ISP doesn't necessarily mean that the same service is the best one for you. After all, you may have different needs. Your aunt may live in a metropolitan area where the provider has several telephone access numbers, but you may live in a rural community or isolated area where the provider doesn't have a local telephone access number and you would get stuck with long-distance charges to use the same provider. Or your brother may subscribe to a provider that gives him only e-mail access, but you want to browse the Internet and keep abreast of the genealogy newsgroups. Because your needs may be different, we recommend that you ask several questions when considering any ISP, whether it's a national, international, or local provider:

- What services — e-mail, Internet access, space for a Web site, *FTP* (*File Transfer Protocol,* which is a way to transfer files from your computer to another, or vice versa, over the Internet), newsgroups, and so on — does the ISP provide?

- Does the ISP provide the software that you need to access its system? Can you use your own software if you prefer?

- What is the ISP's pricing policy? Does it have a set rate for unlimited access, or does it have a tiered system where you pay for a set number of hours of access per month, and then get charged a certain amount for each hour that you go over?

- Does the provider have local telephone access numbers available in the area where you live? If not, does it have free 800 telephone access numbers that you can use and, if so, do you have to pay extra for access to them? (*Access numbers* are the phone numbers your modem calls to log you into the ISP's servers so that you can get online.)

- If your subscription includes space for a Web site, does the ISP provide support services to help you set up your home page?

- How does the ISP handle customer support? Do you have to post an e-mail message and, if so, how quickly does it respond? Do you have to call a long-distance telephone number to speak to a customer service representative? What are the provider's hours of customer support?

Shop around to see who gives you the better deal and can best address your Internet needs — a local ISP or one of the national or international providers. You can find a local ISP a few different ways. You can look in your local phone directory or the newspaper, ask your friends and coworkers, or go to the directory Web site at www.thelist.com, which has listings of ISPs by area code. And to help you comparison shop, here are the names and Web addresses (Web addresses are technically known as *Uniform Resource Locators,* or *URLs*) for several of the better-known commercial online services. (Keep in mind that these aren't the only major providers available — they're just a sampling.)

- **America Online (AOL):** www.newaol.com
- **AT&T WorldNet:** www.att.net
- **CompuServe:** www.compuserve.com
- **EarthLink:** www.earthlink.net
- **Microsoft Network (MSN):** free.msn.com/msncom
- **Prodigy:** www.prodigy.com

Of course, visiting Web sites to find out about Internet access is a catch-22 if you don't yet have Internet access. So, to help you along until you can make up your own mind, we provide free software for the AT&T WorldNet Service on the CD-ROM accompanying this book.

Freenets

Freenets are Internet service providers that are locally-based and offer access to people in the community either free of charge or for a minimal charge. (Yes, it is a contradiction to say that there may be a minimal charge for a freenet — which is why you also hear freenets called *community networks* these days.) Some freenets can give free access to individuals because they have corporate sponsorship, and others are associated with educational institutions. Freenets are rather hard to find and may limit the types of service available. For example, they may provide e-mail and FTP (File Transfer Protocol) access but not World Wide Web-browsing. To see if a freenet is in your area, flip through your local phone directory or watch the newspaper. You may also want to ask at the local library or use a friend's or relative's Internet access to check out the directory Web site at www.thelist.com, which identifies ISPs by area code.

Types of Internet Resources

When you prepare to go online, knowing the types of Internet resources available to you is helpful. By reviewing what the resources are and what they're called, you become more familiar with some terms that you may encounter on the Internet after you go online.

Bulletin Board Systems

Although *Bulletin Board Systems* (BBSs) technically aren't Internet resources, you can get to some BBSs via the Internet. A *BBS* is a computer (or maybe more than one computer) that answers the telephone and communicates with other computers that call it, letting users of the other computers post information or messages to the BBS. Some BBS administrators began trading files with other BBSs as the systems became popular, and BBS networks were formed. The best-known BBS network is FidoNet.

E-mail

Electronic mail — commonly called *e-mail* — is just what it sounds like: mail (or a message, if you prefer) that's sent from one person to another electronically over the Internet. Because you can communicate with others worldwide on any given topic (surname, geographic location, types of records, and so on), e-mail is the best Internet tool when it comes to online genealogical research.

How you get an e-mail program varies. If you subscribe to a commercial ISP, the communications software that the ISP provides should include e-mail software. An e-mail program may have come with your computer when you bought it, or your World Wide Web browser may have one. You can also purchase an e-mail program or download one off the Internet. Regardless of how you get your e-mail software, most work generally the same way.

To use your e-mail software, install the program following the instructions provided with the software.

Sending e-mail

When you want to send a message, follow these general steps:

1. **Open your e-mail program.**

   You generally do this by double-clicking the program's icon (the icon varies depending on the program that you use) or by using your Start program menu.

2. **Click the button that lets you create a new message. (Or you can usually use a drop-down menu to tell the software that you want to create a new message.)**

3. **In the To field, type the e-mail address for the message's recipient.**

The protocol for an e-mail address is this: [user name]@[name of the person's ISP]. For example, April's e-mail address is: ahelm@tbox.com (ahelm is her user name, and tbox.com is her ISP through which she gets her e-mail messages).

Depending on your e-mail program, you may be able to enter more than one person's e-mail address if you plan to send the message to more than one person. If you do have multiple addresses, separate each e-mail address with a comma or semicolon. Or (again, depending on your program) you can use the CC (meaning *carbon copy*) field to enter additional addresses.

4. **In the Subject field, type a brief note stating what the message is about.**

5. **In the message box, type the message that you want to send to the other person.**

6. **After you finish your message, click the Send button or use a dropdown menu to tell the software to send the message.**

Receiving and reading e-mail

When you install your e-mail program, you're prompted with questions or dialog boxes to finish configuring your computer and ISP account to receive e-mail. Contact your ISP if you have problems setting the configurations. After you set the configurations, e-mail that others send to you automatically arrives in your inbox, which sits on your ISP account and is accessible whenever you access the Internet. After you log onto your ISP and open your e-mail inbox, you can read any messages that you receive by double-clicking the message line in the Inbox or highlighting the message that you want to read and clicking the Open button. (Of course, if you want to reply to the message after reading it, your e-mail software probably provides a Reply button or drop-down menu option to do so.)

Check out Chapters 3 and 10 for more information on using e-mail for particular genealogical purposes and to learn about *netiquette* (guidelines for communicating effectively and politely with e-mail).

To find out more about your particular e-mail software, consult the user's manual or other documentation that came with the software. That information tells you about special features that the program has and how to use them. Contact your ISP when configuring your software to get your ISP's specific server settings. For even more information on using e-mail programs, we recommend *E-Mail For Dummies,* 2nd Edition, by John R. Levine, Carol Baroudi, Margaret Levine Young, and Arnold Reinhold (published by IDG Books Worldwide, Inc.).

Finding e-mail addresses for other people

You're probably asking, "Who can I e-mail?" You can e-mail anyone with an e-mail address. So where can you get addresses for other genealogical researchers? For the most part, you get e-mail addresses from people when they contact you or when you post a message to a mailing list, post a query, or put up a Web site. However, sometimes you may be looking for a particular person's e-mail address and can't find it (whether you've lost it or never had it), which is when online directories come in pretty handy.

An *online directory* is just that — a listing of names and addresses (e-mail and/or regular mail, depending on the directory) that you can access and search on the Internet. Most directories are accessible on the World Wide Web (we cover the World Wide Web in more detail later). Here's how to use an online directory to look for a particular person's e-mail address:

1. **Open your World Wide Web browser.**

   You generally do this by double-clicking the program's icon or using the Start program menu.

2. **In your browser's URL field, type the Yahoo! People Search Web address** (`people.yahoo.com`).

   The Yahoo! People Search page comes up.

3. **In the First Name field, type the person's first name (if you know it).**

   For this example, we look for April in the People Search directory. In the First Name field, we type **April**.

4. **In the Last Name field, type the person's last name.**

   We type **Helm**.

5. **If you happen to know the *domain* (the name of the person's Internet service provider's computer), type it in the Domain field.**

   Most of the time, you won't know the domain name for the person's e-mail account — that's probably why you're looking for the e-mail address in the first place! So leaving this field blank is perfectly fine.

6. **Click Search.**

   Yahoo! executes the search and brings up an E-mail Basic Search Results page showing any matches that it found or informing you that it doesn't find anyone with that name. For each match, the Search Result page provides the person's name, e-mail address, and location. Each name is a link to more information. For our example, one of April's e-mail addresses came up as the first match.

Directories like Yahoo! People Search are great when you're trying to track down the e-mail addresses for just a few people that you want to contact. However, online directories do have their limitations. If you're searching for someone who has a common name — like John Martin or Elizabeth Smith — you're in for a challenge when you use an online directory. You need to know a little bit more about people with common names to effectively search for their e-mail addresses. Information such as where they live is helpful. Although Yahoo! provides only the country of the person's e-mail address, other online directories provide full address information.

Another twist to online directories that you may encounter is that they can turn up more than one e-mail address for the same person. If you'd run a search on Matthew's name instead of April's in the steps above, three or four of the many Matthew Helms who showed up on the results page would have been the Matthew you were looking for. (The reason for this is that Matthew has three or four different e-mail accounts.)

Use online directories only to find others you know are into genealogy or from whom you know you can get specific information that can guide you in your genealogical pursuits. Unless you want to receive a lot of negative e-mail from people you don't know, don't use an online directory to identify everyone who has a certain surname that you're interested in and then e-mail them with questions of how they're related to you or the ancestor that you're researching. (We discuss this tactic and why it isn't a good idea in more detail in Chapter 3.)

Mailing lists

Mailing lists are closely related to e-mail in that they involve e-mailing other people, but you e-mail others en masse instead of one-on-one. (You may hear mailing lists referred to as *listservs,* although technically Listserv is a software program for managing mailing lists and not a mailing list itself.) Mailing lists are formed by groups of people who share common interests. In terms of genealogical research, the common interest may be a specific surname, locality, or ethnic group.

Here's how mailing lists work: You join (or subscribe to) a mailing list and then receive any e-mail messages sent to the mailing list. (The list consists of the e-mail address of each person who joins the group.) When you want to send a message to the entire group, you send it to a single e-mail address, and your message is forwarded to everyone who subscribes to the list. When responding to a message posted by another subscriber, you can send your response directly to the person who posted the first message or to the entire mailing list. Which you choose to do depends on whether the information that you're sending is of interest to just that one person or to everyone on the list.

We discuss mailing lists and posting queries to them in Chapter 3, along with an example of how to subscribe to a mailing list. In general, to subscribe to a mailing list, all you have to do is send an e-mail message to a designated e-mail address with the word **subscribe** in the subject line. (If a particular mailing list has different instructions for subscribing, the site where you find information about the mailing list should tell you so and provide more detailed instructions.)

For more information about mailing lists, including the ins and outs of how they work and step-by-step instructions for subscribing or unsubscribing, we recommend *Internet For Dummies,* 7th Edition, by John R. Levine, Carol Baroudi, and Margaret Levine Young, and *MORE Internet For Dummies,* 4th Edition, by John R. Levine and Margaret Levine Young (both books published by IDG Books Worldwide, Inc.).

Telnet

Telnet is a text-based program that enables you to log on to another computer and view files or documents that are available for public access. You can't download the files, and you can't upload your files to the other computer, either. To log on to another computer, you need a telnet client (software) or a World Wide Web browser (such as Netscape Navigator and Microsoft Internet Explorer) that launches a telnet client. (For more on browsers, see the "World Wide Web" section later in this appendix.)

As the World Wide Web became more popular over the past few years, telnet started to fall by the wayside, and most of the telnet sites that still exist and are of interest to genealogists are library card catalogs. However, many of these card catalogs have moved to the World Wide Web, and you can usually link to and view those that haven't moved by using your browser.

For more information about telnet and how to use telnet sites, take a look at *Internet For Dummies,* 7th Edition, by John R. Levine, Carol Baroudi, and Margaret Levine Young, and *MORE Internet For Dummies,* 4th Edition, by John R. Levine and Margaret Levine Young (both published by IDG Books Worldwide, Inc.).

File Transfer Protocol

File Transfer Protocol (FTP) is a way to transfer files from your computer to another, or vice versa, over the Internet. You must have software that enables you to transfer files over the Internet, and you can only log on to other computers that allow FTP access. After you log on to a computer that allows FTP access, you can download files that are available for FTP or, in some instances, upload your own file to that computer.

How you get to an FTP site on another computer to log on and download or upload files depends on the other site and the FTP software that you use. The general gist of it is this: Using your software, you tell your computer to transfer files into the other computer. The other computer asks you to login (you must provide a password), and then gives you access to the FTP files that you're allowed to download. If, for some reason, you aren't authorized to transfer files into the other computer, your attempt is rejected. A lot of computer systems allow you to download things *anonymously,* meaning that you can log in to a machine that you don't know the password for by simply typing **anonymous** for the username and your e-mail address for the password.

Some World Wide Web pages have FTP files available for downloading directly from the Web pages. All you have to do is click the link to the file, and your computer asks where you want the file to be saved.

For more detailed information about FTP, we recommend *Internet For Dummies,* 7th Edition, by John R. Levine, Carol Baroudi, and Margaret Levine Young, and *MORE Internet For Dummies,* 4th Edition, by John R. Levine and Margaret Levine Young (both published by IDG Books Worldwide, Inc.).

Gopher

Gopher was developed at the University of Minnesota as a way to hierarchically categorize data on the Internet. Gopher uses a series of text-based menus through which you can browse. You click menu choices to get to other levels of information and eventually to the particular file or document that you're looking for. Gopher was popular before the World Wide Web and has, for the most part, been replaced by Web sites.

You can access Gopher sites in several different ways. You can use a Gopher client (or software) or your World Wide Web browser. (Actually, because you can use your Web browser, Gopher software has basically become obsolete.) Depending on which way you decide to go, your instructions for getting to

Gopher sites vary. However, the method for navigating within a Gopher site is the same: Clicking menu choices takes you to submenus down through the hierarchy.

For more information about Gopher sites and software, we recommend *Internet For Dummies,* 7th Edition, by John R. Levine, Carol Baroudi, and Margaret Levine Young, and *MORE Internet For Dummies,* 4th Edition, by John R. Levine and Margaret Levine Young (both published by IDG Books Worldwide, Inc.).

Newsgroups

Newsgroups are places to post messages of interest to groups of people at large. Newsgroups are similar to mailing lists in that you use e-mail to send a message that several people can read. However, instead of the message being sent individually to everyone on a mailing list, the message is posted to a news server, which in turn copies the message to other news servers. The other news servers wait for people who are interested in the topic to request the latest postings.

Newsgroups are categorized into hierarchies. Each hierarchy has a top-level label like `soc` or `alt`. Beneath the top level is a second hierarchy, followed by a third level, and so on. The majority of traffic pertaining to genealogical research flows through the `soc.genealogy` hierarchy (although some traffic does come through the `alt.genealogy` newsgroup).

We discuss newsgroups, their hierarchies, and posting messages to them in greater detail in Chapter 3, as well as provide information on how to access the newsgroups to read the messages posted on them. In general, you have a few ways to get to the newsgroups or the messages posted to them:

✔ If your Internet service provider (ISP) has a news feed, you can use a news reader that's configured to pick up the news feed and connect you to the news server. If you use Netscape Navigator or Internet Explorer, a newsreader is built in. (To use this method of access, we recommend that you consult the manual or other instructions provided by your individual ISP to configure your news reader. Your ISP will tell you what your specific news server settings should be.)

✔ If your Internet service provider doesn't have a news feed or you don't have the software necessary to access it, you can get to some newsgroups through the World Wide Web (one such site is Deja.com at `www.deja.com`). (We prefer to access newsgroups through the Web because it's easy and requires only a World Wide Web browser. For more on browsers, see the "World Wide Web" section later in this appendix. To find out how to access and use DejaNews, keep reading.

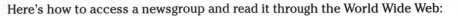

> ✔ If the newsgroup is gatewayed with a mailing list, you can receive the messages posted to the newsgroup through that mailing list. (*Gatewayed* means that traffic from the newsgroup is relayed to a mailing list and vice versa.)

Here's how to access a newsgroup and read it through the World Wide Web:

1. **Open your World Wide Web browser.**

   You usually do this by double-clicking the program's icon or using the Start program menu.

2. **In your browser's URL field, type the Web address for DejaNews** (`www.dejanews.com/usenet`).

3. **Click the <u>soc</u> link.**

   This takes you to a page with a list of the `soc` newsgroups, including `soc.genealogy`.

4. **Select the <u>matches</u> link.**

   A page listing all the `soc.genealogy` newsgroups pops up. From here, you can select any of these to explore the messages posted to that particular group.

Be sure to take a look at Chapter 3 for detailed information about posting to newsgroups before you do so. It gives you a few guidelines on what to post and how to format your message.

World Wide Web

The *World Wide Web* is a system for viewing and using multimedia documents on the Internet. The documents that you view on the Web are written in a code called *Hypertext Markup Language* (HTML) that is translated into graphical pages (which may have sound and motion attached) by software called a *Web browser*. (For general information about features of a browser and how to use one, see the section "Web browsers" in this appendix. For more on HTML, take a look at Chapter 12.)

The pages of the multimedia documents usually have hypertext links that you can click to get to other sites. You can navigate the Web by typing the address of a Web site — also called a *Uniform Resource Locator* (URL) — in the appropriate field of your browser and pressing Enter, or by clicking the links on a page to get to other pages.

Although you hear the Web referred to as the Internet, the Web is *not* the Internet. The Web is a resource *on* the Internet; it doesn't make up the Internet all by itself. (Other sections of this appendix explain various Internet resources in addition to the Web.)

Web browsers

Several different Web browser programs are available. You can download some browsers for free off the Internet; others come loaded on your computer with software packages; some you buy separately; and still others come with your subscription to an Internet service provider. Most offer similar standard navigation features, and almost all are easy to use.

The two most popular browsers are Netscape Navigator and Microsoft Internet Explorer. Here are some of the common features of these two browsers and how to use those features:

- Both browsers have a field in which you enter the address, or URL, to get to a Web page. Navigator calls its address field *Location* or *Netsite,* and Internet Explorer calls its field *Address.*

- The Stop button halts a page that's loading into your browser.

- The Back button on the button bar takes you back to the previous page. Similarly, the Forward button takes you forward to the site that you were viewing before you hit the Back button.

- The Reload button (Navigator) and the Refresh button (Internet Explorer) reload the page that you're looking at. If any changes to the page occurred while you were online, reloading or refreshing the page picks up those changes and reflects them.

- Clicking the Print button prints a copy of the page that you're looking at. If the Web page is too long to fit on one regular sheet of paper, the browser tells the printer where to split the Web page to print on multiple sheets of paper.

- *Bookmarks* (Navigator) and *Favorites* (Internet Explorer) give you a shortcut list to pages that the software manufacturers think you may be interested in or looking for. Additionally, you can add your own bookmarks or favorites for your frequently visited sites by choosing Bookmarks⇨Add Bookmark in Navigator or Favorites⇨Add to Favorites in Internet Explorer.

- Both programs have Help drop-down menus for more information on using the browser and its features.

Search engines

Search engines are programs that search large indexes of information gathered by robots sent out to *catalog* (sort and record) resources on the Internet. (*Robots* are programs that travel throughout the Internet and collect information on the various sites and resources that they run across.) You can access the information contained in search engines through an *interface* (an online form or page).

Some of the better-known search engines are

- **Google:** www.google.com
- **Lycos:** www.lycos.com
- **AltaVista:** www.altavista.com
- **HotBot:** www.hotbot.com
- **Excite:** www.excite.com

Although each search engine has its own variations, all of them function similarly. All search engines have an interface with a form in which you enter keywords to search for in the search engine's index. Each search engine then runs a search of its index, returning its findings to you with links directly to the pages where the search engine's robot identified the keywords.

Chapter 3 explores genealogical-specific search engines and walks you through a search. Check out The *Genealogy Online For Dummies* Internet Directory for even more information on particular search engines.

Chat rooms

Chat rooms are Internet sites where you can log on and participate in real-time (or with just a few seconds delay) conversations. And although you may not encounter and use chat rooms a lot in your genealogical research, we did want you to know that they exist.

A few chat rooms discuss genealogy specifically. Typically, the genealogy chat rooms (or in some cases, sessions that are pre-arranged) are hosted by or are available through the commercial Internet service providers (particularly America Online) or the Internet Relay Chat (IRC) network.

The IRC hosts several areas (called *channels*) where you can find discussions about genealogy. To access and use a chat channel on IRC, you have to use chat software. For more information about the genealogy-related chat channels, visit the Home Page for Genealogy on IRC (`www.genealogy.org/~jkatcmi/genealogy-irc/welcome.html`). Not only does this home page tell you what's available, its FAQ (Frequently Asked Questions) section provides detailed instructions for downloading the chat software and joining chat channels as well.

In addition to chat rooms, there are other ways to communicate with researchers "in real time." Products such as AOL/Netscape Instant Messaging and ICQ allow researchers to communicate with each other. For more information on AOL/Netscape Instant Messaging, see `home.netscape.com/aim/index.html?cp=hop10hb4`. Information on ICQ can be found at `www.cnet.com/internet/0-3782.html`.

Appendix B

What Does This Mean? (A Glossary of Terms)

•••

Abstract: A brief overview or summary of what a document or Web site contains.

Administration: Handling of the estate of a person who died intestate.

Admon: Abbreviation for *administration*.

Ahnentafel: A well-known genealogical numbering system. Ahnentafel is a method of numbering that has a mathematical relationship between parents and children. The word itself means *ancestor* and *table* in German; also referred to as the ***Sosa-Stradonitz System*** of numbering.

Albumen print: A type of photograph that was produced on a thin piece of paper coated with albumen and silver nitrate and usually mounted on cardboard; typically taken between 1858 and 1910.

Ambrotype: A type of photograph that was printed on thin glass and usually had a black backing; typically taken between 1858 and 1866.

America Online: One of the most popular commercial Internet service providers.

Ancestor: A person from whom you are descended.

Ancestor chart: A chart that runs horizontally across a page and identifies a primary person (including that person's name, date and place of birth, date and place of marriage, and date and place of death), his/her parents, and then each of their parents, and so on until the chart runs off the page. Usually called a ***Pedigree chart.***

Ancestral file: A database created and maintained by the Church of Jesus Christ of Latter-day Saints with millions of names available in Family Group Sheets and Pedigree charts; part of the FamilySearch collection of CD-ROMs, which are accessible at Family History Centers. See also ***Family History Center*** and ***Family History Library.***

Archive: A physical location where historical documents and records are stored.

Automoderator: A computer program that determines whether a post to a newsgroup is appropriate, and if so, posts it to the newsgroup.

Backbones: High-speed data lines that support the Internet.

Bandwidth: The capacity that a particular phone line or other networking cable has to carry traffic to and from the Internet or computer network.

Banns: See marriage banns.

Baptismal certificate: A certificate issued by a church at the time of baptism; sometimes used to approximate birth in the absence of a birth certificate.

BBS: Acronym for Bulletin Board System.

Bibliography: A list of books or other materials that were used in research; also a list of books or other materials that are available on a particular topic.

Biographical sketch: A brief written account of a person's life.

Biography: A detailed written account of a person's life.

Birth certificate: A legal record stating when and where a person was born.

Bookmark: A method for saving links to your favorite Web sites within your Web browser so you can easily return to them.

Bounce: When e-mail doesn't reach the intended party for whatever reason and is returned to the sender.

Bounty land: Federal land given to a person in exchange for military service or some other civic service.

Browser: See *World Wide Web browser.*

Bulletin Board System: One or more computers that answer a telephone in order to communicate with other computers that call. Bulletin Board Systems allow users of the other computers to post information or messages to them. Also called *BBS.*

Bureau of Refugees, Freedmen, and Abandoned Lands: Established in 1865, the bureau had programs to assist ex-slaves after the American Civil War. Also called *Freedman's Bureau.*

Cabinet card: A larger version of the carte-de-visite photograph; typically taken between 1865 and 1906.

Cable connection: Direct access to the Internet using cable lines.

Cache: A directory on your computer where your Web browser stores information about Web pages and images that it has downloaded. This enables the browser to load that page faster if you visit it again within a specified period of time.

Canon Code: A code that explains the bloodline relationship in legal terms by identifying how many degrees of separation (or steps) exist between two people related by blood. Canon law counts only the number of steps from the nearest common ancestor of both relatives.

Carte-de-visite: A type of photograph that was a small paper print mounted on a card; collections were usually bound together in photo albums. Typically taken between 1858 and 1891.

CD-ROM: Acronym for Compact Disk-Read Only Memory; used in your computer's compact disc drive. A CD-ROM stores large amounts of information (including multimedia) that can be retrieved by your computer.

Census: The counting of a population undertaken by a government.

Census index: A listing of people who are included in particular census records, along with references indicating where you can find the actual census records.

Census return: The record/form on which census information is collected. Also called a *census schedule.*

Census schedule: Another term for a *census return* form.

Channel: An area within Internet Relay Chat where you can find discussions on particular topics, including genealogy.

Charter: A formal or informal document that defines the scope of a newsgroup.

Chat room: An Internet site where you can log in and participate in real-time conversations.

Cite: To name the source of some information and provide reference to the original source.

Civil Code: A code that explains the bloodline relationship in legal terms by identifying how many degrees of separation (or steps) exist between two people related by blood; civil law counts each step between two relatives as a degree.

Civil records: Government documents that contain information on the civic duties of your ancestors, proceedings of municipal governments, or any other records of your ancestors' interaction with the government; often found in local and state archives or courthouses.

Civil registration: Primary record of a vital event in life: birth, death, or marriage; for the most part, originals are kept by local governments. Also called *vital records* in the United States and Canada.

Commercial Internet service provider: A company or organization that supplies access to the Internet for a fee.

Community network: An Internet service provider that's locally based and offers access to people in the community (usually free of charge). Also called *freenet.*

Comprehensive genealogical site: A Web site that identifies a large number of other genealogical sites containing information on a number of families, locations, or a variety of other genealogically-related subjects.

CompuServe: A popular commercial Internet service provider.

Cookies: Pieces of information that are sent to your computer by other computers when you visit certain Web pages. Generally, cookies are used for navigation purposes or by commercial sites that want to rotate banner advertisements for you so you don't get tired of the same old advertisement.

Copyright: Copyright is the exclusive right of a creator to reproduce, prepare derivative works, distribute, perform, display, sell, lend, or rent his/her creations.

County clerk: The clerk of the county court that records or maintains records of transactions and events in that county. Sometimes called the *county recorder.*

Cyberspace: A slang term for the Internet.

Daguerreotype: A type of photograph that required a long exposure time and was taken on silver-plated copper; typically taken between 1839 and 1860.

Database: A collection of information that is entered, organized, stored, and used on a computer.

Death certificate: A legal record stating when and where a person died.

Declaration of intent: A sworn statement by a person who intends to become a naturalized citizen of the United States.

Deed: A document that records the transfer of ownership of a piece of property or land.

Descendant: A person who descended from a particular ancestor.

Descendant chart: A chart that contains information about an ancestor and spouse (or particular spouses if there was more than one), their children and their spouses, grandchildren and spouses, and so on down the family line; usually formatted vertically on a page like a list.

Dial-up connection: A method of connecting to the Internet wherein your computer uses a telephone line to call in to an *Internet service provider.*

Digest mode: An option for receiving postings to some mailing lists in which several messages are batched together and sent to you instead of each message being sent separately.

Digital camera: A camera that captures images to memory instead of to film, and then downloads the images to your computer.

Digital Subscriber Line (DSL): Direct access to the Internet using specialized phone lines. This service is faster than a dial-up connection, which uses traditional phone lines.

Digitized record: A copy or image of a record that has been made using electronic means.

Direct connection: Direct access to the Internet from your home. There are four ways in which you can have a direct connection: You can access the Internet through an Internet line that comes directly into your home or business and is hooked up to your computer(s); a cable connection; a Digital Subscriber Line (DSL); or a satellite connection.

Directory: A collection of information about individuals who live in a particular place.

Download: Getting a file (information or a program) to your computer from another computer.

Earthlink: A popular commercial Internet service provider.

Electronic mail: Messages that are sent from one person to another electronically over the Internet. Also called *e-mail.*

E-mail: Short for *electronic mail.*

Emigrant: A person who leaves or moves away from one country to settle in another country.

Emoticons: Graphics created by combinations of keys on the keyboard to express an emotion within a message.

Enumeration district: The area assigned to a particular enumerator of the census.

Enumerator: A person who collected details on individuals during a census.

Estate: The assets and liabilities of a person who dies.

Family association: An organized group of individuals who are researching the same family.

Family association site: A Web site that's designed and posted by an organization devoted to researching a particular family.

Family group sheet: A summary of a particular family, including biographical information about a husband, wife, and their children.

Family history: The written account of a family's existence over time.

Family History Center: Local branches of the *Family History Library.*

Family History Library: The Church of Jesus Christ of Latter-day Saints' main library in Salt Lake City, Utah. The Family History Library has the world's largest collection of genealogical holdings, including print sources and microfilmed records, as well as records and other information shared by genealogical researchers worldwide.

Family History Library Catalog: A listing of records (books, films, microfiche, CDs, cassette tapes, videos, and microfilms) available at the Family History Library in Salt Lake City, Utah; part of the FamilySearch collection of CD-ROMs, which are accessible at Family History Centers.

Family outline report: A list of the descendants of a particular ancestor.

FamilySearch: A collection of information compiled by the Church of Jesus Christ of Latter-day Saints; it includes the Ancestral File, Family History Library Catalog, International Genealogical Index, Military Index, Social Security Death Index, and Scottish Church Records.

FAQ: Acronym for Frequently Asked Questions.

FHC: Acronym for Family History Center.

FHL: Acronym for Family History Library.

File Transfer Protocol: A way to transfer files from your computer to another, or vice versa, over the Internet. Also called *FTP.*

Flame: A verbal (written) attack online.

Forum: A subject-specific area where members post messages and files.

Fraternal order: A service club or organization of persons.

Freedman's Bureau: Abbreviated name for the Bureau of Refugees, Freedmen, and Abandoned Lands.

Freedman's Savings and Trust Company: Established in 1865, this was a bank for ex-slaves.

Freenet: An Internet service provider that's locally based and offers access to people in the community free of charge. Also called *community network.*

Freeware: Software that you usually obtain and use for free by downloading it off the Internet.

Frequently Asked Questions: A Web page or message posted to a mailing list or newsgroup that explains answers to the most-asked questions to the particular Web site, mailing list, or newsgroup. Usually serves as a starting point for people new to a site or resource.

FTP: Acronym for File Transfer Protocol.

Gateway: Computer(s) that forward messages and route data between networks.

Gatewayed: When traffic from a newsgroup is relayed to a related mailing list and vice versa.

Gazetteer: Geographical dictionary that provides information about places.

GEDCOM: Acronym for GEnealogical Data COMmunication.

Genealogical database: Software in which you enter, store, and use information about ancestors, descendants, and others relevant to your genealogy.

Genealogical Data Communication: The standard file format for exporting and importing information between genealogical databases; intended to make data translatable between different genealogical software programs so you can share your family information easily.

Genealogically-focused search engine: A program that indexes the full text of Web sites that are of interest and value to genealogists, and allows you to search the index for particular keywords.

GENDEX: An index of online genealogical databases that comply with the GED2HTML indexing format.

Genealogical society: An organized group that attempts to preserve documents and history for the area in which the society is located; often a genealogical society has a second purpose, which is to help its members research their ancestors.

Genealogy: The study of *ancestors, descendants,* and family origins.

Geographic-specific Web site: A Web site that has information pertaining to a particular locality (town, county, state, country, or other area).

Glass plate negative: A type of photograph made from light-sensitive silver bromide immersed in gelatin; typically taken between 1848 and 1930.

Gopher: A way to hierarchically categorize data on the Internet using a series of text-based menus through which you can browse and click; developed at the University of Minnesota.

Helm Online Family Tree Research Cycle: A five-phase research model that explains the ongoing process of genealogical research.

Henry System: A widely-used and accepted genealogical numbering system, it assigns a particular sequence of numbers to the children of the progenitor and subsequent generations.

Hierarchy: In terms of a newsgroup, a hierarchy is the major grouping to which a newsgroup belongs; for example, `soc.genealogy.computing` belongs to the `soc` hierarchy.

Historical society: An organized group that attempts to preserve documents and history for the area in which the society is located.

Home page: The entry point for a World Wide Web site.

HTML: Acronym for HyperText Markup Language.

HyperText Markup Language: The programming language of the World Wide Web. HTML is a code that's translated into graphical pages by software called a World Wide Web browser.

IGI: Acronym for International Genealogical Index.

Immigrant: A person who moves into or settles in a country.

Immigration record: A record of the entry of a person into a specific country where he or she was not natively born or naturalized.

Index: A list of some sort. An index can be a list of Web sites, types of records, and so on.

Interface: An online form or page.

Interlibrary loan: A system in which one library loans a book or other material to another library for a person to borrow or use.

International Genealogical Index: A list of births and marriages of deceased individuals reflected in records collected by the Church of Jesus Christ of Latter-day Saints. The International Genealogical Index is part of the FamilySearch collection of CD-ROMs which are accessible at Family History Centers.

Internet: A system of computer networks joined together by high-speed data lines called *backbones*.

Internet Relay Chat: A network providing channels (or areas) where you can find real-time discussions about genealogy and participate using chat software. Also called *IRC*.

Internet service provider: A company or other organization that provides people with access to the Internet through a direct connection or dial-up connection. Also called *ISP*.

Intestate: A person who died without leaving a valid will.

IRC: Acronym for Internet Relay Chat.

ISP: Acronym for Internet service provider.

Kinship report: A list of family members and how they relate directly to one particular individual in your database; usually kinship reports include the Civil Code and Canon Code for the relationship to the individual.

Land grant: Permission to purchase land or a gift of land in exchange for military service or other civic service.

Land patent: A document that conveyed the title of a piece of land to a new owner after that person met required conditions to own the land.

Land record: A document recording the sale or exchange of land; most land records are maintained at a local level where the property is located.

Listowner: A person who oversees a mailing list.

Listserv: A software program for managing electronic mailing lists.

Lurking: Reading messages that others post to a mailing list or newsgroup without posting any messages of your own.

Maiden name: A woman's surname prior to marriage; sometimes reflected as "née" on records and documents.

Mail mode: The method for mailing lists in which each message is sent to you separately as it's posted.

Mailing list: An e-mail exchange forum that consists of a group of people who share common interests; e-mail messages posted to the list come directly to your e-mail in full-format (mail mode) or digest mode; the list consists of the names of everyone who joins the group. When you want to send a message to the group, you post it to a single e-mail address that subsequently delivers the message to everyone on the list.

Manumission papers: Documents granting slaves their freedom.

Marriage banns: A proclamation made in front of a church congregation expressing one's intent to marry.

Marriage bond: A financial contract guaranteeing that a marriage was going to take place; usually posted by the groom and another person (often the father or brother of the bride).

Marriage certificate: A legal document certifying the union of two individuals.

Marriage license: A document granting permission to marry from a civil or ecclesiastical authority.

Maternal: Relating to the mother's side of the family.

Microfiche: A clear sheet that contains tiny images of documents, records, books, and so on; you must read it with a microfiche reader or other magnifying equipment.

Microfilm: A roll of clear film that contains tiny images of documents, records, books, and so forth; you must read it with a microfilm reader.

Microsoft Network: A popular commercial Internet service provider.

Military Index: A list of those killed in the Korean and Vietnam Wars; part of the FamilySearch collection of CD-ROMs, which are accessible at Family History Centers.

Modem: A piece of equipment that allows your computer to talk to other computers through a telephone or cable line; modems can be internal (inside your computer) or external (plugged into one of your computer's serial ports or card).

Moderator: A person who determines whether a post to a newsgroup or mailing list is appropriate, and if so, posts it.

Mortgage: Legal agreement to repay money borrowed with real property as collateral.

Muster record: A type of military pay record reflecting who was present with a military unit at a particular time and place.

Naturalization: The process of becoming a citizen or subject of a particular country in a manner other than birth in that country.

Naturalization record: The legal document proving one is a naturalized citizen.

Netiquette: Simple guidelines for communicating effectively and politely on the Internet.

Newbie: A person who is new to the Internet.

News reader: Software required to read messages posted to a newsgroup.

News server: One or more computers that replicate newsgroups over the Internet.

Newsgroup: A place to post messages of a particular focus so that groups of people at large can read them online; messages are posted to a news server which, in turn, copies the messages to other news servers.

Notebook computer: A compact computer that's portable.

Obituary: An account of one's death that usually appears in a newspaper or other type of media.

One-name study: A page on the World Wide Web that focuses on research involving one particular surname regardless of the geographic location in which it appears.

Online: Gaining access to and using the Internet; available through the Internet.

Orphan: An infant or child whose parents are both deceased. In some early times and places, a child was considered an orphan if his/her father had died but the mother was still living.

Palmtop: A hand-sized computer that is portable and can contain some of the same programs that are housed on desktop computers.

Passenger list: Listing of the names of passengers who traveled from one country to another on a particular ship.

Paternal: Relating to the father's side of the family.

Pedigree chart: A chart that runs horizontally across a page, identifying a primary person (including that person's name, date and place of birth, date and place of marriage, and date and place of death), his/her parents, and then each of their parents, and so on until the chart runs off the page. Sometimes called an *ancestor chart.*

Pension record: A type of military record reflecting the amount of a pension that the government paid to an individual who served in the military; pension records also showed the amount of pension paid to the widow or orphan(s) of such an individual.

Personal Web page: A page on the World Wide Web that was designed and posted by an individual or family.

Petition for land: An application your ancestor may have filed for a land grant.

Plat map: A map of lots within a tract of land, usually showing the owners' names.

Platinum print: A type of photograph with a matte surface that appeared to be embedded in the paper. Images were often highlighted with artistic chalk, giving the photo a hand-drawn quality; typically taken between 1880 and 1930.

Primary source: A document, oral account, photograph, or any other item that was created at the time a certain event occurred; information for the record was supplied by a witness to the event.

Probate: Settlement of one's estate after death.

Probate records: Types of court records that deal with the settling of an estate upon one's death. Probate records include contested wills and will readings; often the file contains testimonies and the ruling.

Prodigy: A popular commercial Internet service provider.

Professional researcher: A person who will research your genealogy — particular family lines — or obtain copies of documents for you for a fee.

Progenitor: The farthest-back ancestor you know about in a particular family line.

Query: A research question that you post to a particular Web site, mailing list, or newsgroup so that other researchers can help you solve your genealogical research problems/challenges.

Research groups: A group of people who coordinate their research and share resources to achieve success.

Robot: A program that travels throughout the Internet and collects information about sites and resources that it comes across. Also called a *spider.*

Roots Surname List: A list of surnames, their associated dates, and locations accompanied by the contact information for persons researching those surnames. Also called *RSL.*

RSL: Acronym for Roots Surname List.

Satellite connection: Direct access to the Internet using a satellite dish and signals.

Scanner: A device that captures digital images of photographs and documents into your computer.

Search engine: A program that searches either a large index of information generated by robots or a particular Web site.

Secondary source: A document, oral account, or any other record that was created after an event took place or for which information was supplied by someone who was not an eyewitness to the event.

Server: A computer that makes information available for access by other computers.

Service record: A type of military record that chronicles the military career of an individual.

Shareware: Software that you can try before you pay to license and use it permanently; usually you download shareware off the Internet.

Shotgun approach: A bad idea; the process of sending mass e-mails to anyone you find with your surname through one of the online white pages sites.

Signature file: A file that you can create and attach to the bottom of your e-mail messages that gives your name, contact information, surnames that you're researching, or anything else you want to convey to others.

Site: One or more World Wide Web pages; also called a *Web site.*

Snail mail: Mail delivered by hand — such as U.S. Mail.

Social Security Death Index: An index of those persons for whom Social Security death claims were filed with the United States government. The Social Security Death Index is part of the FamilySearch collection of CD-ROMs, which are accessible at Family History Centers; also available online (www.ancestry.com/search/rectype/vital/ssdi/main.htm).

Sosa-Stradonitz System: See *ahnentafel*.

Sound card: An internal computer device that enables you to hear any audio that comes on software or audio files that you download off the Internet.

Soundex: A system of indexing the U.S. federal census that places names that sound alike but are spelled differently into groups; the Soundex code for a name includes a letter followed by three numbers.

Source: Any person or material (book, document, record, periodical, and so on) that provides information for your research.

Spam: Unsolicited junk e-mail that tries to sell you something or offers a service.

Spider: A program that travels throughout the Internet and collects information about sites and resources it comes across. Also called a *robot.*

Stereographic card: A type of photograph that was curved and rendered a three-dimensional effect when used with a viewer; developed in the 1850s.

Surname: A last name or family name.

Survey: Detailed drawing and legal description of the boundaries of a land parcel.

SYSOP: A person who oversees forums or areas provided to members of commercial Internet service providers or Bulletin Board Systems.

Tax record: A record of any tax paid, including property, inheritance, and church taxes; most taxes were collected at the local level, but the records have now been turned over to government archives.

Telnet: A text-based program that allows you to log in to another computer and view files or documents that are available for public access; you need a telnet client (software) to use telnet.

Thread: A group of messages with a common subject on a newsgroup.

Tintype: A type of photograph that was made on a metal sheet; the image was often coated with a varnish. Typically taken between 1858 and 1910.

Tiny tafel: A compact way to show the relationships within a family database. Tiny tafel provides a Soundex code for a *surname* and the dates and locations where that surname may be found according to the database.

Toggling: The process of flipping back and forth between open programs on your computer by using the Alt and Tab keys in Windows or the Application Switcher in Macintosh.

Tract book: A book describing the lots within a township or other geographic area.

Transcribed record: A copy of the content of a record that has been duplicated word for word.

Uniform Resource Locator: A way of addressing resources on the World Wide Web; also called *URL.*

URL: Acronym for Uniform Resource Locator.

U.S. Colored Troops database: An online database of information on more than 230,000 soldiers of African descent who served in the U.S. Colored Troops; part of the Civil War Soldiers and Sailors System sponsored by the National Park Service.

Video-capture board: A device that enables your computer to grab images from your video camera or VCR.

Vital record: Primary record of a vital event in life — birth, death, or marriage; for the most part, originals are kept by local governments. Often called *civil registrations* outside the United States.

Warrant: A certificate to receive land when your ancestor's petition for a land grant was approved.

Web site: One or more World Wide Web pages created by an individual or organization; also called a *site.*

Webmaster: A person responsible for creating and maintaining a particular Web site.

WebTV: A console containing a small computer with limited functions that hooks directly into your television set and enables you to connect to the WebTV Internet service provider for access to e-mail, the World Wide Web, and newsgroups.

Will: A legal document that explains how a person wishes his/her estate to be settled or distributed upon death.

Witness: One who attests that he/she saw an event.

World Wide Web: A system for viewing and using multimedia documents on the Internet; Web documents are created in HyperText Markup Language (HTML) and are read by World Wide Web browsers.

World Wide Web browser: Software that enables you to view HTML documents on the Internet.

World Wide Web page: A multimedia document that is created in HTML and is viewable on the Internet with the use of a World Wide Web browser.

XML: Similar to HTML in that it's a code that uses tags to describe information. However, XML has a broader purpose; it's designed not only to display information, but also to describe the information.

Zip disk: A computer disk that you use with an Iomega Zip drive; stores up to 250MB of data.

Appendix C

About the CD

● ●

*H*ere's some of what you can find on the *Genealogy Online For Dummies,* 3rd Edition, CD-ROM:

- ✔ AT&T WorldNet Service, a popular Internet service
- ✔ Family Tree Maker for Windows, a trial version of the popular genealogy database
- ✔ Homesite 4.5, an evaluation copy of the popular HTML editor

System Requirements

Make sure your computer meets the following minimum system requirements. If your computer doesn't match up to most of these requirements, you may have problems using the contents of the CD:

- ✔ A PC with a Pentium or faster processor, or a Mac OS computer with a 68040 or faster processor.
- ✔ Microsoft Windows 95 or later, or Mac OS system software 7.55 or later.
- ✔ At least 32MB of total RAM installed on your computer. For best performance, we recommend at least 64MB of RAM installed.
- ✔ At least 500MB of hard-drive space available to install all the software from this CD. (You need less space if you don't install every program.)
- ✔ A CD-ROM drive — double-speed (2x) or faster.
- ✔ A sound card for PCs. (Mac OS computers have built-in sound support.)
- ✔ A monitor capable of displaying at least 256 colors or grayscale.
- ✔ A modem with a speed of at least 33,600 bps (56K recommended).

If you need more information on the basics, check out *PCs For Dummies,* 7th Edition, by Dan Gookin; *Macs For Dummies,* 6th Edition by David Pogue; *iMacs For Dummies,* by David Pogue; *Windows 95 For Dummies,* 2nd Edition, or *Windows 98 For Dummies* both by Andy Rathbone (all published by IDG Books Worldwide, Inc.).

Using the CD with Microsoft Windows

1. **Insert the CD into your computer's CD-ROM drive.**

2. **Open your browser.**

   If you don't have a browser, we include Microsoft Internet Explorer and Netscape Communicator on the CD-ROM. They can be found in the Programs folders at the root of the CD.

3. **Click Start⇨Run.**

4. **In the dialog box that appears, type** D:\START.HTM.

   Replace *D* with the proper drive letter if your CD-ROM drive uses a different letter. (If you don't know the letter, see how your CD-ROM drive is listed under My Computer.)

5. **Read through the license agreement, nod your head and smile, and click the Accept button if you want to use the CD.**

   After you click Accept, you jump to the Main Menu.

   This action displays the file that walks you through the content of the CD.

6. **To navigate within the interface, simply click any topic of interest to go to an explanation of the files on the CD and how to use or install them.**

7. **To install the software from the CD, simply click the software name.**

   You see two options — the option to run or open the file from the current location or the option to save the file to your hard drive. Choose to run or open the file from its current location and the installation procedure continues. After you are done with the interface, simply close your browser as usual.

To run some of the programs, you may need to keep the CD inside your CD-ROM drive. This is a Good Thing. Otherwise, the installed program would have required you to install a very large chunk of the program to your hard drive space, which would have kept you from installing other software.

How to Use the CD Using the Mac OS

To install the items from the CD to your hard drive, follow these steps:

1. **Insert the CD into your computer's CD-ROM drive.**

   In a moment, an icon representing the CD you just inserted appears on your Mac desktop. The icon may look like a CD-ROM.

2. **Double click the CD icon to show the CD's contents.**

3. In the window that appears, double click the START.HTM icon.

4. Read through the license agreement, nod your head and smile, and click the Accept button if you want to use the CD — after you click Accept, you jump to the Main Menu.

   This action displays the file that walks you through the content of the CD.

5. To navigate within the interface, simply click any topic of interest to be taken to an explanation of the files on the CD and how to use or install them.

6. To install the software from the CD, simply click the software name.

   After you're done with the interface, simply close your browser as usual.

What You Get on the CD

Here's a summary of the software on this CD.

AT&T WorldNet Service, from AT&T

This service is for both Windows and Mac OS, and you can find it in the Internet Tools category or in the Internet AT&T folder. In case you don't have an Internet connection, the CD includes sign-on software for AT&T WorldNet Service, an Internet service provider. For more information and updates of AT&T WorldNet Service, visit the AT&T WorldNet Web site at www.att.com/worldnet.

If you already have an Internet service provider, please note that AT&T WorldNet Service software makes changes to your computer's current Internet configuration and may replace your current provider's settings.

When you are asked for a registration number while installing this program, type **L5SQIM631** if you use AT&T as your home's long-distance service or type **L5SQIM632** if you use another long-distance service.

Genealogy programs

Ancestral Quest 3.0
For Windows. Demo version.

Ancestral Quest is a Windows program for storing and organizing your genealogical findings. Included on this disk is the demonstration version of the program. Detailed information about the software is available at www.ancquest.com/.

AniMap Plus
For Windows. Demo version.

This is a demonstration version of the AniMap & SiteFinder program. AniMap is an interactive historical atlas that helps you track your family's movements and county boundary changes over time. Information about the full program is available at `www.goldbug.com/AniMap.html`.

Brother's Keeper
For Windows. Shareware version.

Brother's Keeper 5.2G is genealogical shareware that enables you to store information about your family and create charts and reports using that information. It includes versions in English, French, Norwegian, Danish, Swedish, German, and Dutch. If you decide you want to keep and register your copy after trying it out, you can follow the instructions at the Brother's Keeper for Windows Web site (`ourworld.compuserve.com/homepages/Brothers_Keeper/`).

Brother's Keeper
For DOS. Shareware version.

This is the MS-DOS brother program to Brother's Keeper 5.2B (described earlier). It's a genealogy shareware program that stores data on your ancestors and enables you to create charts and reports. It includes versions in English, French, Norwegian, Danish, Swedish, German, Finnish, and Dutch. If you decide to keep and pay for the shareware after you try it, the Brother's Keeper for DOS Web site (`home.sprynet.com/sprynet/steed/`) provides instructions for you to follow.

Family Origins
For Windows. Demo version.

This is a demonstration version of the genealogy database software. Family Origins features a multimedia scrapbook, detailed reports, and heirloom quality trees. This demo is limited to 50 people, but does allow you to print reports. A sample database is included. You can find more information on Family Origins at `formalsoft.com`.

Family Tree Maker
For Windows. Trial version.

Genealogy.com provides a limited Version 6.0 of its popular genealogical database called Family Tree Maker. The program is easy to use and enables you to produce a variety of charts and reports, as well as record information on an unlimited number of people. The only limitation of this version is that you are not able to use the FamilyFinder Index functionality that is standard with the full Version 6.0. To find more information about the most recent version of Family Tree Maker and how to upgrade to it, visit www.familytreemaker.com.

GED2HTML
For Windows. Shareware version.

This program converts your GEDCOM to an HTML file so that you can post data contained within it on the Web. It's shareware that you must register if you decide to keep it when the trial period is over. The GED2HTML Web site (www.gendex.com/ged2html/) provides additional information about the program. GED2HTML is a trademark of Gene Stark.

GEDClean
For Windows. Shareware version.

This GEDClean freeware assists you by stripping out information about living persons from your GEDCOM file per your specifications. For more information about GEDClean or about the new commercial version for Windows 95/98 called GEDClean32, check out www.raynorshyn.com/gedclean/ or e-mail the author at GEDClean@rynorshyn.com.

GenBrowser
For Windows. Shareware version.

GenBrowser is shareware that searches the Internet for sites with genealogy indices created with GEDCOM files. It retrieves the information that you request and converts the HTML back to GEDCOM for you to use with your genealogical database. For more information about GenBrowser features and how to register your copy if you decide to keep it, see www.pratt.lib.md.us/~bharding/rippleeffect/GenBrowser/GenBrowser.html.

Genelines
For Windows. Demo version.

This is a demonstration version of Genelines, a charting utility for files produced by Family Tree Maker and Personal Ancestral File, as well as GEDCOM files. Genelines produces five types of historical bar charts, including the individual geneline, comparative geneline, pedigree, direct descendant, and family group. For more information, see Progeny Software's site at www.progenysoftware.com.

Legacy Family Tree
For Windows. Full version.

The Millennia Corporation has provided a fully functional, basic version of its genealogical database software, called Legacy Family Tree. It stores data on an unlimited number of people and produces various charts and reports. For a detailed list of features and information about upgrading to the newest version of Legacy Family Tree, check out www.legacyfamilytree.com/.

Reunion
For Mac. Demo version.

This is the demonstration version of the popular genealogical program for Macintosh. It allows you to document, store, and display information about your family. The demo version limits you to information about 35 people. If you find that you like Reunion after using the demo, you can purchase the full version. For more information about Reunion, visit its Web site at www.LeisterPro.com/Default.html.

Sparrowhawk
For Mac. Shareware version.

Sparrowhawk is Macintosh shareware that converts your GEDCOM file into HTML so that you can post part or all of it on the Web. It requires that you have OS 7.0 or higher. Its Web page provides detailed information about the program — how to use it and how to register it if you decide to keep it after the trial period. The Web address is www.tjp.washington.edu/bdm/genealogy/sparrowhawk.html.

Internet tools

Eudora
For Windows and Mac. Shareware version.

Eudora Light from Qualcomm, Inc., is a free, powerful e-mail program. If you have an Internet e-mail account, you can use Eudora Light to send e-mail to and receive e-mail from any of the tens of millions of other people around the world who are connected to the Internet. In addition to text messages, Eudora Light lets you attach files to e-mail, so you can use it to transmit electronic pictures, sound clips, or any other kind of data that is stored in files. To learn more or to purchase the more powerful commercial version of Eudora Pro, go to the Web site at www.eudora.com.

Free Agent
For Windows. Freeware version.

If your Internet service provider has a news feed and you want to access the `soc.genealogy` and `alt.genealogy` newsgroups in the traditional way (not using the Web), this is a program that can help you. Free Agent, from Forté, Inc., is a free (for personal use) Windows program that lets you read and participate in ongoing group discussions that take place on the Internet via Usenet newsgroups. Among its features is its capability to let you read newsgroup articles offline, which could conceivably save you Internet connection charges and phone charges. For more information about how to use Free Agent, visit their Web site at `www.forteinc.com`.

HomeSite
For Windows. Evaluation version.

HomeSite 4.5, from Allaire, is a popular shareware HTML editor for Windows 95/98. If you're interested in creating your own Web site, this program makes creating and editing documents with HTML (the programming language used to make a Web page) a breeze. Get more information on HomeSite at `www.allaire.com`.

HotDog Professional 5.5 Webmaster Suite
For Windows. Trial version.

HotDog, from Sausage Software, is a powerful but easy-to-use Windows shareware program that helps you create Web pages. This is shareware from Sausage Software that you can use and evaluate for 30 days before deciding whether to purchase it. For more information about HotDog, visit the program's Web site (`www.sausage.com`).

HTML Web Weaver
For Mac. Lite version.

This is a shareware version of Miracle Software's commercially available World Wide Web Weaver. Though it doesn't have many of the stronger features of its commercial sibling, HTML Web Weaver Lite is easy to use and takes up only a bit of your hard drive space and memory, making it a perfect editor for older Macs. To learn more or to purchase the commercial version, check out the Web site at `www.miracleinc.com`.

Internet Explorer

For Windows.

Internet Explorer 5.5 for Windows 95 or higher is the latest version of the popular Web browser from Microsoft. To learn more or to check for updated versions, go to the Microsoft Web site at www.microsoft.com.

NetNanny

For Windows. Evaluation version.

NetNanny is just what it sounds like: It's a program that monitors and blocks Internet content that is unsuitable for your children (or other young viewers). This is a 30-day free trial version. You can find additional information at www.netnanny.com.

Netscape Communicator

For Windows.

Netscape Communicator 4.7, from Netscape Communications Corporation, is a Web suite from the folks at Netscape. It features enhancements like faster start-up time, faster loading plug-ins and Java applets, and drop-down menus for quicker and easier navigation. For more information about the Navigator family of products, go to the Web site at home.netscape.com.

WebWhacker

For Windows and Mac. Trial version.

WebWhacker, from Blue Squirrel, enables you to save Web pages (the text, graphics, and HTML links) to your hard drive so that you can open and view them quickly and offline. The copy on your CD-ROM is a demonstration version and expires after you've used it for 15 days. If you like it after trying it, you can purchase the software from the Web site at www.bluesquirrel.com/products/whacker/whacker.html.

WS_FTP Pro

For Windows. Trial version.

WS_FTP Pro, from Ipswitch, Inc., is a free (for noncommercial use) Windows File Transfer Protocol (FTP) program. With it, you can transfer files (also called uploading and downloading) between your PC and a computer on the Internet that supports FTP. Why would you need it? It is handy if you want to download an FTP copy of a GEDCOM file from someone's Web or FTP site or upload your Web page to your Internet service provider's server. To learn more, check out the Web site at www.ipswitch.com.

Utilities

Acrobat Reader

For Windows and Mac. Evaluation version.

Acrobat Reader 4.0, from Adobe Systems, is a free program that lets you view and print Portable Document Format, or PDF, files. The PDF format is used by many programs that you find on the Internet for storing documentation because it supports the use of such stylish elements as assorted fonts and colorful graphics. You can also get more information by visiting the Adobe Systems Web site (www.adobe.com).

GraphicConverter

For Mac. Shareware version.

GraphicConverter 3.7.2, by shareware author Thorsten Lemke, is a Macintosh program that lets you view images in virtually any graphics format that you're likely to encounter on the Internet. For more information, check out the Lemke Software Web site at www.lemkesoft.de.

Paint Shop Pro

For Windows. Evaluation version.

Paint Shop Pro, from JASC, Inc., is a multipurpose graphics tool for Windows. This superb shareware program lets you view images in virtually any graphics format that you're likely to encounter on the Internet. In addition, it lets you edit and crop images, convert images from one file format to another, and even create pictures from scratch — all of which can be useful in helping to create your own Web pages. Visit the program's Web site (www.jasc.com/psp.html) for more information.

StuffIt Expander

For Mac. Commercial version.

StuffIt Expander, from Aladdin Systems, Inc., is an invaluable file-decompression freeware utility for the Macintosh. Many files on the Internet are compressed — or shrunken in size via special programming tricks — both to save storage space and to cut down on the amount of time that they require to be downloaded. You may also occasionally receive compressed files as e-mail attachments. After you have a compressed file on your hard drive, you should use StuffIt Expander to decompress it and make it useable again. To learn more, check out the Web site at www.aladdinsys.com.

DropStuff with Expander Enhancer
For Mac. Shareware version.

DropStuff with Expander Enhancer is a complementary shareware product that not only creates StuffIt archives, but also enables StuffIt Expander to handle a wider variety of compression formats and to decompress files more quickly on Power Macintosh computers. For more information about StuffIt Expander and DropStuff with Expander Enhancer, visit the Web site at www.aladdinsys.com.

WinZip 8.0
For Windows. Shareware version.

WinZip 8.0, from Nico Mak computing, is an invaluable file compression and decompression Windows shareware utility. Many files that you find on the Internet are compressed — or shrunken in size via special programming tricks — both to save storage space and to cut down on the amount of time that they require to be downloaded. You may also occasionally receive compressed files (ZIP files) as e-mail attachments. After you have a compressed file on your hard drive, you can use WinZip to decompress it and make it useable again. To learn even more about WinZip, visit the program's Web site (www.winzip.com).

Understanding the Difference between Freeware and Shareware

Freeware is a program that the creator makes available for public use on a free-of-charge basis. Usually, you download freeware off the Internet (although some exceptions exist in which you can get freeware — like the CD-ROM that accompanies this book — and it doesn't require that you register your copy. You can use freeware for as long as you like with no obligations.

Shareware is another story. Shareware isn't free — it is commercial software that you're allowed to use on a trial basis for no charge. After the trial period is over, you must decide whether to keep it and pay for it or delete it from your computer. (Sometimes, the copy that you downloaded becomes unusable after the trial period expires.) If you decide to buy the shareware, you should follow the registration instructions that come with it.

Using the Directory Links

The *Genealogy Online for Dummies* Internet Directory in this book provides many URLs for sites that we recommend you visit to get an idea of what is available in various categories. Rather than make you flip page by page through the directory to find these URLs, we thought we'd save you some time and paper cuts! We've put links to all of the sites identified in the directory here! Isn't that convenient? Here's what you need to do to use these links:

1. **With the CD-ROM in your drive, launch your Web browser.**

2. **Choose File⇨Open (or Open File, depending on your browser).**

   An Open dialog box appears.

3. **If you're using Windows, type** D:\LINKS\LINKS.HTM **in the Open text box. (If your CD-ROM drive isn't D, be sure to use the correct letter for your drive.)**

   If you're using Mac OS, use the Open dialog box to display the contents of the CD-ROM. Select the Links.htm file from the Links folder and press Return or Enter.

4. **Click the link for any site that you want to visit.**

   This opens a second browser window that takes you to the Web site that you selected. The links page remains open in the original browser window so you can toggle back to it to select another link. Each time you select a new link, the selected Web site pops up in that second browser window, so don't worry that you're going to end up with several browser windows open at one time.

If You've Got Problems (Of the CD Kind)

We tried our best to compile programs that work on most computers with the minimum system requirements. Alas — your computer may differ, and some programs may not work properly for some reason.

The two likeliest problems are that you don't have enough memory (RAM) for the programs that you want to use, or you have other programs running that are affecting installation or running of a program. If you get error messages like Not enough memory or Setup cannot continue, try one or more of these methods and then try using the software again:

✔ Turn off any anti-virus software that you have on your computer. Installers sometimes mimic virus activity and may make your computer incorrectly believe that a virus is infecting it.

✔ Close all running programs. The more programs you're running, the less memory is available to other programs. Installers also typically update files and programs. So if you keep other programs running, installation may not work properly.

✔ Have your local computer store add more RAM to your computer. This is, admittedly, a drastic and somewhat expensive step. However, if you have a Windows 95 PC or a Mac OS computer with a PowerPC chip, adding more memory can really help the speed of your computer and allow more programs to run at the same time. This may include closing the CD interface and running a product's installation program from Windows Explorer.

If you still have trouble with installing the items from the CD, please call the Customer Service phone number: 800-762-2974 (outside the U.S.: 317-572-3993).

Index

• T •

Wiley Publishing, Inc.
End-User License Agreement

READ THIS. You should carefully read these terms and conditions before opening the software packet(s) included with this book "Book". This is a license agreement "Agreement" between you and Wiley Publishing, Inc. "WPI". By opening the accompanying software packet(s), you acknowledge that you have read and accept the following terms and conditions. If you do not agree and do not want to be bound by such terms and conditions, promptly return the Book and the unopened software packet(s) to the place you obtained them for a full refund.

1. **License Grant.** WPI grants to you (either an individual or entity) a nonexclusive license to use one copy of the enclosed software program(s) (collectively, the "Software" solely for your own personal or business purposes on a single computer (whether a standard computer or a workstation component of a multi-user network). The Software is in use on a computer when it is loaded into temporary memory (RAM) or installed into permanent memory (hard disk, CD-ROM, or other storage device). WPI reserves all rights not expressly granted herein.

2. **Ownership.** WPI is the owner of all right, title, and interest, including copyright, in and to the compilation of the Software recorded on the disk(s) or CD-ROM "Software Media". Copyright to the individual programs recorded on the Software Media is owned by the author or other authorized copyright owner of each program. Ownership of the Software and all proprietary rights relating thereto remain with WPI and its licensers.

3. **Restrictions On Use and Transfer.**

    (a) You may only (i) make one copy of the Software for backup or archival purposes, or (ii) transfer the Software to a single hard disk, provided that you keep the original for backup or archival purposes. You may not (i) rent or lease the Software, (ii) copy or reproduce the Software through a LAN or other network system or through any computer subscriber system or bulletin- board system, or (iii) modify, adapt, or create derivative works based on the Software.

    (b) You may not reverse engineer, decompile, or disassemble the Software. You may transfer the Software and user documentation on a permanent basis, provided that the transferee agrees to accept the terms and conditions of this Agreement and you retain no copies. If the Software is an update or has been updated, any transfer must include the most recent update and all prior versions.

4. **Restrictions on Use of Individual Programs.** You must follow the individual requirements and restrictions detailed for each individual program in the About the CD Appendix of this Book. These limitations are also contained in the individual license agreements recorded on the Software Media. These limitations may include a requirement that after using the program for a specified period of time, the user must pay a registration fee or discontinue use. By opening the Software packet(s), you will be agreeing to abide by the licenses and restrictions for these individual programs that are detailed the About the CD Appendix and on the Software Media. None of the material on this Software Media or listed in this Book may ever be redistributed, in original or modified form, for commercial purposes.

Notes

Notes

Notes